Mallo

& Menorca

THE ROUGH GUIDE

There are more than one hundred Rough Guide titles
covering destinations from Amsterdam to Zimbabwe

Forthcoming titles include
Argentina • Croatia • Ecuador • Money Online • Switzerland

Rough Guide Reference Series
Classical Music • Drum 'n' Bass • English Football • European Football
House • The Internet • Jazz • Music USA • Opera • Reggae
Rock Music • Techno • World Music

Rough Guide Phrasebooks
Czech • Dutch • Egyptian Arabic • European Languages • French
German • Greek • Hindi & Urdu • Hungarian • Indonesian
Italian • Japanese • Mandarin Chinese • Mexican Spanish • Polish
Portuguese • Russian • Spanish • Swahili • Thai • Turkish • Vietnamese

Rough Guides on the Internet
www.roughguides.com

Rough Guide Credits

Text Editor:	Gavin Thomas
Series Editor:	Mark Ellingham
Editorial:	Martin Dunford, Jonathan Buckley, Jo Mead, Kate Berens, Amanda Tomlin, Ann-Marie Shaw, Paul Gray, Chris Schüler, Helena Smith, Kieran Falconer, Judith Bamber, Olivia Eccleshall, Orla Duane, Ruth Blackmore, Sophie Martin, Geoff Howard, Claire Saunders, Anna Sutton, Alexander Mark Rogers (UK); Andrew Rosenberg, Andrew Taber (US)
Online Editors:	Alan Spicer, Kate Hands (UK); Geronimo Madrid (US)
Production:	Susanne Hillen, Andy Hilliard, Link Hall, Helen Ostick, James Morris, Julia Bovis, Michelle Draycott, Cathy McElhinney
Picture Research:	Eleanor Hill, Louise Boulton
Cartography:	Melissa Flack, Maxine Burke, Nichola Goodliffe, Ed Wright
Finance:	John Fisher, Katy Miesiaczek
Marketing & Publicity:	Richard Trillo, Simon Carloss, Niki Smith, David Wearn (UK); Jean-Marie Kelly, SoRelle Braun (US)
Administration:	Tania Hummel, Charlotte Marriott

Acknowledgements

Special thanks to Maria Peterson for her help with Spanish; Dave Robson for his advice on wine; Johnny and Carole Moore for updating the hikes – and writing the new one to Cala Bóquer; and for the perceptive contributions of Ruth Rigby. Further thanks are also due to Martha Crean, and Emma and Cathy Rees.

At Rough Guides, I'm grateful to my editor Gavin Thomas, who made this second edition a painless experience; to James Morris for typesetting; Cameron Wilson and Nick Thomson for research in Australia and the US; Stratigraphics for cartography; and Russell Walton for proofreading.

The publishers and authors have done their best to ensure the accuracy and currency of all information in *The Rough Guide to Mallorca and Menorca*; however, they can accept no responsibility for any loss, injury, or inconvenience sustained by any traveller as a result of information or advice contained in the guide.

This second edition published May 1999 by Rough Guides Ltd, 62–70 Shorts Gardens, London WC2H 9AB. Reprinted May 2000. Previous edition published 1996, reprinted 1997.

Distributed by the Penguin Group:
Penguin Books Ltd, 27 Wrights Lane, London W8 5TZ.
Penguin Books USA Inc, 375 Hudson Street, New York, NY 10014, USA.
Penguin Books Australia Ltd, 487 Maroondah Highway, PO Box 257, Ringwood, Victoria 3134, Australia.
Penguin Books Canada Ltd, 10 Alcorn Avenue, Toronto, Ontario M4V 1E4, Canada.
Penguin Books (NZ) Ltd, 182–190 Wairau Road, Auckland 10, New Zealand.

Printed in the United Kingdom by Clays Ltd, St Ives PLC.
Typography and original design by Jonathan Dear and The Crowd Roars.
Illustrations throughout by Edward Briant.

ISBN 1-85828-408-2

Mallorca
& Menorca

THE ROUGH GUIDE

Written and researched by
Phil Lee

THE ROUGH GUIDES

Help us update

We've gone to a lot of trouble to ensure that this second edition of *The Rough Guide to Mallorca & Menorca* is completely up to date and accurate. However, things do change: hotels and restaurants come and go, opening hours are notoriously fickle, and prices are volatile. We'd appreciate any suggestions, amendments or contributions for future editions of the guide. We'll credit all letters and send a copy of the next edition (or any other *Rough Guide*) for the best.

Please mark all letters "Rough Guide to Mallorca & Menorca Update" and send to:

Rough Guides, 62–70 Shorts Gardens, London WC2H 9AB or
Rough Guides, 375 Hudson St, 3rd Floor, New York, NY 10014.

Email should be sent to:
mail@roughguides.co.uk

Online updates about Rough Guide titles can be found on our Web site at *www.roughguides.com*

The author

Phil Lee has been writing for Rough Guides for over a decade. His other books in the series include Canada, Norway, the Pacific Northwest, Toronto and Brussels. He lives in Nottingham, where he was born and raised.

Readers' letters

Many thanks also to all the readers of the previous edition who took the time to write in with their suggestions and comments: Hilary Bradts, Garry Brooks, Rob Duckett, J. Jagger, Igor Jülich, Jeronimo Bauza Llado, Patrick Marks, Rosemary Morlin, Helen Sandelands, Derek Wilde and John Woodhouse.

Rough Guides

Travel Guides • Phrasebooks • Music and Reference Guides

We set out to do something different when the first Rough Guide was published in 1982. Mark Ellingham, just out of university, was travelling in Greece. He brought along the popular guides of the day, but found they were all lacking in some way. They were either strong on ruins and museums but went on for pages without mentioning a beach or taverna. Or they were so conscious of the need to save money that they lost sight of Greece's cultural and historical significance. Also, none of the books told him anything about Greece's contemporary life – its politics, its culture, its people, and how they lived.

So with no job in prospect, Mark decided to write his own guidebook, one which aimed to provide practical information that was second to none, detailing the best beaches and the hottest clubs and restaurants, while also giving hard-hitting accounts of every sight, both famous and obscure, and providing up-to-the-minute information on contemporary culture. It was a guide that encouraged independent travellers to find the best of Greece, and was a great success, getting shortlisted for the Thomas Cook travel guide award, and encouraging Mark, along with three friends, to expand the series.

The Rough Guide list grew rapidly and the letters flooded in, indicating a much broader readership than had been anticipated, but one which uniformly appreciated the Rough Guides' mix of practical detail and humour, irreverence and enthusiasm. Things haven't changed. The same four friends who began the series are still the caretakers of the Rough Guide mission today: to provide the most reliable, up-to-date and entertaining information to independent-minded travellers of all ages, on all budgets.

We now publish more than 100 titles and have offices in London and New York. The travel guides are written and researched by a dedicated team of more than 100 authors, based in Britain, Europe, the USA and Australia. We have also created a unique series of phrasebooks to accompany the travel series, along with the acclaimed series of music guides, and a best-selling pocket guide to the Internet and World Wide Web. We also publish comprehensive travel information on our Web site: *www.roughguides.com*

Contents

Introduction   ix

Part One   Basics   1

Getting there from Britain   3   Costs, money and banks   28
Getting there from Ireland   9   Getting around   30
Getting there from the US and   Accommodation   34
  Canada   10   Eating and drinking   37
Getting there from Australia and   Post, phones and the media   45
  New Zealand   13   Opening hours and public holidays   47
Getting there from the rest of Spain   15   Festivals, the bullfight and football 48
Visas and red tape   19   Trouble, the police and sexual
Insurance   20   harassment   51
Travellers with disabilities   22   Finding work   54
Information and maps   23   Directory   55
Health   27

Part Two   The Guide   57

Chapter 1   Palma and around   59

Arrival, orientation and information   61   Nightlife and entertainment   87
Accommodation   65   Listings   89
The city   68   Around Palma   91
Eating and drinking   84

Chapter 2   Northwest Mallorca   102

Sóller and around   105   Beyond Sóller: Cala Tuent to the
Down the coast from Deià to Port   Cap de Formentor   134
  d'Andratx   114   Alcúdia and around   152

Chapter 3   Southeast Mallorca   161

East from Palma to Artà   163   The south coast   186
The east coast   172

Chapter 4   Menorca   194

Maó and around   197   Central Menorca   217
Southeast Menorca   209   Ciutadella and around   225
Fornells and the northeast coast   212

Part Three   Contexts

A history of Mallorca and Menorca   241   Books   259
A chronology of Spanish history   251   Language   262
Flora and fauna   255   Glossary   267

Index

269

List of maps

Mallorca and Menorca x–xi
Air and sea connections 17
Chapter divisions 57
Palma and around **60**
Palma 62–63
Central Palma 69
Northwest Mallorca **103**
Sóller 107
Port de Sóller 110
A coastal walk from Deià to
 Port de Sóller 118
Valledemossa to Puig des Teix 126

Massanella 139
Pollença 142
Port de Pollença 146
Port de Pollença to Cala Bóquer 150
Port d'Alcúdia 155
Southeast Mallorca **162**
Cala Rajada 175
Porto Cristo 179
Colònia de Sant Jordi 188
Menorca **195**
Maó 198
Ciutadella 226

MAP SYMBOLS

═════ Motorway	🏛 Country mansion
═══ Main road	♟ Monastery
── Minor road	♦ Prehistoric site
▭▭▭ Steps	▲ Mountain peak
- - - - Footpath	Cliff
▬▬▬ Railway	⌒ Cave
++++ Tram line	🛈 Lighthouse
─── Waterway	�☆ Viewpoint
— — Ferry route	ⓘ Tourist office
– – – Chapter division boundary	✉ Post office
✕ Airport	★ Bus stop
P Parking	✉ Gate
◉ Hotel	✚ Church (town maps)
▣ Restaurant	Park
⚠ Campsite	Nature reserve
♦ Church (regional maps)	Beach
♖ Castle	

Introduction

F ew Mediterranean holiday spots are as often and as unfairly maligned as **Mallorca**. The largest of the Balearic Islands, an archipelago to the east of the Spanish mainland which also comprises Menorca, Ibiza and Formentera, Mallorca is commonly perceived as little more than sun, sex, booze and high-rise hotels – so much so that there's a long-standing Spanish joke about a mythical fifth Balearic island called "Majorca" (the English spelling), inhabited by an estimated four million tourists a year. However, this image, spawned by the helter-skelter development of the 1960s, takes no account of Mallorca's beguiling diversity.

Until well into this century, Mallorca was a sleepily agrarian backwater, left behind in the Spanish dash to exploit the Americas from the sixteenth century onwards. Mass tourism has reversed the island's fortunes since World War II, bringing the highest level of disposable income per capita in Spain, but the price has been profound social transformation and the disfigurement of tracts of the coastal landscape. However, the spread of development is surprisingly limited, essentially confined to the Bay of Palma, a thirty-kilometre strip flanking the island capital, and a handful of mega-resorts notching the east coast. Elsewhere, Mallorca is much less developed than many other parts of Spain. **Palma** itself, the Balearics' one real city, is a bustling, historic place whose grandee mansions and magnificent Gothic cathedral defy the expectations of many visitors. To the east of the capital stretches **Es Pla**, an agricultural plain that fills out the centre of the island, sprinkled with ancient and seldom visited country towns. On either side of the plain are coastal mountains. In the northwest, the rugged **Serra de Tramuntana** hides beautiful cove beaches, notably Cala de Deià and Platja de Formentor, and deep sheltered valleys. Crisscrossed with footpaths, the range is ideal hiking country, particularly in the cooler spring and autumn. Tucked away here too are a string of picturesque villages, such as Orient and Fornalutx, and a pair of intriguing monasteries at Valldemossa and Lluc. The gentler, greener **Serres de Llevant** shadow the coves of the east coast and culminate in the pine-clad headlands and medieval hill

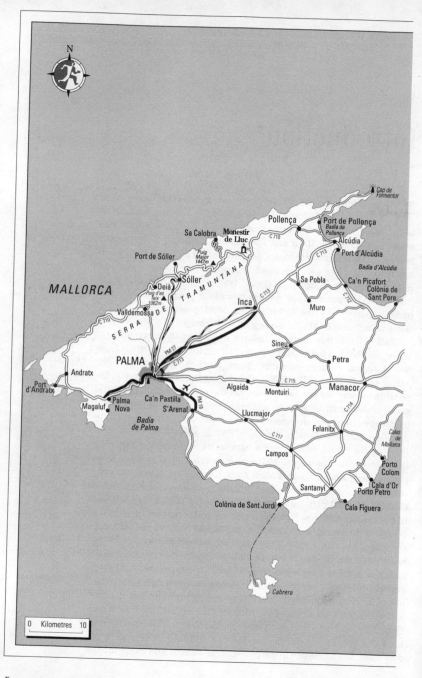

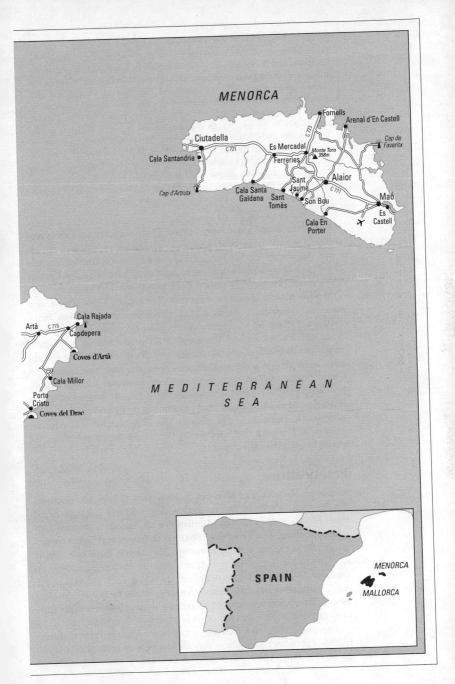

towns of the island's northeast corner. There's a startling variety and physical beauty to the land, which, along with the mildness of the climate, has drawn tourists to visit and well-heeled expatriates to settle here since the nineteenth century, including artists and writers of many descriptions, from Robert Graves to Roger McGough.

Smaller, flatter **Menorca**, next door, has escaped character assassination, principally because the development has been more restrained. Here on the most easterly Balearic, resorts and villa-villages are spread around the coast, with ready access to pristine coves and the rolling agricultural scenery of the interior. The resorts have been kept at a discreet distance from the two main towns, the island capital of **Maó**, with its magnificent harbour, and the beguiling old port of **Ciutadella**, arguably the prettiest settlement in the Balearics. Menorca's other claim to fame is its liberal smattering of **prehistoric remains**, most notably the cone-shaped stone heaps known as *talayots* and, unique to the island, the mysterious, T-shaped megaliths called *taulas*.

Practicalities

Access to Mallorca and Menorca is easy from Britain and northern Europe, with plenty of charter flights and complete package deals, some of which drop to absurd prices out of season or through last-minute booking. From mainland Spain, both ferries and flights are frequent and comparatively inexpensive. The islands have one airport and one major ferry port apiece, at Palma on Mallorca and Maó on Menorca. From these points of arrival, the rest of each island is within easy striking distance by car, and to a large extent by public transport as well; it only takes an hour or so to drive across Menorca, while from one corner of Mallorca to the other is a three- or four-hour trip.

The main constraint for travellers is accommodation. From mid-June to mid-September rooms are in very short supply on both islands. If you go at this time, you're well advised to make a reservation several months in advance or to book a package. Out of season on Mallorca, things ease up and you can idle round, staying pretty much where you want. Two or three weeks are sufficient to see most of the island; on a shorter visit, head for Palma and the northwest coast. Bear in mind also that six of Mallorca's monasteries rent out renovated cells at exceptionally inexpensive rates – it's well worth sampling at least one. On Menorca, most tourist facilities close down from November to April – the best bases are Maó, Fornells and Ciutadella, each of which has a small cache of all-year hotels and *hostals*.

Climate

There's little significant difference between the climates of Mallorca and Menorca. Spring and autumn are the ideal times for a visit, when the weather is comfortably warm, with none of the oven-like temperatures which bake the islands in July and August. It's well worth considering a winter break too – even in January, temperatures are usually high enough during the day to sit out at a café in shirtsleeves. Both islands see occasional rain in winter, however, and the Serra de Tramuntana mountains, which protect the rest of Mallorca from inclement weather, are often buffeted by storms, while Menorca, where there's no mountain barrier, can be irritatingly windy.

Palma climate table

	J	F	M	A	M	J	J	A	S	O	N	D
Highest recorded temp (°C)	22	23	24	26	31	37	39	37	35	31	26	24
Average daily max. temp (°C)	14	15	17	19	22	26	29	29	27	23	18	15
Average daily min. temp (°C)	6	6	8	10	13	17	20	20	18	14	10	8
Lowest recorded temp (°C)	-3	-4	-1	1	5	8	12	11	4	1	1	-1
Average hours of sunshine per day	5	6	6	7	9	10	11	11	8	6	5	4
Average number of days with rain	8	6	8	6	5	3	1	3	5	9	8	9

Part 1

The Basics

Getting there from Britain 3

Getting there from Ireland 9

Getting there from the US and Canada 10

Getting there from Australia and New Zealand 13

Getting there from the rest of Spain 15

Visas and red tape 19

Insurance 20

Travellers with disabilities 22

Information and maps 23

Health 27

Costs, money and banks 28

Getting around 30

Accommodation 34

Eating and drinking 37

Post, phones and the media 45

Opening hours and public holidays 47

Festivals, the bullfight and football 48

Trouble, the police and sexual harassment 51

Finding work 54

Directory 55

Getting there from Britain

The easiest and often the cheapest way to reach Mallorca and Menorca from Britain is to fly, which takes a little over two hours from London, and two and three-quarter hours from Manchester on a non-stop flight. More arduous is the long drive to the east coast of Spain, where regular car ferries depart for both islands from Barcelona and, further south, from Valencia; these same ports also offer a summertime hydrofoil service to Mallorca. If you do decide to drive, it's worth considering the ferries linking Plymouth with Santander, and Poole or Portsmouth with Bilbao, both of which cut many hours off the driving time. The train journey from London to Barcelona takes between twelve and twenty hours depending on which route you use.

By air

Hundreds of aircraft, mostly **charter** planes, shuttle back and forth between Britain and Mallorca and Menorca during the summer season and, although the charters are heavily subscribed by package-tour operators well in advance, there are usually spare seats for independent travellers once these package firms have taken their allocation. Excellent deals are available, with tickets averaging around £170 return – though you can pay up to £100 less. As a general rule, prices are at their highest during July and August. On these flight-only deals, waiting until the last minute to book won't gain you much advantage: you won't save much (if any) cash and you have to be prepared to fly from any UK airport at any time of the day or night.

As far as **scheduled flights** are concerned, your choices are limited to a handful of direct flights a day to Mallorca and a few more daily services to both islands via Barcelona. A full fare on a scheduled flight to either Mallorca or Menorca can cost more than twice the average charter price, but scheduled tickets on special offer or with certain restrictions can be reasonably good value, especially as the departure times of scheduled flights are often more sociable than those of charters.

It's also worth considering buying a **package holiday** (see p.5) – even if you've no intention of using the accommodation provided, package prices, especially at the last minute, can be so low that they represent a reasonable deal for the flight alone.

Each island's **airport** is a short hop from its capital – Palma in Mallorca, and Menorca's Maó.

Charter flights

There are frequent **charter flights** from London and almost all of Britain's regional airports to Mallorca and Menorca during the summer, with flights from the major airports throughout the year. For an idea of current prices and availability, contact any high street travel agent or a specialist operator. A good source of last-minute bargains is Teletext or, increasingly, the Internet. The widest selection of ads for London departures is invariably found in the classified pages of the London listings magazine *Time Out* or in the *Evening Standard*. For regional departures, scan the local newspapers and the travel pages of the weekend broadsheets. Otherwise, the operators and agents listed in the boxes on p.4 and p.6 are a good starting point. First Choice, for example, offer twice-weekly flights to Mallorca and weekly flights to Menorca during the summer from most UK airports. Depending on seat availability, prices range from £100 to £240 return to Mallorca and from £125 to £240 to Menorca for stays of seven and fourteen nights, with additional supplements payable for three- and four-week returns.

Airlines

British Airways, 156 Regent St, London W1R 5TA; 146 New St, Birmingham B2 4HN; 32 Frederick St, Edinburgh EH2 2JR; 66 Gordon St, Glasgow G1 3RS; 41–43 Deansgate, Manchester M3 2AY (all enquiries ☎0345/222111). Internet: *www.britishairways.com* (online booking and information).

British Midland, Donington Hall, Castle Donington, Derby DE74 2SB ☎0345/554554. Internet: *www.iflybritishmidland.com* (online booking and information).

EasyJet, "Easyland", London Luton Airport, Luton, Beds LU2 9LS (enquiries ☎01582/702900; reservations ☎0870/333 0870). Internet: *www.easyjet.com.*

Iberia, 27–29 Glasshouse St, London W1R 6SU ☎0990/341341. Internet: *www.iberia.com* (online booking and information).

Discount flight agents

Avro, Vantage House, 1 Weir Rd, London SW19 8UX ☎0181/715 0000. *A wide range of bargains.*

Cheapflights, Internet: *www.cheapflights.co.uk This UK Web site searches for the best fare bargains and provides links to the agents.*

Dial-a-Flight, London ☎0171/334 0994; Croydon ☎0181/401 6670; Maidstone ☎01622/617200; Manchester ☎0161/962 9799. *First-rate bargains with over-the-phone booking.*

STA Travel, Telephone sales ☎0171/361 6161. 117 Euston Rd, London NW1 2SX ☎0171/465 0484; 38 Store St, London WC1E 7BZ

☎0171/580 7733; 86 Old Brompton Rd, London SW7 3LQ ☎0171/581 4132; 30 Upper Kirkgate, Aberdeen AB10 1BA ☎01224/658222; 38 North St, Brighton BN1 1RH ☎01273/728282; 25 Queens Rd, Bristol BS8 1QE ☎0117/929 4399; 38 Sidney St, Cambridge CB2 3HX ☎01223/366966; 184 Byres Rd, Glasgow G12 8SN ☎0141/338 6000; 88 Vicar Lane, Leeds LS1 7JH ☎0113/244 9212; 75 Deansgate, Manchester M3 2BW ☎0161/834 0668; 36 George St, Oxford OX1 2OJ ☎01865/792800; plus branches at universities around the country. Internet: *www.statravel. co.uk. Worldwide specialists in low-cost flights and tours for students and under-26s.*

Travel Bug, 597 Cheetham Hill Rd, Manchester M8 5EJ ☎0161/721 4000. *Large range of discounted tickets.*

Usit Campus, 52 Grosvenor Gardens, London SW1W 0AG ☎0171/730 3402; 110 High St, Aberdeen AB24 3HE ☎01224/273559; 541 Bristol Rd, Bournbrook, Selly Oak, Birmingham B29 6AU ☎0121/414 1848; 61 Ditchling Rd, Brighton BN1 4SD ☎01273/570226; 39 Queen's Rd, Clifton, Bristol BS8 1QE ☎0117/929 2494; 5 Emmanuel St, Cambridge CB1 1NE ☎01223/324283; 20 Fairfax St, Coventry CV1 5RY ☎01203/225777; 53 Forest Rd, Edinburgh EH1 2QP ☎0131/668 3303; 122 George St, Glasgow G1 1RF ☎0141/553 1818; 166 Deansgate, Manchester M3 3FE ☎0161/273 1721; 105–106 St Aldates, Oxford OX1 1BU ☎01865/242067. Internet: *www.campustravel.co.uk.*

Student/youth travel specialists, with branches also in YHA shops and on university campuses all over Britain.

The principal disadvantage of charter flights is the **fixed return date** – a maximum of four weeks from the outward journey. Some return charters are, however, good value even if you only use half, but for more flexibility you'll probably want to buy a ticket for a scheduled flight.

Scheduled flights

Spain's national carrier, **Iberia**, is the main operator of scheduled flights from Britain to Mallorca and Menorca. They operate a one-stop service from Heathrow, which takes around four and a half hours to reach either Mallorca (three–four times daily in summer, once in winter) or Menorca (two–three times daily in summer, once in winter) via Barcelona or Madrid. Iberia also run a daily service from Manchester to Palma via Barcelona, with a journey time of around five hours. Their principal competitors are **British Midland**, who operate non-stop services from Heathrow (daily; 2hr 15min) and from East Midlands (2–3 weekly; 2hr 30min) to Mallorca and **EasyJet**, who fly from Luton to Mallorca (daily; 2hr 30min). British Midland can also provide good connections on to Mallorca via Heathrow from several other British airports: Edinburgh (1 daily; 6hr), Glasgow (1 daily; 6hr), Leeds (1 daily; 5hr) and Teesside (1 daily; 5hr). **British Airways** offer five non-stop flights weekly from Gatwick to Palma (2hr 30min) on its franchised carrier, GB Airways. Otherwise, BA operate frequent one-stop flights to Barcelona from six regional British airports as well as non-stop flights from London and Manchester. Connecting flights from Barcelona to the islands can be booked through BA but it may be cheaper to book the final leg of your trip separately with Iberia (for more information on flights to the islands from the Spanish mainland, see p.16).

Scheduled tickets at the cheapest **prices** carry almost as many restrictions as charter flights. Usually they are only valid for one month, need to be booked a minimum of fourteen days in advance, require you to stay at least one Saturday night, and don't allow for cancellation or change. For instance, Iberia's Economy Class return ticket from London to Mallorca (on which the above restrictions apply) costs around £300 in summer, £205 in winter, whereas a ticket without restrictions will set you back over £500 return; their flights from Manchester cost an additional £20 for Economy Class and an extra £100 plus for more flexible tickets. Similarly, British Midland's full-fare return to Palma (with no restrictions) can cost over £500 from East Midlands Airport. On the other hand, its restricted Economy Class return fares begin at £150 in the off-season, increasing to £200 mid-season, and £230 in the high season. The cheapest flight is with EasyJet, whose high-season return costs in the region of £90, although you'll need to book well in advance. Look out also for the **special offers** which the scheduled airlines sometimes run on their Economy Class tickets. Another option is Iberia's **open-jaw tickets**, whereby you fly into one island and return from the other, with an inter-island flight as part of the arrangement if you require it: London–Palma and Maó–London costs around £224 in low season, £235 in high without the inter-island flight, an extra £30 with.

Packages

Few places on earth provide the **package tourist** with as many choices as Mallorca and Menorca, but unfortunately for the islands' reputations it's the ugly high-rise hotels – along with the drunken antics of some of their clientele – that have grabbed most of the media attention. However, there are also plenty of countrified villas and apartments, genteel pensions and ritzy hotels on offer from companies such as Magic of Spain and Mundi Color, as well as walking holidays around the islands' lesser-known beauty spots.

High street travel agents will help you trawl through a wide range of packages, some of which are excellent value. If the price is right, it can also be worth booking a package simply for the flight: after all, there's no compulsion to stick around at your hotel for the full period of your holiday and it's handy to have your lodgings sorted out at least for a night or two at each end of your trip. Packages are especially worth considering at the height of the season when island accommodation can be very hard to find through independent means, and the last minute deals advertised in travel agents' windows can work out almost cheaper than staying at home.

To give yourself a general idea of prices, you could start by looking at the Thomson brochures in any travel agent. Prices per person for seven nights in a self-catering **apartment** with pool access, including the return flight, start at around £185 in the low season and rise to £365 in July and August. An equivalent Menorcan holiday will cost between £205 and £370. Thomson's **hotel** holidays begin at about £280 in May (£400 in August) for a week in a standard high-rise with half-board on Mallorca, and £345–485 on Menorca. By comparison, Magic of Spain offers a week's half-board in a medium-sized four-star hotel for £525 per person (£690 in high season), and spacious **villas** for two to six people, with car rental and private pool, for £330 per person per week (£590 in high season). Mundi Color send their customers to some of the finest hotels on the island, such as *La Residencia* in Deià (seven nights B&B including car hire from £990).

Packaged **activity holidays** are another option, with **walking** in Mallorca an especially popular pastime. The best hiking is in the Serra de Tramuntana mountains of northwest Mallorca, and going with a guide makes sense as the available hiking maps are not wholly reliable. Globespan, for example, specialize in this type of holiday in Mallorca, running over twenty different hikes with an average length of around 12km. Their seven-night package (Sept–May only), including three or four guided walks and self-catering accommodation, but not flights, costs as

Package tour operators

Alternative Mallorca, 60 Steinbeck Rd, Leeds LS7 2PW ☎ 0113/278 6862.
All-in and accommodation-only packages at a wide range of prices in lesser-known parts of Mallorca, as well as walking holidays and courses in birdwatching.

First Choice, First Choice House, Peel Cross Rd, Salford, Manchester M4 2AN ☎ 0870/750 0001. Internet: *www.first-choice.com*.
The standard range of package holiday fare, with a flight-only booking option.

Freelance Holidays (Mallorca), 40b Grove Rd, Stratford upon Avon, Warwickshire CV37 6PB ☎ 01789/297705.
A wide variety of self-catering accommodation in beautiful locations, including the Serra de Tramuntana.

Globespan, Colinton House, 10 West Mill Rd, Colinton Village, Edinburgh EH13 0NX ☎ 0131/441 1388.
Seven- and fourteen-night hiking holidays (Sept–May), including self-catering accommodation but not flights.

Ilkeston Co-op, 12 South St, Ilkeston, Derbyshire DE7 5SG ☎ 0115/932 3546.
A wide range of package holidays, often at extraordinarily cheap prices, plus bargain-basement charter flights to both Mallorca and Menorca, especially from Birmingham and East Midlands airports.

The Individual Traveller's Spain, Manor Courtyard, Bignor, Pulborough, West Sussex RH20 1QD ☎ 0179/886 9485.
Deluxe farmhouses, villas, cottages and village houses on both Mallorca and Menorca.

Magic of Spain, 227 Shepherd's Bush Rd, London W6 7AS ☎ 0181/748 4220.
Upmarket hotel and villa holidays, often in out-of-the-way places, on both Mallorca and Menorca.

Minorca Sailing Holidays, 58 Kew Rd, Richmond, Surrey TW9 2PQ ☎ 0181/948 2106.
Specializing in dinghy sailing and windsurfing holidays with a range of accommodation options and tuition available.

Mundi Color, 276 Vauxhall Bridge Rd, London SW1V 1BE ☎ 0171/828 6021.
Quality hotel package holidays across Mallorca.

Thomson, Greater London House, Hampstead Rd, London NW1 7SD ☎ 0990/502555.
One of the largest UK package-tour companies, with holidays to both Mallorca and Menorca. Brochures on all manner of holidays to suit most budgets are available at any high-street travel agent, including vacations in villas and apartments, family-owned hotels and luxury hotels, as well as city breaks in Palma.

little as £140 in November, increasing to around £170 at the end of May. Increasingly popular **sailing and windsurfing** holidays are more expensive, with Minorca Sailing offering one week in shared 'pot luck', self-catering accommodation at £580 in May and £850 in July and August, including flight, tuition and the use of equipment.

By train

Travelling by **train** from London, it can take as little as twelve hours to reach **Barcelona**, from where there are regular ferries to Palma and Maó (see p.16). The first leg of the journey involves taking a **Eurostar** train from London's Waterloo Station via the Channel Tunnel to either Lille or Paris, from where a **TGV** will take you on to Barcelona. The journey takes two hours to Lille, from where you can catch the TGV to Barcelona

via Montpellier, a daytime journey of around ten hours. Alternatively, Eurostar trains continue from Lille to Paris, arriving an hour later at the Gare du Nord. In Paris you have to change stations to the Gare de Lyon to catch the TGV to Montpellier. The only advantage of travelling via Paris is the slightly greater number of trains: there are two or three daily from Lille; four or five from Paris.

Another, cheaper, option is to reach Paris using the **Dover–Calais ferry**, though this increases the journey time to about twenty hours. From Paris, an alternative to using the TGV is to take the direct overnight train, the **Talgo**, which leaves the Gare Austerlitz in Paris daily at 8.47pm and arrives in Barcelona at 8.53am. It's slower and more expensive than the TGV but has the benefit of arriving in the morning to connect with ferry departures. In Barcelona, the Estació Marítim for

Train information

Eurostar ☎ 0990/186186.
Internet: *www.eurostar.com*.

National Rail Enquiries ☎ 0345/484950 for UK rail travel. See also the Railtrack timetable information on the Internet at *www.railtrack.co.uk*.

Rail Europe Information Line ☎ 0990/848848

SNCF, Internet: *www.sncf.fr*

Bus information

Eurolines UK ☎ 0990/143219 plus agents nationwide. Internet: *www.eurolines.co.uk*

National Express ☎ 0990/808080. Internet: *www.nationalexpress.co.uk* (for timetable and fares information).

ferries to the Balearics is at the foot of La Rambla, in the heart of the city and some 4km from the Estació-Sants train station, where all the trains mentioned above pull in – take metro line no.3 from Estació-Sants to Drassanes.

The **price** of a standard rail ticket from London to Barcelona via the Channel Tunnel (available from some travel agents, Rail Europe (see box above) and major train stations) fluctuates with the season and in accordance with restrictions similar to those of an airline ticket. To get the cheaper fares, you need to be away on a Saturday night and book at least eight days in advance. A sample fare in July from London to Barcelona within these restrictions costs £229 return via Lille with Eurostar/TGV, whilst the Eurostar/Talgo option via Paris weighs in at £264 return – £99 to Paris with Eurostar and £165 for the return journey from Paris to Barcelona on the Talgo (including compulsory sleeping accommodation). It's recommended to book well in advance in summer.

By bus

The main **bus route** between Britain and north-east Spain connects London with Barcelona (from where you can reach the Balearics by ferry – see p.16) via Calais, Perpignan and Girona. Bus services are operated by Eurolines in Britain, with departures from London's Victoria Station three times weekly. Eurolines sell tickets, including through-transport to London, at all British National Express bus terminals, and through many travel agents. The return **fare** from London to Barcelona is £119; there's also a **youth fare** (for under 25s) of £109 return.

The journey time from London to Barcelona is around 26 hours, long but just about bearable if you take enough to eat, drink and read. There are stops for around twenty minutes every four to five hours, and the routine is also broken by the cross-Channel ferry (included in the cost of a ticket). A small amount of French currency is useful for coffees and snacks. Buses arrive at the Barcelona–Sants bus terminal, close to the Estació-Sants train station and some 4km north of the Balearic ferry dock, which is in the town centre at the foot of La Rambla – take metro line no.3 from Estació-Sants to Drassanes.

By car

The traditional route **by car** to Spain involves taking a ferry across the Channel and driving through France, for which you should allow at least two days – unless, that is, you can share the driving and manage to travel non-stop. You can book your vehicle onto a **cross-Channel ferry** or **hovercraft** through a travel agent or direct with the company. As a rough guide, a low-season return fare on P&O's **Dover–Calais** ferry costs around £155 for a driver, passenger and average-sized car, increasing to around £210 in the summer. Dover–Calais is the obvious – and fastest – choice, but you could also **travel Dover–Boulogne** or **Ramsgate–Dunkerque**. If your starting point is to the west of London, or if you simply want to cut down on driving time through France, it may well be worth **crossing to Normandy or Brittany** via one of the other south coast ports: potentially useful routings are Newhaven to Dieppe, and Portsmouth, Weymouth or Poole to Le Havre, Caen or Cherbourg.

For details of ferries from mainland Spain to the Balearics, see p.16.

Via The Shuttle

Taking **The Shuttle's** drive-on/drive-off service through the Channel Tunnel, rather than a cross-Channel ferry, cuts a couple of hours off the journey time to Spain. Le Shuttle operates trains 24 hours a day, carrying cars, motorcycles, buses and their passengers, and taking 35 minutes between Folkestone and Coquelles, near Calais. At peak times services operate every fifteen minutes; during the night they run every 45 minutes.

Ferry companies and The Shuttle

Brittany Ferries ☎ 0990/360360.
Internet: *www.brittany-ferries.com*
(timetable information and special offers).
To Santander, Roscoff, St Malo, Cherbourg and Caen.

Hoverspeed ☎ 0990/240241.
Internet: *www.hoverspeed.co.uk* (timetable, fares information and booking by email).
To Boulogne, Ostend and Calais.

P&O European Ferries ☎ 0990/980555.
Internet: *www.poef.com/portsmouth*

(timetable, special offers and online booking).
To Cherbourg, Le Havre and Bilbao.

P&O Stena Line ☎ 0990/980980. Internet:
www.posl.com (timetables, offers information and online booking). *To Calais and Dieppe.*

SeaFrance ☎ 0990/711711.
Internet: *www.seafrance.com*
(fares, schedules and booking). *To Calais.*

The Shuttle ☎ 0990/353535.
Internet: *www.eurotunnel.com*
(timetable and price information).

Fares vary with the season and the time of day you travel, with standard returns beginning at £136 from October to March and increasing to £220 on July and August weekends between 6am and 10pm. Tickets cover the car and all its passengers. The five-day limit on most return tickets means you may be better off buying two singles, generally half the price of a return. There's also a bargain £15 return bicycle ticket.

Via Santander or Bilbao

Although they're expensive, the direct car and passenger ferry services from England to northern Spain greatly reduce the driving time to Barcelona. Brittany Ferries sail from **Plymouth to Santander** twice weekly most weeks from March to mid-November, with a sailing time of 24 hours,

and from **Portsmouth or Poole to Santander** once weekly for the rest of the year. This is a thirty-hour trip from Portsmouth, 28 hours from Poole. P&O's twice-weekly ferry service from **Portsmouth to Bilbao** takes 35 hours. From Santander it's about nine hours' drive to Barcelona; from Bilbao about eight.

Ticket prices vary enormously according to the season and the number of passengers carried. As an illustration, a return with Brittany Ferries would cost around £360 for two adults and car in low season, £645 in peak season, including pullman seats for sleeping. Two-berth cabins are available from £104 return in low season, £142 in high season. Tickets are best booked in advance, either directly with the company by phone or through any major travel agent.

Getting there from Ireland

Summer charter flights direct to Mallorca and Menorca are easy to pick up from either Dublin or Belfast. Prices are at their highest during August – reckon on around £230/IR£245 return – but drop a little in the months either side. If you're prepared to book at the last minute, you'll sometimes get a cheaper deal, though you won't necessarily get the departure date you want. As another option, you might find that taking a budget flight from Dublin (with Aer Lingus or British Midland) or Belfast (British Airways, Iberia or British Midland) to London, and then a London–Palma charter flight will save you a few pounds. Buying a Eurotrain ticket (through USIT) from Dublin to London may cut costs slightly again, but by this time you're starting to talk about a journey of days rather than hours. Students – and anyone under 31 – should contact USIT, who generally have the best discounts on Balearic flights.

Iberia have **scheduled flights** from Dublin to Mallorca via Barcelona daily, with the cheapest return fare costing IR£380 in July and August. These cheapest, Economy Class fares have several restrictions – you can't change your departure date and you can't extend your visit beyond

---

Airlines in Ireland

Aer Lingus, 46–48 Castle St, Belfast BT1 1HB; 2 Academy St, Cork; 40 41 O'Connell St, Dublin 1; 136 O'Connell St, Limerick; all enquiries ☎0645/737747.

British Airways, Suite 1, Fountain Centre, College St, Belfast BT1 6ET ☎0345/222111; c/o Aer Lingus, 38 Patrick St, Cork; c/o Aer Lingus, 13 St Stephen's Green, Dublin 2; all enquiries in Eire ☎1800/626747.

British Midland, Suite 2, Fountain Centre, College St, Belfast BT1 6ET ☎0345/554554; Nutley, Merrion Rd, Dublin 2 ☎01/283 8833.

Iberia, 54 Dawson St, Dublin 2 ☎01/677 9846.

Travel agents in Ireland

J Barter Travel, Unit 2, Douglas Shopping Centre, Cork ☎021/894084. *Reliable agent, good for cheap flights.*

Thomas Cook, 11 Donegal Place, Belfast BT1 5AJ ☎01232/554455; 118 Grafton St, Dublin 2 ☎01/677 1721.

Internet: *www.thomascook.com*.
Package holiday and flight agent, with occasional discount offers.

Tommy Tobin Travel, 10 Chatham Lane, Dublin 2 ☎01/694100.
Good and efficient general travel agent.

Tony Roche Travel, Travel House, Walkinstown Cross, Dublin 12 ☎01/456 7311.
Specialist in last-minute bookings.

USIT, Fountain Centre, College St, Belfast BT1 6ET ☎01232/324073; 10–11 Market Parade, Patrick St, Cork ☎021/270900; 33 Ferryquay St, Derry BT48 6JB ☎01504/371888; 19–21 Aston Quay, O'Connell Bridge, Dublin 2 ☎01/602 1600; Victoria Place, Eyre Square, Galway ☎091/565177; Central Buildings, O'Connell St, Limerick ☎061/415064; 36–37 Georges St, Waterford ☎051/872601; plus offices at Athlone, Coleraine, Jordanstown and Maynooth. Internet: *www.usit.ie*. *Student and youth specialist for flights and trains.*

a maximum of one month. The same ticket without restrictions runs to about IR£720 return all year. For Menorca, you change at Barcelona; the fares are the same as for Dublin–Mallorca. Iberia also operate a once-daily flight from Belfast to Barcelona via London, a route that's followed three times daily by British Airways. Both these carriers have additional services to Mallorca and Menorca from London (see p.4). Watch out for special offers from the scheduled airlines, which can reduce fares by anything up to forty percent.

A two-week **package holiday** to Mallorca or Menorca (based on four people in a reasonably comfortable self-catering apartment) will cost about £260 per person in low season, rising to £480 high season, from Belfast, and from about IR£300 (low) to IR£480 (high) from Dublin. You may well find you're routed via London, with an add-on fare for the connection from Ireland.

Getting there from the US and Canada

There are no direct flights from any part of North America to Mallorca or Menorca. The nearest you'll get are Iberia's one- or two-stop flights from Los Angeles, New York, Chicago, Miami and Montréal via Madrid to Palma, Mallorca. Iberia offer competitive rates for their transatlantic flights, so they should be your first line of enquiry. The most obvious alternative is to search for the least expensive transatlantic fare offered by any airline to Madrid or Barcelona, from where an Iberia domestic flight will shuttle you across to the islands.

Shopping for tickets

Barring special offers, the cheapest of the airlines' published fares are usually **Apex** tickets, although these carry certain restrictions concerning the length of your stay (usually a maximum of one month, and including a Saturday night), and the latest date for payment for your ticket (usually 14 or 21 days before departure); you will also be penalized if you change your schedule. Some airlines offer youth or student fares to **under 26s**; a passport or driving licence are sufficient proof of age, though these tickets are subject to availability and can have eccentric booking conditions.

You might be able to cut costs further by going through a **specialist flight agent** – either a **consolidator**, who buys up blocks of tickets from the airlines and sells them at a discount, or a **discount agent**, who in addition to dealing with discounted flights may also offer special student and youth fares and a range of other travel-related services such as travel insurance, rail passes, car rentals, tours and the like. Bear in mind, though, that penalties for changing your plans can be stiff. Remember too that these companies make their money by dealing in bulk – don't expect them to answer lots of questions. Some agents specialize in **charter flights**, which may be cheaper than anything available on a scheduled flight, but again departure dates are fixed and withdrawal penalties are high (check the refund policy). If you travel a lot, **discount travel clubs** are another option – the annual membership fee may be worth it for benefits such as cut-price air tickets and car rental.

Don't automatically assume that tickets purchased through a travel specialist will be cheapest – once you get a quote, check with the airlines and you may turn up an even better deal. Be advised also that the pool of travel companies is swimming with sharks – exercise caution and never deal with a company that demands cash up front or refuses to accept payment by credit card.

A further possibility is to see if you can arrange a **courier flight** to Madrid, although the hit-or-miss nature of these makes them most suitable for the single traveller who travels light and has a very flexible schedule. You get a discounted ticket in return for shepherding a parcel through customs and possibly giving up your baggage allowance. A couple of courier outfits are listed in the box overleaf.

Regardless of where you buy your ticket, the **fare** will, most likely, depend on season. As a general rule, you can expect fares to Spain to be highest from around mid-May to the end of September; they drop during the "shoulder" seasons (October, April to mid-May and mid-December to mid-January); you'll get the best deals during the low season, November through March (excluding the weeks around Christmas/New Year). Remember that these seasonal boundaries can vary from airline to airline and from year to year, so if you want to make sure you're getting the best deal, always double check. Note that flying on weekends ordinarily adds around $50/CDN$70 to the return fare; price ranges quoted in the following sections assume midweek travel and exclude taxes (around $50 or CDN$55).

From the US

On Iberia's daily flights to Palma, Mallorca via Madrid, the Apex fare (maximum stay one month, payment 21 days before departure) from Los Angeles (12hr) is $1259 high season, $931 low season; from New York (8hr) $1013 high, $685 low; from Chicago (9hr) $975 high, $685 low; and from Miami (8hr) $1105 high, $777 low. Travelling on any of these tickets, however, you can't break your journey in Madrid. If you want a stopover in

---

Airlines in North America

Air Europa ☎1-800/327-1225; *www.easyspain.com.* *Flies each Monday, Thursday and Friday from New York to Madrid.*

Air France ☎1-800/237-2747; in Canada ☎1-800/667-2747; *www.airfrance.fr.* *Flies daily from New York, Chicago, Atlanta, Miami, San Francisco, Los Angeles, Washington DC, Toronto and Montréal to Paris and then on to Madrid, Barcelona and Sevilla.*

American Airlines ☎1-800/433-7300; *www.americanair.com.* *Daily non-stop flights from Miami to Madrid.*

British Airways ☎1-800/247-9297; in Canada ☎1-800/668-1059; *www.britishairways.com.* *Flies daily via London from Montréal, Toronto and Vancouver plus 21 gateway cities in the US to Madrid and Barcelona.*

Continental Airlines ☎1-800/231-0856; *www.flycontinental.com.* *Daily flights from Newark to Madrid.*

Delta Airlines ☎1-800/241-4141; *www.delta-air.com. Daily direct flights from New York to Madrid and Barcelona with* connections from most other major North American cities.

Iberia ☎1-800/772-4642; in Canada ☎1-800/423-7421; *www.iberiausa.com.* *Flights to Palma, Mallorca via Madrid from New York, Chicago, Miami and Montréal, plus special deals such as fly-drive.*

Lufthansa ☎1-800/645-3880; *www.lufthansa-usa.com.* *Flights from many US cities to Madrid, Barcelona, Valencia, Bilbao and Palma, all via Frankfurt.*

Northwest/KLM ☎1-800/447-4747 or 1-800/374-7747; *www.nwa.com.* *Flights from major US and Canadian cities, via Amsterdam, to Madrid and Barcelona.*

Sabena ☎1-800/955-2000; *www.sabena.com.* *Flights from East Coast and Midwest cities to Barcelona, Madrid and Bilbao via Brussels.*

TAP Air Portugal ☎1-800/221-7370; *www.tap-airportugal.pt. New York and Boston to Madrid and Barcelona, via Lisbon.*

TWA ☎1-800/892-4141; *www.twa.com.* *New York to Madrid and Barcelona via Lisbon.*

---

mainland Spain, you'll need to purchase one ticket for the transatlantic leg and then a separate ticket for the onward flight to Mallorca or Menorca (see "Getting there from the rest of Spain", p.15). The price of an Iberia Apex fare to Madrid from Los Angeles is $1155 ($855 low); from New York $900 ($415 low); from Chicago $895 ($525 low); and from Miami $1015 ($490 low). You should also look out for special promotional offers.

The box overleaf details leading airlines with services to Spain. Other companies worth investigating are Lufthansa, who currently quote a return New York–Palma via Frankfurt fare of $500 ($1260 high season), and Delta, whose direct low-season return special from New York to Barcelona costs just $356 ($934 high season). The advantage of Barcelona as an intermediate destination is its proximity to Mallorca and Menorca, with frequent onward Iberia flights to Palma costing $134 round-trip.

From Canada

There's not much choice when it comes to flying direct from Canada to Spain, never mind the Balearics. Iberia operate the only service, thrice-weekly flights from **Montréal** via Madrid to Palma, Mallorca. The Iberia Apex fare to Mallorca from Montréal is around CDN$1225 in high season, CDN$935 in low. Fares are the same from Toronto as from Montréal, whilst from Vancouver expect to pay in the region of CDN$1775 (high), CDN$1315 (low). Travelling on these tickets, however, you can't break your journey in Madrid. If you want to stopover there, you'll need to purchase one ticket for the transatlantic leg and then a separate ticket for an onward flight to Mallorca or Menorca (see "Getting there from the rest of Spain", p.15). The price of an Iberia Apex fare to Madrid from Montréal or Toronto is around CDN$995 (high season) or CDN$835 (low), and from Vancouver approximately CDN$1455 (high) or CDN$1215 (low). You should also check out other airlines through a discount agent such as Travel Cuts. Travelling from Toronto, for instance, they may be able to route you through a European city such as Frankfurt for a return fare of roughly CDN$1000 (high season) or CDN$800 (low).

Discount travel companies in North America

Air Courier Association, 191 University Blvd, Suite 300, Denver, CO 80206 ☎1-800/282-1202 or 303/215-0900; *www.aircourier.org*.
Courier flight broker.

Airtech, 588 Broadway, Suite 204, New York, NY 10017 ☎1-800/575-8324 or 212/219-7000; *www.airtech.com*.
Stand-by seat broker, courier agent and consolidator.

Council Travel, 205 E 42nd St, New York, NY 10017 ☎1-800/226-8624, 888/COUNCIL or 212/822-2700; *www.ciee.com*. Other branches in San Francisco, Los Angeles, Boston, Chicago, Washington DC.
Nationwide specialists in student travel.

Educational Travel Center, 438 N Frances St, Madison, WI 53703 ☎1-800/747-5551 or 608/256-5551; *www.edtrav.com*.
Student/youth and consolidator fares.

International Association of Air Travel Couriers, 8 South J St, PO Box 1349, Lake Worth, FL 33460 ☎561/582-8320; *www.courier.org*.
Courier flight broker.

STA Travel, 10 Downing St, New York, NY 10014 ☎1-800/777-0112 or 212/627-3111; *www.sta-travel.com*. Other branches in Los Angeles, Chicago, San Francisco, Philadelphia and Boston.
Worldwide discount travel firm specializing in student/youth fares; also student IDs, travel insurance, car rental, train passes, etc.

TFI Tours International, 34 W 32nd St, New York, NY 10001 ☎1-800/745-8000 or 212/736-1140. *Consolidator*.

Travac, 989 Sixth Ave, New York, NY 10018 ☎1-800/872-8800 or 212/563-3303.
Consolidator and charter broker mostly to Europe; has another office in Orlando.

Travel Avenue, 10 S Riverside, Suite 1404, Chicago, IL 60606 ☎1-800/333-3335 or 312/876-6866; *www.travelavenue.com*.
Discount travel company.

Travel Cuts, 187 College St, Toronto, ON M5T 1P7 ☎1-800/667-2887 or 416/979-2406; *www.travelcuts.com*. Branches in Montréal, Vancouver, Calgary and Winnipeg.
Canadian discount travel organization.

Tour operators in North America

North American travellers are hardly spoiled for choice when it comes to finding a tour operator offering deals to Mallorca/Menorca. Don't expect anything more imaginative than the basic air/hotel beach resort combo with maybe a sightseeing tour thrown in and the option of reduced-rate car rental. The companies in the box below either have set packages available or will help you customize one of your own. As a very rough estimate of price, for a low-season six-night air-hotel package expect to pay upwards of $950.

Tour operators in North America

Auto Europe ☎ 1-800/223-5555; *www.autoeurope.com. Air-hotel deals and car rental.*

Central Holidays, 120 Sullivan Ave, Englewood Cliffs, NJ 07632 ☎ 1-800/227-5858; *www.centralholidays.com. Agents for the Iberia tour department's Discover Spain Vacations.*

EC Tours, 12500 Riverside Drive, Suite #210, Valley Village, CA 91607-3423 ☎ 1-800/388-0877; *www.ectours.com.*

Escapade Tours, c/o Isram World of Travel, 630 Third Ave, New York, NY 10017 ☎ 1-800/356-2405; *www.isram.com.*

International Gay Travel Association ☎ 1-800/448-8550. *Trade group with lists of gay-owned or gay-friendly travel agents, accommodations and other travel businesses.*

M.I. Travel, 450 Seventh Ave, Suite 1805, New York, NY 10123 ☎ 1-800/848-2314 or 212/967-6565; *www.stoa.spain.com.*

Petrabax Tours, 9745 Queens Blvd, Rego Park, NY 11374 ☎ 1-800/634-1188; *www.petrabax.com.*

Saga Holidays, 222 Berkely St, Boston, MA 02116 ☎ 1-800/343-0273. *Group travel for seniors.*

Travel Go Round, 90-05 Jericho Turnpike, Mineola, NY 11501 ☎ 1-800/293-0076; *www.travelgoround.com.*

Getting there from Australia and New Zealand

There are no direct flights to any part of Spain from Australia or New Zealand, but various airlines offer one-stop services to Madrid and Barcelona. British Airways (via London), KLM (via Amsterdam), Alitalia (via Milan), Singapore Airlines (via Singapore) and Thai Airways (via Bangkok) have reasonably frequent flights and competitive fares; Lauda Air's connections (via Vienna) are less convenient, but may be worth checking for special offers. From Barcelona or Madrid there are regular direct flights to Mallorca and Menorca (see "Getting there from the rest of Spain", p.15). Alternatively, it may be worth considering a

Airlines in Australia and New Zealand

Alitalia, 9/118 Alfred St, Milson's Point, North Sydney ☎ 02/9922 1555; local-call rate ☎ 1300/653 747; 6th floor, 229 Queen St, Auckland ☎ 09/379 4455.
Three connections a week to Madrid and Barcelona from Sydney and Melbourne via Milan.

British Airways, Level 19, 259 George St, Sydney ☎ 02/8904 8800; cnr Queen & Customs streets, Auckland ☎ 09/356 8690.
Daily to seven cities in Spain, via Bangkok or Kuala Lumpur and London, from Sydney, Melbourne, Perth and Auckland; daily from Brisbane via Singapore and London.

Iberia, c/o Aerolineas Argentinas, Level 2, 580 George St, Sydney ☎ 02/9238 3660; Level 6, 80 Collins St, Melbourne ☎ 03/9650 7111.
No flights to Europe from Australasia, but easily the widest range of flights into Mallorca and Menorca from London and other European destinations.

KLM, 5 Elizabeth St, Sydney ☎ 02/9231 6333; toll-free ☎ 1800/505 747.
Three times a week from Sydney to Madrid or Barcelona via Amsterdam.

Lauda Air, 11th Floor, 143 Macquarie St, Sydney ☎ 02/9251 6155; toll-free ☎ 1800/642 438.
Three flights a week from Sydney and Melbourne to Barcelona, with a one-night stopover in Vienna.

Qantas, 70 Hunter St, Sydney ☎ 02/9951 4294; reservations ☎ 13/1211; Qantas House, 154 Queen St, Auckland ☎ 09/357 8900 or 0800/808 767.
Twice-daily flights to London from all the mainland state capitals, connecting with British Airways for destinations in Spain.

Singapore Airlines, 17 Bridge St, Sydney ☎ 02/9350 0121; reservations ☎ 131960; Lower Ground Floor, West Plaza Building, cnr Customs and Albert streets, Auckland ☎ 09/379 3209 or 0800/808 909.
Twice a week from Melbourne and Sydney to Madrid via Singapore. Daily from Auckland to Madrid via Singapore (one-night stopover).

Thai Airways, 75 Pitt St, Sydney ☎ 02/9251 1922; reservations ☎ 1300/651 960; 1st Floor, 22 Fanshawe St, Auckland ☎ 09/377 3886; reservations ☎ 0800/100 992.
Sydney/Auckland to Madrid via Bangkok three times a week.

---

cheap flight to London, from where bargain fares to the islands are generally easy to pick up (see "Getting there from Britain", p.3). Any of the agents listed opposite can help with deals to Spain or London, or ticket you right through to the Balearics. Booking ahead as far as possible is the best way to secure the most reasonable prices.

Fares

Fares to Europe change according to the time of year you travel. Mid-May to the end of August, December and the first half of January are the high season; mid-January to the end of February, October and November the low season; and the rest of the year the shoulder

season. The current lowest standard return fares to Spain are around A$1700/2300 (low/high season) from Australia, NZ$2000/2800 from New Zealand; to London, fares are around A$1400/1900 from Australia, NZ$2150/2500 from New Zealand.

Though they charge heavily for cancellations or alterations, **discount agents** generally offer better deals than the airlines themselves. Full-time students and those aged under 26 or over 60 may also be eligible for special fares, although availability tends to vary according to the season. Some useful discount agents are listed in the box opposite, and others can be found in the travel sections of the major weekend newspapers.

Travel and discount agents in Australia and New Zealand

Accent on Travel, 545 Queen St, Brisbane ☎07/3832 1777.

Anywhere Travel, 345 Anzac Parade, Kingsford, Sydney ☎02/9663 0411.

Budget Travel, 16 Fort St, Auckland ☎09/366 0061; other branches around the city (☎09/366 0061 or 0800/808 040 for nearest branch).

Destinations Unlimited, 3 Milford Rd, Milford, Auckland ☎09/373 4033.

Flight Centre, Australia: 82 Elizabeth St, Sydney ☎02/9235 3522; 19 Bourke St, Melbourne ☎03/9650 2899; plus branches nationwide (☎13/1600 for nearest branch). New Zealand: National Bank Towers, 205–225 Queen St, Auckland ☎09/309 6171; other branches countrywide (☎0800/FLIGHTS for nearest branch).

Northern Gateway, 22 Cavenagh St, Darwin ☎08/8941 1394.

Passport Travel, 401 St Kilda Rd, Melbourne ☎03/9876 3888.

STA Travel, Australia: 855 George St, Sydney ☎02/9212 1255; 256 Flinders St, Melbourne ☎03/9654 7266, plus branches nationwide (☎13/1776 for nearest branch).

Travellers' Centre, 10 High St, Auckland ☎09/309 0458; 132 Cuba St, Wellington ☎04/385 0561; 90 Cashel St, Christchurch ☎03/379 9098; other offices in Dunedin, Palmerston North, Hamilton and major universities.

Thomas Cook, Australia: 175 Pitt St, Sydney ☎02/9229 6611; 257 Collins St, Melbourne ☎03/9282 0333; plus other city branches (nearest branch ☎13/1771). New Zealand: 159 Queen St, Auckland ☎09/379 3924 (nearest branch ☎0800/500 600).

Topdeck Travel, 65 Grenfell St, Adelaide ☎08/8232 7222.

Tymtro Travel, 428 George St, Sydney ☎02/9223 2211.

UTAG Travel, 122 Walker St, North Sydney ☎02/9956 8399; branches throughout Australia.

Getting there from the rest of Spain

Menorca and especially Mallorca are easily reached by plane and ferry from mainland Spain and from Ibiza. Obviously, the main advantage of a flight over a ferry journey is its speed: Barcelona to Palma, for example, takes just forty minutes, compared to the ferry trip of eight hours. By plane, there's also the advantage of a wider range of jumping-off points: regular scheduled flights link many of Spain's major cities with Mallorca and several with Menorca too. By ferry and hydrofoil you're confined to three departure ports for Mallorca – Ibiza, Valencia and Barcelona – and two ports (but no hydrofoil) for Menorca – Valencia and Barcelona. Ticket prices also favour aircraft travel: it is less expensive by ferry, but not by all that much, and not enough to justify the extra time and trouble – unless, that is, you're in or near one of the departure ports anyway. However, if you're taking your own vehicle over to the islands, you will have to travel by boat. For details of ferries and flights between Mallorca and Menorca, see p.33.

By air from the mainland

The vast majority of **flights** from the mainland to Mallorca and Menorca are operated by Spain's national carrier, Grupo Iberia, a multi-headed conglomerate whose subsidiaries include Iberia and Aviaco. These two companies combine to link a range of mainland cities with Mallorca and – to a far lesser degree – Menorca. The Iberia group has sales offices in every major Spanish city and most capital cities abroad. Seat availability isn't usually a problem and fares are very reasonable – a flight to Mallorca from Valencia, for instance, costs 12,000ptas, from Madrid 21,500ptas, and from Barcelona 11,600ptas, whilst from Barcelona to Menorca costs 10,300ptas. Normal return fares are roughly double, but there are a variety of excursion fares available at discounted prices; Iberia features special offers on its Web site (*www.iberia.com*). Alternatively, it's sometimes possible to get a cheaper ticket on a charter flight to the Balearics (mostly from Madrid), but you'll have to plod around local travel agents once in Spain; they're listed under *viajes agencias* in the yellow pages.

By ferry from the mainland

At present, Trasmediterranea is the only company operating **ferry and hydrofoil** services between the Spanish mainland and the Balearics. How long this monopoly will last it's impossible to say: Trasmediterranea's principal rival, Flebasa, suspended most of its passenger services in 1998 and may or may not resume operations. Trasmediterranea's ferry routes are from **Barcelona to Maó** (2–3 weekly; 9hr); **Barcelona to Palma** (1–2 daily; 8hr); **Valencia to Palma** (2–3 weekly; 9hr); and **Valencia via Palma to Maó** (1 weekly; 9hr to Palma; 14hr to Maó). They also operate hydrofoils from **Barcelona to Palma** (mid-June to mid-Sept 3 weekly; 4hr 15min) and from **Valencia via Ibiza to Palma** (mid-June to mid-Sept 3 weekly; 5hr 15min). Trasmediterranea also run ferries linking Barcelona and Ibiza (2–4 weekly; 9hr) and Valencia and Ibiza (1 weekly; 6hr). There are no services from early December to the end of January.

Tickets can be purchased from the Trasmediterranea office at the port of embarkation either in advance or on arrival. The company also has a sales office in Madrid and authorizes certain travel agents to sell its tickets both in other Spanish cities and, far more infrequently, elsewhere in Europe. Within Spain, ask at the local tourist office for the address; abroad, Spanish National Tourist Offices will have the details (see the box on p.23). In the UK, the official agent is Southern Ferries, 179 Piccadilly, London W1V 9DB ☎0171/491 4968 (Internet: *www.seafrance.co.uk*).

Iberia offices and flight frequencies

In addition to their many mainland offices, Iberia have a nationwide domestic flight reservation and information line in Spain on ☎902 400500 (English spoken). The route frequencies given below cover direct flights to Mallorca unless otherwise specified.

Alicante Doctor Gadea 12 ☎96 521 86 13 (3 daily, 45min).

Barcelona Passeig de Gràcia 30 ☎93 412 70 20; and Plaça Espanya s/n ☎93 325 73 58 (Mallorca 10 daily, 40min; Menorca 3–6 daily, 35min).

Bilbao Ercilla 20 ☎94 424 19 35 (1 daily, 1hr 10min).

Ibiza Town Passeig Vara de Rey 15 ☎971 302580 (4 daily, 30min).

Madrid Velázquez 130 ☎91 587 87 87 or 91 587 47 47 (Mallorca 6–9 daily, 1hr 10min; Menorca 1–3 daily, 1hr 10min).

Maó, Menorca Aeroport Menorca ☎971 157025.

Palma, Mallorca Avgda Joan March 8 ☎971 757151.

Sevilla Almirante Lobo 2 ☎95 422 89 01 (4 weekly, 1hr 15min).

Valencia Paz 14 ☎96 352 75 52 (Mallorca 3 daily, 55min; Menorca 3 weekly, 1hr 10min).

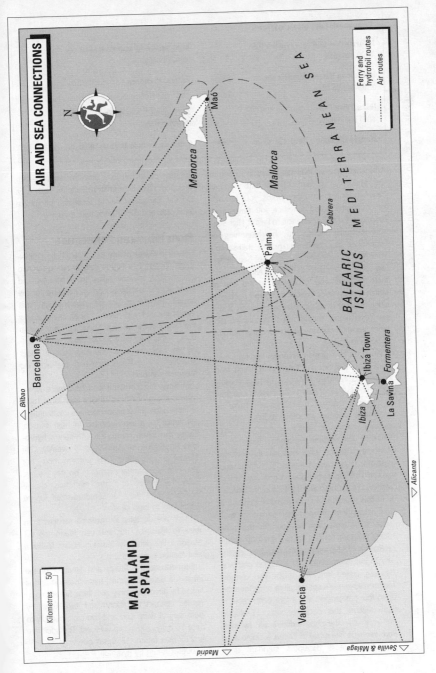

AIR AND SEA CONNECTIONS

MAINLAND SPAIN

MEDITERRANEAN SEA

BALEARIC ISLANDS

Menorca

Maó

Mallorca

Cabrera

Palma

Barcelona

Ibiza Town

Formentera

Ibiza

La Savina

Valencia

▷ Bilbao

▷ Alicante

▷ Madrid

▷ Sevilla & Malaga

- - - Ferry and hydrofoil routes
.... Air routes

N

0   Kilometres   50

Trasmediterranea offices

Information and reservation line:
☎ 902 454645.

Barcelona Estació Marítim s/n
☎ 93 443 25 32.

Ibiza Town Estació Marítim s/n
☎ 971 315000.

Madrid Obenque 4 ☎ 91 423 85 00.

Maó, Menorca Moll Comercial s/n
☎ 971 366050.

Palma, Mallorca Estació Marítim 2
☎ 971 405014.

Tarragona Nueva de San Olegario 16
☎ 977 225506.

Valencia Estació Marítim ☎ 96 367 65 12.

Trasmediterranea ferry **fares** vary according to the season, but, surprisingly, hardly at all between routes – in other words, your fare will be much the same whether you travel from Barcelona to Maó or Valencia to Palma. High season is from mid-July to the beginning of September, plus the Easter period; mid-season from April to early July, plus most of September; low season from October to early December, and then from the end of January to the end of March. Setting aside special deals and packages, a return ticket is about twice as much as a single. Reservations, though not obligatory, are recommended for the ferry and, especially, hydrofoil in July and August.

The price of a single passenger fare on a ferry from either Barcelona or Valencia to Palma, Maó or Ibiza is currently 6660ptas in high season, 4350ptas in low; children (2–12 years old) travel half-price, infants (under 2) go free. There are night-time sailings on most routes, when a **cabin** is extremely useful, especially if you're travelling with children. From either Barcelona or Valencia to Palma, Maó or Ibiza, the inclusive cost of a single cabin starts at 20,950ptas, doubles at 16,950ptas per person one way in high season (14,450ptas and 10,450ptas respectively in low season); a triple cabin is charged at 13,450ptas high season per person, a four-berth 10,960ptas high season. On the same routes, the tariff for cars up to 2.4m long in high season is 18,560ptas, with caravans costing 38,735ptas. Motorbikes cost 4845ptas and bicycles are carried free. You might also consider Trasmediter-ranea's special all-in price for a car, up to four passengers and a four-berth cabin. In high season, this package costs 51,440ptas one-way. On the Trasmediterranea hydrofoil from Valencia (via Ibiza) to Palma, a single adult passenger fare is 8150ptas, standard class.

Vehicles up to 6m long (the maximum permitted) and 1.8m high cost 18,560ptas each way. On the Barcelona–Palma route the prices are 7660ptas and 17,320ptas respectively.

From Ibiza and Formentera

Getting to Mallorca from Ibiza couldn't be simpler. Iberia operate four **flights** daily between the two islands. The journey takes thirty minutes and costs around 8400ptas one-way (double for the return). There's usually no problem with seat availability, but you need to book ahead during the height of the season. There are, however, no direct flights from Ibiza to Menorca – you're routed via Mallorca at a one-way cost of about 16,500ptas. For flights between Mallorca and Menorca see p.33.

By **ferry**, Trasmediterranea runs a twice-weekly, four-and-a-half-hour service from Ibiza Town to Palma; the adult passenger fare costs around 3500ptas for a one-way trip in high season. Plying the same route, the company's **hydrofoils** (mid-June to mid-Sept 3 weekly; 2hr 15min) charge about forty percent more, but also offer substantial discounts on day returns. Both the ferries and the hydrofoils charge 9280ptas one way for standard-sized (up to 1.8m) cars in high season.

There are no ferry or hydrofoil services from Ibiza to Menorca, but you can island-hop via Mallorca. For details of ferries between Mallorca and Menorca, see p.33.

Formentera, the fourth and smallest of the inhabited Balearic Islands, has no airport and is linked by direct ferry only with Ibiza. Several companies connect the island and Ibiza Town by both ferry (4 daily; 1hr) and hydrofoil (mid-July to Sept 10 daily; 20min; no vehicles). The adult fare is 2200ptas return (1350ptas one-way) by ferry, 3800ptas return by hydrofoil.

Visas and red tape

Citizens of EU countries (and Norway and Iceland) need only a valid national identity card to enter Spain for up to ninety days. Since Britain has no identity card system, however, British citizens do have to take a passport. US and Canadian citizens don't need a visa but do require a passport valid for a minimum of either 6 months (US) or 3 months (Canada) and can stay for up to ninety days. Australians do not need a visa for stays of up to thirty days; for a longer visit (up to ninety

days) a visa should be obtained before departing for Spain. New Zealanders can stay up to ninety days without a visa. Visa requirements do change, however, and it is always advisable to check the current situation.

To **stay longer**, EU nationals (and citizens of Norway and Iceland) can apply for a *permiso de residencia* (residence permit) from within Spain. You'll either have to produce proof that you have sufficient funds (officially 5000ptas per day) to be able to support yourself without working – easiest done by keeping bank exchange forms every time you change money – or a contract of employment (*contrato de trabajo*), or something to prove you are self-employed (for example as a teacher), which involves registering at the tax office. Other nationalities will either need to get a special visa from a Spanish consulate before departure (see below for addresses); or can apply for one ninety-day visa extension, showing proof of sufficient funds, once in Spain. In Mallorca, further advice can be obtained from the various consulates listed on p.90; nationalities not represented should contact their representative in Madrid.

Spanish embassies and consulates abroad

Australia 15 Arkana St, Yarralumla, Canberra, ACT 2600 ☎02/6273 3555; Level 24, 31 Market St, Sydney, NSW 2000 ☎02/9261 2433; 4th floor, 540 Elizabeth St, Melbourne, VIC 3000 ☎03/9347 1966.

Canada 74 Stanley Ave, Ottawa, Ontario K1M 1P4 ☎613/747-2252; 1 Westmount Square #1456, Montréal, Québec H3Z 2P9 ☎514/935-5235; Simcoe Place, 200 Front St, #2401, PO Box 15, Toronto, Ontario M5V 3K2.

Ireland 17A Merlyn Park, Ballsbridge, Dublin 4 ☎01/269 1640.

New Zealand: no representation.

UK 39 Chesham Place, London SW1X 8SB ☎0171/235 5555; Suite 1a, Brook House, 70 Spring Gardens, Manchester M2 2BQ

☎0161/236 1213; 63 North Castle St, Edinburgh EH2 3LJ ☎0131/220 1843. Premium-rate visa information line ☎0891/600123.

USA 2375 Pennsylvania Ave NW, Washington, DC 20009 ☎202/728-2330; 150 E 58th St, New York, NY 10155 ☎212/355-4090; 545 Boylston St #803, Boston, MA 02116 ☎617/536-2506; 180 N Michigan Ave #1500, Chicago, IL 60601 ☎312/782-4588; 1800 Berins Drive #660, Houston, TX 77057 ☎713/783-6200; 5055 Wilshire Blvd #960, Los Angeles, CA 90036 ☎213/938-0158; 2655 Lejeune Rd #203, Coral Gables, Miami, FL 33134 ☎305/446-5511; 2102 World Trade Center, 2 Canal St, New Orleans, LA 70130 ☎504/525-4951; 1405 Sutter St, San Francisco, CA 94109 ☎415/922-2995.

Insurance

As an EU country, Spain has free reciprocal health agreements with other member states. To take advantage, British citizens will need form E111, available from most post offices. Treatment within this scheme is, however, only provided by practitioners within the Spanish health care system, the Instituto Nacional de la Salud, whereas most doctors on the islands are more accustomed to – or only deal with – private insurance work (see also "Health", p.27). Taking out your own medical insurance means you won't have to hunt around for a doctor who will treat you for free, and will also cover the cost of items not within the EU scheme's purview, such as dental treatment and repatriation on medical grounds. It will usually also cover your baggage and tickets in case of theft, as long as you get a report from the local police. Non-EU residents will need to insure themselves for all eventualities, including medical costs.

Note that some **bank** and **credit cards** have medical or other insurance included, and travel insurance is sometimes covered if you pay for your trip with a credit or charge card.

Insurance in Britain and Ireland

In **Britain** and **Ireland**, standard travel insurance schemes (around £25–35 per person for a fortnight, £30–40 for a month) are sold by almost every travel agent and bank, and direct by several specialist insurance firms. Please note that if you're

engaging in high-risk outdoor activities (mountaineering or rock-climbing, for example) you'll probably have to pay an extra premium; ask your insurers for advice. Conversely, many insurers offer cheaper policies providing only the most basic medical and luggage cover.

Travel insurance contacts in Britain and Ireland

Columbus Travel Insurance, 279 High St, Croydon CR0 1QH ☎0171/375 0011. Internet: *www.columbusdirect.com* (online purchasing).

Endsleigh Insurance, 97–107 Southampton Row, London WC1B 4AG ☎0171/436 4451. Internet: *www.endsleigh.co.uk*.

Frizzell Insurance, Frizzell House, County Gates, Bournemouth, Dorset BH1 2NF ☎01202/292333.

Royal & Sun Alliance, 13–17 Dawson St, Dublin 2 ☎01/677 1851.

USIT, Fountain Centre, College St, Belfast BT1 6ET ☎01232/324073; 19–21 Aston Quay, O'Connell Bridge, Dublin 2 ☎01/602 1600. Internet: *www.usit.ie*.

North American insurance

Before buying an insurance policy, check that you're not already covered. **Canadian provincial health plans** typically provide some overseas medical coverage, although they are unlikely to pick up the full tab in the event of a mishap. Holders of official **student/teacher/youth cards** are entitled to accident coverage and hospital in-patient benefits – the annual membership is far less than the cost of comparable insurance. **Students** may also find that their student health coverage extends during the vacations and for one term beyond the date of last enrolment. **Homeowners' or renters'** insurance often covers theft or loss of documents, money and valuables while overseas.

After exhausting the possibilities above, you might want to contact a specialist **travel insur-**

ance company; your travel agent can usually recommend one, or see the box above.

Travel insurance **policies** vary: some are comprehensive while others cover only certain risks (accidents, illnesses, delayed or lost luggage, cancelled flights, etc.). In particular, ask whether the policy pays medical costs up front or reimburses you later, and whether it provides for medical evacuation to your home country. For policies that include lost or stolen luggage, check exactly what is and isn't covered, and make sure the per-article limit will cover your most valuable possession.

The best **premiums** are usually to be had through student/youth travel agencies – STA policies (see p.4), for example, come in two forms:

with or without medical coverage. The current rates are $45/35 (for up to 7 days); $60/45 (8–15 days); $110/85 (1 month); $140/115 (45 days); $165/135 (2 months); $50/35 (for each extra month). If you're planning to do any "dangerous sports" (skiing, rock-climbing), be sure to ask whether these activities are covered: some companies levy a surcharge.

Australasian insurance

In **Australia** and **New Zealand**, travel insurance is put together by the airlines and travel agent groups (see box below) in conjunction with insurance companies. They're all comparable in premium and coverage – a typical policy for Europe will cost A$180/NZ$210 for a month, A$260/NZ$300 for two months and A$330/NZ$380 for three months. Most adventure sports are covered, but check the policy first.

Travellers with disabilities

Despite their popularity as holiday destinations, Mallorca and Menorca pay scant regard to their disabled visitors, with facilities lagging way behind those of most other EU regions. That said, there are hotels on both islands with wheelchair access and other appropriate facilities, and attitudes are beginning to change — by law all new public buildings in Spain are required to be fully accessible.

Flying to the islands may pose difficulties, although all the scheduled airlines concerned, including the main carrier, Iberia, will assist disabled travellers to some degree. If you're driving down, the Brittany Ferries crossing from Plymouth to Santander offers good facilities, as do most of the cross-Channel ferries. On Mallorca and Menorca themselves, however, transport is a real problem, as buses and trains are not equipped for wheelchairs, and none of the islands' car rental firms have vehicles with adaptations — though at least the taxi drivers are usually helpful. Note also that the more remote roads along the coast and out in the countryside have very rough surfaces. Toilet facilities for disabled visitors are a rare sight anywhere.

Contacts for travellers with disabilities

GENERAL

European Commission: Mobility International, 18 Boulevard Badouin, B-1000 Brussels, Belgium. Internet: *www.europa.eu.int/en/comm/dg23/tourisme/publications/spain.pdf. Travel guides for tourists with disabilities. Their forty-page guide to Spain covers tour operators, travel agencies and information services, transport, accommodation and places to visit. It also provides other useful contacts across Spain and the Balearics.*

Organización Nacional de Ciegos de España (ONCE), Plaça Bisbe Berenguer de Palou, Palma, Mallorca ☎971 469311.
ONCE, the Spanish organization for the visually impaired, is active and influential, thanks in part to its huge lottery. It sells braille maps and can arrange trips: write for details.

Spanish National Tourist Office (see box opposite for addresses). *Publishes a fact sheet listing addresses and some accessible accommodation, but it's far from comprehensive.*

Australia and New Zealand

ACROD (Australian Council for Rehabilitation of the Disabled), PO Box 60, Curtin, ACT 2605 ☎02/6282 4333; 24 Cabarita Rd, Cabarita ☎02/9743 2699.
General travel information.

Disabled Persons Assembly, 173 Victoria St, Wellington (☎04/801 9100).
Advice and general travel information.

UK and Ireland

Access Travel, 16 Haweswater Ave, Astley, Lancashire M29 7BL ☎01942/888844.
Private operator specializing in overseas holidays for wheelchair users including Mallorca.

Disability Federation of Ireland, 2 Sandyford Office Park, Sandyford, Dublin 18 ☎01/295 9344.
General information and advice.

Holiday Care Service, 2nd floor, Imperial Building, Victoria Rd, Horley, Surrey RH6 9HW ☎01293/774535.
Information on all aspects of travel. Issues factsheets on both Mallorca and Menorca which include detailed descriptions of wheelchair-accessible and other suitable hotels and apartments. Also offers a reservations service on ☎01293/771500.

RADAR, 12 City Forum, 250 City Rd, London EC1V 8AS ☎0171/250 3222; minicom ☎0171/250 4119. Internet: *www.radar.org.uk. A good source of advice on holidays and travel abroad.*

Tripscope, The Courtyard, Evelyn Rd, London W4 5JL ☎0345/585641 with minicom. *Travel information for disabled people.*

USA and Canada

Directions Unlimited, 720 N Bedford Rd, Bedford Hills, NY 10507 ☎1-800/533-5343. *Tour operator specializing in custom tours for people with disabilities.*

Jewish Rehabilitation Hospital, 3205 Place Alton Goldbloom, Chomedy Laval, PQ H7V 1R2 ☎450/688-9550 ext 226. *Guidebooks and travel information.*

Mobility International USA, PO Box 10767, Eugene, OR 97440 (Voice and TDD ☎541/343-1284). *Information and referral services, access guides, tours and exchange programmes. Annual membership $35 (includes quarterly newsletter).*

Society for the Advancement of Travel for the Handicapped (SATH), 347 Fifth Ave, New York, NY 10016 ☎212/447-7284. *Non-profit-making travel industry referral service that passes queries on to its members as appropriate.*

Travel Information Service ☎215/456-9600. *Telephone-only information and referral service for disabled travellers.*

Twin Peaks Press, Box 129, Vancouver, WA 98666 ☎206/694-2462 or 1-800/637-2256. *Publisher of the Directory of Travel Agencies for the Disabled ($19.95), listing more than 370 agencies worldwide;* Travel for the Disabled *($19.95); the* Directory of Accessible Van Rentals *($9.95) and* Wheelchair Vagabond *($14.95), loaded with personal tips.*

Information and maps

The Spanish National Tourist Office (SNTO) produces and gives away a wide range of maps, pamphlets and special interest leaflets on Mallorca and Menorca. Contact, or better still visit, one of their offices before you leave and stock up. In particular, try to get hold of the booklet listing all the Balearic Islands' hotels, *hostals* and campsites, as this is printed in Madrid and can be difficult to obtain on the islands themselves.

SNTO offices abroad

Australia c/o Spanish Tourism Promotions, 178 Collins St, Melbourne ☎03/9650 7377; toll-free ☎1800/817 855.

Canada 2 Bloor St W, Toronto, Ontario M4W 3E2 ☎416/961-3131. Internet: *www.tourspain.es.*

UK 22–23 Manchester Square, London W1M 5AP (general enquiries ☎0171/486 8077; brochure requests, premium line ☎0891 669920).

USA ☎888/OK SPAIN; 666 Fifth Ave, New York, NY 10103 ☎212/265-8822; 845 N Michigan Ave, Chicago, IL 60611 ☎312/642-1992; San Vicente Plaza Bldg, 8383 Wilshire Blvd, Beverly Hills, Los Angeles, CA 90211 ☎213/658-7188; 1221 Brickell Ave, Miami, FL 33131 ☎305/358-1992. Internet: *www.okspain.org.*

Information offices in Mallorca and Menorca

In **Mallorca**, the main provincial and municipal **tourist offices** in Palma (see p.64) will provide free maps of the town and the island, and leaflets detailing all sorts of island-wide practicalities – from bus and train timetables to lists of car rental firms, ferry schedules and boat excursion organizers. Outside of Palma, many of the larger settlements and resorts have seasonal tourist offices (addresses are detailed in the guide). These vary enormously in quality, and while they are generally extremely useful for local information, they cannot be relied on to know anything about what goes on outside their patch. In **Menorca**, there are efficient year-round tourist offices in the two main towns, Maó and Ciutadella, but nowhere else. **Opening hours** vary considerably, but the larger tourist offices are all open at least from Monday to Friday, from 8am or 9am to 2pm or 3pm. The smaller concerns operate from April or May to September or October, usually from Monday to Friday in the mornings. We've given details of opening times throughout the guide, though you can't always rely on the officially posted hours in remoter spots.

Maps

For most visitors, the **maps** in this guide – supplemented by the free road and town maps issued by the tourist offices – will suffice, though if you're planning to explore the islands' nooks and crannies by bike or car, you'll need a more detailed road map. Many alternatives are widely available from island newsagents, filling stations, souvenir shops and bookshops, and you shouldn't pay more than 500ptas for any of the road maps detailed below. If you buy supplementary maps, it's important to remember that all town and street **signs** on the islands have recently been translated into the local language, **Catalan**, making Castilian (ie Spanish) maps obsolete. To ensure you're buying a Catalan map, check out the spelling of Port de Pollença on Mallorca (Puerto de Pollença in Castilian) and, on Menorca, Maó (Mahón in Castilian). Just to confuse matters, however, some maps switch between the two languages for no apparent reason.

The best Catalan map of **Mallorca**, entitled *Mallorca*, is published by the Ministerio de Obras Públicas (Ministry of Public Works). This accurately portrays the island's most important highways and principal byways, and provides topographical details too. It's not, however, as easy to get as most of its rivals – to buy a copy you'll need to consult a specialist map shop either before you go (see box) or in Mallorca. More widely available alternatives include the easy-to-follow, Catalan *Collins Mallorca Holiday Map* (1:175,000), which usefully indicates distances between settlements, marks salient geographical features and provides a street plan and index of central Palma. In Mallorca, the largely Catalan *Mallorca and Palma* (1:175,000) is a widely available and inexpensive local government publication equipped with a large-scale, indexed plan of Palma and brief descriptions of the city's tourist attractions. Its only drawbacks are the absence of topographical features and some waywardness when it comes to depicting the island's byroads.

For **Menorca**, the most detailed and veracious Catalan map is produced by Distrimapas Telstar (1:75,000) and is reasonably easy to obtain at newsagents and bookshops on the island. The Eurotour map is good too – there's an English version titled *Minorca* (1:75,000). Both these maps show all the island's major and minor roads, the only problem being that they don't effectively indicate which country lanes are easily driveable and which aren't. The same caution applies to the clear and accurate Firestone map of Menorca (1:75,000; no. E-54), which also has the drawback that the nomenclature is a mix of Castilian and Catalan.

Serious **hikers** are poorly provided for: there are no really reliable maps with walking trails marked. The IGN (Instituto Geográfico Nacional) issues **topographical maps** of the Balearics at the 1:25,000 and 1:50,000 scales, based on an aerial survey of 1979, but many minor roads and footpaths simply don't appear and even crags and cliffs are not always shown. As a precaution, some hikers cross-check IGN maps with their rather out-of-date predecessors, the Mapa Militar (military maps), which are available at both 1:50,000 and 1:25,000 scales. These maps are available from bookshops in Palma, Maó and Ciutadella (see the relevant "Listings" in the guide for addresses), or (more expensively) from a few specialist suppliers overseas.

Map outlets

Australia

Mapland, 372 Little Bourke St, Melbourne ☎ 03/9670 4383.

The Map Shop, 16a Peel St, Adelaide ☎ 08/8231 2033.

Perth Map Centre, 884 Hay St, Perth ☎ 08/9322 5733.

Travel Bookshop, 3/175 Liverpool St, Sydney ☎ 02/9261 8200.

Worldwide Maps and Guides, 187 George St, Brisbane ☎ 07/3221 4300.

Britain

Blackwell's Map and Travel Shop, 53 Broad St, Oxford OX1 3BQ ☎ 01865/792792. Internet: *bookshop.blackwell.co.uk.*

Daunt Books, 193 Haverstock Hill, London NW3 4QL ☎ 0171/794 4006; 83 Marylebone High St, London W1M 3DE ☎ 0171/224 2295.

Heffers Map Shop, 19 Sidney St, Cambridge CB2 3HL ☎ 01223/568467. Internet: *www.heffers.co.uk.*

John Smith and Sons, 57–61 St Vincent St, Glasgow G2 5TB ☎ 0141/221 7472. Internet: *www.johnsmith.co.uk.*

National Map Centre, 22–24 Caxton St, London SW1H 0QU ☎ 0171/222 2466. Internet: *www.mapsworld.com.*

Stanfords, 12–14 Long Acre, London WC2E 9LP ☎ 0171/836 1321; at Campus Travel, 52 Grosvenor Gardens, London SW1W 0AG ☎ 0171/730 1314; at British Airways, 156 Regent St, London W1R 5TA ☎ 0171/434 4744; 29 Corn St, Bristol BS1 1HT ☎ 0117/929 9966.

The Travel Bookshop, 13–15 Blenheim Crescent, London W11 2EE ☎ 0171/229 5260. Internet: *www.thetravelbookshop.co.uk.*

Waterstone's, 91 Deansgate, Manchester M3 2BW ☎ 0161/832 1992. Internet: *www.waterstones.co.uk.*

Maps by **mail order** are available from Stanfords ☎ 0171/836 1321. Internet: *sales@stanfords.co.uk.*

Canada

International Travel Maps & Books, 552 Seymour St, Vancouver, V6B 3J6 ☎ 604/687-3320. Internet: *www.itmb.com.*

Open Air Books and Maps, 25 Toronto St, Toronto, ON M5C 2R1 ☎ 416/363-0719.

Ulysses Travel Bookshop, 4176 St-Denis, Montréal H2W 2M5 ☎ 514/843-9447. Internet: *www.ulysses.ca.*

Ireland

Easons Bookshop, 40 O'Connell St, Dublin 1 ☎ 01/873 3811.

Fred Hanna's Bookshop, 27–29 Nassau St, Dublin 2 ☎ 01/677 1255.

Hodges Figgis Bookshop, 56–58 Dawson St, Dublin 2 ☎ 01/677 4754.

Waterstones, Queens Building, 8 Royal Ave, Belfast BT1 1DA ☎ 01232/247355; 69 Patrick St, Cork ☎ 021/276522; 7 Dawson St, Dublin 2 ☎ 01/679 1415.

New Zealand

Specialty Maps, 58 Albert St, Auckland ☎ 09/307 2217.

USA

Book Passage, 51 Tamal Vista Blvd, Corte Madera, CA 94925 ☎ 1-800/999-7909 or 415/927-0960.

The Complete Traveler Bookstore, 3207 Fillmore St, San Francisco, CA 94123 ☎ 415/923-1511. Internet: *www.completetraveler.com.*

The Complete Traveller Bookstore, 199 Madison Ave, New York, NY 10016 ☎ 212/685-9007.

Elliot Bay Book Company, 101 S Main St, Seattle, WA 98104 ☎ 1-800/962-5311 or 206/624-6600. Internet: *www.elliotbaybook.com\ebbco\.*

Forsyth Travel Library, 226 Westchester Ave, White Plains, NY 10604 ☎ 1-800/367-7984. Internet: *www.forsyth.com.*

Map Link, 30 S La Patera Lane, Unit 5, Santa Barbara, CA 93117 ☎ 805/692-6777. Internet: *www.maplink.com.*

Mallorca and Menorca on the Internet

The **Internet** is a useful source of travel information for Menorca and, more especially, Mallorca. At present, most sites emanating from the islands themselves are rudimentary and many are not regularly updated. The best are given below.

Govern Balear

www.caib.es/kfcont.htm
The official site of the Balearic provincial government. An excellent and well-presented source of general information. The tourist information section is presented in several languages, including English, and gives links to sites offering information on accommodation, eating and drinking, sports, etc.

Mallorca Cycling – Tourist Guide

www.baleares.com/tourist.guide/cycling/cycling.htm
Details of eight different cycle routes on Mallorca, from 70km to 320km. Routes are designed to avoid busy roads and to provide sections on the flat as well as steep climbs. In several languages, including English.

Mallorca Highway

www.malhigh.com
Expat heaven, this site hosts private ads from German and English expatriates. Useful and amusing in equal measure.

Palma Airport

www.aena.es/ae/pmi/evuedia.htm
Real-time arrivals and departures. Likely to cover Ibiza and Menorca airports soon.

Tot Menorca

www.menorca.net/
A Catalan/English site with a cultural bent, giving details of places of archeological, historical and ecological interest, plus standard tourist information.

Spanish Meteorological Institute Weather Information

www.inm.es/wwb
A source of daily weather forecasts for the whole of Spain.

Health

No inoculations are required for the Balearics and the only likely blight to your holiday may be an upset stomach or a ferocious hangover. To avoid the former, wash fruit and avoid *tapas* dishes that look like they were cooked last week. Many islanders also avoid consuming mayonnaise during the summer.

Pharmacies, doctors, emergencies and dentists

If you should fall ill, for minor complaints it's easiest to go to a *farmàcia* – there are plenty of them and they're listed in the Balearic islands' yellow pages (details of several in the main towns are given in the guide). Pharmacists are highly trained, willing to give advice (often in English), and able to dispense many drugs which would be available only on prescription in many other countries. Most keep usual shop hours (ie 9am–1pm & 4–7pm); in Palma and Maó some open late and at weekends, and a rota system keeps at least one open 24 hours a day. In both towns, the rota is displayed in the window of every pharmacy, or you can check at reception in one of the better hotels. Outside the towns, you'll find a *farmàcia* in most of the larger villages, though there's not much chance of late-night opening or of an English-speaking pharmacist unless you're staying in a resort area.

In more serious cases you can get the address of an **English-speaking doctor** from your consulate, hotel, local *farmàcia* or tourist office. If you're seeking free treatment under the EU health scheme, double check that the doctor is working within the Spanish health care system (the Instituto Nacional de la Salud). Even within the EU agreement, you still have to pay forty percent of **prescription charges** (senior citizens are exempt). Neither do most private insurance policies help cover prescription charges – their "excesses" are usually greater than the cost of the medicines.

In medical **emergencies**, telephone the **Creu Roja** (Red Cross), which operates the islands' main ambulance service – in Mallorca ☎202220, in Menorca ☎361180. If you're reliant on free treatment within the EU health scheme, try to remember to make this clear to the ambulance staff and, if you're whisked off to hospital, to the medic you subsequently encounter. It's a good idea to hand over a photocopy of your E111 on arrival at hospital, or else you may be mistaken for a private insurance job and billed accordingly. Hospital charges are as much as 14,000ptas per visit (see also "Insurance" on p.20).

Dentists are all private – you'll pay around 5000ptas for having a cavity filled. A comprehensive list of *dentistas* can be found in the yellow pages, or ask at your hotel or *hostal* reception.

Contraceptives

Condoms no longer need to be smuggled into Spain as they did during the Franco years. They're available from most *farmàcias*, and from all sorts of outlets – like bars and vending machines – in the resorts. It's a good job: a recent survey of 18- to 30-year-old visitors found that the average time between arrival and first sexual contact was three hours and forty two minutes.

Costs, money and banks

In terms of food, wine and transport, Mallorca and Menorca remain budget destinations for northern Europeans, North Americans and Australasians. However, Balearic hotel prices have increased considerably over the last few years, so independent travellers on any kind of budget will have to plan their accommodation carefully and, in summer, when vacant rooms are scarce, reserve well in advance. Another serious expense may be partying: nightclubs can rush you thousands of pesetas in the space of a few hours.

More precise costs for places to stay are given in the guide, and you should consult the box on p.34 for general guidelines on accommodation prices. On average, if you're prepared to buy your own picnic lunch, stay in inexpensive *hostals* and hotels, and stick to the cheaper bars and restaurants, you could get by on around £20–25 (approximately US$30–40) a day per person. If you intend to stay in three-star hotels and eat at quality restaurants, then you'll need more like £50/$75 a day per person, with the main variable being the cost of your room – and bear in mind that room prices rise steeply as the season progresses. On £80/$120 a day and upwards, you'll be limited only by your energy reserves – unless you're planning to stay in a five-star hotel, in which case this figure won't even cover your bed. On both islands, **eating out** is excellent value, and even in a top-notch restaurant in Palma a superb meal will only set you back around £15/US$23 – though, of course, you may pay well over the odds for food and drink in the tourist resorts. As always, if you're travelling alone you'll spend much more than you would in a group of two or more – sharing rooms saves a lot of money.

One other cost is **IVA**, a seven percent sales tax levied on most goods and services. Check in advance to see if IVA is included in the price of your bigger purchases; otherwise, especially in more expensive hotels and restaurants, you may be in for a bit of a shock.

Money and the exchange rate

Pending the introduction of the euro, the Spanish currency is the **peseta**, indicated in this book as "ptas". **Coins** come in denominations of 1, 5, 10, 25, 50, 100, 200 and 500 pesetas; **notes** as 1000, 2000, 5000 and 10,000 pesetas.

The **exchange rate** for the Spanish peseta at the time of writing was around 230 to the pound sterling, 210 to the Irish punt, 140 to the US dollar, 105 to the Canadian dollar, 90 to the Australian dollar and 76 to the NZ dollar. You can take in as much money as you want (in any form), although amounts over one million pesetas must be declared; you can take a maximum of 500,000 pesetas out – unless, that is, you can prove that you brought more with you in the first place.

The euro

Spain is one of eleven countries who have opted to join the European monetary union and, from January 1, 1999, is beginning to phase in the single European currency, the **euro**. Initially, however, it will only be possible to make paper transactions in the new currency (if you have, for example, a euro bank or credit card account), and the peseta will remain the normal unit of currency in Spain. Euro notes and coins are scheduled to be issued at the beginning of 2002, and to replace the peseta entirely by July of that year.

Travellers' cheques and credit cards

The safest way to carry your funds is in **travellers' cheques**; the usual fee for their purchase is one percent of face value. Make sure to keep the purchase agreement and a record of cheque serial numbers safe and separate from the cheques themselves. In the event that cheques are lost or stolen, the issuing company will expect you to report the loss forthwith. Consequently, when you buy your travellers' cheques, ensure you have details of the company's emergency contact numbers or the address of their local office. Most companies claim to replace lost or stolen cheques within 24 hours. American Express cheques are sold through most North American, Australasian and European banks, and they're the most widely accepted cheques in Spain. American Express also have offices in Palma and Port de Pollença in Mallorca, and Maó in Menorca – see the relevant chapters for addresses. When you cash your cheques in the Balearics, guard against outrageous **commissions** (usually they're 400–500ptas per transaction); if commission is waived, make sure that the exchange rate doesn't deteriorate drastically to compensate the bank.

If you have an ordinary British/EU bank account you can use **Eurocheques** with a Eurocheque card in many banks and can write out cheques in pesetas in shops and hotels. Most Eurocheque cards, many Visa, Mastercard and British bank/cash cards, as well as US cards, can also be used for withdrawing cash from **ATMs** in Spain; check with your bank to find out about these reciprocal arrangements – the system is highly sophisticated and can often give instructions in a variety of languages. Make sure you have a personal identification number (PIN) that's designed to work overseas.

Credit cards are particularly useful for car rental, cash advances (though these attract a high rate of interest from the date of withdrawal) and hotel bills. American Express, Visa and Mastercard are all widely accepted.

Changing money

Spanish **banks** and **savings banks** have branches in all but the smallest of Balearic towns, and nearly all of them will change foreign currency and travellers' cheques (albeit with occasional reluctance for the more obscure brands). The Banco de Bilbao, Banco March, Banco de Credito Balear and Banco de Santander are four of the most widespread banks, while Sa Nostra and La Caixa are the biggest savings banks on the islands. All of them also handle Eurocheques, and most give cash advances on credit cards.

Banking hours are generally Monday to Friday 9am–2pm and Saturday (except in summer) 9am–1pm. Outside these hours, most major hotels and many travel agents will change money at less generous rates and with variable commissions, as will the many **exchange kiosks** that are concentrated in the tourist areas. Legally, exchange rates must be on public display.

Wiring money

Having money **wired** from home is never convenient or inexpensive, and should be considered a last resort. One option is to have your own bank send the money through; for that you need to nominate a receiving bank in the Balearics. Any local branch will do, but those in Maó, Palma and Ciutadella will probably be more familiar with the process. Naturally, you need to confirm the cooperation of the local bank before you set the wheels in motion back home. The sending bank's fees are geared to the amount being transferred and to the urgency of the service you require – the fastest transfers, taking two or three days, start at around £20 for the first £300–400. The receiving bank charges a commission too – expect a 2000ptas charge on amounts up to £300–400.

Money can also be wired via American Express, with the funds sent by one office and available for collection at the company's local offices, in Palma and Port de Pollença, Mallorca, and Maó, Menorca, within minutes – see the relevant chapters for addresses. All transactions are done in US dollars. Again, charges depend on the amount being sent, but as an example, wiring $400 from Britain to Spain will cost $20, $5000 will cost $190. The maximum that can be sent in one go is $20,000.

Getting around

On both Mallorca and Menorca, you're spoiled for choice when it comes to transport. There's a reliable bus network between all the major settlements, a multitude of taxis, a plethora of car rental firms (which keeps prices down to a minimum, especially off-season), plenty of bicycles and mopeds to rent, as well as a couple of minor rail lines on Mallorca. Distances are small and consequently the costs of travel limited, whether in terms of petrol or the price of a ticket. Even on Mallorca, the larger of the two islands, it's only 110km from Andratx in the west to Cala Rajada in the east, and from Palma on the south coast to Alcúdia on the north shore is a mere 60km. Menorca has only one major road, which traverses the island from Ciutadella in the west to Maó in the east, a distance of just 45km.

Hopping from one island to the other is easy and economical too, as there are regular and inexpensive inter-island flights – though you're advised to book well in advance in July and August.

Buses

Both Mallorca and Menorca have an extensive network of **bus services** linking the main towns – Palma, Maó and Ciutadella – with most of the villages and resorts of the coast and interior. These main bus routes are supplemented by more intermittent local services between smaller towns and between neighbouring resorts. Ticket

prices are reasonable: the one-way fare from Palma to Colònia de Sant Jordi is 640ptas, from Palma to Cala Rajada 890ptas, and from Maó to Ciutadella 550ptas. Only Palma is large enough to have its own public transit system, with a multiplicity of bus services linking the city centre with the suburbs and beach resorts that surround it – see p.93 and p.101 for more on this – though the larger resorts all have some form of local transport, either bus or electric mini-train.

On all island bus services, destinations are marked on the front of the bus. Passengers enter the bus at the front and buy tickets from the driver, unless they've been bought in advance at a bus station. Bus stops are mostly indicated with the word *parada*. A confusing variety of bus companies operate the various routes on Mallorca, while all buses on Menorca are run by Transportes Menorca; a timetable is readily available from most tourist offices.

On the whole buses are reliable and comfortable enough, the only significant problem being that many country towns and villages do not have a bus station or even a clearly marked *parada*, which can be very confusing, as in some places buses leave from the most obscure parts of town. Remember also that bus services are drastically reduced on **Sundays** and **holidays**, and it's best not even to consider travelling out in the sticks on these days. The Catalan words to look out for on timetables are *diari* (daily), *feiners* (workdays, including Saturday), *diumenge* (Sunday) and *festius* (holidays).

Trains

Mallorca has its own electric **railways**, with 914mm-gauge trains travelling through the mountains from Palma to Sóller (28km), and across the flatland of the interior from Palma to Inca (29km). Each line has its own station, next door to each other on Palma's Plaça Espanya. Neither line is as fast as the bus, but the trip to Sóller takes you through some of Mallorca's most magnificent scenery (the line to Inca passes through some of its most tedious). The standard return fare from Palma to Sóller is 760ptas and to Inca 500ptas.

Taxis

The excellence of the islands' bus services means it's rarely necessary to take a **taxi**, though it is a fast and easy way of reaching your resort from the airport and, perhaps more importantly, of getting back to your hotel after a day's hiking. In the latter case, you should arrange collection details before you set out – there's no point wandering round a tiny village hoping a taxi will show. Throughout the Balearics, the taxis of each town and resort area have their own livery – Palma taxis, for example, are black with a cream-coloured roof and bonnet. Local journeys are all metered, though there are supplementary charges for each piece of luggage and for night and Sunday travel. For longer journeys there are official prices, which are displayed at the islands' airports and at some taxi stands and tourist offices. Naturally, you're well advised to check the price with the driver *before* you set out. Fares are reasonable, but not cheap: the journey from the airport to downtown Palma, a distance of around 11km, will cost you in the region of 2000ptas, while the fare from Palma airport to Port d'Andratx (37km) is about 5000ptas, Maó to Ciutadella (45km) 5300ptas.

Driving and vehicle rental

Getting around on public transport is easy enough, but you'll obviously have a great deal more freedom if you have your own vehicle; on Menorca especially, the more attractive and secluded beaches are only accessible under your own steam. Major roads are generally good, though side roads are very variable – unpaved minor roads are particularly lethal after rain. Traffic is generally well behaved (even if Spain does have one of the highest incidences of traffic accidents in Europe), but noisy, especially in Palma, where the horn is used as a recreational tool as well as an instrument of warning. **Fuel** (*gasolina*) comes in four grades. Different companies use different brand names, but generally *Super Plus* is 98-octane fuel, selling at about 120ptas per litre; *Super* is 96-octane, equivalent to four-star in the UK, selling at about 110ptas per litre, and almost always without lead (*sense plom*); and *Mezcla*, or *Normal*, is 90-octane, equivalent to 2-star, available for about 100ptas per litre. Diesel (*gasoleo* or *gasoil*) costs about 90ptas per litre. Both Menorca and Mallorca are well supplied with filling stations; a few are open 24 hours a day, seven days a week, though most close around 9pm or 10pm and on public holidays.

Most foreign **driving licences** are honoured in Spain – including all EU, US and Canadian ones – but an **International Driver's Licence** (available at minimal cost from your home motoring organization) is an easy way to set your mind at rest. If you're bringing your own car, you must have adequate insurance, a green card (available from your insurers or motoring organization), and a **bail bond** (a document to be shown to the police if you're involved in anything but the most trivial of accidents – without it, they'll almost certainly imprison you and impound your vehicle pending an investigation). Extra insurance coverage for unforeseen legal costs is also well worth having, as is an appropriate **breakdown** policy from a motoring organization. In Britain, for example, the RAC and AA charge about £90 for a month's Europe-wide breakdown cover, with all the appropriate documentation, including green card and bail bond, provided. Note, however, that rates vary depending on the age of the vehicle and increase if you're towing anything.

Throughout the Balearics speed **limits** are posted – the maximum on urban roads is 60kph, on other roads 90kph, on motorways 120kph – and on the main highways speed traps are fairly frequent. If you're stopped for any violation, the Spanish police can (and usually will) levy a stiff on-the-spot fine of up to 10,000ptas before letting you go on your way, their draconian instincts reinforced by the fact that few tourists are likely to appear in court to argue the case. Most **driving rules** and regulations are pretty standard (seat belts are compulsory and "Stop" signs mean exactly that), but remember that a single, unbroken white line in the middle of the road means no overtaking, even if the rule is frequently ignored – note also that drivers often sound their horns when overtaking. You yield to traffic coming from the right at all junctions, whether or not there's a give way sign; and be prepared for road signs that give very little, if any, warning of the turning you might require. On major trunk roads, turnings that take vehicles across oncoming traffic are being phased out and replaced by semi-circular minor exits that lead round to traffic lights on the near side of the major road. Finally, drivers do not have to stop (and usually don't) at zebra crossings, which merely indicate a suitable pedestrian crossing place. If you come to an abrupt stop at a crossing, as you might do in Britain, the pedestrians will be amazed and someone may well crash into your rear end. As ever, don't drink and drive.

Car rental agencies

AUSTRALIA

Avis	☎ 1800/225 533
Budget	☎ 13/2727
Hertz	☎ 13/3039

IRELAND

Avis	☎ 01/874 5844
Budget	☎ 0800/973159
Europcar	☎ 01/874 5844
Hertz	☎ 01/676 7476
Holiday Autos	☎ 01/872 9366

NEW ZEALAND

Avis	☎ 09/526 2847
Budget	☎ 03/375 2222
Hertz	☎ 09/367 6350

NORTH AMERICA

Auto Europe	☎ 1-800/223-5555
Avis	☎ 1-800/331-1084
Budget	☎ 1-800/527-0700
Dollar	☎ 1-800/800-6000
Hertz in US	☎ 1-800/654-3001
in Canada	☎ 1-800/263-0600

UK

Avis	☎ 0990/900500
Budget	☎ 0800/181181
Europcar	☎ 0345/222525
Hertz	☎ 0990/996699
Holiday Autos	☎ 0990/300400

Car rental

There are scores of companies on Mallorca and Menorca offering **car rental** (still rendered in Castilian, *coches de alquiler*), their offices thronging the islands' resorts, larger towns and airports: most of the major international players have outlets and dozens of small companies make up the remainder. Several useful addresses are given in the Palma, Maó and Ciutadella "Listings"; comprehensive lists are available from the islands' tourist offices. To rent a car, you'll have to be 21 or over (and have been driving for at least a year), and you'll probably need a credit card – though some places will accept a hefty deposit in cash and some smaller companies simply ignore all the normal regulations. However, no car rental firm will allow you to transport their vehicles from one Balearic island to another. If you're planning to spend much time driving the islands' rougher tracks, you'll probably be better off with a moped, or even a four-wheel drive (about thirty percent more expensive than the average car and available from larger rental agencies).

Rental **charges** vary enormously: out-of-season costs for a standard car can come down to as little as 2000ptas per day with unlimited mileage; in July and August, by comparison, the same basic vehicle could set you back 6000ptas a day (though weekly prices are slightly better value, and special rates operate at the weekend). The big companies all offer competitive rates, but you can often get a better deal through someone in contact with local vehicle rental firms, such as Holiday Autos (see above). If you choose to deal directly with smaller, local companies, proceed with care. In particular, check the policy for the excess applied to claims, and ensure that it includes a bail bond (see above), collision damage waiver (applicable if an accident's your fault) and, in general, adequate levels of financial cover. **Fly-drive** deals are well worth investigating. In Britain, for example, Iberia offer Avis cars from just £112 a week in the low season, £154 in high season (including unlimited mileage, collision damage waiver, bail bond, insurance and VAT), as long as you book your flight to Mallorca or Menorca with Iberia.

Moped rental

Widely available on both islands, **mopeds** are a popular means of transport, especially for visiting remoter spots. Prices start at about 2000ptas per day, including insurance and crash helmets, which must be worn. Be warned, however, that the insurance often excludes theft – always check with the company first. You will generally be asked to show some kind of driving licence (particularly for mopeds over 50cc), and to leave a deposit on your credit card, though most places will accept cash as an alternative. We've listed names and addresses of rental companies throughout the guide where most appropriate; tourist offices on the islands will provide comprehensive lists of suppliers.

Cycling

Cycling can be an inexpensive and flexible way of getting around both Menorca and far hillier Mallorca, and of seeing a great deal of the country that would otherwise pass you by. The Spanish are keen cycling fans, which means that you'll be well received and find reasonable facilities, while cars will normally hoot before they pass – though this can be alarming at first. Scenic Mallorca is especially popular with cyclists – and its tourist office produces a free specialist leaflet, the *Guia del Ciclista* (in Spanish only), which details suggested itineraries and indicates distances and levels of difficulty. **Renting a bike** (about 1500ptas per day, 6500ptas per week) is easy enough as there are dozens of suppliers (there's usually one at every resort) and tourist offices will provide a list or advise you of the nearest outlet; we've also listed a few in the guide. If you've brought your own bike, **parts** can often be found at auto repair shops or garages – look for Michelin signs – and there are bike shops in the larger towns.

Getting your own bike to the islands should present few problems. Most **airlines** are happy to take them as ordinary baggage provided they come within your allowance (though it's sensible to check first: crowded charter flights may be less obliging). Deflate the tyres to avoid explosions in the unpressurized holds. **Ferries** between the islands and from the mainland transport bikes for free.

Flights and ferries between Mallorca and Menorca

Iberia, who have a monopoly on **inter-island flights**, fly four times a day from Mallorca to Menorca and vice versa. Flying time is just thirty minutes and fares are cheap, with a one-way ticket costing 5900ptas (9500ptas return) throughout the year. There's rarely a problem with availability, except in the peak season when it's a good idea to reserve a seat ahead of time by phoning any Iberia office (see p.16 for addresses of their offices in Spain, the "Getting there" sections for offices abroad).

Trasmediterranea operate a once-weekly car and passenger **ferry** service between **Palma** and **Maó**; the sailing time is six hours and the one-way adult fare is about 3300ptas, with a standard-size car costing 7700ptas (9300ptas high season). Reservations are not required, but are a good idea in summer. Addresses and phone numbers for Trasmediterranea are given on p.18. **Other ferry services** linking Mallorca and Menorca are in a state of flux: the main operator, Flebasa, has suspended most passenger services and it's difficult to predict what will happen next. It's possible that Flebasa will be refloated (they used to operate hydrofoil and ferry services between Mallorca's Port d'Alcúdia and Menorca's Ciutadella). One local company, Cape Balear de Cruceros (see p.176), are currently operating passenger-only hydrofoil services between Mallorca's Cala Rajada and Ciutadella, a 75-minute journey which costs around 7500ptas in summer, 6000ptas in winter. At present there are between one and three sailings daily, though this situation is likely to change.

Accommodation

Although package-tour operators have a stranglehold on thousands of hotel rooms, villas and apartments in both Menorca and Mallorca, reasonably priced rooms are still available to the independent traveller, even though options are severely limited at the height of the season. Off season you should be able to get a simple, medium-sized double room with shower and sink for around 3500ptas, whereas in August the same double, if available, can set you back as much as 4500ptas – though this still compares reasonably well with much of the rest of Europe. You can, however, comfortably spend 10,000ptas and upwards in hotels with three or more stars – some of them being very firmly in the super-luxury class.

Vacant rooms are at their scarcest from late June to early September, when advance **reservations** are strongly recommended. Most hoteliers speak at least a modicum of English, so visitors who don't speak Catalan or Spanish can usually book over the phone, but a confirming letter or fax is always a good idea. In Mallorca the easi-est place to get a room is Palma, with Sóller lagging not far behind, but don't forget the five monasteries on the island that offer accommodation – they're a good bet for vacancies, even in high summer. In Menorca, accommodation is far thinner on the ground than in Mallorca – only Maó, Ciutadella and possibly Fornells are likely bases for a visit.

It's often worth **bargaining** over room prices, especially outside of peak season and at fancier hotels, since the posted tariff doesn't necessarily mean much. Many hotels have rooms at different prices, and tend to offer the more expensive ones first. If there are more than two of you, most places have rooms with three or four beds at not a great deal more than the double-room price, which represents a real saving. On the other hand, people travelling alone invariably get the rough end of the stick. We've detailed where to find places to stay in most of the destinations listed in the guide, from the most basic of rooms to luxury hotels, and given a price range for each (see box below). We've also indicated where an establishment closes over the winter – this is the case with a few hotels in Mallorca, while in Menorca almost all tourist facilities close down from November to March.

Fondas, casas de huéspedes, pensions, hostals and hotels

The one thing all travellers need to grasp is the elaborate diversity of types of places to stay – though in practice the various categories often overlap. The least expensive places are **fondas**,

---

Accommodation price codes

After each accommodation entry in this book you'll find a symbol that corresponds to one of nine price categories. These categories represent the minimum you can expect to pay for a double room in high season; for a single room, expect to pay around two-thirds the price of a double. The only ① options are youth hostels, where you'll get a dorm bed, and the monasteries.

Note that in the more upmarket *hostals* and *pensions*, and in anything calling itself a hotel, you'll pay a **tax** (IVA) of seven percent on top of the room price.

① Under 3000ptas	④ 6000–8000ptas	⑦ 14,000–20,000ptas
② 3000–4000ptas	⑤ 8000–10,000ptas	⑧ 20,000–25,000ptas
③ 4000–6000ptas	⑥ 10,000–14,000ptas	⑨ Over 25,000ptas

Accommodation signs

The various categories of accommodation in Spain are identifiable by square blue signs inscribed with the following letters in white.

F	CH	P	H^S	HR^S	H
fonda	casa de huéspedes	pensió	hostal	hostal-residencia	hotel

casas de huéspedes and pensions (*pensiones* in Castilian); further categorized with either one or two stars. Establishments in these categories are few and far between in the Balearics, and the distinctions between them blurred, but in general you'll find food served at *fondas* and *pensions* (some will only rent rooms on a meals-inclusive basis), while *casas de huéspedes* – literally "guesthouses" – are often used as long-term lodgings. Confusingly, the name of many *pensions* does not follow their designation – lots of *pensions* call themselves *hostals* and vice versa. As a result, the name isn't always a reliable guide to the establishment's price, though the sign outside usually is (see box above).

Slightly more expensive are **hostals** (*hostales* in Castilian) and **hostal-residencias**, categorized from one to three stars; a one-star *hostal* generally costs about the same as a *pensió*. Many *hostals* offer good, functional rooms, often with a private shower; the *residencia* designation means that no meals other than breakfast are served.

Moving up the scale, **hotels** are also star-graded by the authorities, from one to five stars. One-star hotels cost no more than three-star *hostals* (sometimes they're cheaper), but at three stars you pay a lot more, and at four or five you're in the luxury class with prices to match. There are also a handful of *hotel-residencias*, where the only meal provided is breakfast.

It's safe to assume that bedrooms in a hotel will be adequately clean and furnished, but in the lower categories you're well advised to ask to see the room before you part with any money. Standards vary greatly between places in the same category (even between rooms in the same *hostal*) and it does no harm to check that there's hot water if there's supposed to be, or that you're not being stuck at the back in an airless box. Note that bathrooms in many *pensions* and *hostals* (some hotels too) will not actually have baths, only showers.

A word about **complaints**: by law, each establishment must display its room rates and there should be a card on the room door showing the prices for the various seasons. If you think you're being overcharged, take it up first with the management; you can usually produce an immediate resolution by asking for one of the *hojas de reclamaciones* (complaints forms) that all places are obliged by law to keep. The threat of filling in a form is usually in itself enough to make the proprietor back down.

Monasteries

In recent times Mallorca's **monasteries** have become severely underpopulated and several now let out empty cells to visitors of both sexes. They're all in delightful settings in the mountains: the Santuari de Sant Salvador near Felanitx; the Ermita de Nostra Senyora de Bonany near Petra; the Ermita de Nostra Senyora del Puig outside Pollença; the Monastir de Nostra Senyora de Lluc; and the Santuari de Nostra Senyora de Cura on Puig Randa near Algaida (specific details of each are given in the guide). There's an increasing demand for this simple, cheap form of accommodation so, although it's possible just to turn up and ask for a room, you'd be well advised to either telephone ahead or, if your Spanish isn't good enough, get the local tourist office to make a reservation on your behalf. For a double room, you can expect to pay around 1500ptas at most of these monasteries, though it's a little more than twice that at Lluc (3500ptas), the most visited and commercialized of the five. Reasonably priced food is usually available, but check arrangements when you book.

Youth hostels

There are only two **youth hostels** (*albergues juveniles*) on Mallorca – one near Palma, the other outside Alcúdia – and none on Menorca. Both are open in the high season only and tend to be block-booked by school groups, so unless you reserve a bed well in advance you shouldn't rely on either as a viable source of cheap accommodation. At both, the price of a bed is about 1300ptas (1700ptas if you're over 26) and you'll need a sheet sleeping bag. The hostels are operated by Hostelling International (HI) and they expect you to have a membership card, available from your home hostelling organization, although it is possible to buy a card on the spot. Specific details of each hostel are given in the guide.

Fincas

Many of Mallorca's old stone **fincas** (farmhouses) have been snaffled up for use as second homes, and some are now leased by the owners to package-tour operators for the whole or part of the season – Individual Traveller's Spain (see p.6) has one of the best selections. Out of the tour operators' main season, these *fincas* often stand idle – ask around the villages of the northwest coast to see if someone's prepared to rent one out informally. At any time of the year, though preferably well in advance of your holiday, it's worth approaching the Associació Agroturisme Balear, Avgda Gabriel Alomar i Villalonga, 07006 Palma (☎971 721508, fax 971 717317), which issues a booklet detailing most of the finest *fincas* and takes bookings. Some are very luxurious and situated in remote, beautiful spots – though others form part of a working farm – and they're not cheap: prices range from 6000ptas to 12,000ptas per person per night, and a minimum length of stay is often stipulated.

Camping

There are just two official **campsites** (*càmpings*) on Mallorca: the *Sun Club Picafort*, beside the main road between Port d'Alcúdia and Ca'n Picafort, and the *Club San Pedro* (June to mid–Sept), outside the village of Colònia de Sant Pere, at the east end of the Badia d'Alcúdia (Bay of Alcúdia). Both are Class 1C campsites occupying seaside locations, but whereas the first is well-maintained and smart, the second badly needs an overhaul. Each has about five hundred pitches – taking tents, trailer caravans and motor caravans – and a comprehensive range of facilities, including a grocery store, laundry room, swimming pool, bicycle and pedalo rental, bars and restaurants and all sorts of sports amenities. *Sun Club Picafort* is very popular and heaves with campers in the summer, when it's best to make a reservation well ahead of time. Menorca's facilities are modest, the better of two authorized campsites being the *S'Atalaia*, a Class 3C affair that can accommodate a hundred campers, just outside the resort of Cala Santa Galdana. Prices and specific details of each site are given in the relevant chapters.

Camping off-site is legal, but not encouraged, and has various restrictions attached. Spanish regulations state that you're not allowed to camp "in urban areas, areas prohibited for military or touristic reasons, or within 1km of an official campsite". What this means in effect is that you can't camp on resort beaches (though there is some latitude if you're discreet), but you can camp out almost anywhere in the countryside, providing you act sensitively and use some common sense: whenever possible ask locally first and/or get the permission of the landowner.

Eating and drinking

In the "Eating and drinking" section that follows we've generally given the **Catalan** names for food and drink items. Most restaurants, cafés and bars have **multilingual** menus (including English), but out in the sticks, in the cheaper cafés and restaurants, there may only be a Catalan (or Castilian) menu, or maybe no menu at all, in which case the waiter will rattle off the day's dishes in Catalan. Though Catalan is the islands' first language, Castilian (ie Spanish) is also used or understood by almost all restaurateurs. With these factors in mind, we've given the **Castilian** names alongside the Catalan names wherever it's useful.

Traditional Balearic food, which has much in common with Catalan food, is far from delicate, but its hearty soups and stews, seafood dishes and spiced meats can be delicious. In common with other areas of Spain, this regional cuisine has, after many years of neglect, experienced something of a renaissance, and nowadays restaurants offering *Cuina Mallorquína* are comparatively commonplace and should not be missed. Neither should a visit to one of the islands' many pastry shops (*pastisserias*), where you'll find the sweetest of confections and the Balearics' gastronomic pride and joy, *ensaimadas* (spiralled flaky pastries).

On both islands, the distinction between **cafés** (or *cafeterias*) and **restaurants** is blurred. The bulk serve both light snacks and full meals, with the best deals often appearing as the *menú del día* (menu of the day). At either end of the market, however, the differences become more pronounced: in the more expensive restaurants, there is usually a *menú del día*, but the emphasis is on à la carte; by contrast, the least expensive cafés only serve up simple snacks, and in their turn are often indistinguishable from the islands' **bars**, also known as *cellers* or *tavernas*. Before the tourist boom, these snacks always consisted of traditional dishes prepared as either *tapas* (small snacks) or *racions* (larger ones). Today, it's often chips, pizzas and sandwiches, but in Palma there's still a lively *tapas* scene, allowing you to move from place to place sampling a wide range of local specialities.

Opening hours vary, but as a general rule cafés and *tapas* bars open from around 9am until at least early in the evening, many till late at night; restaurants are open from around noon until 2, 3 or sometimes 4pm, before reopening in the evening from around 6 or 7pm until 10 or 11pm. Those restaurants with their eye on the tourist trade often stay open all day and can be relied upon on Sundays, when many local spots close. There's rarely any need to **reserve** a restaurant table in Mallorca or Menorca – for the few places where it's advisable, we've given the phone numbers in the guide.

Breakfast, snacks and sandwiches

For **breakfast** you're best off in a bar or café. Some *hostals* and most hotels will serve the "continental" basics, but it's generally cheaper and more enjoyable to go out to breakfast. A traditional Balearic breakfast (or lunch) dish is *pa amb tomàquet* (*pan con tomate* in Castilian) – a massive slice of bread rubbed with tomato, olive oil and garlic, which you can also have topped with ham – washed down with a flagon of wine. *Pa amb oli* (bread rubbed with olive oil) arrives in similar style, but dispenses with the tomato. If that sounds like gastric madness, other breakfast standbys are *torradas* (*tostadas*; toasted rolls)

Some common fillings for bocadillos are:		
Catalan	**Castilian**	**English**
Butifarra	Butifarra	Catalan sausage
Cuixot dolç	Jamón York	Cooked ham
Formatge	Queso	Cheese
Llom	Lomo	Loin of pork
Pernil salat	Jamón serrano	Cured ham
Salami	Salami	Salami
Salxitxó	Salchichón	Sausage
Tonyina	Atún	Tuna
Truita	Tortilla	Omelette
Xoriç	Chorizo	Spicy sausage

with oil or butter and jam, and *xocolata amb xurros* (*chocolate con churros*) – long, fried tubular doughnuts that you dip into thick drinking chocolate. Most places also serve *ou ferrat* (*huevo frito*; fried egg) and cold *truita* (*tortilla*; omelette), both of which make an excellent breakfast.

Coffee and **pastries** (*pastas*), particularly croissants and doughnuts, are available at some bars and cafés, though for a wider selection of cakes you should head for a *pastisseria* (pastry shop) or *forn* (bakery), which have an excellent reputation, as in the rest of Spain. These often sell a wide array of appetizing baked goods besides the obvious bread, croissants and *ensaimadas*. For ordering coffee see "Soft drinks and hot drinks" (p.44).

Some bars specialize in **sandwiches** (*bocadillos*), both hot and cold, and as they're usually outsize affairs in French bread they'll do for breakfast or lunch. In a bar with *tapas* (see below), you can have most of what's on offer put in a sandwich, and you can often get them prepared (or buy the materials to do so) at grocery shops as well. Menorcan cheese (*formatge*) is popular throughout Spain – the best is hard with a rind, similar to British cheddar.

Tapas

Tapas are small portions, three or four chunks of fish, meat or vegetables, cooked in a sauce or served with a dollop of salad, which traditionally used to be provided free with a drink. These days you have to pay for anything more than a few olives, but a single helping rarely costs more than 200–350ptas unless you're somewhere very

flashy. *Racions* (*raciones* in Castilian) are simply bigger plates of the same, served with bread and costing around 450–650ptas, and are usually enough in themselves for a light meal. (Make it clear whether you want a *ració* or just a *tapa*.) The more people you're with, of course, the better, and half a dozen or so different dishes can make a varied and quite filling meal for three or four people.

One of the advantages of eating *tapas* in bars is that you are able to experiment. Most places have food laid out on the counter, so you can see what's available and order by pointing without necessarily knowing the names; others have blackboards (see the lists opposite).

Meals and restaurants

Regular meals are usually eaten in a *cafeteria* or *restaurant*, though the distinction between the two, particularly at the cheaper end of the market, is often very blurred. In similar fashion, cafeterias blend seamlessly into café-bars and bars, almost all of which serve at least some food. That said, the average price of an average meal in an average establishment does slide down the scale from restaurant to cafeteria to café-bar to bar. At a **cafeteria** offering something like egg, steak or chicken and chips, or *calamars* and salad, a meal will generally cost in the region of 500–900ptas, excluding drink, whereas the price of a main course at a good quality restaurant averages about 1400ptas. **Restaurants** run from simple formica table and check-tablecloth affairs to expense-account palaces. Many have a daily set menu – the **menú del día** – which is usually on offer alongside the à la carte menu, though some of the more basic places might *only* serve a *menú del día*. This consists of three or four courses, including bread, wine and service, and usually costs 900–1300ptas, quite a bit more in flash restaurants and at seaside resorts.

In terms of cuisine, *restaurants*, *cafeterias* and bars in Mallorca and Menorca, especially in the resort areas, are reliant on the tourist industry and many ignore the strong flavours of traditional Balearic and Spanish food for the blandness of pizzas, hamburgers and pastas, or else dish up a hotch-potch of sanitized local favourites such as omelettes, paella and grilled meats. However, there are still plenty of places – highlighted in the guide – where the food is more

Tapas and racions

Catalan	Castilian	English
Anxoves	Boquerones	Anchovies
Bollit	Cocido	Stew
Calamars	Calamares	Squid, usually deep fried in rings
Calamars amb tinta	Calamares en su tinta	Squid in ink
Cargols	Caracoles	Snails, often served in a spicy/curry sauce
Cargols de mar	Berberechos	Cockles
Calamarins	Chipirones	Whole baby squid
Carn amb salsa	Carne en salsa	Meat in tomato sauce
Croqueta	Croqueta	Fish or chicken croquet
Empanada petita	Empanadilla	Fish/meat pasty
Ensalada Russa	Ensaladilla	Russian salad (diced vegetables in mayonnaise)
Escalibada	Escalibada	Aubergine and pepper salad
Faves	Habas	Broad beans
Faves amb cuixot	Habas con jamón	Beans with ham
Fetge	Hígado	Liver
Gambes	Gambas	Prawns
Musclos	Mejillones	Mussels (either steamed, or served with diced tomatoes and onion)
Navallas	Navajas	Razor clams
Olives	Aceitunas	Olives
Ou bollit	Huevo cocido	Hard-boiled egg
Pa amb tomàquet	Pan con tomate	Bread, rubbed with tomato and oil
Patates amb all i oli	Patatas alioli	Potatoes in mayonnaise
Patates cohentes	Patatas bravas	Fried potato cubes with spicy sauce and mayonnaise
Pilotes	Albóndigas	Meatballs, usually in sauce
Pinxo	Pincho moruno	Kebab
Pop	Pulpo	Octopus
Prebes	Pimientos	Peppers
Ronyons amb Xeres	Riñones al Jerez	Kidneys in sherry
Sardines	Sardinas	Sardines
Sípia	Sepia	Cuttlefish
Tripa	Callos	Tripe
Truita Espanyola	Tortilla Española	Potato omelette
Truita Francesa	Tortilla Francesa	Plain omelette
Tumbet	Tumbet	Pepper, potato, pumpkin and aubergine stew with tomato puree
Xampinyons	Champiñones	Mushrooms, usually fried in garlic
Xoriç	Chorizo	Spicy sausage

distinctive and flavoursome. Fresh **fish and seafood** can be excellent, though it's almost always expensive – much of it is imported, despite the local fishing industries around the Balearics and on the Catalan coast. Nevertheless, you're able to get hake, cod (often salted) and squid at very reasonable prices, while fish stews and rice-based *paellas* are

often truly memorable. **Meat** can be outstanding too, usually either grilled and served with a few fried potatoes or salad, or – like ham – cured or dried and served as a starter or in sandwiches. Veal is common, served in great stews, while poultry is often mixed with seafood (chicken and prawns) or fruit (chicken/duck with prunes/pears).

Balearic dishes and specialities

Many of the specialities that follow come from the Balearics' shared history with Catalunya. The more elaborate fish and meat dishes are generally only found in fancier restaurants.

Pastries (*Pastas*)

Cocaroll	Pastry containing vegetables and fish
Ensaimada	Flaky spiral pastry with fillings such as *cabello de ángel* (sweetened citron rind)
Panades sobrasada	Pastry with peas, meat, (see below) or fish

Soup (*Sopa*)

Carn d'olla	Mixed meat soup
Escudella	Mixed vegetable soup
Sopa d'all	Garlic soup
Sopas Mallorquínas or Menorquínas	Vegetable soup, sometimes with meat and chick peas

Salad (*Amanida*)

Amanida Catalana	Salad with sliced meat and cheese
Escalivada	Aubergine, pepper and onion salad
Esqueixada	Dried cod salad with peppers, tomatoes, onions and olives

Starters

Entremesos	Hors d'oeuvres of mixed meat and cheese
Espinacs a la Catalana	Spinach with raisins and pine nuts
Fideus a la cassola	Baked vermicelli with meat
Llenties guisades	Stewed lentils
Pa amb oli	Bread rubbed with olive oil, eaten with ham, cheese or fruit
Samfaina	Ratatouille-like stew of onions, peppers, aubergine and tomato
Truita (d'alls tendres, de xampinyons, de patates)	Omelette/tortilla (with garlic, mushrooms or potato); don't order trout (*truita*) by mistake – ask for a *tortilla*

Rice dishes

Arròs negre	"Black rice", cooked with squid ink
Arròs a banda	Rice with seafood, the rice served separately
Arròs a la marinera	Paella: rice with seafood and saffron
Paella a la Catalana	Mixed meat and seafood paella; sometimes distinguished from a seafood paella by being called *Paella a Valencia*

Meat (*Carn*)

Albergínies en es forn	Stuffed aubergines filled with grilled meat
Botifarra amb mongetes	Spicy blood sausage with white beans
Conill (all i oli)	Rabbit (with garlic mayonnaise)
Escaldum	Chicken and potato stew in an almond sauce
Estofat de vedella	Veal stew
Fetge	Liver
Fricandó	Veal casserole
Frito Mallorquín	Pigs' offal, potatoes and onions cooked with oil
Mandonguilles	Meatballs, usually in a sauce with peas
Perdius a la vinagreta	Partridge in vinegar gravy
Pollastre (farcit, amb gambas, al cava)	Chicken (stuffed, with prawns, or cooked in *cava*,
Porc (rostit)	Pork (roast)
Sobrasada	Finely minced pork sausage, flavoured with paprika

Fish (*Peix*) and shellfish (*marisc*)

Bacallà (amb samfaina)	Dried cod (with ratatouille)
Caldereta de llagosta	Lobster stew
Cloïsses	Clams, often steamed
Espinagada de Sa Pobla	Turnover filled with spinach and eel

Greixonera de peix	Menorcan fish stew, cooked in a pottery casserole		Crema Catalana	Crème caramel, with caramelized sugar topping
Guisat de peix	Fish and shellfish stew		Gelat	Ice cream
Llagosta (amb pollastre)	Lobster (with chicken in a rich sauce)		Mel i mató	Curd cheese and honey
			Postres de músic	Cake of dried fruit and nuts
Lluç	Hake, a common dish either fried or grilled		Turrón	Almond fudge
Musclos al vapor	Steamed mussels		Xurros	Deep-fried doughnut sticks (served with hot chocolate)
Pop	Octopus			
Rap a l'all cremat	Monkfish with creamed garlic sauce		Yogur	Yoghurt

Market shopping

Vegetables (Verdures/Llegumes)

Sarsuela	Fish and shellfish stew
Suquet	Fish casserole
Tonyina	Tuna
Truita	Trout (sometimes stuffed with ham, a la Navarre)

Albergínies	Aubergines
Cebes	Onions
Concombre	Cucumber
Espàrrecs	Asparagus
Mongetes	Beans
Pastanagues	Carrots
Patates	Potatoes
Pèsols	Peas
Tomàquets	Tomatoes
Xampinyons (also bolets, setes)	Mushrooms

Sauces and terms

Salsa mahonesa	Mayonnaise
Allioli	Garlic mayonnaise
Salsa romesco	Spicy tomato and wine sauce to accompany fish (from Tarragona)
A la planxa/ a la brasa	Grilled
Rostit	Roast
Fregit/frit	Fried
Farcit	Stuffed/rolled
Guisat	Casserole

Fruit (Fruita)

Plàtan	Banana
Maduixes	Strawberries
Meló	Melon
Pera	Pear
Pinya	Pineapple
Poma	Apple
Préssec	Peach
Raïm	Grapes
Taronja	Orange

Desserts (Postres)

Arròs amb llet	Rice pudding

Vegetables rarely amount to more than a few chips or boiled potatoes with the main dish, though there are some splendid vegetable concoctions to watch out for, such as *tumbet* (pepper, potato, pumpkin and aubergine stew with tomato purée). It's more usual to start your meal with a **salad**, either a standard green or mixed affair, or one of the islands' own salad mixtures, which come garnished with various vegetables, meats and cheeses. **Dessert** in the cheaper places is nearly always fresh **fruit** or *flam*, the local version of *crème caramel*; look out also for *crema Catalana*, with a caramelized sugar coating, the Catalan version of *crème brûlée*, and *músic*, dried fruit-and-nut cake.

In all but the most rock-bottom establishments it is customary to leave a small **tip**; the amount is up to you, though ten to fifteen percent of the bill is sufficient. Service is normally included in a *menú del día*. The other thing to take account of is **IVA**, a sales tax of seven percent which is either included in the given prices (in which case it should say so on the menu) or added to your bill at the end.

Some common Catalan and Castilian food terms

English	Catalan	Castilian
Basics		
Bread	*Pa*	*Pan*
Butter	*Mantega*	*Mantequilla*
Cheese	*Formatge*	*Queso*
Eggs	*Ous*	*Huevos*
Oil	*Oli*	*Aceite*
Pepper	*Pebre*	*Pimienta*
Salt	*Sal*	*Sal*
Sugar	*Sucre*	*Azúcar*
Vinegar	*Vinagre*	*Vinagre*
Garlic	*All*	*Ajo*
Rice	*Arròs*	*Arroz*
Fruit	*Fruita*	*Fruta*
Vegetables	*Verdures/*	*Verduras/*
	Llegumos	*Legumbres*

	Catalan	Castilian
Meals		
to have breakfast	*Esmorzar*	*Desayunar*
to have lunch	*Dinar*	*Almorzar*
to have dinner	*Sopar*	*Cenar*
In the restaurant		
Menu	*Menú*	*Carta*
Bottle	*Ampolla*	*Botella*
Glass	*Got*	*Vaso*
Fork	*Forquilla*	*Tenedor*
Knife	*Ganivet*	*Cuchillo*
Spoon	*Cullera*	*Cuchara*
Table	*Taula*	*Mesa*
The bill	*El compte*	*La cuenta*

Vegetarians and special diets

If you eat fish but not meat you should relish your holiday – the range of seafood is magnificent. The *menú del día* nearly always features a fish dish, and there are plenty of vegetable and egg dishes, as well as fruit, to be going on with. Even out in the country, you'll often find trout on the menu. If you're a **vegetarian**, however, your diet will be a little more limited. Palma has a couple of vegetarian restaurants (see p.86) and most of the resorts are accustomed to having vegetarian guests, but elsewhere the choice isn't so great and is essentially confined to large salads, fried eggs and chips or omelettes.

If you're a **vegan**, you're either going to have to compromise or accept weight loss if you're away for any length of time. Some salads and vegetable dishes are strictly vegan – like *espinacs a la Catalana* (spinach, pine nuts and raisins) and *escalivada* (aubergine and peppers) – but they're few and far between. Fruit and nuts are widely available though, and most pizza restaurants will

serve you a vegetarian pizza without cheese – ask for *vegetal sense formatge* (in Castilian, *vegetal sin queso*).

For vegetarian and vegan **shopping**, use the markets – where you can buy ready-cooked lentils and beans, and pasta – or look out for shops marked *Aliments regim* (*dietetica* in Castilian), which sell soya milk and desserts, vegetarian biscuits, and so on.

Wine

Wine (*vi* in Catalan, *vino* in Castilian), either red (*negre, tinto*), white (*blanc, blanco*) or rosé (*rosada, rosado*), is the invariable accompaniment to every meal and is, as a rule, inexpensive. In bars, cafés and budget restaurants, it may be whatever comes out of the barrel, or the house bottled special (ask for *vi/vino de la casa*). In a bar, a small glass of wine will generally cost anything from 40 to 100ptas; in a restaurant prices start at around 250ptas a bottle, and even in the poshest of places you'll be able to get a bottle of house wine for under 1000ptas. If you're having the *menú del día*, house wine will be included in the price – you'll get a third- to a half-litre per person.

On both islands, all the more expensive restaurants, the supermarkets, and some of the cheaper cafés and restaurants carry a good selection of Spanish wines. The thing to check for is the appellation **Denominació d'Origen (DO)**, which indicates the wine has been passed as of sufficiently high quality by the industry's watchdog,

Vegetarian phrases

In **Catalan**, try *Sóc vegetarià/ana. Es pot menjar alguna cosa sense carn?* (I'm a vegetarian. Is there anything without meat?); in **Castilian**, that's *Soy vegetariano/a. Hay algo sin carne?* Or you may be better understood if you simply say – in Catalan – *No puc menjar carn* (I can't eat meat).

the Instítuto Nacional de Denominaciónes d'Origen (INDO). Forty regions of Spain currently carry DO status, including the north central region that produce's Spain's most famous and widely distributed **red wine, Rioja**. Even though there's now a profusion of reds being produced all over the country, it's hard to match Rioja for reliability and finesse. The wines are generally made of the *tempranillo* and *garnacha* grapes and are classified according to their age. At one end of the scale, *joven* indicates a young, inexpensive, straightforward wine which has spent no time in wood. Wines labelled *con crianza* (with breeding) or *reserva* have received respectively moderate and generous ageing in oak casks and in the bottle. At the top of the scale, in both price and quality, are the *gran reserva* wines, which are only produced in the best years and which have to spend at least two years in the cask followed by three in the bottle before being offered for sale. The names to look for in red Rioja include **Martínez-Bujanda**, **Tondonia** and **Monte Real**.

The region of **Navarra** also produces excellent wine using similar techniques and grape varieties at a fraction of the price. The labels to watch for here are **Chivite** and **Señorío de Sarría**. Around Barcelona, the region of **Penedès** was long renowned for its heavy and coarse red wines, responsible for countless hangovers. These days things have improved and the vinous produce of firms like **Torres** and **Masía Bach** have already established a solid reputation. Nevertheless, it is

---

Mallorcan wine

Wine production has flourished in the Balearics since classical times. In the nineteenth century, sweet "Malvasia" – wine similar to Madeira – was exported in great quantity, until the vineyards were devastated by the *phylloxera* louse whose activities changed the course of European wine history in the 1870s. Vine cultivation never re-established itself on Ibiza or Menorca, and, with the best will in the world, Mallorcan wines were regarded as being of only average quality.

In the last few years, however, a concerted attempt has been made to raise the standards of Mallorcan wine-making, driven on one side by the tourist industry and on the other by the realization amongst local producers that the way forward lay in exporting wine that matched international standards. This meant new methods and new equipment. Mallorca's leading wine is **Binissalem**, from around the eponymous village northeast of Palma. Following vigorous local campaigning, it was justifiably awarded its *Denominación d'Origen* credentials in 1991.

Red Binissalem is a robust and aromatic wine made predominantly of the local *mantonegro* grape. It is not unlike Rioja, but it has a distinctly local character, suggesting cocoa and strawberries. The best producer of the wine is **Franja Roja**, who make the **José Ferrer** brand – well worth looking out for, with prices starting at around 350ptas per bottle, 1200ptas for the superior varieties. Red Binissalem is widely available throughout Mallorca, and the Franja Roja Bodega, c/Conquistador 103, Binissalem, welcomes visitors by prior appointment (☎971 511050). White and rosé Binissalem struggle to reach the same standard as the red. However, the **Binissalem Blanco** made by **Herederos de Ribas** is a lively and fruity white that goes well with fish. Also around the island are various country wineries making inexpensive and unpretentious wine predominantly for local consumption, such as the **Muscat Miguel Oliver** or the **Celler Son Calo**. The best places to sample these local, coarser wines is in the *cellers* and bars of the country towns of the interior – we've recommended several in the guide.

If you're visiting the Balearics in late September, you can catch Binissalem's **Festival of the Grape Harvest** (Festa d'es Verema), which takes place during the week leading up to the last Sunday of the month. Saturday is the best day, with a procession of decorated floats and a good deal of free wine. On a more sedate level, Palma's **Food Week** (Setmana de Cuina Mallorquína) takes place in the middle of May all over the centre of town, with stalls featuring the cuisine and wine of the island. The best selection of wines available in Mallorca is at Palma's **El Centro del Vino y del Cava**, c/Bartomeu Rossello-Porcel 19 (☎971 452990); in Menorca, try Maó's **Xoriguer**, Plaça Carme 16 (☎971 362611).

---

the reds of the **Ribera del Duero** region, 120km north of Madrid, which have attracted most recent attention, with wines such as **Protos, Viña Pedrosa** and **Pesquera** offering the smooth integration of fruit and oak that is the hallmark of good Spanish wine.

Spain's **white wines** have not enjoyed the same reputation as the reds. Traditionally, they tended to be highly alcoholic and over-oaked. Spain's best white, the **Rioja Blanca** made by **Marqués de Murrieta**, descends from this tradition, but it offers a smooth-tasting marriage of oak and lemony fruit. The demands of the export market have recently led to new approaches to white wine-making, and the result has been clean, fruity and dry wines that tend to be competent rather than memorable. The best of this style has to be **Marqués de Riscal Blanco** from Rueda, just south of Valladolid.

Spain's growing reputation for **sparkling wine** has been built on the performance of two producers, Freixenet and Codorníu, which hail from a small area west of Barcelona. Local grape varieties are used and the best examples, known as *cava*, are made by the same double-fermentation process as is used in champagne production.

Other alcoholic drinks

Fortified wines and spirits in the Balearics are those you can find throughout Spain. The classic Andalucian wine, **sherry** – *vino de Jerez* – is served chilled or at room temperature, a perfect drink to wash down *tapas*. The main distinctions are between *fino* or *Jerez seco* (dry sherry), *amontillado* (medium), and *oloroso* or *Jerez dulce* (sweet), and these are the terms you should use to order. In mid-afternoon – or even at breakfast – many islanders take a *copa* of **liqueur** with their coffee. The best – certainly to put *in* your coffee – is **coñac**, excellent Spanish brandy, mostly from the south and often deceptively smooth. If you want a brandy from Mallorca, try the mellow, hard-hitting Suau, and from Catalunya, look for Torres. Other good brands include Magno, Veterano and Soberano. Most other spirits are ordered by brand name, too, since there are generally cheaper Spanish equivalents for standard imports. Larios **gin** from Málaga, for instance, is about half the price of Gordons, but around two-thirds the strength and a good deal rougher. The Menorcans, who learnt the art of gin-making from the British, still produce their own versions of the liquor, in particu-

lar the waspish Xoriguer. Always specify *nacional* to avoid getting an expensive foreign brand.

Almost any **mixed drink** seems to be collectively known as a *Cuba Libre* or *Cubata*, though strictly speaking this is rum and Coke. For mixers, ask for orange juice (*suc de taronja* in Catalan) or lemon (*llimona*); tonic is *tònica*.

Cervesa, pilsner-type beer (more usually seen in Castilian, *cerveza*), is generally pretty good, though more expensive than wine. The two main brands you'll see everywhere are San Miguel and Estrella, though keep an eye out in Palma for draught *cerveza negra* – black fizzy beer with a bitter taste. Beer generally comes in 300ml bottles or, for a little bit more, on tap – a *cana* of draught beer is a small glass, a *cana gran* larger. Equally refreshing, though often deceptively strong, is **sangría**, a wine-and-fruit punch which you'll come across at *festas* and in tourist resorts.

Soft drinks and hot drinks

Soft drinks are much the same as anywhere in the world, but one local favourite to try is *orxata* – *horchata* in Castilian – a cold milky drink made

Drinks		
English Alcohol	**Catalan**	**Castilian**
Beer	*Cervesa*	*Cerveza*
Wine	*Vi*	*Vino*
Champagne	*Xampan/Cava*	*Champan/Cava*
Hot drinks		
Coffee	*Café*	*Café*
Espresso coffee	*Café sol*	*Café solo*
White coffee	*Café amb llet*	*Café con leche*
Decaff	*Descafeinat*	*Descafeinado*
Tea	*Te*	*Té*
Drinking chocolate	*Xocolata*	*Chocolata*
Soft drinks		
Water	*Aigua*	*Agua*
Mineral water (sparkling)	*Aigua mineral (amb gas)*	*Agua mineral (con gas)*
(still)	*(sense gas)*	*(sin gas)*
Milk	*Llet*	*Leche*
Juice	*Suc*	*Zumo*
Tiger nut drink	*Orxata*	*Horchata*

from tiger nuts. Also, be sure to try a *granissat* (iced fruit-squash); popular flavours are *granissat de llimona* or *granissat de café*. You can get these drinks from **orxaterias** and from **gelaterias** (ice cream parlours; *heladerías* in Castilian).

Although you can drink the **water** almost everywhere, it usually tastes better out of the bottle – inexpensive *aigua mineral* comes either sparkling (*amb gas*) or still (*sense gas*).

Coffee – served in cafés, bars and restaurants – is invariably espresso, slightly bitter and, unless you specify otherwise, served black (*café sol*). A slightly weaker large black coffee is called a *café Americano*. If you want it white ask for *café cortado* (small cup with a drop of milk) or *café amb llet* (*café con leche* in Castilian) made with hot milk. For a large cup ask for a *gran*. Black coffee is also frequently mixed with brandy, cognac or whisky, all such concoctions being called *carajillo*; liqueur mixed with white coffee is a *trifásico*. **Decaffeinated** coffee (*descafeinat*) is increasingly available, though in fairly undistinguished sachet form. Tea (*te*) comes without milk unless you ask for it, and is often weak and insipid. If you do ask for milk, chances are it'll be hot and UHT, so your tea isn't going to taste much like the real thing.

Better are the **infusions** that you can get in most bars, like mint (*menta*), camomile (*camamilla*) and lime (*tiller*).

Where to drink

You'll do most of your everyday drinking – from morning coffee to nightcap – in a **bar** or **café** (between which there's little difference). Very often, you'll eat in here too, or at least snack on some *tapas*. Bars situated in old wine cellars are sometimes called *cellers* or *tavernas*; *bodegas* traditionally specialize in wine. In Palma you also have the choice of drinking in rather more salubrious surroundings in the the so-called *bars modernos* – designer bars, for want of a better description. Some of these are extraordinarily chic and stylish, sights in their own right, but their drinks are invariably expensive – locals hang out for hours while imbibing very little.

Bar **opening hours** are difficult to pin down, but you should have little difficulty in getting a drink somewhere in Palma until 2am or perhaps 3am. Elsewhere you're OK until at least 11pm, sometimes midnight. The islands' nightclubs tend to close by 2am or 3am. Some bars close on Sundays and, in the resorts, don't expect much to be happening out of season.

Post, phones and the media

On Mallorca and Menorca there are post offices (*correus*) in every town and many villages, most of them handily located on or near the main square. Opening hours are usually Monday to Friday 9am–2pm, though the main post offices in Palma and Maó open through the afternoon and on Saturday mornings too. All post offices close on public holidays. You can send letters to any post office by addressing them "Poste Restante", followed by the surname of the addressee (preferably underlined and in capitals), and then the name of the town and island. To collect, take along your passport or identity card and – if you're expecting post and your initial enquiry produces nothing – ask the clerk to check under all of your names as letters are often filed under first or middle names. Alternatively, American Express, which has agents in Maó, Port de Pollença and Palma (addresses in the guide), will hold incoming mail for a month on behalf of card and travellers' cheque holders.

Outbound post is slow but reasonably reliable, with letters or cards taking around a week to ten days to reach Britain and Ireland, ten days to a fortnight for North America, and about three weeks to Australasia. You can buy **stamps** (*segells*) at tobacconists (look for the brown and yellow; *tabac* or *tabacos* sign) and at scores of souvenir shops as well as at post offices. Post boxes are yellow; on those where there's a choice of posting slots, pick the flap marked *províncies i estranger* or *altres destinos*. Postal rates are inexpensive, with postcards and small letters attracting two tariffs: one to anywhere in Europe; the other worldwide.

Telephones

You can make domestic and international phone calls with equal ease from Spanish public **telephones**, which generally work well. Alternatively, if you can't find one, many bars have pay phones you can use. Most hotel rooms have phones, though there's always an exorbitant surcharge for their use. The majority of public telephones display instructions in English (amongst several languages) and a list of Spanish provincial and some overseas dialling codes. They take 25-, 100- and 500ptas pieces or phonecards of 1000ptas or 2000ptas, which can be purchased at tobacconists. Mallorca's yellow pages is a useful source of information and includes an introductory section and index in English, as will the upcoming Menorca edition. Within Spain, the **ringing tone** is long, whereas **engaged** is shorter and rapid; the standard response to a call anywhere in Spain is to the point – *digáme* (speak to me). For international calls, you're best off shovelling in at least 300ptas to ensure a connection – and make sure you have a good stock of 100-peseta pieces on hand if you're intending to have a conversation of any length. If you have a mobile phone, it's worth asking your supplier if it can be used in the Balearics – with Vodafone, for example, you just get them to lift the international bar code and you're in business.

International and domestic **rates** are slightly cheaper after 10pm and before 8am, and after 2pm on Saturday and all day Sunday. Making a **collect** or **reverse-charge call** (*cobro revertido*) can be a bit of a hassle, especially if your Spanish, the language in which the phone company conducts its business, is poor: it's best to ring the international operator for advice.

Newspapers and magazines

British and other European newspapers, as well as *USA Today* and the *International Herald Tribune*, are all widely available in the resort areas and larger towns of Mallorca and Menorca. These are supplemented by a ragbag of locally produced English papers and journals, the most informative of them being the *Majorca Daily Bulletin*. Of the **Spanish newspapers**, the best two are *El País* – liberal, and the only one with much serious analysis or foreign news coverage – and its rival, *El Mundo*, a left-of-centre broadsheet. Other national papers include *ABC*, solidly elitist with a hard moral line against abortion and

---

Area code

All Mallorca, Menorca and Ibiza telephone numbers begin with the same **regional prefix**: ☎971. This prefix is part of the telephone number: you have to dial it whether you're phoning from within or from outside the region.

Useful telephone numbers
Directory enquiries ☎003
European operator ☎008
International operator ☎025

Phoning abroad from the Balearics
To Australia: dial 00 + 61 + area code (minus first 0) + number.

To Britain: dial 00 + 44 + area code (minus first 0) + number.

To US & Canada: dial 00 +1 + area code + number.

Phoning the Balearics from abroad
From Australia: dial 0011 + 34 (Spain) + number including 971, the Balearic prefix.

From Britain: dial 00 + 34 (Spain) + number including 971, the Balearic prefix.

From US & Canada: dial 011 + 34 (Spain) + number including 971, the Balearic prefix.

divorce, and the equally conservative *La Vanguardia*. Printed in Catalan, *Avui* is the chief nationalist paper, but its main competitor, the Catalan *El Diari de Barcelona*, is more liberal. On the Balearics, there are several rather modest local papers, of which *Ultima Hora* and *Diario de Mallorca* are the most substantial.

Amongst a plethora of glossy **magazines**, Spain's most interesting offering is *Ajo Blanco*, a monthly from Barcelona with an eclectic mix of politics, culture and style. The more arty and indulgent *El Europeo*, a massive quarterly publication from Madrid, can also be worth a browse. And, of course, Spain is the home of *Holà* – the original of *Hello*.

TV and radio

In general, Spaniards love their **TV** and consequently you'll catch more of it than you might expect sitting in bars and cafés. On the whole it's hardly riveting stuff, the bulk being a mildly entertaining mixture of kitsch game shows and foreign-language films and TV series dubbed into Spanish. Soaps are a particular speciality, either South American *culebrones* ("serpents" – they go on and on), which take up most of the daytime programming, or well-travelled British or Australian exports, like *EastEnders* (*Gent del Barri*) and *Neighbours* (*Veins*). Sports fans are well catered for, with regular live coverage of football and basketball matches – in the football season, you can watch one or two live matches a week in many bars. The number of TV stations is increasing all the time, but you could look out for the two main national TV channels, TVE1 and TVE2, or the Catalan TVE3 and Canal 33.

If you have a **radio** that picks up short wave, you can tune in to the BBC World Service, broadcasting in English for most of the day on 648, 3955, 6195, 9410, 12095 and 15575 KHz. The *Majorca Daily Bulletin* and other English papers printed in the Balearics detail frequencies and broadcasting schedules.

Opening hours and public holidays

Although there's been some movement towards a North European working day in Mallorca and Menorca – especially in Palma and the major tourist resorts – most shops and offices still close for a siesta of at least two hours in the hottest part of the afternoon. There's a lot of variability, but basic working hours are generally 9am–1pm and 4–7pm; notable exceptions are the extended hours operated by the largest department stores, some important tourist attractions and most tourist/souvenir shops.

Museums and churches

Almost without exception, **museums** take a siesta, closing between 1pm and 3pm in the afternoon, while many close on Mondays and some on Saturdays and Sundays too. Don't be surprised if the official opening times of the less-visited museums are disregarded. Admission charges are usually in the region of 300ptas per person, irrespective of the size of the collection or the quality of the exhibits.

Palma Cathedral, arguably the islands' key sight, attracts an entrance fee of 400ptas, but other **churches** are almost always free. They generally open every weekday and sometimes on the weekend, but nearly all close for a two- or three-hour siesta. That said, the less significant churches are often kept locked, opening (if at all) only for worship in the early morning and/or the evening (around 6–9pm). In these cases, either time your visit to coincide with the Mass, or find someone with a key. This is not as difficult as it sounds as a sacristan or custodian almost always lives nearby – and someone will know where to direct you. You're often expected to give a small donation.

Public holidays

January 1: New Year's Day (*Año Nuevo*)
January 6: Epiphany (*Reyes Magos*)
March 19: St Joseph's Day (*Sant Josep*)
Good Friday (Castilian *Viernes Santo*;
   Catalan *Divendres Sant*)
May 1: Labour Day (*Dia del Trabajo*)
Corpus Christi (early or mid-June)
June 24: St John's Day (*Sant Joan*, the king's
   name-day)
June 29: St Peter and St Paul
   (*Sant Pere i Sant Pau*)
July 25: St James's Day (*Santiago*)

August 15: Assumption of the Virgin
   (*Asunción*)
October 12: Discovery of America Day
   (*Día de la Hispanidad*)
November 1: All Saints (*Todos los Santos*)
December 6: Constitution Day
   (*Día de la Constitución*)
December 8: Immaculate Conception
   (*Inmaculada Concepción*)
December 25: Christmas Day
   (Castilian *Navidad;* Catalan *Nadal*)

Public holidays

Public holidays – as well as scores of local festivals (see below) – may well disrupt your travel plans at some stage. There are ten Spanish national holidays per year and these are supplemented by five holidays fixed by the regions. In the Balearics, the resorts are generally oblivious to public holidays, but elsewhere almost all businesses and shops close, and it can prove difficult to find a room. Similarly, vacant seats on planes and buses (which are in any case reduced to a skeleton service) are at a premium.

Festivals, the bullfight and football

It's hard to beat the experience of arriving in a town to discover the streets decked out with flags and streamers, a band playing in the square and the entire population out celebrating the local festa (in Castilian, fiesta). Everywhere in Mallorca and Menorca takes at least one day off a year to devote to partying. Usually it's the local saint's day, but there are celebrations, too, of harvests, deliverance from the Moors, of safe return from the sea – any excuse will do.

Each festival is different, with a particular local emphasis, but there is always music, dancing, traditional costume and an immense spirit of enjoyment. The main event of most *festas* is a parade, either behind a revered holy image or a more celebratory affair with fancy costumes and *gigantones*, giant carnival figures that run down the streets to the delight, or terror, of children.

Although these *festas* take place throughout the year – and it's often the obscure and unexpected event which proves to be most fun – Holy Week (*Setmana Santa*) stands out, its passing celebrated in many places with magnificent processions.

The box overleaf gives the highlights of Mallorca and Menorca's festival year; for information about less prominent festivals, try local tourist offices. Remember that, although outsiders are nearly always welcome at a *festa*, you will have difficulty finding a room, and should try to book your accommodation well in advance.

The Bullfight

In recent years the popularity of the **Bullfight** (*Los Toros*) has declined across Spain, though it was never as big a deal in Catalunya and the Balearics as elsewhere. Yet Mallorca does have two main rings – one in Palma, the other in Muro – which still attract large crowds. The spectators turn up to see the *matadores* dispatch the bulls cleanly and with "artistic merit", which they greet with thunderous applause and the waving of handkerchiefs; a prolonged and messy kill will get the audience whistling. Some Spaniards do, of course, object to the whole spectacle, but opposition is not widespread and if Spaniards tell you that bullfighting is controversial, they are more likely to be referring to new refinements to the "sport", especially the widespread but illegal shaving down of bulls' horns. The horns are as sensitive as fingernails a few millimetres in, and the paring down deters the animals from charging and affects their balance, thereby reducing the danger to the *matador*.

Whether you attend a bullfight, obviously, is down to you. If you spend any time at all in Mallorca and Menorca during the season (which runs from March until October), you may well encounter *Los Toros* on a bar TV, and that will probably make up your mind. Many neutrals are particularly offended by the use of horses: padded up for protection, the horses are repeatedly charged by the bulls, which clearly terrifies them – though they can't make their feelings heard as their vocal chords have been cut out. If you want to know more about the **opposition to bullfighting**, Spain's Anti-Bullfight Campaign can be contacted at ABC International, c/Pere Verges 1, 10.3 Edifici Piramidon, 08020 Barcelona, Spain. (Internet: *www.intercom.es/adda*).

The corrida

Highly stylized, each bullfighting programme (*corrida*) begins with a **procession**, to the accompaniment of a *paso doble* by the band. Leading the procession are two *algauziles* or "constables", on horseback and in traditional costume, followed by the three *matadores*, who will each fight two bulls, and their personal teams, each comprising two mounted assistants – *picadores* – and three *banderillas*. At the back are the mule teams who will drag off the dead bulls. The beast is softened up by the *picadores*, who stab pikes into its withers, and then by the *banderillas*, who stick beribboned and sharpened sticks into the bull in preparation for the *matador*, who kills the animal off.

Tickets for *corridas* cost 2000ptas and up – much more for the prime seats and prestigious fights. The cheapest seats are *gradas*, the highest rows at the back, from where you can see everything that happens without too much of the detail; the front rows are known as the *barreras*. Seats are also divided into *sol* (sun), *sombra* (shade) and *sol y sombra* (shaded after a while), though these distinctions have become less relevant as more and more bullfights start later in the day, at 6pm or 7pm, rather than the traditional 5pm. The *sombra* seats are more expensive not so much for the spectators' personal comfort as for the fact that most of the action takes place in the shade. On the way in, you can rent **cushions** – two hours sitting on concrete is not much fun. Beer and soft drinks are sold inside.

Football

To foreigners, the bullfight is easily the most celebrated of Spain's spectacles. In terms of popular support in modern Spain, however, it ranks far below **futbol** (football or soccer). For many years, the country's two dominant teams have been Real Madrid and FC Barcelona, and these have shared the League title and Cup honours with repetitive regularity. Both teams are in Division 1 – La Primera Liga – of Spain's four-division League (Divisions 1, 2A, 2B and 3), and it's here you'll also find the excellent, Palma-based Real Club Deportivo Mallorca, easily the Balearics' best team. A good way behind, in Division 3, come Atletico Baleares, who are also based in Palma. A visit to a match is good fun, the crowd noisy, enthusiastic and usually good-humoured. Real Club Deportivo Mallorca play in the Estadi Lluis Sitjar, just to the north of Palma city centre on Avgda Argentina, near Plaça Madrid. Atletico Baleares play in the Estadi Baleares, near the Via Cintura. The football season runs from early September to mid-June with a short Christmas break. Most matches are on Sunday afternoons and tickets, which are available at the turnstiles, cost between 3000ptas and 6000ptas.

Festival calendar for Mallorca and Menorca

January

16 The *Revetla de Sant Antoni Abat* (Eve of St Antony's Day) is celebrated by the lighting of bonfires (*foguerons*) in Palma and several of Mallorca's villages – especially Sa Pobla, where the inhabitants move from fire to fire, dancing round in fancy dress and eating traditional eel and vegetable patties, *espinagades*. Also observed in Maó.

17 *Beneides de Sant Antoni* (Blessing of St Antony). St Antony's feast day is marked by processions in many of Mallorca's country towns, notably Sa Pobla and Artà, with farmyard animals herded through the streets to receive the saint's blessing and protection against disease.

17 *Processó d'els Tres Tocs* (Procession of the Three Knocks). Held in Ciutadella (Menorca), this procession commemorates the victory of Alfonso III over the Muslims here on January 17, 1287. There's a mass in the cathedral first and then three horsemen – dressed in black evening suits and riding boots – lead the way to the old city walls, where the eldest of the trio knocks three times with his flagstaff at the exact spot the Catalans first breached the walls.

19 *Revetla de Sant Sebastià*. Palma has more bonfires, singing and dancing for St Sebastian.

20 *Festa de Sant Sebastià*. This feast day is celebrated in Pollença (Mallorca) with a procession led by a holy banner (*estenard*) picturing the saint. It's accompanied by *cavallets* (literally "merry-go-rounds"), two young dancers each wearing a cardboard horse and imitating the animal's walk. Of medieval origin, you'll see *cavallets* at many of the islands' festivals.

February

Carnaval Towns and villages throughout the islands live it up during the week before Lent with marches and fancy dress parades. The biggest and liveliest are in Palma, where the shindig is known as *Sa Rua* (the Cavalcade).

March/April

Setmana Santa (Holy Week) is as widely observed as everywhere else in Spain. On Maundy Thursday in Palma, a much venerated icon of the crucified Christ, *La Sang*, is taken from the eponymous church on the Plaça del Hospital (off La Rambla) and taken in procession through the city streets. There are also solemn Good Friday (*Divendres Sant*) processions in many towns and villages, with the more important taking place in Palma, Sineu (Mallorca) and Maó. Most holy of all, however, is the Good Friday *Davallament* (The Lowering), the culmination of Holy Week in Pollença. Here, in total silence and by torchlight, the inhabitants lower a figure of Christ down from the hilltop Oratori to the church of Nostra Senyora dels Àngels below. During Holy Week there are also many *romerias* (pilgrimages) to the islands' holy places, with one of the most popular being the climb up to the Ermita Santa Magdalena, near Mallorca's Inca. The Monestir de Lluc, which possesses Mallorca's most venerated shrine, is another religious focus during this time, with the penitential trudging round its Camí dels Misteris del Rosari (The Way of the Mysteries of the Rosary).

Mid-May

The *Festa de Nostra Senyora de la Victòria* in Port de Sóller, Mallorca, features mock battles between Christians and infidels in commemoration of the thrashing of a band of Arab pirates in 1561. Lots of booze and firing of antique rifles (in the air).

June

Corpus Christi At noon in the main square of Pollença an ancient and curious dance of uncertain provenance takes place – the *Ball de les Àguiles* (Dance of the Eagles) – followed by a religious procession.

23–25 In Ciutadella, the midsummer *Festa de Sant Joan* has been celebrated since the fourteenth century. There are jousting competitions, folk music, dancing, processions and pilgrimages. A particular highlight is on the Sunday before the 24th, when the *S'Homo d'es Bé* (the Man of the Lamb) leads a party of horsemen through the town. Clad in animal skins and carrying a lamb in honour of St John, he invites everyone to the forthcoming knees-up.

July

15–16 *Día de Virgen de Carmen*. The day of the patron saint of seafarers and fishermen is celebrated in many coastal settlements – principally Palma, Port de Sóller, Colònia de Sant Pere, Porto Colom, Cala Rajada and Maó – with parades and the blessing of boats.

Third week The Reconquest of Menorca is celebrated in a festival in Mercadal.

Last Sunday The *Festa de Sant Jaume* in Alcúdia (Mallorca) celebrates the feast day of St James with a popular religious procession followed by all sorts of fun and games – folk dances, fireworks and the like. Similar festivities in Es Castell, Menorca, too.

August

2 *Mare de Déu dels Àngels*. Moors and Christians battle it out again, this time in Pollença.

Second weekend High jinks on horseback through the streets of the town, in the *Festa de Sant Llorenç* in Alaior (Menorca).

20 *Cavallet* (see opposite) dances in Felanitx, Mallorca.

Throughout August International Festival at Pollença, including art and sculpture exhibitions and chamber music.

September

Second week In Alaró (Mallorca), the *Nativitat de Nostra Senyora* (Nativity of the Virgin) is honoured by a pilgrimage to a hilltop shrine near the Castell d'Alaró.

October

Third Sunday *Festa d'es Butifarra* (Sausage Festival). Of recent origins, this festival follows on from tractor and automobile contests held in the Mallorcan village of Sant Joan. It features folk dancing and traditional music as well as the eating of specially prepared vegetable pies (*coca amb trampó*) and sausages (*berenada de butifarra*).

December

Christmas (*Nadal*) is especially picturesque in Palma, where there are Nativity plays in the days leading up to the 25th.

Trouble, the police and sexual harassment

Many North European expatriates love Mallorca and Menorca for their lack of crime – and with good reason. In the islands' villages and small towns petty crime is unusual, and serious offences, from burglary to assault and beyond, extremely rare. Of the three larger towns, only Palma presents any problems, mostly low-key stuff such as the occasional fight and minor theft – commonsense precautions are normally enough to keep you out of any trouble. However, you should also be aware that some of the late-night bars of the seedier resorts are commonly colonized by noisy and aggressive male tourists. In this regard, S'Arenal and Magaluf have the worst reputations, but it's more a question of which bar you're in, rather than the resort you're staying at. If you've accidentally dropped into a rough house, get out while the going is good.

If for some reason you do have dealings with the Spanish police, remember that, although they are polite enough in the normal course of events, they can be extremely unpleasant if you get on the wrong side of them. At all times, keep your cool.

Avoiding trouble

Almost all the problems tourists encounter in the Balearics are to do with **petty crime** – pickpocketing and bag-snatching – rather than more serious physical confrontations, so it's as well to be on your guard and know where your possessions are at all times. Sensible **precautions** include: carrying bags slung across your neck and not over your shoulder; not carrying anything in pockets that are easy to dip into; having photocopies of your passport, airline ticket and driving licence; leaving passports and tickets in the hotel safe; and noting down travellers' cheque and credit card numbers. When you're **looking for a hotel room**, never leave your bags unattended. If you have a **car**, don't leave anything in view when you park. Vehicles are rarely stolen, but luggage and valuables left in cars do make a tempting target. At **night** in Palma, avoid unlit streets, don't go out brimming with valuables, and try not to appear hopelessly lost.

Thieves often work in pairs and, although theft is far from rife on the Balearics, you should be aware of certain **ploys**, such as: the "helpful" person pointing out "birdshit" (shaving cream or something similar) on your jacket, while someone else relieves you of your money; the card or paper you're invited to read on the street to distract your attention; the move by someone in a café for your drink with one hand (the other hand is in your bag as you react to save your

drink); and if you're studying postcards or papers at stalls, watch out for people standing unusually close.

What to do if you're robbed

If you're robbed, you need to **go to the police** to report it, not least because your insurance company will require a police report. Don't expect a great deal of concern if your loss is relatively small – and expect the process of completing forms and formalities to take ages. In the unlikely event that you're **mugged** or otherwise threatened, *never* resist, and try to reduce your contact with the robber to a minimum. Either just hand over what's wanted, or throw money in one direction and take off in the other. Afterwards, go straight to the police, who will be more sympathetic and helpful on these occasions – tourism is, after all, the islands' economic lifeblood, and many officers on the Balearics speak English.

The police

Franco created a **police force** of labyrinthine complexity and since his death political parties of all persuasions have dodged the fundamental reorganization that is really needed. The reason is simple: no one wants to take them on.

There are three main types of police: the Guardia Civil, the Policía Nacional and the Policía Municipal, all of them armed. Dressed in green uniforms, the **Guardia Civil** police the highways and the countryside, but they are generally regarded as being officious and best avoided. Even now, many Spaniards are deeply suspicious of them, remembering their enthusiastic support of Franco and the unsuccessful coup led by one of their colonels, Tejero, when he held the Cortes hostage in February 1981. They have, however, had their sails trimmed in recent years – improbably, they've even assumed some environmental responsibilities – and the loathed tricorn hat has been abandoned except for ceremonial occasions. The brown-uniformed **Policía Nacional** have made a better fist of the transition to democracy despite their disagreeable origins as Franco's brutal security police, the Policía Armada – they were even instrumental in Tejero's failure. They are mainly seen in the cities, armed with submachine guns and guarding key installations. They are also used to control crowds and demonstrations and – despite their democratic credentials – are not known for their sensitivity.

If you do need the police – and above all if you're reporting a serious crime – you should always try to go to the more sympathetic **Policía Municipal**, who wear blue and white uniforms. The problem is that they only operate in the towns – in the **countryside** you'll usually have no choice but to throw yourself on the tender mercies of the Guardia Civil, and although their rural officers are often more helpful than their urban colleagues, they are inclined to resent the suggestion that any crime exists on their turf. Indeed, you may end up feeling as if you're the one who stands accused.

Offences

Should you be **arrested** on any charge, you have the right to contact your local consulate in Palma (see p.90 for the addresses). Unfortunately, many consulates are notoriously reluctant to get involved, though most are required to assist you to some degree if you have your passport stolen or lose all your money. If you've been detained for a drugs offence, don't expect any sympathy or help. You also ought to be aware of a couple of **offences** that you might commit unwittingly:

• In theory you're supposed to carry some kind of **identification** at all times, and the police can stop you in the streets and demand it. In practice they're rarely bothered if you're clearly a foreigner.

• **Nude bathing** or **unauthorized camping** (see p.36) are activities more likely to bring you into contact with officialdom, though a warning to cover up or move on is more likely than any real confrontation. Topless tanning is commonplace at all the resorts, but in country areas, where attitudes are more traditional, you should take care not to upset local sensibilities.

Sexual harassment

Spain's macho image has faded in the post-Franco years and these days there are few parts of the Balearics where foreign women, travelling alone, are likely to feel threatened, intimidated, or attract unwanted attention. The tendency of Spaniards to move around in mixed crowds, filling central bars, clubs and streets late into the night, also helps to make you feel less exposed. If you are in any doubt as to your safety, there are always taxis – plentiful and reasonably priced.

The major tourist **resorts** have their own artificial holiday culture, which has much to do with sex. The men (of all nationalities) who hang around in nightclubs and bars here pose no greater or lesser a threat than similar operators at home, though the language barrier makes it harder to know who to trust. Amongst Spaniards, "dejame en paz" ("leave me in peace") is a fairly standard rebuff. The **remoter parts of the interior** can pose problems for women too. In some areas you can walk for hours without seeing a soul or coming across an inhabited farm or house. It's rare that this poses a threat – help and hospitality are much more the norm – but you are certainly more vulnerable, and local men less accustomed to women being on their own.

Finding work

Unless you've some particular skill and have applied for a job advertised in your home country, the only real chance of long-term work in the Balearics is in language schools. However, there is much less work about than in the boom years of the early 1980s – schools are contracting rather than expanding – and you'll need to persevere if you're to come up with a rewarding position. To give yourself any kind of chance, you'll need some sort of recognized qualification, like a TEFL (Teaching English as a Foreign Language) or ESL (English as a Second Language) certificate.

Teaching and language work

Finding a **teaching** job is mainly a question of pacing the streets, stopping in at every language school around and asking about vacancies. For the addresses of schools look in the yellow pages under *academias*. The best time to try is from the middle to the end of September when the schools know how many replacement teachers they need. Reputable schools will require you to have undergone at least a one-month intensive teacher training course and to give a demonstration lesson. If you intend to stay in the Balearics for any length of time, you'll need a *permiso de residencia* – see "Visas and red tape" p.19.

Other options are to try advertising **private lessons** (better paid, but harder to make a living at) in the local press or, if you speak good Spanish, **translation work**, most of which will be business correspondence – look in the yellow pages under *traducciones*. If you intend doing translation work, you'll usually need access to a fax and a PC.

Temporary work

If you're looking for **temporary work**, the best chances are in the **bars and restaurants** of the larger resorts. This may help you have a good time but it's unlikely to bring in much money; pay (often from British bar owners) will reflect your lack of official status. If you turn up in spring and are willing to stay through the season you might get a better deal – also true if you're offering some special skill like windsurfing. Occasionally there are jobs on offer at **yacht marinas**, scrubbing down and servicing the boats of the well-heeled; just turn up and ask around, but don't be too hopeful.

Directory

ADDRESSES These are usually abbreviated to a standard format – c/Bellver 7 translates as Bellver street (*carrer*) no. 7; Plaça Reina 9 as Reina square (*plaça*) no. 9; Plaça Rosari 5, 2è means second floor at no. 5 Plaça Rosari; Passeig d'es Born 15, 1–C means suite C, first floor, at no. 15; Passeig d'es Born s/n (*sense número*) means without a number. In Franco's day, most avenues and boulevards were named after Fascist heroes and, although the vast majority were redesignated years ago, there's still some confusion in remoter spots. Another source of bafflement can be house numbers: some houses carry more than one number (the by-product of half-hearted reorganizations), and on many streets the sequence is impossible to fathom.

AIRPORT TAX There's no departure tax.

CHILDREN Most *hostals, pensions* and hotels welcome children and many offer rooms with three or four beds; restaurants and cafés almost always encourage families too. Many package holidays have child-minding facilities as part of the deal. For babies, food seems to work out quite well (some places will prepare food specially) though you might want to bring powdered milk – babies, like most Spaniards, are pretty contemptuous of the UHT stuff generally available. Disposable nappies and other basic supplies are widely available in the resort areas and the larger towns.

ELECTRICITY The current is 220 volts AC, with standard European-style two-pin plugs. Brits will need an adaptor to connect their appliances, North Americans both an adaptor and a transformer.

LAUNDRIES Although there's the occasional self-service launderette (usually rendered in Castilian, *lavandería automática*), mostly you'll have to leave your clothes for a full (and somewhat expensive) laundry service. A dry cleaner is a *tintorería* (also Castilian).

TIME Spain is one hour ahead of the UK, six hours ahead of Eastern 'Standard Time, nine hours ahead of Pacific Standard Time, nine hours behind Australian Eastern Standard Time and eleven behind New Zealand except for brief periods during the changeovers made in the respective countries to and from daylight saving. In Spain the clocks go back on the last Sunday of March and forward again on the last Sunday of September.

TOILETS Public toilets, which remain rare, are averagely clean but almost never have any paper (best to carry your own). They're commonly referred to as *los servicios* or *el lavabo*. *Dones* or the Castilian *Damas* (Ladies) and *Homes* or the Castilian *Caballeros* (Gentlemen) are the usual signs, though you may also see *Señoras* (Women) and *Señores* (Men).

The Guide

Chapter 1   Palma and around   59

Chapter 2   Northwest Mallorca   102

Chapter 3   Southeast Mallorca   161

Chapter 4   Menorca   194

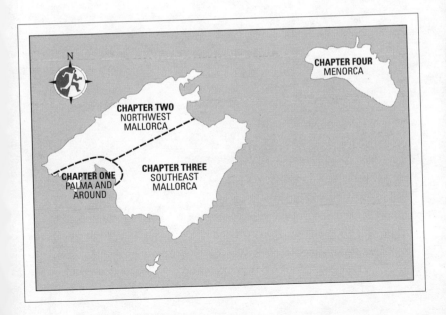

Palma and around

P ALMA is an ambitious city. In 1983 it became the capital of one of Spain's newly established autonomous regions, the Balearic Islands, and since then it's shed the dusty provincialism of yesteryear, developing into a go-ahead and cosmopolitan commercial hub of 320,000 people. The new self-confidence is plain to see in the city centre, a vibrant and urbane place of careful coiffures and well-cut suits, which is akin to the big cities of the Spanish mainland – and a world away from the heaving tourist enclaves of the surrounding bay. There's still a long way to go – much of suburban Palma remains obdurately dull and somewhat dilapidated – but the centre now presents a splendid ensemble of lively shopping areas, mazy lanes and refurbished old buildings, all enclosed by what remains of the old city walls and their replacement boulevards. This geography encourages downtown Palma to look into itself and away from the sea, even though its harbour – now quarantined by the main highway – has always been the city's economic lifeline.

The Romans were the first to recognize the site's strategic value, establishing a military post here, but real development came with the Moors who made their **Medina Mayurka** a major seaport protected by no fewer than three concentric walls. Jaume I of Aragón captured the Moorish stronghold in 1229 and promptly started work on the **cathedral**, whose mellow sandstone still towers above the waterfront, presenting from its seaward side – in the sheer beauty of its massive proportions – one of Spain's most stunning sights.

As a major port of call between Europe and North Africa, Palma boomed under both Moorish and medieval Christian control, but its wealth and prominence came to a sudden end with the Spanish exploitation of the New World: from the early sixteenth century, Madrid looked west across the Atlantic and Palma slipped into Mediterranean obscurity. One result of its abrupt decline has been the preservation of much of the **old town**, whose narrow, labyrinthine streets and high-storeyed houses are at their most beguiling behind the cathedral. This district possesses few specific

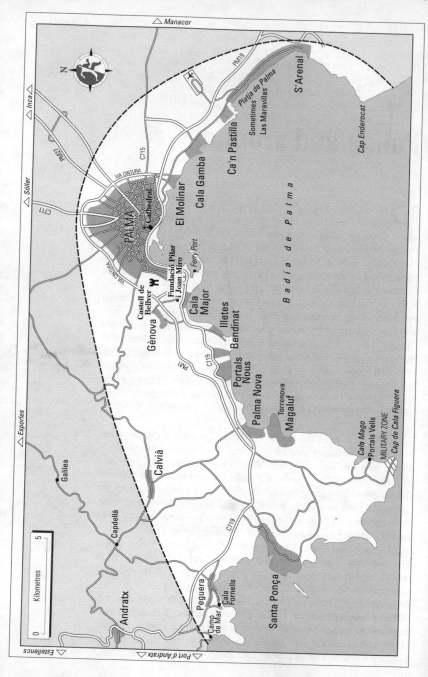

sights, but it's a delightful place to wander, especially as an ambitious renovation programme is rapidly returning the area to its old elegance. The pick of Palma's other historic attractions are the fourteenth-century **Castell de Bellver** and the heavyweight Baroque of the **Basílica de Sant Francesc**.

Yet for most visitors, Palma's main appeal is its sheer vitality: at night scores of excellent **restaurants** offer the best of Spanish, Catalan and Mallorcan cuisine, while the city's **cafés** buzz with purposeful chatter. Palma also boasts **accommodation** to match most budgets, making it a splendid base from which to explore the island. In this respect, the city is far preferable, at least for independent travellers, to the string of resorts along the **Badia de Palma** (Bay of Palma), where nearly all the accommodation is block-booked by tour operators. If you are tempted by a cheap package, it's as well to bear in mind that the more agreeable of the resorts lie to the west of the city, where a hilly coastline of rocky cliffs and tiny coves is punctuated by mostly small, sandy beaches. Development is ubiquitous, but well-to-do **Illetes** has several excellent hotels and a couple of lovely cove beaches; pint-sized **Cala Fornells** has a fine seashore setting and a pair of good hotels, with the spacious sandy shoreline of family-oriented **Peguera** in easy reach; and then there's **Camp de Mar**, set in an attractive wooded bay fringed by another good beach. Places to avoid include the massive villa complex of **Santa Ponça**, lager-swilling **Magaluf** and all the resorts to the east of Palma. Here the pancake-flat shoreline is burdened by a seamless band of skyscrapers stretching from **Ca'n Pastilla** to **S'Arenal** – behind what is, admittedly, one of the island's longest and most impressive beaches, the **Platja de Palma**.

Arrival, orientation and information

Mallorca's gleaming new international **airport** is 11km east of Palma, immediately behind the resort of Ca'n Pastilla. It has one enormous terminal, which handles both scheduled and charter flights, with separate floors for arrivals (below) and departures (above). Both floors have an airport information desk. The arrivals area has 24-hour **cash card and credit card machines**, **car rental** and **currency exchange** facilities as well as a provincial **tourist office**, with public transport timetables, taxi rates, maps and general island information (Mon–Sat 9am–2pm & 3–8pm, Sun 9am–2pm). The tourist office has lists of hotels and *hostals*, but will not help arrange **accommodation**. The dozen or so travel agents scattered round the arrivals hall, however, will: it's a good idea to shop around, but you could start with Prima Travel, who have a wide selection of hotels, apartments and villas.

For full details of accommodation in Palma see p.

If you're collecting someone from the airport by car, there's a free five-minute stop zone, plus an enormous if slightly confusing **car park**: when you arrive, grab a ticket from the machine at the car park entrance; before departure, take the ticket to one of the pay machines, which allow you twenty minutes' grace to find your vehicle and leave.

The airport is linked to the city and the Bay of Palma resorts by a busy highway (*autopista*) which shadows the shoreline from S'Arenal in the east to Magaluf in the west. The least expensive way to reach Palma from the airport is by **bus #17** (daily, every 20min from 6am to midnight, plus 1am, 1.35am and 2.10am; 290ptas one way). These leave from the main entrance of the terminal building – just behind the taxi rank – and reach the city's inner ring road near the foot of Avgda Gabriel Alomar i Villalonga, at the c/Joan Maragall junction; they then head on to Plaça Espanya, on the north side of the centre,

before continuing west to the Passeig Mallorca and then south to the top of Avgda Jaume III. There are frequent stops along the way. A taxi from the airport to the city centre will set you back about 2000ptas; taxi rates are controlled and a list of island-wide fares is displayed in the arrivals hall (and in the window of the provincial tourist office).

The Palma **ferry terminal** is about 4km west of the city centre, linked to town by bus #1; to catch it, walk 200m out of the ferry terminal to the main road; the bus stop on the near (harbour) side of the road is for Palma. Buses (175ptas) run every hour to the Plaça de la Reina and the Plaça Rei Juan Carles I, at either end of the Passeig d'es Born, and then continue to the Plaça Espanya. They operate from 8am to 9pm, but beware of reduced services on Sundays and holidays. There's also a taxi rank outside the ferry terminal building; the fare to the city centre is about 700ptas.

Arrival, orientation and information

For full details of ferries and flights between the Balearic Islands and from the Spanish mainland, see Basics.

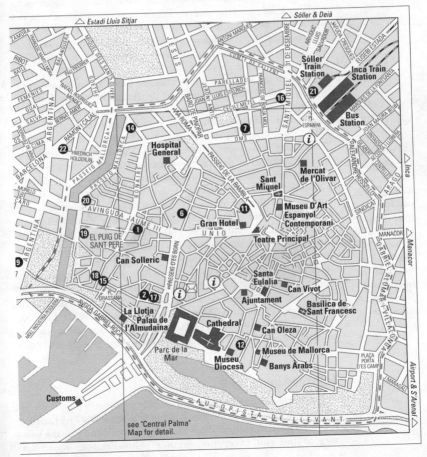

Orientation

Almost everything of interest in Palma is located in the city centre, a roughly circular affair whose southern perimeter is largely defined by the cathedral and the remains of the old city walls, which in turn abut the coastal motorway and the harbour. The city centre's landward limits are determined by a zigzag of wide boulevards built beside or in place of the old town walls – **Avinguda de la Argentina** and **Avinguda Gabriel Alomar i Villalonga** connect with the coastal motorway, thereby completing the circle. The **Via Cintura**, the ring road around the suburbs, loops off from the coastal motorway to create a much larger, outer circle. The city centre itself is crossed by four interconnected avenues, **Passeig d'es Born**, **Avinguda Jaume III**, **c/Unió** (which becomes **c/Riera** at its eastern end) and **Passeig de la Rambla**. Your best bet is to use these four thoroughfares to guide yourself round the centre – Palma's jigsaw-like side streets and squares can be very confusing. Central Palma is about 2km in diameter, roughly thirty minutes' walk from one side to the other. If you're in a hurry, take a **taxi**: fares are reasonable and there are ranks outside all the major hotels.

To reach the city's outskirts, take the **bus**. City buses are operated by EMT (Empresa Municipal de Transports) and almost all their services pass through Plaça Espanya, linking the centre with the suburbs and the nearer tourist resorts. In the city centre, each EMT bus stop sports a large route map with timetable details. Tickets, available from the driver, cost 175ptas per journey within the city limits, a few pesetas more for the resorts. Under the Bono-Bus scheme, a book of ten tickets valid for city-wide travel costs 1500ptas; books are available from most newsagents or tobacconists (look for the brown and yellow *tabacs* or *tabacos* signs) and from the EMT information kiosk on the Plaça Espanya. **Island-wide buses** are operated by several other companies. Most use the bus station on the northeast side of the Plaça Espanya, though a few leave from the surrounding side streets; the most significant of these are the services run by Bus Nord Balear to Valldemossa, Deià, Sóller and Port de Sóller, which stop outside the *Bar La Granja*, c/Arxiduc Lluis Salvador 1. Timetable information for all island-wide services is available in Spanish and Catalan on ☎971 176970. The island's two tiny **train stations** are by the bus station on the northeast side of the Plaça Espanya – one line goes to Inca, the other to Sóller.

For details of the frequencies and journey times of buses and trains from Palma, see p.101. For further information on the delightful train journey from Palma to Sóller, see p.105.

Information

The provincial **tourist office** is just off the Passeig d'es Born at Plaça de la Reina 2 (daily 9am–2.30pm & 3–8pm; ☎971 712216), while the main municipal office is at c/Sant Domingo 11, in the subway at the end of c/Conquistador (Mon–Fri 9am–8pm, Sat

9am–1pm; ☎971 724090). Both provide city- and island-wide information, dispensing free maps, accommodation lists, bus schedules, ferry timetables, lists of car rental firms, boat trip details and all sorts of special-interest leaflets, including the useful *Artesanía*, which lists specialist suppliers of everything from pottery and pearls to books and handicrafts. The smaller municipal tourist office on Plaça Espanya (Mon–Fri 9am–8pm, Sat 9am–1pm) just provides the basics.

Accommodation

There are about twenty *hostals* and thirty hotels dotted around Palma, but nevertheless demand still tends to outstrip supply from the middle of July through to the third week in August. If you haven't got a reservation and you're travelling during this period, you should either phone around or contact a **travel agent**, at the airport (see p.60) or in the city centre (see p.91), where Viajes Iberia should be able to find you somewhere if anyone can. At other times of the year, things are much easier: you could select somewhere from the list overleaf and contact them direct; or get the official list of all the city's accommodation from either the municipal or the provincial tourist office – though neither will help you actually book a room.

A full list of all Palma's travel agents is given in the yellow pages under agències de viatges.

The bulk of Palma's **budget accommodation** is in the centre and, fortunately enough, this is by far the most diverting part of the city – the immediate suburbs are quite unprepossessing. There's a cluster of places along the narrow, cobbled side streets off the Passeig d'es Born and – rather less appetizingly – around the Plaça Espanya. The most convenient concentration of **smarter hotels** is on the Passeig Mallorca, a particularly attractive portion of the inner ring road where two sections of old city wall run down the middle of the boulevard to either side of an ancient watercourse. Another cluster is to the west of the centre, overlooking the waterfront along Avinguda Gabriel Roca.

The nearest youth hostel to Palma is in the resort of Sometimes, a 25-minute bus ride from town – see p.94.

Inexpensive

Hostal Apuntadores, c/Apuntadors 8 ☎ & fax 971 713491. Appealingly laid-back, youthful one-star *hostal* in an old house down a cramped and bustling side street off Passeig d'es Born. Rooms are simple but adequate with wash-basins but not showers. Next door to the *Ritzi* (see below). ②.

Hostal-residencia Bonany, c/Almirall Cervera 5 ☎971 737924. Faded one-star *hostal* on a quiet residential street, about 3km west of the city centre, close to Castell de Bellver. Take bus #3, #4 or #21 from Plaça Espanya and get off at the start of Avgda Joan Miró. Closed November to March. ③.

Hotel Cannes, c/Cardenal Pou 8 ☎971 726943. Unprepossessing fifty-room, two-star hotel in a grittily modern part of town by the Plaça Espanya, and close to the principal shopping areas. ③.

Hostal-residencia Cuba, c/Sant Magí 1 ☎971 738159. Attractive, well-appointed rooms in a beautifully restored *Modernista* stone house of 1904 with a pretty little tower and balustrade. Overlooks the harbour and the bottom of busy Avgda Argentina. Rooftop sun terrace. Twenty rooms. ④.

Hostal-residencia Monleón, Passeig de la Rambla 3 ☎971 715317. Gloomy and slightly battered *hostal* in an old-fashioned 1950s building at the foot of La Rambla; often has vacancies when others don't. ②.

Hostal-residencia Pons, c/VI 8 ☎971 722658. Simple rooms in a lovely old house with a courtyard and house plants. In the old part of town, near the Passeig d'es Born. ③.

Hostal-residencia Regina, c/Sant Miquel 77 ☎971 713703. Just ten frugal rooms above some shops in this dreary, two-storey modern building bordering a main commercial street to the north of the old part of town. ③.

Hostal Ritzi, c/Apuntadors 6 ☎971 714610. Spartan one-star rooms in an ancient and well-tended five-storey house off the Passeig d'es Born. Of the 17 rooms, those with their own shower cost about 1000ptas more than those with a washbasin. ②.

Hostal-residencia Terminus, c/Eusebi Estada 2 ☎971 750014. Two-star establishment beside the train station, with a quirkily old-fashioned foyer and fairly large bedrooms. ③.

Hostal-residencia Valencia, c/Ramon i Cajal 21 ☎971 733147. Modern, 30-room *hostal* on the northern edge of the city centre. Spruce, almost antiseptic rooms, some with balconies overlooking the street. ③.

Moderate

Hotel Araxa, c/Alférez Cerdá 22 ☎971 731640, fax 971 731643. Attractive, three-storey modern hotel with pleasant gardens and an outdoor swimming pool. Most rooms have balconies. In a quiet residential area about 2km west of the centre, not far from the Castell de Bellver. Take bus #3, #4 or #21 from Plaça Espanya or bus #4 or #21 from Plaça de la Reina and get off at the start of Avgda Joan Miró. ⑥.

Hotel-residencia Born, c/Sant Jaume 3 ☎971 712942, fax 971 718618. This delightful hotel has an excellent downtown location and occupies a refurbished mansion with big wooden doors and a lovely courtyard where you can have breakfast under the palm trees. The rooms, most of which face onto the courtyard, are comfortable if a little plain. It's a popular spot, so try to book early if you're visiting in summer. ⑥.

Hotel Costa Azul, Avgda Gabriel Roca 7 ☎971 731940, fax 971 731971. Standard high-rise, popular with package tours, with balconied rooms overlooking the bay. ⑥.

Hotel Mirador, Avgda Gabriel Roca 10 ☎971 732046, fax 971 733915. Flanked by much larger and higher hotels down by the waterfront ten minutes' walk to the west of the city centre, this unassuming, slightly old-fashioned hotel is popular with Spanish business folk. Considering its bayside location, room rates are very reasonable. ⑥.

Hotel-residencia Palladium, Passeig Mallorca 40 ☎971 713945, fax 971 714665. Proficient three-star hotel offering spick and span accommodation in a modern tower overlooking the handsome Passeig Mallorca. ⑥.

Hotel Sol Jaime III, Passeig Mallorca 14 ☎971 725943, fax 971 725946. Agreeable three-star with smart modern rooms, mostly with balconies. Front rooms overlook the Passeig Mallorca. Very reasonable prices. ⑥.

Expensive

Hotel-residencia Almudaina, Avgda Jaume III, 9 ☎971 727340, fax 971 722599. Dapper modern rooms overlooking one of Palma's busiest streets. Right in the centre. ⑦.

Hotel Bellver, Avgda Gabriel Roca 11 ☎971 735142, fax 971 731451. Well-maintained chain hotel with balconies overlooking the harbour, a 15-minute walk west of the city centre. Standard high-rise, but the rooms are very comfortable. ⑦.

Hotel-residencia Palacio Ca Sa Galesa, c/Miramar 8 ☎971 715400, fax 971 721579. Charmingly renovated seventeenth-century mansion amongst the narrow alleys of the oldest part of town, a couple of minutes' walk from the cathedral. There's also an indoor heated swimming pool and fine views of the city from the roof terrace. Just a dozen luxurious and tastefully furnished rooms and suites. ⑨.

Hotel Palas Atenea, Avgda Gabriel Roca 29 ☎971 281400, fax 971 451989. Classy and classic 1960s-style foyer leads to attractively furnished, comfortable rooms with balconies overlooking the bay. ⑨.

<table>
<tr><td>Accomm-
odation</td><td>

Hotel-residencia San Lorenzo, c/Sant Llorenç 14 ☎971 728200, fax 971 711901. Delightful four-star hotel set in a luxuriously modernized seventeenth-century mansion, with a rooftop swimming pool. Located among the ancient side streets west of the Passeig d'es Born. Six rooms only, so reservations are essential. ⑧.

Hotel Saratoga, Passeig Mallorca 6 ☎971 727240, fax 971 727312. Excellent, newly refurbished hotel with rooftop swimming pool. Most rooms have balconies overlooking the boulevard. ⑦.

Hotel Son Vida, c/Son Vida ☎971 790000, fax 971 790017. Sumptuous five-star hotel, with its own golf course, in a refurbished eighteenth-century mansion, 5km northwest of Palma. ⑨.

</td></tr>
</table>

The City

There's not much argument as to where to start a tour of Palma – it's got to be the **cathedral**, which dominates the waterfront from the crest of a hill. Next door, Palma's other landmark is the **Palau de l'Almudaina**, an important royal residence from Moorish times, though successive modifications have destroyed most of its character and nowadays it's only worth a visit on a rainy day. Spreading northeast behind the cathedral are the narrow lanes and ageing mansions of the most intriguing part of the **old town**. A stroll here is a pleasure in itself and, tucked away among the side streets, there are two good diversions: the **Museu de Mallorca**, the island's most extensive museum, and the Baroque **Basílica de Sant Francesc**. North of the old town lies the heart of the early twentieth-century city, where the high-sided tenements are graced by a sequence of flamboyant buildings in the **Modernista** style (the Spanish, and especially Catalan, form of Art Nouveau), particularly on and around **Plaça Weyler**.

West of the city centre, you should consider a visit to the **Castell de Bellver**, an impressive hilltop castle, and perhaps also to the much less intriguing **Poble Espanyol**, which comprises detailed reproductions of important and typical buildings from every region of Spain.

The cathedral

Legend has it that when Jaume I of Aragón and Catalunya and his invasion force stood off Mallorca in 1229, a fierce gale threatened to sink the fleet. The desperate king promised to build a church dedicated to the Virgin Mary if the expedition against the Moors was successful; it was, and Jaume fulfilled his promise, starting construction work the next year. The king had a political point to make too – he built his cathedral, a gigantic affair of golden sandstone, bang on top of the Great Mosque, inside the Almudaina, the old Moorish citadel. The Reconquest was to be no temporary matter.

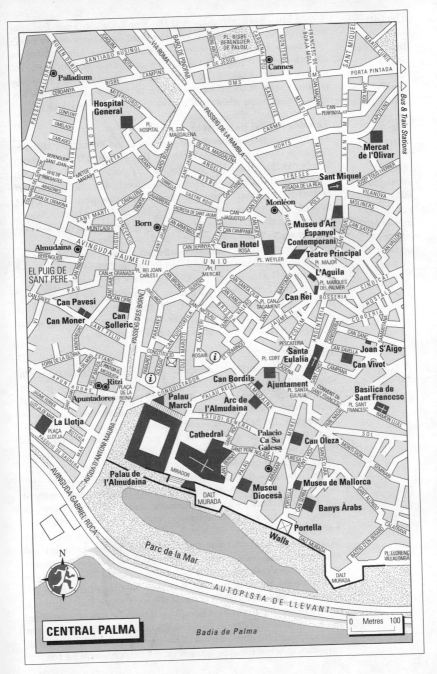

The City

The cathedral is open April–Oct Mon–Fri 10am–6pm, Sat 10am–2pm; Nov–March Mon–Fri 10am–3pm, Sat 10am–2pm; 400ptas. For the background to Jaume I's invasion, see p.244.

As it turned out, the cathedral (*La Seu* in Catalan) was five hundred years in the making. Nonetheless, although there are architectural bits and bobs from several different eras, the church remains essentially Gothic, with massive exterior buttresses – its most distinctive feature – taking the weight off the pillars within. The whole structure derives its effect from sheer height, impressive from any angle but startling when viewed from the waterside esplanade.

The doors and bell tower

The finest of the cathedral's three doors is the **Portal del Mirador** (Lookout Door), which overlooks the Bay of Palma from the south facade. Dating from the late fourteenth century, the weathered Mirador features a host of Flemish-style, ecclesiastical figurines set around a tympanum where heavily bearded disciples sit at a Last Supper. In contrast, the west-facing **Portal Major** (Great Door), across from the Almudaina, is a neo-Gothic disaster, an ugly reworking – along with the sixty-metre-high flanking turrets – of a far simpler predecessor that was badly damaged in an earthquake of 1851. On the north side is a third door, the **Portal de l'Almoina**, decorated in a simple Gothic design of 1498. Up above rises the solid squareness of the **bell tower** (closed to the public), an incongruous, fortress-like structure that clearly did not form part of the original design. When the largest of the bells, the 5700-kilo N'Eloi, was tolled in 1857 it shattered most of the cathedral's windows.

The interior

The cathedral is entered through the museum (see p.72) on the north side, but the majestic proportions of its interior are seen to best advantage from the western end, from the Portal Major. In the central nave, fourteen beautifully aligned, pencil-thin pillars rise to 21 metres before their ribs branch out – rather like fronded palm trees – to support the single-span, vaulted roof. The nave, at 44 metres high, is one of the tallest Gothic structures in Europe and its length – 121 metres – is of matching grandeur. This open, hangar-like construction, typical of Catalan Gothic architecture, was designed to make the high altar visible to the entire congregation, and to express the mystery of the Christian faith, with kaleidoscopic floods of light filtered in through the **stained-glass windows**. Most of the original glass was lost long ago, but recent refurbishment has returned several windows to their former glory and, now that many others have been un-bricked and cleaned, the cathedral has re-emerged from the gloom imposed by Renaissance, Baroque and neo-Gothic architects. There are seven rose windows, the largest of which crowns the triumphal arch of the apse and boasts over 1200 individual pieces of glass. The cathedral's designers also incorporated a specific, carefully orchestrated artifice: twice a year, at 6.30am on Candlemas and St Martin's Day, the sun shines through the stained glass of the eastern window onto the wall immediately below the rose window on the main, western facade.

The first attempt to return the church to something like its original splendour was made at the beginning of the twentieth century when an inspired local bishop commissioned the *Modernista* Catalan architect **Antoni Gaudí** to direct a full-blown restoration. At the time, Gaudí was renowned for his fancifully embellished metalwork, and his functionalist extrapolation of Gothic design was still evolving. This experimentation led ultimately to his most famous and extravagant opus, the church of the Sagrada Família in Barcelona, but here in Palma his work was relatively restrained. Flattened by a Barcelona tram, Gaudí died in 1926; it was only in the 1960s that his techniques were championed and copied across western Europe, and he was acknowledged as crucial to the development of modernism.

Gaudí worked on Palma's cathedral intermittently from 1904 to 1914, during which time he removed the High Baroque altar and shifted the ornate choir stalls from the centre of the cathedral, placing them flat against the walls of the presbytery. The new high altar, a medieval alabaster table of plain design, was then located beneath a phantasmagorical giant **baldachin**, suspended from the roof. This wrought-iron canopy, whose flowing lines are enhanced by hanging lanterns, is supposed to symbolize the Crown of Thorns – it's not a great success, though to be fair, Gaudí never had time to complete it so it's impossible to say what the final version would have looked like.

Other examples of Gaudí's distinctive workmanship are dotted around the cathedral. The railings in front of the high altar are twisted into shapes inspired by Mallorcan window grilles, while the wall on either side of the Bishop's Throne, at the east end of the church, sports ceramic inlays with brightly painted floral designs. Yet Gaudí's main concern was to revive the Gothic tradition by giving light to the cathedral. To this end he introduced electric lighting, bathing the apse in bright artificial light and placing lamps and candelabra throughout the church. At the time, Gaudí's measures were deeply controversial; no choir had ever before been removed in Spain and electric lighting was a real novelty. The artistic success of the whole project, though, was undeniable, and it was immediately popular.

The aisles on either side of the central nave are flanked by a long sequence of chapels, dull affairs for the most part, dominated by dusty Baroque altars of gargantuan proportions and little artistic merit. The exception, and the cathedral's one outstanding example of the Baroque, is the **Capella de Corpus Christi**, at the head of the aisle to the left of the high altar. Begun in the sixteenth century, the chapel's tiered and columned altarpiece features three religious scenes, cramped and intense sculptural tableaux of – from top to bottom – *The Temptations of St Anthony*, *The Presentation of Jesus in the Temple* and *The Last Supper*. The massive stone pulpit next to the chapel was moved here by Gaudí, a makeshift location for this excellent illustration of the Plateresque style. Dated to 1531, the pulpit's intricate floral patterns and bustling Biblical scenes cover a clumsy structure whose upper portion is carried by telamons, male counterparts of the more usual caryatids.

Though you can't get to it today – it's at the east end of the church directly behind the high altar – the **Capella de la Trinidad** (Trinity Chapel) is also of interest. Completed in 1329, this tiny chapel accommodates the remains of Jaume II and III, two notable medieval kings of Mallorca. Initially, the bodies were stored in a tomb that operated rather like a filing cabinet, allowing the corpses to be venerated by the devout, but this gruesome practice was finally discontinued – alabaster sarcophagi now enclose the royal bones.

The Museu de la Catedral

The ground floor of the bell tower and two adjoining chapterhouses have been turned into the **Museu de la Catedral** to accommodate an eclectic mixture of ecclesiastical treasures. The first room's most valuable exhibit, in the glass case in the middle, is a gilded silver monstrance of extraordinary delicacy, its fairy-tale decoration dating from the late sixteenth century. On display around the walls are assorted chalices and reliquaries and a real curiosity, the portable altar of Jaume I, a wood and silver chess board with each square containing a bag of relics.

Further works by the Mallorcan Primitives are displayed at the Museu de Mallorca – see pp.75–77.

The second room is mainly devoted to the Gothic works of the **Mallorcan Primitives**, a school of painters who flourished on the island in the fourteenth and fifteenth centuries, producing strikingly naive devotional works of bold colours and cartoon-like detail. The work of two of the school's leading fourteenth-century practitioners is displayed here, the so-called **Master of the Privileges**, whose love of minute detail and warm colours reveals an Italian influence, and the **Master of Bishop Galiana**, who looked to his Catalan contemporaries for his sense of movement and tight draughtsmanship. Later, the work of the Mallorcan Primitives shaded into the new realism of the Flemish style, which was to dominate Mallorcan painting throughout the sixteenth century: **Joan Desi**'s (unlabelled) *Panel of La Almoina* (c. 1500) illustrates the transition – it's the large panel showing St Francis, complete with stigmata, at the side of Christ. In terms of content, look out for the tribulations of **St Eulalia**, whose martyrdom fascinated and excited scores of medieval Mallorcan artists. A Catalan girl-saint, Eulalia defied the Roman Emperor Diocletian by sticking to her Christian faith despite all sorts of ferocious tortures, which are depicted in ecstatic detail here in a painting by the Master of the Privileges. Ultimately she was burnt at the stake and, at the moment of her death, white doves flew from her mouth.

The third and final room, the **Baroque chapterhouse**, is entered through a playful Churrigueresque doorway, above which a delicate Madonna is overwhelmed by lively cherubic angels. Inside, pride of place goes to the High Baroque altar, a gaudy, gilded affair surmounted by the Sacred Heart, a gory representation of the heart of Jesus that was very much in vogue during the eighteenth century. Some imagination went into the designation of the reliquaries displayed round the room – there's a piece of the flogging post, three thorns from Christ's crown and even a piece of the gall and vinegared sponge that was offered to the crucified Jesus. Of more appeal are a pair of finely carved, Baroque crucifixes, each Christ a study in perfect muscularity swathed in the flowing folds of a loincloth.

The Museu Diocesà

Immediately behind – and clearly signposted from – the cathedral, the **Museu Diocesà** (in Castilian, *Museo Diocesano*), on c/Mirador, just about merits a visit. It's situated within the Bishop's Palace, a mostly seventeenth-century structure built around an expansive courtyard presided over by a statue of the Sacred Heart. The museum has only two rooms, beginning with a tiny antechamber in which is displayed a panel-painting by the Master of Bishop Galiana (see p.72). It's an intriguing work, a didactic cartoon-strip illustrating the life of St Paul, who is shown with his Bible open and sword in hand, a militant view of the church that must have accorded well with the preoccupations of the powerful bishops of Mallorca. Look out also for the way the artist portrays the conversion on the road to Damascus, with Saul/Paul struck by a laser-like beam of light. Beyond, in the main room, there's a mildly diverting assortment of Moorish and Mudéjar tiles as well as the clumsy eighteenth-century sarcophagus built to house the remains of King Jaume II, but it's mostly stuffed with dull religious artefacts, including some spectacularly unsuccessful sculptures.

The Museu Diocesà is open April–Oct Mon–Fri 10am–1.30pm & 3–8pm, Sat & Sun 10am–1pm; Nov–March Mon–Fri 10am–1pm & 3–6pm; 300ptas.

The Palau de l'Almudaina and around

Opposite the cathedral entrance stands the **Palau de l'Almudaina**, originally the palace of the Moorish *walis* (governors) and later of the Mallorcan kings. The present structure, built around a compact courtyard, owes much of its appearance to Jaume II (1276–1311), who spent the last twelve years of his life in residence here. Jaume converted the old fortress into a lavish palace that incorporated both Gothic and Moorish features, an uneasy mixture of styles conceived by the Mallorcan Pedro Selva, the king's favourite architect. The two most prominent "Moorish" attributes are the fragile-looking outside walls, with their square turrets and dainty crenellations, and the delicate arcades of the loggia, which is best viewed from down below on the waterside esplanade.

The City

The Palau de l'Almudaina is open April–Sept Mon–Fri 10am–6.30pm, Sat 10am–2pm; Oct–March Mon–Fri 10am–2pm & 4–6pm, Sat 10am–2pm; 450ptas, free to EU citizens on Wed.

Once Mallorca was incorporated within the Aragonese kingdom, the Palau de l'Almudaina became surplus to requirements, though it did achieve local notoriety when the eccentric Aragonese king Juan I (1387–1395) installed an alchemist in the royal apartments, hoping he would replenish the treasury by turning base metal into gold.

Today, the palace serves a variety of official functions, housing the island's legislature, its military – whose camera-shy guards stand outside one of the entrances – and a series of state apartments kept in readiness for visiting dignitaries. Sometimes you're allowed to walk round the palace unescorted, but usually you'll get roped into one of the regular guided tours, whose energetic commentaries are repeated in three languages. Most of what you see – and there are considerable parts cordoned off – is really rather tedious, with the medieval rooms almost entirely devoid of ornamentation and the state apartments spruce and sterile. Saving graces are few and far between, but there are several admirable Flemish **tapestries**, fifteenth- and sixteenth-century imports devoted to classical themes such as Cleopatra's suicide. The palace also possesses a handful of **Flemish genre paintings**, fine still-life studies including one by the seventeenth-century Antwerp-based artist Frans Snyders, a contemporary of Rubens – in whose pictures he often painted the flowers and fruit. The guided tour finishes with a quick gallop round the Gothic **Capella de Santa Aina**, which is still used for army officers' masses and weddings.

The city walls and the Parc de la Mar

A flight of steps leads down from between the cathedral and the Palau de l'Almudaina to a handsomely restored section of the Renaissance **city walls**, whose mighty zigzag of bastions, bridges, gates and dry moats once encased the whole city. They replaced the city's medieval walls, portions of which also survive – look back up from the foot of the steps and a large chunk is clearly visible beneath and to either side of the cathedral. Constructed of sandstone blocks and adobe, the earlier fortifications depended on their height for their efficacy, with a gallery running along the top from which the defenders could fire at the enemy. By the middle of the fifteenth century, however, the development of more effective artillery had shifted the military balance in favour of offence, with cannons now able to breach medieval city walls with comparative ease. The military architects of the day soon evolved a new design in which walls were built much lower and thicker to absorb cannon shot, while four-faced bastions – equipped with artillery platforms – projected from the line of the walls, providing the defenders with a variety of firing lines. The whole lot was protected by a water-filled moat with deep, sheer sides. The costs of re-fortifying the major cities of western Europe were astronomical, but every country joined in the rush. In Palma, the Habsburgs ordered work to start to the new design in the 1560s, though the chain of bastions was only completed in 1801.

From the foot of the steps below the cathedral, a wide and pleasant **walkway** travels along the top of the wall, providing fine views of the cathedral and an insight into the tremendous strength of the Renaissance fortifications. Heading west, the walkway leads to the tiered gardens of a small Moorish-style park, which tumble down to the foot of Avinguda d'Antoni Maura, an extension of the tree-lined Passeig d'es Born. In the opposite direction – east from the steps below the cathedral – the walkway passes above the planted palm trees, concrete terraces and ornamental lagoon of the **Parc de la Mar**, an imaginative and popular redevelopment of the disused land that once lay between the walls and the coastal motorway – so popular in fact that the municipality are considering shoving the road underground so that they can extend the park to the seashore. Wall and walkway zigzag along the south side of old Palma before fizzling out at Plaça Llorenç Villalonga. On the way, you'll pass above the double **Portella gateway**, whose inner portal carries the Bourbon coat of arms above its arch; you can come off here for the Banys Àrabs and the old town.

The old town

The medina-like maze of streets at the back of the cathedral constitutes the heart of the **old town**, which extends north to Plaça Cort and east to Avinguda Gabriel Alomar i Villalonga. Long a neglected corner of the city, the district is now being refurbished, an ambitious and massively expensive project that's slowly restoring its antique charms. The area's general appearance is its main appeal, and you can spend hours wandering down narrow lanes and alleys, loitering in the squares, gawping at Renaissance mansions and peering up at imposing Baroque and Gothic churches.

The Banys Àrabs

If you leave the city wall walkway at the Portella gate, you'll find yourself in the old town at the foot of c/Portella. North of the gate, take the first turning right for the **Banys Àrabs**, at c/Can Serra 7. One of the few genuine reminders of the Moorish presence, this tenth-century brick *hammam* (bath house) consists of a small horseshoe-arched and domed chamber which was once heated through the floor. The remains are reasonably well preserved, but if you've been to the baths in Girona or Granada, these are anticlimactic; the garden outside, with tables where you can picnic, is perhaps nicer.

The Museu de Mallorca

Close by, back on c/Portella, the **Museu de Mallorca** occupies Can Aiamans, a Renaissance mansion whose rambling rooms are a delightful setting for an enjoyable medley of Mallorcan artefacts, the earliest dating from prehistoric times, and featuring a superb assortment of Gothic paintings.

The Banys Àrabs is open daily: April–Sept 9.30am–8pm; Oct–March 10am–6pm; 150ptas. Cafeteria Sa Murada, at the bottom of c/Portella, is a good spot for a drinks break – see p.86.

The Museu de Mallorca is open Tues–Sat 10am–2pm & 4–7pm, Sun 10am–2pm; 300ptas, but free on Sat afternoon and Sun.

The collection begins on the ground floor, to the right of the entrance, with half a dozen rooms filled with all sorts of bits and pieces retrieved from old buildings and archeological digs. Highlights include a selection of exquisite Arab and Moorish jewellery and some beautiful, highly decorated wooden panelling that's representative of Mudéjar artistry. Retracing your steps, you'll come across a hotchpotch of prehistoric archeological finds in the room just down from the entrance desk and, carrying on up the stairs, the first of a couple of rooms devoted to the **Mallorcan Primitive** painters. On display in this first room are works by the Masters of Bishop Galiana, Montesion and Castellitx and, best of the lot, a painting entitled *Santa Quiteria*, whose precisely executed, lifelike figures – down to the wispy beard of the king – are typical of the gifted Master of the Privileges. In the same room, there's also a curious thirteenth-century work of unknown authorship dedicated to St Bernard, with the saint on his knees devotedly drinking the milk of the Virgin Mary.

For more on the Master of the Privileges and the Mallorcan Primitives, see p.72.

Beyond a room of religious statues and carved capitals, the second room of Gothic paintings is distinguished by a sequence of works by **Francesc Comes** (1379–1415), whose skill in catching the subtle texture of skin echoes his Flemish contemporaries and represents a softening of the early Mallorcan Primitives' crudeness. In his striking *St George*, the saint – girl-like, with typically full lips – impales a lime-green dragon with more horns than could possibly be useful. One of the last talented exponents of the

---

Mansions in Palma

Most of medieval Palma was destroyed by fire, so the patrician mansions that characterize the old town today generally date from the reconstruction programme of the late seventeenth and early eighteenth centuries. Consequently they were built in the fashionable Renaissance style, with columns and capitals, loggias and arcades tucked away behind outside walls of plain stone, three or four storeys high. Surprisingly uniform in layout, entry to almost all of these mansions was through a great arched gateway that gave onto a rectangular courtyard around which the house was built. Originally, the courtyard would have been cheered by exotic trees and flowering shrubs, and equipped with a fancy stone and iron-work well-head, where visitors could water their horses. From the courtyard, a stone outside staircase led up to the main public rooms of the first floor – with the servants' quarters below and the family's private apartments up above.

Very few of these mansions are open to the public, and all you'll see for the most part is the view from the gateway – the municipality have actually started to pay people to leave their big wooden gates open. Several have, however, passed into the public domain, the Can Aiamans, now the home of the Museu de Mallorca, being the prime example; others worth making a detour to see are Can Bordils, Can Oleza (see p.77), Can Vivot (p.77) and Can Solleric (p.80).

Mallorcan Gothic, the **Master of the Predellas** – most probably a certain Joan Rosató – is represented by his Bosch-like *Santa Margarita*, each crowd of onlookers a sea of ugly, deformed faces and merciless eyes. The work outlines the life of **Margaret of Antioch**, one of the most venerated saints in medieval Christendom. During the reign of the Roman Emperor Diocletian (284–305 AD), she refused to marry a pagan prefect and was consequently executed after being tortured with extravagant gusto. As if this wasn't enough, she also had to resist more metaphysical trials: Satan, disguised as a dragon, swallowed her, but couldn't digest her holiness, so his stomach opened up and out she popped unharmed. This particular tribulation made Margaret the patron saint of pregnant women.

The Església de Santa Eulalia

Continuing on up the hill from the museum, c/Portella leads to c/Morei where, at no. 9, you'll find the **Can Oleza**, a sixteenth-century mansion with a cool and shaded courtyard embellished by a handsome balustrade and a trio of Ionic columns. Just up the street, it's worth detouring left along c/Almudaina for a peek at the chunky remains of the old east gate – the **Arc de L'Almudaina** – a remnant of the Moorish fortifications, and to see the recently renovated **Can Bordils**, one of the city's oldest mansions, at no. 9.

Built on the site of a mosque in the mid-thirteenth century, the **Església de Santa Eulalia** took just 25 years to complete and consequently possesses an architectural homogeneity that's unusual for Palma – though there was some later medieval tinkering, and nineteenth-century renovators added the belfry and remodelled the main (south) facade. The church is typically Gothic in construction, with a yawning nave originally designed – as in the cathedral – to give the entire congregation a view of the high altar. Today, however, the bricked-up windows keep out most of the light and ruin the effect. Framing the nave, the aisles accommodate twelve chapels, several of which – notably the first chapel on the right – sport fine Gothic paintings; in kitsch contrast, the hourglass-shaped high altarpiece is a Baroque extravagance of colossal proportions. This holy ground witnessed one of the more disgraceful episodes of Mallorcan history. During Easter week of 1435, a rumour went round that Jewish townsfolk had enacted a blasphemous mock-up of the Crucifixion. There was no proof, but the Jews were promptly robbed of their possessions and condemned to be burnt at the stake unless they adopted Christianity – the ensuing mass baptism was held at Santa Eulalia.

Around the back of the church, at c/Can Savella 2, is the eighteenth-century **Can Vivot**, another opulent mansion, with a spacious main courtyard of red marble columns, graceful arches and a slender staircase.

Can Oleza, Can Bordils and Can Vivot are all closed to the public.

The Església de Santa Eulalia is open Mon–Fri 7am–1pm & 5.30–8pm, Sat & Sun 8am–1pm & 6–8pm. See p.72 for more on St Eulalia's life.

The sociable Ca'n Joan de S'Aigo, behind Santa Eulalia at c/Can Sanç 10, is a good place for a drinks stop and ensaimadas (pastries) – see p.40.

The Basílica de
Sant Francesc
is open daily
9.30am–12.30
pm & 3.30–
6pm; closed
Sun afternoon;
100ptas.

The Basílica de Sant Francesc

A brief walk away from the Plaça Santa Eulalia along c/Convent de
Sant Francesc is the **Basílica de Sant Francesc**, a domineering pile
that occupies the site of the old Moorish soap factory. Built for the
Franciscans towards the end of the thirteenth century, the original
church was a vast Gothic edifice which benefited from royal patronage after Jaume II's son, also named Jaume, became a member of the
order in 1300. Subsequent Gothic remodellings replaced the initial
wooden ceiling with a single-span, vaulted stone roof of imposing
dimensions and added stately chapels to the nave and apse. The
Basílica became the most fashionable church in medieval Palma and
its friars received handsome kickbacks for entombing the local nobility inside its precincts. Increasingly eager to enrich themselves, the
priests came to compete for possession of the corpses, while the various aristocratic clans vied with each other in the magnificence of
their sarcophagi. These tensions exploded when a clansman, a certain Jaume Armadams, had a jug of water emptied over his head on
All Saints' Day, 1490. The congregation, gathered to pray before the
tombs of the dead, went berserk and over 300 noblemen fought it out
in the nave before the priests finally restored order. The ensuing
scandal caused the Basílica to be closed for several decades.

In the seventeenth century the church was badly damaged by lightning, prompting a thoroughgoing reconstruction which accounts for
most of its present-day appearance. Dating from this period, the main
facade displays a stunning severity of style, with its great rectangular
sheet of dressed sandstone stretching up to an arcaded and balustraded
balcony. The facade is pierced by a gigantic rose window of Plateresque
intricacy and embellished by a **Baroque doorway**, whose tympanum
features a triumphant Virgin Mary engulfed by a wriggling mass of sculp-
tured decoration. Above the Madonna is the figure of St George, and to
either side and below are assorted saints – look out for the scholar and
missionary Ramon Llull, who is shown reading a book. The strange statue in front of the doorway – of a Franciscan monk and a young Native
American – celebrates the missionary work of **Junipero Serra**, a
Mallorcan priest despatched to California in 1768, who subsequently
founded San Diego, Los Angeles and San Francisco.

For further
details on the
life and times
of Junipero
Serra, see
p.167.

The church's interior, approached through a trim Gothic cloister,
is disappointingly gloomy – too dark, in fact, to pick out all but the
most obvious of its features, though fortunately you can push a
switch to light the monumental high **altar**, a gaudy, Baroque affair of
balustrades, lattice-work and clichéd figurines beneath a monk-made
St George and the Dragon. Less overblown are the rolling scrolls
and trumpeteer-angel of the eighteenth-century **pulpit**, on the wall of
the nave, and the ornate Gothic-Baroque frontispiece of the nearby
organ. The second chapel on the left of the ambulatory shelters the
tomb of Ramon Llull, whose bones were brought back to Palma
after his martyrdom in Algeria in 1315. Considering the sanctity of

Ramon Llull

Beloved of Catholic propagandists, the life of Ramon Llull (1235–1315) was an exercise in redemption following carnal excess. As a young man, Llull was an ebullient rake in the retinue of the future Jaume II. His sexual adventures were not in the least impeded by his marriage, but they ground to a dramatic halt when, having pursued Ambrosia de Castillo, the woman of his immediate desire, into the church of Santa Eulalia on horseback, she revealed to him her diseased breasts. A deeply shocked Llull devoted the rest of his life to the Catholic faith, becoming a fearless missionary and dedicated scholar of theology, philosophy and alchemy. Exemplifying the cosmopolitan outlook of thirteenth-century Mallorca, Llull learnt to read, write and speak several languages, including Arabic, and travelled to France, much of Spain and North Africa. He also founded a monastery and missionary school on Puig Randa, 35km east of Palma, where he spent ten years in seclusion and wrote no fewer than 250 books and treatises. It was Llull's scholarship that attracted the attention of his old friend Jaume II, who summoned him to court in 1282. With royal patronage, Llull then established a monastic school of Oriental languages near Valldemossa, where he trained his future missionary companions. Llull was killed on his third evangelical excursion to Algeria in 1315, his martyrdom ensuring his subsequent beatification.

the man's remains, it's an odd and insignificant-looking affair, with Llull's alabaster effigy set in the wall to the right of the chapel altarpiece at a disconcertingly precarious angle.

Plaça Cort
Leaving the basilica, you can either wander the labyrinth of ancient side streets that stretches southeast as far as Avinguda Gabriel Alomar i Villalonga, or retrace your steps west to the Plaça Santa Eulalia, from where it's a brief walk along c/Cadena to the elegant nineteenth-century facades of the bustling **Plaça Cort**. One side of the square is dominated by the **Ajuntament** (Town Hall), a debonair example of the late Renaissance style. Pop in for a look at the grand and self-assured foyer, which mostly dates from the nineteenth century, and the four folkloric *gigantones* (giant carnival figures) stored here – two in a corner, the others tucked against the staircase.

From Plaça Cort, it's a pleasant five-minute stroll to the Passeig d'es Born via either c/Palau Reial or **c/Sant Domingo**, which weaves downhill lined by an attractive ensemble of nineteenth-century town houses with wrought-iron grilles and stone balconies.

Nothing remains of Llull's foundations, but the site of the missionary school is now occupied by the Santuari de Nostra Senyora de Cura – see p.165.

Around the Passeig d'es Born

Distinguished by the stone sphinxes at its top and bottom, the **Passeig d'es Born** has been the city's principal promenade since the early fifteenth century, when the stream that ran here was diverted following a disastrous flash flood. Nowadays, this leafy avenue is too traffic-congested to be endearing, but it's still at the heart of the city

The City

The Can Solleric is open Tues–Sat 10.30am–1.30pm & 5.30–8pm, Sun 10am–1.30pm; free. The contemporary Spanish art collection of the March family is displayed at the Banca March – see p.82.

and in the immediate vicinity are some of Palma's most fashionable bars and restaurants. At no. 10, overlooking the *passeig*, is the fine Italianate loggia of **Can Solleric**, a lavish mansion of heavy wooden doors, marble columns and vaulted ceilings built for a family of cattle and olive oil merchants in 1763. Recently restored, the house now displays temporary exhibitions of modern art.

From Plaça de la Reina, the tiny square at the foot of the Passeig d'es Born, a wide and elegant flight of steps, the **Costa de la Seu**, leads up to the cathedral. At the foot of the steps is another noteworthy mansion, the **Palau March**, a heavyweight affair whose arcaded galleries, chunky columns and large stone blocks were erected in the 1930s in the general style of the city's earlier Renaissance mansions. It was built for the Mallorcan magnate and art collector **Joan March** (1880–1962), who became the wealthiest man in Franco's Spain by skilfully reinvesting the profits he made from his control of the government monopoly in tobacco – though his enemies always insisted that it was smuggling that really made him rich. Most of the Palau March is not open to the public, but a few rooms have been turned into the **Biblioteca Bartomeu March Servera**, one of several privately funded libraries dotted round the city.

The Biblioteca Bartomeu March Servera is open Mon–Fri 9.30am–2pm; free.

Beyond Plaça de la Reina, **Avinguda d'Antoni Maura** runs down to the wide breakwater which marks the start of Palma harbour. The avenue takes its name from **Antoni Maura** (1853–1925), a Mallorquin who served as prime minister of Spain four times between 1903 and 1921. An outstanding orator and extraordinarily forceful personality, Maura was a conservative who opposed universal suffrage as "the politics of the mob", preferring a limited franchise and a constitution which gave power to the middle classes, as long as they marched to the tune of the church and the crown. Needless to say, these credentials were quite enough for Franco to have this avenue named after him.

El Puig de Sant Pere

West of the Passeig d'es Born and Avgda d'Antoni Maura, in between Avgda Jaume III and Plaça Drassana, lies the ancient neighbourhood of **El Puig de Sant Pere** (Saint Peter's Mount), whose narrow lanes and alleys shelter another sprinkling of patrician mansions – though most of the old houses were divided up into apartments years ago to cater for the district's sailors, dockers and fishermen. Again, it's the general flavour of the area that appeals rather than specific sights, but it's still worth seeking out the late Renaissance facades of **Can Moner** and **Can Pavesi**, at c/Sant Feliu 8 and 10 respectively. There's a gruesome story behind the name of a lane off c/Estanc: **La Mà del Moro**, "the hand of the Moor", harks back to Ahmed, an eighteenth-century slave who murdered his master. After the subsequent execution, Ahmed's hand was chopped off and stuck above the doorway of the house down this alley where the murder was committed.

Along the harbourfront – La Llotja and Parc Cuarentena

From the bottom of Avinguda d'Antoni Maura, it's a couple of minutes' walk west along the harbourfront to the fifteenth-century Llotja, the city's former stock exchange. This carefully composed late Gothic building, with its four octagonal turrets and tall windows, now hosts frequent and occasionally excellent exhibitions. The distinguished building next door – the **Consolat de Mar** – was built in the 1660s to accommodate the Habsburg officials who supervised maritime affairs in this part of the empire. Today, as the home of the president of the Balearic Islands, it's closed to the public, but the outside is worth a second look for its pair of crusty old cannons and elegant Renaissance gallery. The forlorn-looking gate in between the two buildings – the **Porta Vella del Moll** – originally stood at the end of Avinguda d'Antoni Maura, where it was the main entrance into the city from the sea; the gate was moved here when portions of the town wall were demolished in the 1870s.

The various marinas, shipyards, fish docks and ferry and cargo terminals that make up Palma's **harbourfront** extend west for several kilometres from the bottom of Avinguda d'Antoni Maura to the edge of Cala Major. The harbour is at its prettiest at this eastern end and it's here that a cycling and walking path skirts the seashore, with boats to one side and bars, restaurants, apartment blocks and the smart hotels of the Avgda Gabriel Roca on the other. At the foot of Avgda Argentina – opposite the breakwater where the fishing boats come in – are the flower beds of a trim little park. These abut both the walled watercourse which once served as the **city moat** and the sheer bastion that anchored the southwest corner of the Renaissance city wall. Pressing on west, it's a further fifteen to twenty minutes' walk along the palm-lined esplanade to the next worthwhile objective, the delightful **Parc Cuarentena**, whose cool and shaded terraces, with their aromatic trees and shrubs, clamber up the hillside from the harbourfront.

During exhibitions only, La Llotja is open Tues–Sat 11am–2pm & 5–9pm, Sun 11am–2pm.

With its pleasant terrace bar, the waterfront Café Port Pesquer, just east of the fish dock, is a great place to stop for a drink – see p.86. The best views of the harbour are from the Castell de Bellver – see p.84.

Along Carrer de la Unió

Back in the city centre, at the top of Passeig d'es Born, the sturdy shopping and office buildings of **Avinguda Jaume III**, dating to the 1940s, march west towards the Passeig Mallorca. Eastwards from the Passeig d'es Born is c/Unió, a new, if rather unimaginative, appellation – it means "unity" – for a street Franco had previously named after **General Mola**, one of the prime movers of the Nationalist rebellion of 1936. Mola was killed in an aeroplane accident during the Civil War, possibly to Franco's relief. Hitler, for one, thought that Mola was the more competent, remarking that his death meant that "Franco came to the top like Pontius Pilate in the Creed."

Carrer Unió leads to tiny **Plaça Mercat**, the site of two identical *Modernista* buildings, commissioned by a wealthy baker, Josep Casasayas, in 1908. Each is a masterpiece of flowing, organic lines tempered by graceful balconies and decorated with fern-leaf and butterfly motifs. Just down the street, on **Plaça Weyler**, stands a further *Modernista* extravagance, the magnificent **Gran Hotel** of 1903. Recently scrubbed and polished, the facade boasts playful arches, balconies, columns and bay windows enlivened with intricate floral trimmings and brilliant polychrome ceramics inspired by Hispano-Arabic designs. The interior houses a café-bar, a good art bookshop and the spacious **art gallery** of the Fundació La Caixa, the cultural arm of the savings bank, who organize an excellent and wide-ranging programme of exhibitions. The permanent collection is confined to a large sample of the work of the Catalan impressionist Hermen Anglada-Camarasa, who produced dozens of evocative Mallorcan land- and seascapes during his sojourn on the island from 1914 to 1936.

The art gallery of the Fundació La Caixa is open Tues–Sat 10am–9pm & Sun 10am–2pm; free.

There's another excellent example of *Modernisme* across the street from the Gran Hotel in the floral motifs and gaily painted wooden doorway of the **Forn des Teatre** (theatre bakery) at Plaça Weyler 9. A few metres away looms the Neoclassical frontage of the **Teatre Principal** – the city's main auditorium for classical music, ballet and opera – whose tympanum sports a fanciful relief dedicated to the nine Muses of Greek mythology.

At the theatre, the main street – now c/Riera – does a quick aboutface to join the **Passeig de la Rambla**, whose plane trees shelter Palma's main flower market. The two statues at the foot of the boulevard, representing Roman emperors, were placed here in 1937 in honour of Mussolini's Italy – one set of Fascists tipping their municipal hats to another.

Around Plaça Major – the Museu d'Art Espanyol Contemporani

On both sides of the theatre, steep flights of steps lead up to **Plaça Major**, a large pedestrianized square built on the site of the headquarters of the Inquisition after their demolition in 1823. The square, a rather plain affair with a symmetrical portico running around its perimeter, once housed the fish and vegetable market, but nowadays it's popular for its pavement cafés.

The busy shopping street of c/Sant Miquel runs north from Plaça Major. Here, at no. 11, the **Banca March** occupies a fine Renaissance mansion whose *Modernista* flourishes date from a tasteful refurbishment of 1917. The building has two entrances, one to the bank, the other to the first-floor **Museu d'Art Espanyol Contemporani**, which features part of the contemporary art collection of the March family. Over fifty works are displayed, each by a different Spanish artist of the twentieth century, the intention being to survey the Spanish contribution to modern art, a theme that's further developed by temporary

Baker's sign, Palma

Stone houses, Fornalutx

Valldemossa

La Llotja, Palma

Plaça Major, Palma

Monastery church, Valldemossa

Castell de Bellver, Palma

Lluc Monastery

Palma Cathedral

Mime artist, Palma

Palma

Renaissance courtyard, Palma

CLINICA DENTAL J.F.KEY

The Palma–Sóller train

Modernista facade, Palma

exhibitions. The earliest piece, *Tête de Femme* (1907), by Picasso, is of particular interest as it's one of the first of the artist's works to be influenced by the primitive forms that were to propel him, over the following decade, from the re-creation of natural appearances into abstract art. Miró and Dalí are also represented, and there's a substantial selection of work by the Spanish Cubist Juan Gris, but the bulk of the collection is remorselessly modern and hard to warm to, especially the allegedly "vigorous" abstractions of both the El Paso (Millares, Saura, Feito, Canogar) and the Parpalló (Sempere, Alfaro) groupings of the late 1950s.

If you're in the vicinity, it's worth continuing a few metres up along c/Sant Miquel to the **Església Sant Miquel**, whose sturdy exterior, the result of all sorts of architectural meddlings, hides a gloomy barrel-vaulted nave and rib-vaulted side chapels. The poorly lit high altarpiece, a Baroque classic with a central image celebrating St Michael, showcases the intricate work of Francesc Herrara, a much-travelled Spanish painter of religious and genre subjects known for his vigorous compositions and tangy realism.

On the south side of Plaça Major lies the much smaller **Plaça Marqués de Palmer**, a cramped setting for two fascinating *Modernista* edifices. The more dramatic is **Can Rei**, a five-storey apartment building splattered with polychrome ceramics and floral decoration, its centrepiece a gargoyle-like face set between a pair of winged dragons. The facade of the adjacent **L'Àguila** building is of similar ilk, though there's greater emphasis on window space, reflecting its original function as a department store.

Continuing south, the shopping area in between Plaça Major and Plaça Cort remains one of the more agreeable parts of Palma. Its old-fashioned air is distilled from the three- and four-storey buildings that flank its main streets – principally pedestrianized **c/Jaume II** – embellished with an abundance of fancy iron-grilled balconies.

The Poble Espanyol

A couple of kilometres west of the old town, and reachable by EMT bus #5 from Placa Espanya – the nearest stop is on c/Andrea Doria – the **Poble Espanyol** (Spanish Village) was built between 1965 and 1967, a kitsch, purpose-made tourist attraction, with Francoist intentions apparent in its celebration of everything Spanish. Walled like a medieval city, the village contains accurate reproductions of about twenty old and important buildings, such as Barcelona's Palau de la Generalitat, Seville's Torre del Oro, a segment of Granada's Alhambra, El Greco's house in Toledo, and the Ermita de San Antonio in Madrid. These are woven round the village's streets and squares, where you'll also find craft workshops, souvenir shops, restaurants and bars. It's all a bit daft – and school parties swamp the place – but it's an easy way of introducing yourself to Spanish architecture.

The Museu d'Art Espanyol Contemporani is open Mon–Fri 10am–6.30pm, Sat 10am–1.30pm; 500ptas.

The Església Sant Miquel is open Mon–Sat 8am–12.30pm & 5–7pm, Sun 10am–1pm & 5–7pm; free.

The Poble Espanyol is open daily: April–Nov 9am–8pm; Dec–March 9am–6pm; 800ptas.

The Castell de Bellver

Boasting superb views of Palma and its harbour from a wooded hill-top some 3km west of the city centre, the **Castell de Bellver** is a handsome, strikingly well-preserved fortress built for Jaume II at the beginning of the fourteenth century. Of canny circular design, the castle's thick walls accommodate three imposing towers, while an overhead, single-span stone arch connects the main structure to a massive, freestanding keep. Dry moats and embankments add further lines of defence, crossed by footbridges set at oblique angles to each other. The castle was also intended to serve as a royal retreat from the summer heat, and so the austere outside walls hide a commodious circular courtyard, surrounded by two tiers of inward-facing arcades that originally belonged to the residential suites. The whole construction is ingenious, incorporating many skilful touches: the flat roof, for example, was designed to channel every drop of rainwater into a huge underground cistern. Improvements in artillery, however, soon rendered the fortress obsolete, and it didn't last long as a royal residence either. As early as the 1350s the keep was in use as a prison, a function it performed until 1915. More recently, part of the castle has been turned into a modest **museum** featuring a rag-bag of archeological finds and a miscellany of Roman sculpture, originally the collection of the eighteenth-century antiquarian Cardinal Antonio Despuig.

The Castell de Bellver is about 1km south of the Poble Espanyol, though not connected to it by bus. From the city centre, take **bus #3** or **#21** from Plaça Espanya or **#4** or **#21** from Plaça de la Reina to Plaça Gomila, which leaves a steep one-kilometre walk up the hill. If you're driving, turn off Avinguda Joan Miró onto the circuitous c/Camilo Jose Cela to reach the castle.

Eating and drinking

Eating well in Palma is less pricey – or can be – than anywhere else in the Balearics. Inexpensive **cafés** and **tapas bars** are liberally distributed around the city centre, with a particular concentration in the side streets off the Passeig d'es Born and Avinguda d'Antoni Maura. Many downtown cafés are up and running by 9am, but with most visitors eating breakfast at their hotel there's not the demand for early-morning places you might expect in a big city. On the other hand, for light lunches and snacks (*tapas*) you're spoiled for choice. You can chomp away in chic modernist surroundings, or join the crowds in simple formica and glass joints where the food more than compensates for the decor – and then there's everything in between.

The distinction between *tapas* bars and **restaurants** is blurred as many of the former serve full meals as well as snacks. Indeed, the differences often have more to do with appearance than food – if you've got a table cloth, for instance, you're almost certainly in a restaurant.

Opening times vary enormously, but most places close one day a week and the majority take a siesta from about 3pm or 4pm to 8pm. Many of Palma's restaurants and *tapas* bars are geared up for the tourist trade, especially those along the harbourfront and amongst the side streets off Avinguda d'Antoni Maura. It is, however, foolish to be snooty about them, as some serve delicious food and are popular with Spaniards also. If you venture a little further into the city centre, you'll discover more exclusively local haunts, some offering the finest of Catalan and Spanish cuisine. A smattering of restaurants specialize in ethnic foods such as Swedish and Italian, and there's a couple of vegetarian café-restaurants too. At all but the most expensive of places, 3500ptas will cover the cost of a starter and main course, as well as a bottle of wine – though you can expect prices to be jacked up in the summer.

Cafés and tapas bars

L'Angel Blau, c/Capiscolat 1. Chic, pint-sized *tapas* bar with classical music and smooth-tasting snacks. You'll walk past the place en route from the cathedral to the Museu Diocesà.

Bar Bosch, Plaça Rei Joan Carles I. One of the most popular and inexpensive *tapas* bars in town, the traditional haunt of intellectuals and usually humming with conversation. At peak times you'll need to be assertive to get served.

Bon Lloc, c/Sant Feliu 7. One of the few vegetarian café-restaurants on the island, centrally situated off the Passeig d'es Born. Informal atmosphere and good food at low prices. Open Mon–Sat 1–4pm and the odd evening, usually Fri till 9pm.

Café Brondo, c/Can Brondo 7. Lively, fashionable *tapas* bar off Plaça Rei Joan Carles I, with the *Restaurante Brondo* downstairs (see below).

Ca'n Joan de S'Aigo, c/Can Sanç 10. A long-established coffee house with wonderful, freshly baked *ensaimadas* (spiral pastry buns) for just 100ptas and fruit-flavoured mousses to die for. Charming decor too, from the kitsch water fountain to the traditional Mallorcan green-tinted chandeliers. Carrer Can Sanç is a tiny alley near Plaça Santa Eulalia – take c/Sant Crist and its continuation c/Canisseria, and turn right. Closed Tues.

Es Cantó de S'Arc, c/Morei 6. Smart *tapas* bar-cum-restaurant with antique furnishings and fittings. *Tapas* from 300ptas per portion. Just off Plaça Santa Eulalia.

La Cueva, c/Apuntadors 9. Small and busy *tapas* bar, one of several on this street, with a rack of liquors behind the bar and hocks of meat hanging up in front. Reasonable prices; tasty food. **Sa Volta**, next door, is very similar.

Dalt Murada, c/Sant Roc 1. Café-restaurant specializing in Mallorcan cuisine. It occupies part of a recently renovated Renaissance mansion, a couple of minutes' walk north of the cathedral. The *tapas* are tasty and there's a shaded terrace where you can take a leisurely break from wandering the streets of the old town – though in the evenings, you may feel a bit out of it if you haven't come here for a full meal.

S'Impremta, c/Morei 2. Amiable neighbourhood café-restaurant offering a delicious range of *tapas* plus a great-value *menú del día* for 950ptas. Closes at 5.30pm.

Cafeteria Jaime III, Avgda Jaume III 20. Popular with office workers and shoppers, this brisk modern café serves up a good line in snacks – try their *pa amb oli* (bread rubbed with olive oil) and smoked ham.

Café Lirico, Avgda d'Antoni Maura 6. Most of Palma's downtown cafés have been modernized, but not this one – its large mirrors, imitation marble and weather-beaten clientele are reminiscent of the Spanish cafés of yesteryear. Not much in the way of food.

Mesón Salamanca, c/Sant Jaume 3. Mostly Castilian cuisine in a cosily refurbished, warren-like town house off Avgda Jaume III. Delicious *tapas* on the ground floor (much better than the stuffy restaurant upstairs).

Cafeteria Sa Murada, in between the two sets of city walls at the foot of c/Portella. Tasty snacks with the emphasis on traditional Mallorcan dishes. If you've been walking the old town, this is a good spot to soak up the sun from the relative quiet of a pedestrianized mini-plaza.

Orient Express, c/Llotja de Mar 6, behind La Llotja. Idiosyncratic café-restaurant with an interior like the inside of a railway carriage. Salads, slightly overpriced, are its speciality; you'll have to wait for a seat at lunchtime.

El Pilon, c/Can Cifre 4. Vibrant, cramped and crowded *tapas* bar serving all manner of Spanish and Mallorcan dishes at very reasonable prices. Bags of atmosphere; on a side street off the north end of Passeig d'es Born.

Café Port Pesquer, Avgda Gabriel Roca s/n. Bright and breezy, gleamingly new café on the harbourfront. The open-air terrace bar is a good spot to soak up the evening sun. A few minutes' walk west of Avgda d'Antoni Maura.

Raixa, c/Can Savella 8. Wholesome, good-value vegetarian food, near the Basílica de Sant Francesc. Daytime only, usually Mon–Sat 1.30–4pm.

Restaurants

Asador Tierra Aranda, c/Concepció 4, off Avgda Jaume III ☎971 714256. A high-class, fairly formal carnivore's paradise in an old mansion: meats either grilled over open fires or roasted in wood-fired ovens, with suckling pig and lamb a speciality. Closed at lunchtime; dinner from 8pm.

Brondo, c/Can Brondo 7. Beneath the *tapas* bar of the same name, this restaurant is a very good bet: the menu is imaginative, but broadly Catalan in style, and every dish is carefully prepared and presented.

Caballito de Mar, across the plaza from La Llotja at Passeig Sagrera 5. There was a time when this trim little restaurant was generally regarded as the best seafood place in town. It doesn't seem so outstanding today – for a start, the vegetables tend to be overcooked – but there's still an extensive range of fish to choose from. The *daurada amb sal al forn* (*dorada à la sal* – sea bream baked in salt) remains excellent. Main courses average around 2500ptas.

Ca'n Carlos, c/Aigua 5. Charming, family-run restaurant featuring exquisite Mallorcan cuisine – cuttlefish, snails, etc. The menu isn't extensive, but everything is beautifully and imaginatively prepared and there's a daily special as well as a fish-of-the-day. Main courses average around 1800ptas. The furnishings and fittings are smart and cheerfully modern. It's situated near the bottom of c/Aigua, a narrow side street off Avgda Jaume III. Opens for lunch and at 8pm in the evening.

Ca'n Eduardo, Moll Industria Pesquera 4 ☎971 721182. Spick and span restaurant located upstairs in one of the plain modern buildings beside the fish

dock. There's an enjoyable view of the harbour, but the real treat is the fresh
fish – a wonderful range, all simply prepared; first-rate *menú del día* at
around 2500ptas. It's about five minutes' walk west along the harbourfront
from Avgda d'Antoni Maura; the fish dock is just before Avgda Argentina.
Closed Sun and Mon.

Casa Gallega, c/Can Pueyo 6. Long-established place offering quality Galician
cuisine, particularly the seafood. There's a downstairs *tapas* bar and a more
formal restaurant upstairs. It's just north off Plaça Weyler, down the side street
beside the Gran Hotel.

Celler Pagès, off c/Apuntadors at c/Felip Bauza 2. Traditional Mallorcan food
in a tiny, inexpensive restaurant near Passeig d'es Born. Easy-going atmosphere, though stifling hot in the summer. Closed Sun.

Celler Sa Premsa, Plaça Bisbe Berenguer de Palou 8. Justly popular restaurant with delicious seafood cooked in traditional Mallorcan style. A five-minute
walk west of the Plaça Espanya. Old bullfighting photos and posters adorn the
walls amidst a pot-pourri of dusty bygones; you'll probably share a table with
other diners. Prices are surprisingly low – as little as 1600ptas per person for
a three-course meal.

Forn de Sant Joan, c/Sant Joan 4. Smart and extremely popular Catalan
restaurant near La Llotja, one of several busy spots on this narrow alley. Fine
fish dishes for around 1900ptas, *tapas* from 850ptas.

Los Gauchos, c/Sant Magí 78 ☎971 280023. At least once during your stay in
Palma, it's worth trying out South American (ie Spanish colonial) cuisine. This
unassuming Argentine restaurant is one of the best, though it's very meaty –
steaks and brochettes of lamb are the specialities. It's in the slightly dilapidated district of Es Jonquet, the old fishermen's quarter just west of Avgda
Argentina.

S'Olivera, c/Morei 3. This appealingly smart restaurant, with its antique bygones
dotted round the walls, is situated just off Plaça Santa Eulalia. A first-rate range
of *tapas*, at around 500ptas per portion, plus quality Spanish cuisine.

Es Parlament, c/Conquistador 11. All gilt-wood mirrors and chandeliers, this
old and polished restaurant specializes in paella. The tasty and reasonably
priced *menú del día* is recommended too. A favourite hangout of local politi-
cians and lawyers.

Svarta Pannan, c/Can Brondo 5. Comfortable Swedish restaurant convenient-
ly close to Plaça Rei Joan Carles I. The food isn't remarkable, but makes a
refreshing change.

Nightlife and entertainment

Most of the cafés and all the *tapas* bars detailed above are quite
happy just to ply you with drink, making the distinction between
these establishments and the bars we've listed separately below
somewhat artificial. Nonetheless, there's a cluster of lively **late-night
bars** – mostly with music as the backdrop rather than the main event
– amongst the narrow and ancient side streets backing onto Plaça
Llotja. A second concentration of slightly more modish bars embell-
ishes the bayside modernity of Avinguda Gabriel Roca in the vicinity
of **Parc Cuarentena** and west from here out towards the ferry

terminal, about 4km from the city centre. The grimy suburb of El Terreno, also west of the centre, below the Castell de Bellver, once accommodated Palma's best late-night bars. The district has gone downhill, and now features topless "entertainment" and porn shops, but it's here you'll find the occasional offbeat, hippie-flavour bar as well as several gay bars.

Nightclubs (*discotecas*) are not Palma's forte, but there are one or two of some merit on Avinguda Gabriel Roca. They're rarely worth investigating until around 1am and entry charges will rush you anything between 500ptas and 1000ptas, depending on the night and what's happening. The doormen often operate an informal dress code of one sort or another – if you want to get in, avoid beach gear.

Traditionally, Palma has had little to offer in terms of **performing arts**, but matters are on the mend with the resuscitation of the grand nineteenth-century Teatre Principal, Plaça Weyler 16 (booking office ☎971 725548), which features classical concerts and opera, and the revamping of the Teatre Municipal, Passeig Mallorca 9B (☎971 739148), which has a more varied programme of contemporary drama, classic films, dance and ballet.

Late-night bars

Abaco, just off c/Apuntadors at c/Sant Joan 1. Inhabiting a charming Renaissance mansion, this is easily Palma's most unusual bar, with an interior straight out of a Busby Berkeley musical: fruits cascading down its stairway, caged birds hidden amid patio foliage, elegant music and a daily flower bill you could live on for a month. Drinks, as you might imagine, are extremely expensive but you're never hurried into buying one. It is, however, too sedate to be much fun if you're on the razzle.

La Bóveda, c/Boteria 3, off Plaça Llotja. Classy, fashionable bar, one of several on this short alley, with long, wide windows and wine stacked high along the back wall. Be prepared to queue to get in – or come early.

El Globo, at the junction of c/Apuntadors and c/Felip Bauza. Cramped and bustling with modern jazz as the soundtrack. One of several bars at the bottom end of c/Apuntadors

Gotic, Plaça Llotja 4. Tiny bar redeemed by its candle-lit patio/pavement tables which nudge out across the piazza, adding a touch of romance.

Latitude 39, c/Felip Bauza off c/Apuntadors. Tiny, upbeat bar, playing jazz, blues and sometimes classical music.

Lima, just off Avgda Jaume III at c/Concepció 9. Youthful and trendy, pastel-painted bar with lashings of world music and jazz.

La Lonja, opposite La Llotja. A popular, well-established haunt, with revolving doors and pleasantly old-fashioned decor; the background music caters for (almost) all tastes.

Status Pub, Avgda Joan Miró 38. Elegant late-night bar in the El Terreno district. Popular gay hangout.

Twins, c/Sant Joan 7, off Plaça Llotja. Fashionable place with an upbeat tempo and boisterous crowd.

Ses Voltes, Parc de la Mar. Open-air spot which often has live acts – pop, jazz and rock to varying standards.

XL, Avgda Gabriel Roca, next door to Parc Cuarentena. Classy hangout with strikingly conspicuous, abstract decor featuring a series of geometrically arranged poles. Quality cocktails and an upmarket clientele.

Nightclubs

Discoteca Pacha, Avgda Gabriel Roca 42. Loud, popular and raucous disco with a dance floor and a couple of bars inside and another bar outside in the garden. A five-minute walk west of Parc Cuarentena.

Discoteca Tito's, Avgda Gabriel Roca s/n. With its stainless steel and glass exterior, this long-established nightspot looks a bit like something from a sci-fi film set. Outdoor lifts carry you up from Avgda Gabriel Roca to the dance floor, which pulls in huge crowds from many countries. The music lacks conviction, but it's certainly loud. Just on the city centre side of Parc Cuarentena.

Made in Brasil, Avgda Gabriel Roca 27. Alarming tropical decor in this pocket-sized club-cum-bar on the city-centre side of Parc Cuarentena. Great Latin sounds and cocktails.

Listings

Airlines Air France, Avgda Jaume III, 16 (☎971 713500); British Midland, Avgda Joan Miró 16 (☎971 453112; airport ☎971 743377); Iberia, Passeig d'es Born 10 (☎971 710142); Lufthansa, Plaça Rosari 5, 3è (☎971 722840); Sabena, same office and telephone number as Air France; SAS, Avgda Joan Miró 16 (☎971 453112).

Airport information Central switchboard ☎971 789000.

American Express Smart new office at Avgda d'Antoni Maura 10 (March–Oct Mon–Fri 9am–1.30pm & 2–8pm, Sat 10am–2pm & 3–7pm, Sun 9am–2pm; reduced hours – and no Sun opening – off-season; ☎971 722344, fax 971 721090).

Banks There are plenty of banks on and around the Passeig d'es Born and Avgda Jaume III. Banco de Credito Balear has branches at Avgda Jaume III, 27, and Plaça Espanya 1; Banca March at Plaça Rei Joan Carles I, 5, and c/Sant Miquel 30; Banco Santander at c/Jaume II, 18, and c/Bonaire 4. There are also British banks, with Lloyds at Passeig Mallorca 4 and Barclays sharing the premises of the Banco de Credito Balear at Avgda Jaume III, 27. The two biggest savings banks, which also handle currency exchange, have branches all over the city. La Caixa has a handy downtown branch at Passeig d'es Born 23; for Sa Nostra go to Avgda Jaume III, 18. There are 24-hour cash card and credit card machines dotted round the city too.

Beaches The closest beach to the city centre is the narrow strip of sand next to the *autopista* just beyond Avgda Gabriel Alomar i Villalonga. Swimming is not, however, recommended here as the water is too polluted. Instead most locals make the 30-minute trip on bus #15 to the Platja de Palma (see p.94).

Bicycles Rent them at Ciclos Bimont, Plaça Progrés 19 (☎971 731866), for around 3000ptas a day, 12,000ptas a week. They also run a repair service and are one of about twelve city shops to sell bikes, the biggest outlet being Ciclos Mallorca, c/Joan Alcover 23 (☎971 467616).

Listings

Bookshops The biggest department store in town, El Corte Ingles, at Avgda Jaume III, 15 (Mon–Sat 10am–10pm), has a reasonable selection of English-language novels and books about the Balearics, as does the Libreria Fondevila, near the Teatre Principal at Costa de Sa Pols 18 (Mon–Fri 9.45am–1.30pm & 4.30–8pm, Sat 9.45am–1.30pm; ☎971 725616). The latter also has a wide selection of general maps of Mallorca, as well as a fairly comprehensive selection of walking maps.

Bullfights Palma's bullfighting ring, Plaça Toros (☎971 755245), is a few blocks northeast of the Plaça Espanya along c/Reina Maria Cristina. Tickets and details from travel agents and hotel receptions.

Buses Details of all major Mallorcan bus services are available from the main tourist offices. City transit (Empresa Municipal de Transportes – EMT) enquiries on ☎971 711393, and at the kiosk on Plaça Espanya; island-wide bus service information on ☎971 176970.

Car rental Mallorca's four biggest car rental companies have offices at the airport: Atesa-Eurodollar (☎971 789896); Avis (☎971 789187); Betacar (☎971 789135); and Hertz (☎971 789670). In the city, there's a concentration – including many small concerns – along Avgda Gabriel Roca: Hertz are at no. 13 (☎971 732374); Avis at no. 16 (☎971 730720); and Betacar at no. 20 (☎971 455111). The tourist office will supply a complete list of rental companies.

Cinema ABC, near Plaça Espanya at Avgda Alexandre Rossello 38, presents mainstream Spanish films, plus international blockbusters, usually dubbed.

Consulates Belgium, Passeig d'es Born 15 ☎971 724786; Germany, Passeig d'es Born 15 ☎971 722371; Ireland, c/Sant Miquel 68A ☎971 719244; Netherlands, Plaça Rosari 5 ☎971 716493; Norway, c/Unió 2 ☎971 710809; Sweden, c/Unió 2 ☎971 725492; United Kingdom, Plaça Major 3 ☎971 718501; USA, Avgda Jaume III, 26 ☎971 725051.

Doctors and dentists In the resort areas and in Palma most hotel receptions will be able to find an English-speaking doctor or dentist. For complete lists look under *metges* (Castilian *médicos*) or *clíniques dentals* (*clínicas dentales*) in the yellow pages.

Emergencies General emergency number ☎112. **Ambulances** ☎061; fire-fighters ☎080; police (Policia Local) ☎092.

Ferries The main tourist offices have ferry schedules and tariffs. Tickets can be purchased at travel agents or direct from the ferry line Trasmediterranea (Mon–Fri 8am–8pm, Sat 8am–1pm; ☎971 405014), who have offices at the ferry port, about 3.5km west of the city centre along Avgda Gabriel Roca. They operate ferries to Menorca, Ibiza, Barcelona and Valencia.

Gay scene Palma's gay bars and clubs are concentrated in the El Terreno district, just west of the city centre below the Castell de Bellver. Among several popular spots dotted along the first part of Avgda Joan Miró are the *Status Pub*, at no. 38, the *Bikini Bar*, no. 68, and the *Yuppi Pub*, no. 106. The Ben Amics organization, c/Imprenta 1, 1er, 2a, runs an information line (Mon–Fri 7–9pm; ☎971 723058) and produces a bimonthly newssheet that's available free at most gay venues.

Hospital Hospital General, Plaça Hospital 3 ☎971 728484.

Internet Café La Red, c/Felip Bauza 5, near the c/Apuntadors intersection. Half a dozen terminals, though more are planned. Snacks and drinks available too.

Laundry The most convenient self-service laundry is Self-Press at c/Annibal 14, off Avgda Argentina.

Libraries There's a municipal library inside the Ajuntament (Town Hall) on Plaça Cort (Mon–Fri 8.30am–8.30pm, Sat 9am–1pm). The city also has several privately funded libraries-cum-reading rooms – one of the more convenient is the Biblioteca Bartomeu March Servera (see p.80).

Markets Palma's big Rastrillo (flea market) is held every Sat morning, 8am–2pm, on Avgda Gabriel Alomar i Villalonga, between Plaça Porta d'es Camp and c/Manacor. There's a fresh fruit and vegetable market on Plaça Navegació, just west of Avgda Argentina, Mon–Sat 7am–2pm; and a daily flower market on Passeig de la Rambla.

Mopeds RTR Rental, Avgda Joan Miró 338 (☎971 402585).

Pharmacies Farmacia Castañer, Plaça Rei Joan Carles I, 3; Farmacia Llobera, Plaça Santa Eulalia 1; and Farmacia Muret Mayoral, Plaça Weyler 10.

Post office The central *correu* is at c/Constitució 5 (Mon–Fri 8.30am–8.30pm, Sat 9.30am–2pm).

Shopping Palma isn't big enough to sustain a wide range of special-interest stores, but the tourist office's island-wide leaflet *Artesanía* usefully lists shops by category – everything from fancy dress suppliers to crafts and record shops. In the city centre, porcelain and chinaware are sold at Nacar, Avgda Jaume III, 5; imitation pearls manufactured in Manacor (see p.169) at Majórica, Avgda Jaume III, 11; and the handiest record shop is Palma Rock, Avgda Argentina 18. There's a good toy shop, Arlequin, at c/Unió 5, and you can buy a camera and get your films developed at, amongst many places, Casa Vila, Avgda Jaume III, 10. The biggest department store in town is El Corte Ingles, Avgda Jaume III, 15 (Mon–Sat 10am–10pm), and they have a food and drink section in the basement.

Taxis Taxi ranks can be found outside major hotels. Alternatively, telephone Taxis Palma (☎971 401414) or Radio Taxi (☎971 755440).

Trains The tourist office has train timetable details or you can phone direct: Palma to Inca ☎971 752245; Palma to Sóller ☎971 752051.

Travel agencies There are dozens of travel agencies in Palma, listed in full in the yellow pages under *agències de viatges* (Castilian, *agencias de viajes*). Two helpful downtown choices are Wagons-Lits Cook, Avgda d'Antoni Maura 16 (☎971 722129), and Viajes Iberia, Passeig d'es Born 14 (☎971 726743).

Wine Many shops and most supermarkets carry a reasonable range of Spanish wines. Some also feature Balearic vintages – for example the El Corte Ingles department store, at Avgda Jaume III, 15 (Mon–Sat 10am–10pm). For a wider selection, the best place in town is El Centro del Vino y del Cava, c/Bartomeu Rossello-Porcel 19 (Mon–Fri 9am–1.30pm & 4.30–8pm, Sat 9am–1.30pm; ☎971 452990).

Around Palma

Arched around the sheltered waters of the **Badia de Palma** are the package tourist resorts that have made Mallorca synonymous with the cheap and tacky. In recent years the Balearic government have done their best to improve matters – greening resorts, restricting high-rise construction, and redirecting traffic away from the coast –

but their inherited problems remain. In the 1960s and 1970s, the bay experienced a building boom of almost unimaginable proportions as miles of pristine shoreline mushroomed concrete and glass hotel towers, overwhelming the area's farms and fishing villages. There were few (if any) planning controls and the legacy is the mammoth sprawl of development that now extends, almost without interruption, from S'Arenal in the east to Magaluf in the west – with Palma roughly in the middle.

This thirty-kilometre-long stretch of coast is divided into a score or more resorts, though it's often impossible to pick out where one begins and the other ends. Nevertheless, most of the resorts have evolved their own identities, either in terms of the nationalities they attract, the income group they appeal to, or the age range they cater for. **S'Arenal**, to the **east of Palma**, is mainly German and concentrates on the youth scene, with dozens of pounding bars and discos open right through the night. It also fringes one of Mallorca's best beaches, the **Platja de Palma**, which stretches west from S'Arenal as far as **Ca'n Pastilla**, but although the beach is superb, the flat shoreline behind accommodates an unprepossessing, seemingly endless strip of restaurants, bars and souvenir shops.

West of Palma, the coast bubbles up into the low, rocky hills and sharp coves that prefigure the mountains further west. The sandy beaches here are far smaller – and some are actually artificial – but the terrain makes the tourist development seem less oppressive. **Cala Major**, the first stop, was once the playground of the jet set. It's hit hard times, but some of the grand old buildings have survived and the **Fundació Pilar i Joan Miró**, originally the home of Joan Miró and now an exhibition space for his work, makes a fascinating detour. The neighbouring resort of **Illetes** sports comfortable hotels and attractive cove beaches while, moving west again, **Portals Nous** has an affluent and exclusive air born of its flash marina. Next comes British-dominated **Palma Nova**, a major package holiday destination popular with all ages, and then youthful, very British **Magaluf**, where modern high-rise hotels and thumping nightlife back a substantial sandy beach. South of Magaluf there's a real surprise, for here at last is a small portion of the coast that's not been developed – a pine-studded peninsula sheltering the charming cove beach of **Portals Vells**.

West of Magaluf, the coastal highway leaves the Bay of Palma for the dreary villa-land of **Santa Ponça**, and **Peguera** beyond, a large resort with attractive sandy beaches and a relaxed family atmosphere. Next door, tiny **Cala Fornells** occupies a handsome wooded cove, while just 3km along the highway lies **Camp de Mar**, a pleasantly small resort in an impressively large bay.

Camp de Mar is the last significant development within Palma's orbit – further west the scenery assumes a hillier, prettier aspect as you approach Andratx or Port d'Andratx (covered in chapter 2).

Although these resorts boast hundreds of **hotels**, *hostals* and apartment buildings, nearly all are block-booked by the package tourist industry from June – sometimes May – to September or October, with frugal pickings for the independent traveller. Out of season, many places simply close down, but at those which remain open, it's well worth haggling over the price. In the account that follows we've selected some of the more interesting and enjoyable package hotels, as well as picking out several relatively inexpensive places where there's a reasonable chance of finding a vacancy independently in high season. We've concentrated on three smallish resorts where the tourist development is not too oppressive: Illetes, Cala Fornells and Camp de Mar, each with – or within easy striking distance of – a good sandy beach with safe bathing. Nightlife hasn't been a prime concern in this selection as the liveliest discos and clubs are, as a general rule, concentrated in the tackier spots.

There are hundreds of **restaurants** and cafés too, though the choice is not as diverse as you might expect. The vast majority serve either low-price pizzas and pastas or a sort of pan-European tourist menu. For the most part standards are not very high, and the dishes uninspired.

With Palma's Plaça Espanya as the hub, public **transport** along the coast is fast and efficient. EMT bus #15 travels the old coastal road through Ca'n Pastilla to S'Arenal, #21 heads west as far as Palma Nova, and #3 runs through Cala Major to Illetes. The Catalina Marques bus company operate the so-called "Playa Sol" routes, with frequent services to Magaluf, Santa Ponça, Peguera and Camp de Mar. Their buses leave from Plaça Espanya, Plaça Rei Joan Carles I and other city centre points. **Driving** is straightforward too: the *autopista* shoots along the coast from S'Arenal to Palma Nova; or you can take the old coastal road (the C719 west of Palma), which meanders through most of the resorts at a snail's pace.

East to S'Arenal

The *autopista* heads east out of Palma with tourist resorts on one side and the airport on the other. The flatlands backing onto the coast were once prime agricultural land, pastoral days which are recalled by the ruined windmills – built to pump water out of the marshy topsoil – that lie scattered over the landscape. The alternative route, along the old coastal road, is a bit more interesting and a lot slower – take the turning (signposted to C'an Pastilla) off the *autopista* just beyond the city walls. The old road tracks through the gritty suburbs of Portixol and El Molinar en route to **CALA GAMBA**, an unassuming little place with a pleasant horseshoe-shaped harbour. Close by, **CA'N PASTILLA** is the first substantial tourist resort on this part of the coast, its fifty-odd hotels and apartment buildings set in a rough rectangle of land pushed tight against the seashore. The place is short on charm – and certainly too close to the airport for sonic comfort – but it does herald the start of the fine Platja de Palma.

S'Arenal

The **Platja de Palma**, the four-kilometre stretch of sandy beach that defines the three coterminous (and indistinguishable) resorts of **SOMETIMES, LAS MARAVILLAS** and **S'ARENAL**, is crowded with serious sun-seekers, a sweating throng of bronzed and oiled bodies slowly roasting in the heat. The beach is also a busy pick-up point, the spot for a touch of verbal foreplay before the night-time bingeing begins. It is, as they say, fine if you like that sort of thing – though older visitors look rather marooned. Lined by palm trees, a wide and pleasant walkway runs behind the beach and this, in turn, is edged by a long sequence of bars, restaurants and souvenir shops. A toy-town tourist "train" shuttles up and down the walkway, but there's so little to distinguish one part of the beach from another that it's easy to become disoriented. To maintain your bearings, keep an eye out for the series of smart, stainless-steel beach bars, each numbered and labelled, in Castilian, "*balneario*", strung along the shore: Balneario no. 15 is by the Ca'n Pastilla marina, no. 1 beside S'Arenal harbour.

Singling out any part of this massive complex is a pretty pointless exercise, but the area around S'Arenal harbour does at least have a concentration of **facilities**. There's car rental, currency exchange, boat trips and nightclubs, and you can eat well at the lively terrace bar of the harbourside *Club Nautico*, where the paella is mouthwatering. S'Arenal also boasts **Aquacity**, a huge leisure complex of swimming pools, water flumes and kiddies' playgrounds, beside the *autopista*, about 15km east of Palma.

Aquacity is open May–Sept daily 10am–5pm; Oct Mon–Fri & Sun 10am–5pm; 1850ptas.

All three resorts extend a few blocks inland to encompass dozens of **places to stay**. The cheapest accommodation is provided by the **youth hostel**, the *Playa de Palma*, at c/Costa Brava 13, Sometimes (June–Sept; ☎971 260892; ①). To get there, take EMT bus #15 from Plaça Espanya for the 25-minute trip to the resort, and ask to be put off at the giant *Hotel Royal Cristina* on the main road. The youth hostel is a couple of hundred metres further along the road on the left. If you're approaching it from the beach, it's a couple of minutes' walk from Balneario no. 10. The hostel is fairly spick and span, but it only has 65 beds so advance reservations are strongly recommended. At the other end of the market, the four-star *Royal Cristina*, on Arenas de Bilbao (☎971 492550, fax 971 490003; ⑧), offers luxury rooms and apartments. Mid-range options include – amongst many – the three-star *Hotel Torre Azul*, c/Sant Bartoloméu 24 (April–Oct; ☎971 263750; ⑥), a commodious establishment with its own pool about 350m behind S'Arenal harbour; and the three-star, 200-room *Royal Cupido*, a bright modern hotel which backs onto the beach at c/Marbella 32 (☎971 264300, fax 971 265510; ⑦) – a couple of minutes' walk west of the *Royal Cristina*.

West to Cala Major

Crowded **CALA MAJOR** snakes along a hilly stretch of coastline a kilometre or two beyond Palma's ferry port. Overlooking the main street (a section of the C719 coast road), occasional *Modernista* mansions and the newly refurbished *Hotel Nixe Palace* are reminders of halcyon days when the resort was a byword for elegance; the king of Spain still runs a palace here – the Palau Marivent, on the main street, close to the *autopista* at the east end of the resort.

Opposite the palace, a signposted turning (to Gènova) leads up the hill the half-kilometre to the **Fundació Pilar i Joan Miró**, where Miró lived and worked for much of the 1950s, 1960s and 1970s. Initially – from 1920 – the young Miró was involved with the Surrealists in Paris and contributed to all their major exhibitions: his wild squiggles, supercharged with bright colours, prompted André Breton, the leading theorist of the movement, to describe Miró as "the most Surrealist of us all". In the 1930s he adopted a simpler style, abandoning the decorative complexity of his earlier work for a more minimalist use of symbols, though the highly coloured forms remained. Miró returned to Barcelona, the city of his birth, in 1940, where he continued to work in the Surrealistic tradition, though as an avowed opponent of Franco his position was uneasy. In 1957 he moved to Mallorca, its relative isolation offering a degree of safety. His wife and mother were both Mallorcan, which must have influenced his decision, as did the chance to work in his own purpose-built studio with its view of the coast. Even from the relative isolation of Franco's Spain he remained an influential figure, prepared to experiment with all kinds of media, right up until his death in Cala Major in 1983.

With views over the bay, the expansive hillside premises of the Fundació include Miró's old **studio**, an unassuming affair that has been left pretty much as it was at the time of his death. It's worth a quick gander for a flavour of how the man worked – tackling a dozen or so canvases at the same time – but unfortunately you're only allowed to peer through the windows.

Opposite are the angular lines of the bright-white art gallery, the **Edificio Estrella**, which displays a rotating and representative sample of the artist's work drawn from a prodigious supply – Miró was nothing if not productive. The Fundació holds 134 paintings, 300 engravings and 105 drawings, as well as sculptures, gouaches and preliminary sketches, more than six thousand works in all. There are no guarantees as to what will be on display, but you're likely to see a decent selection of his paintings, the familiar dream-like squiggles and half-recognizable shapes that are intended to conjure up the unconscious, with free play often given to erotic associations. The gallery also stores a comprehensive collection of Miró documents and occasionally hosts exhibitions.

The Fundació Pilar i Joan Miró, c/Joan de Saridakis 29, is open from mid-May to mid-Sept Tues–Sat 10am–7pm, Sun 10am–3pm; mid-Sept to mid-May Tues–Sat 10am–6pm, Sun 10am–3pm; 675ptas. EMT bus #4 from Plaça de la Reina to Gènova passes the entrance hourly.

Illetes

At well-heeled **ILLETES**, just along the coast from Cala Major and 7km from Palma, a ribbon of restaurants, hotels and apartment buildings bestrides the steep hills that rise high above the rocky shoreline. There's precious little space left, but at least the generally low-rise buildings are of manageable proportions. A string of tiny cove beaches punctuates the coast, the most attractive being the pine-shaded **Platja Cala Comtesa**, at the southern end of the resort, next door to a restricted military zone. The long main street, Passeig d'Illetes, runs past several good **hotels**. The most enjoyable is the *Bon Sol* (☎971 402111, fax 971 402559; ⑨), about halfway along, which tumbles down the cliffs to the seashore and its own artificial beach. A family-run concern, the hotel has all the conveniences you could want and the better rooms have fine views out over the bay. The clientele is staid and steady, befitting the antique-crammed interior. Another good choice is the *Hotel Albatros* (☎971 402211, fax 971 402154; ⑦), located near the north end of Passeig d'Illetes; rooms have balconies and air conditioning and there's a swimming pool and private access to the sea. There are similar facilities at the luxurious, four-star *Hotel Bonanza Playa* (☎971 401112, fax 971 405615; ⑨), overlooking the seashore close to the *Bon Sol*, while equally spacious lodgings are to be found a couple of minutes' walk south along the coast at the attractive *Hotel-residencia Illetes* (☎971 402411, fax 971 401808; ⑦). Most visitors **eat** in their hotels, but there's a smattering of smart cafés on the main drag, including *Es Parral*, which serves Mallorcan cuisine from premises towards the south end of the resort. Far more expensive is the splendid *Restaurant Bonaire d'Illetes*, about halfway along the main street, whose speciality is oven-baked meat dishes.

Bendinat and Portals Nous

The C719 skirts Illetes but cuts through the peripheries of **BENDI-NAT**, a couple of kilometres further along the coast. On the south side of the road, the resort's leafy streets meander down to the seashore, lined by the villas of the well-to-do. It's a pretty spot and tucked away on a quiet, rocky cove is the charming *Hotel Bendinat*, c/Rossegada (May–Oct; ☎971 675725, fax 971 677276; ⑨), dating from the 1950s and built in the traditional *hacienda* style, with a beautiful arcaded terrace overlooking the sea. You can stay either in the main building, where most of the bedrooms have balconies, or in one of the trim, whitewashed bungalows that dot the gardens.

On its west side, Bendinat merges with the larger **PORTALS NOUS**, another ritzy settlement where polished mansions fill out the green and hilly terrain abutting the coast. There's a tiny beach too, set beneath the cliffs and reached via a flight of steps at the foot of c/Passatge del Mar. In contrast to the studied elegance of the side streets, the resort's main drag (also the C719) is disappointingly drab, though it does lead to the glitzy marina, one of Mallorca's most exclusive, where the boats look more like ocean liners than pleasure yachts. Close by, **Marineland** is one of the tackiest but most popular attractions on the island, with shark tanks, crocodile pounds and an aquarium, as well as exploitative dolphin, sea lion and parrot shows. Kids love the place; adults mostly suffer in silence.

Portals Nous has a number of three-star hotels, but, with much of the shoreline occupied by affluent private villas and apartments, they're restricted to the side streets, well away from the sea. Pick of the bunch is the comfortable *Fabiola*, c/Flores (☎971 675825, fax 971 677006; ⑤), set in the middle of the wealthiest part of town and a short walk from both the marina and the beach. For **food**, try the rows of restaurants and bars down at the marina.

Around Palma

Marineland is open Jan–March & Oct–mid-Nov daily 9.30am–5pm; April–Sept daily 9.30am–6pm; 1800ptas.

Palma Nova and Calvià

Old Mallorca hands claim that **PALMA NOVA**, 4km from Portals Nous, was once a beauty spot, and certainly its wide and shallow bay, with good beaches among a string of bumpy headlands, still has its moments. But for the most part, the bay has been engulfed by a broad, congested sweep of hotels and tourist facilities. With the development comes a vigorous nightlife and a plethora of accommodation on or near the seashore – though, as elsewhere, most places are block-booked by tour operators throughout the season. The summertime **tourist office** (Mon–Fri 9am–1pm & 2.30–5pm; ☎971 682365), beside the beach on Passeig de la Mar, has supplies of *Wot's On*, a monthly freebie detailing local events and entertainments, and issues free maps marking all the **hotels**. The nearby three-star *Playa Trópico*, also on Passeig de la Mar though just off the seafront (☎971 680512, fax 971 682613; ⑤), is a well-maintained and good-looking modern hotel. Other options include the *Hotel Playa Comodoro*, Passeig Cala Blanca (April–Oct; ☎971 682061; ⑧), a standard-issue tower with balconied double rooms looking out over the bay, and the comparable four-star *Hotel Delfín Playa* (☎971 680100, fax 971 680112; ⑦), which faces the beach at the centre of the resort from behind Passeig de la Mar. As you might expect, prices drop as soon as you leave the seashore, at places such as the giant *Hotel Sol Mirlos* on c/Pinzones, a five-minute walk from the beach (☎971 681900, fax 971 681912; ⑥), and its identical neighbour *Hotel Sol Tordos* (April–Oct; ☎971 680250, fax 971 681912; ⑥).

Just 6km north of Palma Nova, tucked away in the hills behind the coast, is the tiny town of **CALVIÀ**, the region's administrative centre – hence the lavish and oversized town hall, paid for by the profits of the tourist industry. The parish church of **Sant Joan Baptista** (daily 10am–1pm) dominates the town, its greying stone dating from 1245, though the Gothic subtleties mostly disappeared during

Beyond Calvià, steep and narrow minor roads twist into the mountains of northwest Mallorca (covered in the next chapter), or you can cut back down to the coast at Santa Ponça (see p.99)

a nineteenth-century refurbishment that left a crude bas-relief carving of the Garden of Gethsemane above the main door. Opposite the church, *Bar Rosita* serves *tapas*, coffee and cakes, and just down the hill, the excellent *Méson Ca'n Torrat* (closed Tues) specializes in roast legs of lamb and suckling pig. EMT **bus #20** links Calvià with Palma via Palma Nova four times daily.

Magaluf and Portals Vells

Torrenova, on the chunky headland at the far end of Palma Nova, is a cramped and untidy development that slides into **MAGALUF**, whose high-rise towers march across the next bay down the coast. Long a bargain-basement package holiday destination, Magaluf has finally lost patience with its youthful British visitors. In 1996 the local authorities won a court order allowing them to demolish twenty downmarket hotels in an attempt to end – or at least control – the annual binge of "violence, drunkenness and open-air sex" that, they argued, now characterized the resort. The high-rise hotels were duly dynamited and an extensive clean-up programme has subsequently freshened up the resort's appearance, but short of demolishing the whole lot there's not too much anyone can do with the deadening concrete of the modern town centre – and, besides, the demolished blocks will be replaced, albeit by more upmarket hotels. Whether these draconian measures will change tourist behaviour remains to be seen, but it doen't help that the resort's British visitors still seem determined to create – or at least patronize – a bizarre caricature of their homeland: it's all here, from beans on toast with Marmite to pubs like *Tom Brown's* and *Benny Hill's*.

Stuck on the western edge of Magaluf are a couple of giant-sized, purpose-built tourist attractions: **Aquapark**, with its swimming pools, water chutes and flumes makes an enjoyable day out if you're travelling with children, but **Dorado**, just opposite, is absolutely dreadful: a Wild West show town-cum-theme park that must be one of the most incongruous sights in Spain. In the unlikely event that you want to find a room in Magaluf, you can get a free map giving the location of all the resort's hotels at the seasonal **tourist office** (June–Aug Mon–Fri 9am–1pm & 3–5pm; ☎971 131126), on the square one block back from the beach at Avgda Pere Vaquer Ramis 1.

Aquapark is open June–Sept daily 10am–6pm; May & Oct daily 10am–5pm; adults 1950ptas, children 1200ptas.

Portals Vells

Things pick up beyond Magaluf, with the pine-clad peninsula that extends to the south of the resort barely touched by the developers. In consequence, however, there aren't any public **buses** down the peninsula – the nearest you'll get is Magaluf – so you'll have to drive, walk or hitch. Follow the road connecting the C719 with Aquapark; 1km beyond Aquapark, when the main road curves to the right, continue straight on along an old country road which heads off into the woods. After about 4km, a steep turning on the left leads down 1km to **Cala Mago** (still signposted in Castilian, "Playa El Mago"), where a rocky little headland with a shattered guard house has lovely beaches to either side. Park and walk down to whichever cove takes your fancy: the nudist beach on the right with its smart café-restaurant, or the delightful pine-shaded strand on the left with its beach bar, tiny port and sprinkling of villas. Both provide sunbeds and showers.

Continuing a further 500m past the Cala Mago turning, a second turning twists for a kilometre down to the cove beach of **PORTALS VELLS**. Despite a bar-restaurant and a handful of villas, it remains a pleasant, pine-scented spot of glistening sand, rocky cliffs and clear blue water, especially appealing early in the morning before it gets crowded. Clearly visible from the beach are the **caves** of the headland on the south side of the cove. A footpath leads to the most interesting, an old cave church where the holy-water stoup and altar have been cut out of the solid rock – the work of shipwrecked Genoese seamen, according to local legend.

Beyond the Portals Vells turning, the road continues for 1.5km as far as a broken-down barbed-wire fence at the start of a military zone. You can't drive any further and you're not supposed to walk beyond the fence either, but some people do, braving the no-entry signs to scramble through the pine woods and out along the headland to reach the solitary **Cap de Cala Figuera** lighthouse after about 1.5km.

From Santa Ponça to Camp de Mar

West of Palma Nova, the C719 trims the outskirts of **SANTA PONÇA**, perhaps the least endearing of all the resorts on this stretch of coast. Mostly a product of the 1980s, this sprawling, still-expanding conurbation has abandoned the concrete high-rises of yesteryear for a pseudo-vernacular architecture that's littered the hills with scores of tedious villas. That said, the aesthetic gloom is at least partly lifted by the setting – with rolling hills flanking a broad bay – and the substantial sandy beach offers safe bathing.

Peguera and Cala Fornells

Sprawling **PEGUERA**, about 6km from Santa Ponça, is strung out along a lengthy, partly pedestrianized main street – the Avinguda de Peguera – immediately behind several generous sandy beaches. There's nothing remarkable about the place, but it does have an easy-going air and is a favourite with families and older visitors alike. Towards the west end of the resort, a signed left turn off the high street, beside the Gigante supermarket, takes you the 1km up to **CALA FORNELLS**, whose chic, *pueblo*-style houses perch on the cliffs that trail round to a minuscule beach and concreted sunbathing slabs. Although Cala Fornells tends to be overcrowded during the daytime, at night the tranquillity returns, and it makes a good base for a holiday. You can also stroll out into the surrounding woods along a wide, dirt track which runs up behind the hotels, cutting across the pine-scented hills towards the stony cove beach of Caló d'es Monjo, 1.5km to the west.

Cala Fornells has two fetching **hotels**, both behind the beach at the end of the access road: the sprucely modern, four-star *Coronado* (April–Sept; ☎971 686800, fax 971 687457; ⑨), where all 150 bedrooms have sea views and balconies, and the more sympathetic, green-shuttered and white-painted *Cala Fornells* (Feb–Oct; ☎971 686950, fax 971 687525; ⑥). If your wallet won't stretch to either of these, consider staying in Peguera, where there are plenty of bargain-basement *hostals* in the characterless side streets sloping up from the seafront. The seasonal **tourist office** (Mon–Sat 9am–1pm & 3–5pm; ☎971 685468), on Avinguda de Peguera at the east end of the resort, issues comprehensive accommodation lists as well as local maps. Try along c/Palmira – a turning off Avinguda de Peguera about 700m east of the Gigante supermarket – where you'll find the no-frills *Hostal-residencia Sutimar* at no. 9 (April–Oct; ☎971 686952; ①); the marginally larger and more agreeable *Hostal-residencia Diamante* at no. 4 (☎971 686629; ③); and the much more comfortable *Hotel Maria Dolores*, with its own heated swimming pool, at Plaça Palmira 29 (☎971 686598; ④).

For **food**, *Pizza Valentino*, Avgda de Peguera 57, is cheap and cheerful, while the *Hotel Cala Fornells* (see above) has a good restaurant. At the top of the range, *La Gran Tortuga* (closed Mon), overlooking the seashore on the road to *Cala Fornells*, serves superb seafood, and has a terrace bar and even its own swimming pool; a three-course dinner will set you back about 4500ptas, but lunches are good too, and far less expensive.

Camp de Mar

Tucked away among the hills just 3km west of Peguera, **CAMP DE MAR** has an expansive beach and fine bathing, but is marred by the presence of two thumping great hotels dropped right on the seashore. All the same, this low-key resort is an amiable spot to soak up the sun and to use as a base for further explorations, though its charm is rapidly being eroded by its all-too-rapid expansion. Both beachside **hotels** are modern high-rises equipped with spacious, balconied bedrooms: the *Hotel Playa* (April–Oct; ☎971 235025, fax 971 208775; ⑤) is a British favourite, whilst the four-star *Club Camp de Mar* (Feb–Oct; ☎971 235200, fax 971 235110; ⑧) caters mainly for Germans. As far as **eating** is concerned, it's hard to resist the eccentric café stuck out in the bay and approached via a rickety walkway on stilts. Or try the *Bar La Siesta*, overlooking the beach, for romantic sunsets and wonderful paellas.

Heading west from Camp de Mar, a minor road twists over wooded hills to Port d'Andratx – see p.132.

Travel details

Local buses

EMT services from **Palma** to: the airport (#17; every 20min; 25min); Cala Major (#3; every 10min; 15min); Calvià (#20; 4 daily; 25min); Capdellà (#20; 3 daily; 50min); Gènova (#4; every 30min; 25min); Illetes (#3; every 10min; 20min); Palma Nova (#21; every 20min; 30min); Portals Nous (#21; every 90min; 25min); S'Arenal (#15; every 10min; 30min).

Catalina Marques services (the "Playa Sol" routes) from **Palma** to: Camp de Mar (May–Oct every 15min, Nov–April every hour; 40min); Magaluf (11 daily; 25min); Palma Nova (11 daily; 20min); Peguera (May–Oct every 15min, Nov–April every hour; 35min); Port d'Andratx (May–Oct every hour, Nov–April every 2hr; 45min); Portals Nous (11 daily; 15min).

Island-wide buses

From **Palma** to: Alaró (2–3 daily; 25min); Alcúdia (May–Oct Mon–Sat 10 daily, 5 on Sun; Nov–April 5 daily; 1hr); Andratx (May–Oct hourly; Nov–April every 2hr; 35min); Artà (Mon–Sat 4 daily, 1 on Sun; 1hr 25min); Banyalbufar (1–3 daily; 35min); Cala d'Or (2–4 daily; 1hr 10min); Cala Figuera (Mon–Sat 1–2 daily; 1hr 20min); Cala Millor (Mon–Sat 5–7 daily, 1–2 on Sun; 1hr 15min); Cala Rajada (Mon–Sat 4 daily, 1–2 on Sun; 1hr 30min); Camp de Mar (May–Oct every 15min; Nov–April hourly; 40min); Ca'n Picafort (2–3 daily; 1hr); Colònia de Sant Jordi (2–5 daily; 1hr); Coves del Drac (Mon–Sat 2–4 daily, 1 on Sun; 1hr); Covetes (for Es Trenc beach; May–Oct 1 daily; 1hr); Deià (5 daily; 45min); Esporles (Mon–Sat 4 daily, 2 on Sun; 20min); Estellencs (1–3 daily; 45min); Felanitx (3–4 daily; 50min); Inca (4–8 daily; 30min); La Granja (Mon–Sat 3 daily, 1 on Sun; 25min); Lluc (1–2 daily; 1hr); Manacor (Mon–Sat 8 daily, 3 on Sun; 45min); Montuiri (2–3 daily; 40min); Muro (2–4 daily; 50min); Petra (2–3 daily; 45min); Platja de Formentor (May–Oct Mon–Sat 1 daily; 1hr 15min); Pollença (3–5 daily; 1hr); Port d'Alcúdia (May–Oct Mon–Sat 10 daily, 5 on Sun; Nov–April 2–5 daily; 1hr 10min); Port d'Andratx (May–Oct 13 daily; Nov–April 2–5 daily; 45min); Port de Pollença (3–5 daily; 1hr 10min); Port de Sóller (5 daily; 35min); Porto Colom (1–3 daily; 1hr 10min); Porto Cristo (Mon–Sat 7 daily, 2 on Sun; 1hr 10min); Porto Petro (2 daily; 1hr 10min); Santanyí (2–4 daily; 1hr); Sóller (5 daily; 30min); Valldemossa (5 daily; 30min).

Trains

From Palma to: Binissalem (hourly; 30min); Inca (hourly; 40min); Sóller (5 daily; 1hr 15min).

Chapter 2

Northwest Mallorca

Mallorca is at its scenic best in the gnarled ridge of the Serra de Tramuntana, the imposing mountain range which stretches the length of the island's northwest shore, its rearing peaks and plunging seacliffs intermittently intercepted by valleys of olive and citrus groves. Midway along and cramped by the mountains is Sóller, an antiquated merchants' town that serves as a charming introduction to the region, especially when it's reached on the dinky rail line from Palma. From here, it's a short hop down to the coast at Port de Sóller, a popular resort on a deep and expansive bay. This geographical arrangement – the town located a few kilometres inland from the eponymous port – is repeated across Mallorca, a reminder of more troubled days when marauding corsairs obliged the islanders to live away from the coast. The mountain valleys in the vicinity of Sóller shelter the bucolic stone-built villages of Fornalutx and Orient, as well as the splendid oasis-like gardens of Alfabia, set beside the main Sóller–Palma road, the C711.

Southwest of Sóller, the main coastal road, the C710, threads up through the mountains to reach the beguiling village of Deià, tucked at the base of formidable cliffs and famous as the former home of Robert Graves. Beyond lies the magnificent Carthusian monastery of Valldemossa, whose echoing cloisters temporarily accommodated George Sand and Frédéric Chopin, and the gracious *hacienda* of La Granja, another compelling stop. Continuing southwest, the C710

Accommodation price codes

All the accommodation prices in this book have been coded using the symbols below, corresponding to the least expensive double room in each establishment in high season, excluding special offers. For a full explanation see p.34.

① Under 3000ptas	④ 6000–8000ptas	⑦ 14,000–20,000ptas
② 3000–4000ptas	⑤ 8000–10,000ptas	⑧ 20,000–25,000ptas
③ 4000–6000ptas	⑥ 10,000–14,000ptas	⑨ Over 25,000ptas

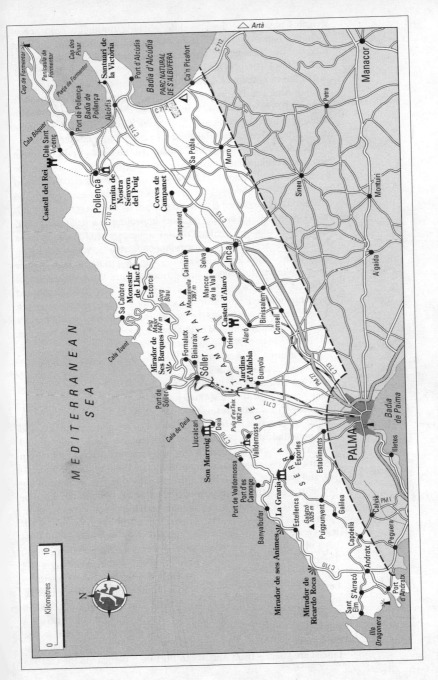

wriggles high above the shoreline, slipping through a sequence of mountain hamlets, of which **Banyalbufar** and **Estellencs** are the most picturesque, their tightly terraced fields tumbling down the coastal cliffs. A few kilometres further and you leave the coast, drifting inland, out of the mountains and into the foothills on the way to the market town of **Andratx**. Beyond, on Mallorca's southwestern tip, lie the safe waters of **Port d'Andratx**, a medium-sized resort draped around a handsome inlet, its villas announcing the start of the intense tourist development that eats up the coast east from Camp de Mar to Palma.

The mountains **northeast of Sóller** are the highest portion of the Serra de Tramuntana – too severe, in fact, to allow for any but the most occasional access to the sea, with the C710 being forced inland to weave its way amongst the craggy peaks. A rare exception is the extraordinary side road that snakes down to the overcrowded mini-resort of **Sa Calobra** and the far more appealing beach at **Cala Tuent**. But it's the expansive, well-appointed monastery of **Lluc** that remains the big draw around here – for religious islanders, who venerate an effigy of the Virgin known as La Moreneta, and tourists alike. Further along the coast, the outstanding attractions are the ancient town of **Pollença**, complete with its fine, cypress-lined Way of the Cross, and the **Península de Formentor**, a rocky finger of land noted for its sea vistas. The peninsula boasts the superb *Hotel Formentor*, but thinner wallets are usually confined to the low-key resort of **Port de Pollença** or the more upbeat and flashy **Port d'Alcúdia**.

The Serra de Tramuntana provides the best walking on Mallorca, with scores of **hiking trails** latticing the mountains. Generally speaking, paths are well marked, though apt to be clogged with thornbushes. There are trails to suit all aptitudes and all levels of enthusiasm, from the easiest of strolls to the most gruelling of long-distance treks. Details of several of the less strenuous walks are given in the text, and four potential hikes, beginning in Valldemossa, Delà, Pollença and Lluc, are described in depth. Spring and autumn are the best times to embark on the longer trails; in mid summer the heat can be enervating and water is scarce. Bear in mind also that the mountains are prone to mists, though they usually lift at some point in the day. For obvious safety reasons, lone mountain walking is not recommended.

As far as **beaches** are concerned, most of the region's coastal villages have no more than a tiny, shingly strip, and only around the bays of Pollença and Alcúdia are there more substantial offerings. The resorts edging these bays have the greatest number of hotel and *hostal* rooms, but from June to early September, and sometimes beyond, vacancies are extremely thin on the ground. Indeed, **accommodation** – especially if you have a tight itinerary and are travelling in the summertime – requires some forethought, though there's a reasonable chance of getting a room on spec in Sóller and in the monasteries at Lluc and just outside Pollença. To compensate, distances are small – from Andratx to Port de Pollença via the C710 is

The train to Sóller

The 28-kilometre train journey from Palma to Sóller is a delight, dipping and cutting through the mountains and fertile valleys of the Serra de Tramuntana. Completed in 1911, the rail line was constructed on the profits of the orange and lemon trade, whose produce the railway was built to transport to Palma – at a time when it took a full day to make the trip by road. First the train has to clear the scratchy suburbs of Palma, but within about fifteen minutes it's running across pancake-flat farmland with an impenetrable-looking line of steep peaks dead ahead. After clunking through the outskirts of Bunyola, the train threads upwards to spend five minutes tunnelling through the mountains, where the noisy engine and dimly lit carriages give the feel of a rollercoaster ride. Beyond, out in the bright mountain air, are the steep valleys and craggy thousand-metre peaks at the heart of the Serra de Tramuntana, and everywhere there are almond groves, which are vivid with pinky-white blossom in January and February. The rolling stock, too, is tremendous, with narrow carriages – the gauge is only 914mm – which seem straight out of an Agatha Christie novel. There are five departures daily from Palma station throughout the year (sometimes six from Sóller), the whole ride taking just under an hour and a quarter. A return costs 760ptas (380ptas one way), though the mid-morning Turist train – whose only distinction is a brief photo-stop in the mountains at the Mirador Pujol d'En Banja – will set you back 1115ptas return (735ptas one way).

only about 130km – the roads are good and the **bus** network is perfectly adequate for most destinations. **Taxis** can work out a reasonable deal too, if you're travelling in a group: the fare for the forty-kilometre trip from Palma to Sóller, for instance, is about 4000ptas.

Sóller and around

At **Sóller**, the terminus of the rail line from Palma, the obvious option is to continue by tram down to the seashore, a rumbling, five-kilometre journey ending at Port de Sóller. If you pass straight through however, you'll miss one of the most laid-back and enjoyable towns on Mallorca, an ideal, and fairly inexpensive, base for exploring the surrounding mountains. To the northeast, Sóller's mellow mansions fade seamlessly into the orchards and farmland that precede the charming hamlets of **Biniaraix** and **Fornalutx**, both within easy walking distance. Further afield, on the landward side of the Serra de Tramuntana, the rustic delights continue amongst the verdant gardens of the **Jardins d'Alfabia**, and at the hamlet of **Orient**, on the road to the remote ruins of the **Castell d'Alaró**. However, most visitors ignore these inland attractions and stick religiously to the coast, the focus of their attention being the popular but mundane resort of **Port de Sóller**. If the seashore is what you're after, there are much nicer bathing spots not far away – especially Cala Deià – but the port does offer good restaurants and a cluster of low-price hotels.

Sóller and around

The quickest route from Palma to Sóller is along the C711, which tunnels straight through the mountains. The twenty-kilometre journey takes about thirty minutes and it costs 505ptas per car to use the three-kilometre tunnel; you can avoid the tunnel by driving along a serpentine road over the mountains, though this adds about 8km to the trip. There's a fast and frequent direct bus service from Palma to Sóller and Port de Sóller via the tunnel; other buses are routed via Valldemossa and Deià. More intermittent services run along the main coastal road, the C710, from Andratx to Valldemossa, and on from Sóller and Port de Sóller to Port de Pollença and Port d'Alcúdia (summertime only). In Palma, buses leave from the Plaça Espanya terminal with the exception of services run by Bus Nord Balear, operators of the Palma–Valldemossa–Deià–Port de Sóller route, whose buses leave from outside *Bar La Granja*, a short walk from the main bus station (see p.64). **Trains** from Palma to Sóller (see p.64) link with the ramshackle old **trams** to Port de Sóller, ex-San Francisco rolling stock from the 1930s. They depart every half-hour or hour daily from 6am to 9pm; the fifteen-minute journey costs 125ptas one way.

Sóller town

Rather than any specific sight, it's the general flavour of **SÓLLER** that appeals, its narrow, sloping lanes cramped by eighteenth- and nineteenth-century stone houses, whose fancy grilles and big wooden doors once hid the region's fruit-rich merchants. All streets lead to the main square, Plaça Constitució, an informal, pint-sized affair of crowded cafés and grouchy mopeds just down the hill from the train station. The square is dominated by the hulking mass of the church of **St Bartomeu**, a crude neo-Gothic remodelling of the medieval original, its only saving grace the enormous and precisely carved rose window stuck high in the main facade. Inside, the cavernous nave is suitably dark and gloomy, the penitential home of a string of gaudy Baroque altarpieces. A couple of minutes' walk northwest at c/Sa Mar 13, the **Museu Municipal** comprises a rather half-hearted sequence of period rooms in a renovated merchant's mansion. It's hardly unmissable, but the antique kitchen, with its majolica plates and old pots and pans, is mildly diverting, and the chapel-shrine showcases some interesting votive offerings.

Retracing your steps to the south end of c/Sa Mar, turn left along c/Bauçà, walk straight across Plaça Constitució and keep going down c/Sa Lluna for the three-kilometre stroll to the pretty village of Biniaraix (see p.109), or turn right down c/Rectoria for the five-minute walk west to the **Museu Balear de Ciències Naturals** (Balearic Museum of Natural Sciences), stuck beside the main Palma–Sóller road. This museum occupies an old merchant's dwelling, although the interior has been stripped out to accommodate a series of modest displays. Temporary exhibitions occupy the top two floors and usually feature Balearic geology and fossils. The

St Bartomeu is open Mon–Thurs 10.30am–1pm & 2.45–5.15pm, Fri & Sat 10.30am–1pm; free.

The Museu Municipal is open Tues–Fri 11am–1pm & 5–8pm; 100ptas.

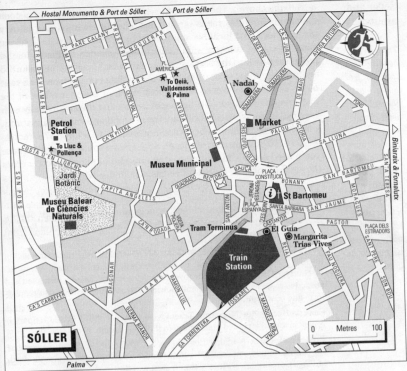

SÓLLER

△ Binaraix & Fornalutx

0 Metres 100

▽ Palma

permanent collection is exhibited on the ground floor and is devoted to the leading botanists of yesteryear – including Archduke Ludwig Salvator (see p.121). The labelling is in Catalan, but English leaflets are available at reception, which also issues a free English-language brochure identifying and illustrating many species of local flora. This is a necessary introduction to the **Jardí Botànic** (botanical garden), which rolls down the hillside in front of the house. The garden is in its infancy, so there's not much horticultural excitement at present, but when there is, you can expect an admission fee to match.

Practicalities

Buses to Sóller from Lluc and Pollença drop passengers beside the petrol station on the main Sóller–Palma road to the west of the town centre. From here, it's a five-minute stroll into the town centre – walk south from the petrol station and take the first left down Costa d'En Llorenç. Buses from Deià, Valldemossa and Palma arrive beside Plaça Amèrica, from where it's about five minutes' walk south to Plaça Constitució, the site of the **Oficina d'Informació Turística** (Mon–Fri 9.30am–1.30pm; ☎971 630200), which has its home in the town hall

The Museu Balear de Ciències Naturals and Jardí Botànic are open April–Sept Tues–Sat 10am–8pm, Sun 10.30am–1.30pm; Oct–March Tues–Sat 10.30am–1.30pm & 5–8pm, Sun 10.30am–1.30pm; 300ptas.

Sóller and around

The buses heading along the coast from Sóller – both to the east and west – are very popular; to make sure of a seat, it's worth travelling down to Port de Sóller, where these services originate, and getting on the bus there.

next to the church. The tourist office has leaflets detailing local accommodation, provides maps of the town and its environs and issue a quick synopsis of local hikes prepared by "Catherine", a local hiking expat who also offers a wide range of well-planned and imformative **guided walks** into the surrounding mountains. These are between 4.5 and 6 hours long, cost from 1500 to 2600ptas per person, and take place 3 to 6 times weekly throughout much of the year. Most of the hikes require a reasonable degree of fitness and the cost usually covers minibus travel to the trailhead, but not food or drink. Reservations, a minimum of 24 hours ahead, are essential on ☎971 633373, mobile ☎909 620226. You can, of course, do the hikes yourself, in which case you'll need an IGN **hiking map** – the **newspaper shop** directly across the square from the tourist office has a limited supply.

Accommodation

Despite the very limited choice of accommodation, in high season there's far more chance of a **room** in Sóller's three hotels and *hostals* than down at the port.

Hotel El Guía, c/Castanyer 2 ☎ & fax 971 630227. Easily the best place in town, this lovely, old-fashioned one-star hotel is approached across a pretty little courtyard. Bygones litter the foyer, which leads to pleasantly furnished and attractive rooms. To get there, walk down the steps from the train station platform and turn right. April–Oct. ⑤.

Casa de Huéspedes Margarita Trías Vives, c/Reial 3 ☎971 634214. Spartan rooms in an old terraced house close to the train station. April–Oct. ②.

Hostal-residencia Nadal, c/Romaguera 27 ☎971 631180. Simple, central two-star, in a modern, neatly decorated house about five minutes' walk north of Plaça Constitució, with over twenty neat and tidy rooms. ③.

Eating and drinking

Sóller's **café-bars** provide an abundance of low-cost snacks and light meals during the day and early evening. The **restaurant** scene is more limited, and although there are a couple of decent spots, you're better heading off to the restaurants down at the port (see p.111).

Bar Turismo, by the tram lines on Avgda d'es Born s/n. Cosy, old-fashioned bar with English lending library, redolent of earlier expatriate days.

Café Es Firo, Plaça Constitució 10. Deep, dark café selling cheap *tapas* and coffee with a kick like a mule.

Café Madrid, just off Plaça Constitució on c/Bauçà 2. Popular, no-frills café-bar, with sandwiches and *tapas* starting at 400ptas.

Cafeteria Soller, Plaça Constitució 14. Tasty snacks and fresh *ensaimadas* in unpretentious surroundings; a good bet for breakfast.

Restaurant El Guía, c/Castanyer 2. In the hotel of the same name, this is a real treat. A little formal for some, but the prices are very reasonable, with a delicious *menú del día* for around 2500ptas. Closed Mon.

Restaurant-bar Oasis, c/Cristófol Colom 5. Situated north of Plaça Constitució by the Port de Sóller tram tracks, this enjoyable restaurant has the added benefit of a shaded terrace. A varied menu features Spanish, Mallorcan and Italian dishes all at low prices – the paella, for instance, costs just 800ptas.

Biniaraix and Fornalutx

Following c/Sa Lluna from Sóller's main square, it takes about half an hour to stroll east to **BINIARAIX**, passing orchards and farmland latticed with ancient irrigation channels and dry-stone walls. The village, nestled in the foothills of the Serra de Tramuntana, is tiny: just a cluster of handsome old stone houses surrounding a dilapidated church and the smallest of central squares. It only takes a few minutes to look around, but Biniaraix is also the starting point for one of Mallorca's busiest hiking routes, commonly called the **Cornadors Circuit**, a thirteen-kilometre trail which takes about six hours to negotiate, weaving a circuitous course through the mountains to finish up in Sóller. To get to the trailhead, walk uphill from the square along c/Sant Josep and, after about 200m, you'll reach a spring and cattle trough. A sign here offers a choice of hiking routes: left for the Camí del Marroig, right for the more interesting **Camí d'es Barranc**, the first, and most diverting, part of the Cornadors Circuit.

The Camí d'es Barranc follows an old cobbled track – originally built for pilgrims on their way to Lluc – which ascends the **Barranc de Biniaraix**, a beautiful gorge of terraced citrus groves set in the shadow of the mountains. After about ninety minutes you'll reach the head of the ravine, where a large barn sporting painted signs on its walls is the obvious landmark. Beyond this point the going gets appreciably tougher and the route more difficult to work out, so you'll need to have a hiking map with you. If you don't fancy completing the Cornadors Circuit by walking all the way back to Sóller you can return the way you came.

Fornalutx

FORNALUTX, a couple of kilometres east of Biniaraix along a narrow, signposted country lane is touted as the most attractive village on the island, and certainly has a superb location. Orange and lemon groves scent the valley as it tapers up towards the settlement, whose honey-coloured stone houses huddle against a mountainous backdrop. Fanning out from the minuscule main square, the centre of Fornalutx is a quaint affair of narrow cobbled streets, stepped to facilitate mule traffic, though nowadays you're more likely to be hit by a Mercedes than obstructed by a mule: foreigners love the place and own about half of the village's three hundred houses. This sizeable expatriate community sustains one excellent **restaurant**, the *Bella Vista*, just off the main square on the road back towards Sóller. Enjoying fabulous views over the valley, it offers seafood and traditional Mallorcan cuisine, with full meals costing around 2500ptas. It's fine just to have a drink here too, or you can head off to the main square, where there are a couple of small, cheap cafés.

As for **accommodation**, the village boasts the charming, one-star *Hostal Ca Ses Monges*, c/Alba 22 (☎971 631997; ⑥), which occupies an attractively furnished and spotlessly clean old stone house with a terraced garden overlooking the orchards behind.

If you're driving from Sóller to Biniaraix, follow the signs from the town centre. It's easy enough to find your way, but note that c/Sa Lluna is a one-way street for traffic entering Sóller from the east.

If you're contemplating hiking the entire Cornadors Circuit, note that there have been problems with access beyond the Barranc de Biniarix, courtesy of a local landowner; before you set out, check the current position at Sóller tourist office.

Sóller and around

Reservations are esssential. To get there, walk down the main street from the square (as for the *Bella Vista*) and take the first left just beyond the conspicuous railings – a minute's walk.

If you've walked to Fornalutx and are heading back to Sóller, you might want to consider a **taxi**. The fare is just 1500ptas – if you don't spot one hanging around, telephone ☎971 630571.

Port de Sóller

PORT DE SÓLLER is one of the most popular resorts on the west coast, and its horseshoe-shaped bay must be the most photographed spot on the island after the package resorts around Palma. The high jinks of the Badia de Palma are about the last thing imaginable down here, though – the place is more than a little staid. There's no point in staying just for the swimming either, since, although the water is warm and calm, it's often surprisingly murky (courtesy of the yachts at anchor), and neither are the two diminutive sandy beaches much to boast about: the (unnamed) one near the boat dock is overlooked on all sides – by the road, hotels and restaurants – while the other, the **Platja d'En Repic**, offers a little more seclusion, but not much. Nevertheless, Port de Sóller does have some merits, especially its selection of excellent seafood restaurants and the enjoyable hour-long hike west to the **lighthouse** (*far*), which guards the cliffs above the entrance to its inlet. From here, the views out over the wild and rocky coast are spectacular, especially at sunset. Directions couldn't be easier as there's a tarmac road all the way: from the jetties on the seafront behind the tram terminus, walk round the southern side of the bay past Platja d'En Repic and keep going, following the signs.

See p.119 for details of an excellent coastal walk from Deià to Port de Sóller.

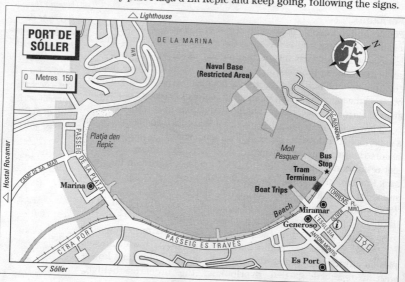

If you're around here in the second week of May, be sure to catch the **Festa de Nostra Senyora de la Victòria**, which commemorates the events of May 1561 when a large force of Arab pirates came to a sticky end after sacking Sóller. The Mallorcans had been taken by surprise, but they ambushed and massacred the Arabs as they returned to their ships and took grisly revenge by planting the raiders' heads on stakes. The story – bar decapitations – is played out in chaotic, alcoholic fashion every year at the festival. The re-enactment begins with the arrival of the pirates by boat, and continues with fancy-dress Christians and Arabs battling it out through the streets of the port, to the sound of blanks being fired in the air from antique rifles. The tourist office can give you a rough idea of the schedule of events, plus details of the dances and parties that follow.

Practicalities

Trams from Sóller shadow the main road and clank to a full stop beside the jetties, bang in the centre of town. From here, it's a couple of minutes' walk east to the **Oficina d'Informació Turística**, beside the church on c/Canonge Oliver (June–Sept Mon–Fri 9.30am–5pm, Sat 9.30am–1.30pm; ☎971 631600). They carry a reasonable range of local information, including restaurant and accommodation lists, maps and boat-trip details. **Bike hire** is available from Vivas, back towards Platja d'En Repic at Passeig Es Través 15 (☎971 630088).

During peak season there's a vague chance of a reasonably priced room at several of the town's hotels, beginning behind the boat dock at either the mundane *Hotel Miramar*, c/de la Marina 12 (April–Oct; ☎971 631350, fax 971 632671; ③), a standard-issue modern block with just thirty frugal rooms, or at the equally unexciting, 100-room *Hotel Generoso*, nearby at c/de la Marina 4 (☎971 631450, fax 971 632200; ④). Moving upmarket, and just a few minutes' walk from the jetties, the three-star *Hotel Es Port*, c/Antoni Montis 43 (☎971 631650, fax 971 631662; ④), boasts lovely gardens, a swimming pool, and a charming reception area set inside a renovated medieval manor house. The hotel's rooms are, however, far less endearing, occupying an unimaginatively modern concrete block. Alternatively, you could try the hotels overlooking the Platja d'En Repic, a quieter and marginally more attractive part of town about 1.5km round the bay from the ferry dock. Easily the best bet here is the smart, two-star *Hotel Marina* (April–Oct; ☎971 631461, fax 971 634182; ⑤); alternatively there's a one-star *hostal*, the unassuming *Los Geranios*, Passeig de Sa Platja 15 (☎971 631440, fax 971 631651; ⑤).

Port de Sóller has several fine **seafood** restaurants within a few steps of the jetties. The pick of the bunch is the spick-and-span *Sa Llotja des Peix* beside Moll Pesquer, the old fishing jetty, where a delicious *menú del día* will set you back a bargain 2300ptas. Other excellent and comparable alternatives are clustered on c/Santa

Caterina d'Alexandria, a narrow side street cutting up from the waterfront next to Moll Pesquer, including *El Pirata*, with its flashy nautical decor at no.7, and the excellent *Es Racó*, next door at no.6.

In the summer, **boats** leave the dock by the tram terminus for day excursions along the coast: south to Cala Deià (1 weekly; 1500ptas) and Sa Foradada (1 weekly; 2000ptas), and north to Sa Calobra (3 daily; 2000ptas) and Cala Tuent (1 weekly; 2000ptas). Cala Deià (see p.117) is the most diverting of the destinations, though each trip is a good way of seeing a chunk of coast. You pay for the round trip, but you don't, of course, have to come back.

The Jardins d'Alfabia

Heading south from Sóller, the road towards Palma tunnels through the mountains to emerge beside the **Jardins d'Alfabia** – though you can, as a scenic alternative, hairpin up and over the mountains, with the road threading its way past the **Coll de Sóller**, a rocky pass with a car park and lookout point offering splendid views out over the coast. Whichever route you choose, stop by the Jardins d'Alfabia, lush and beautiful terraced gardens surrounding a genteel *hacienda*. Shortly after the Reconquest, Jaume I granted the estate of Alfabia to a prominent Moor by the name of Benhabet. Seeing which way the historical wind was blowing, Benhabet, as governor of Pollença, had thrown his support behind Jaume, provisioning the Catalan army during the invasion. There was no way Jaume I could leave his ally in charge of Pollença (and anyway it was already pledged to a Catalan noble), but he was able to reward him with this generous portion of land. Benhabet planned his new estate in the Moorish manner, channelling water from the surrounding mountains to irrigate the fields and fashion oasis-like gardens. Generations of island gentry added to the estate, but without marring Benhabet's original design, thus creating the homogenous ensemble that survives today.

*The Jardins
d'Alfabia are
open Mon–Fri
9.30am–
5.30pm
(June–Aug
9.30am–
6.30pm), Sat
9.30am–1pm;
500ptas.*

From the roadside, visitors follow a stately avenue of plane trees towards the house, but, before reaching the gatehouse, they're directed up a flight of stone steps and into the **gardens**. Here, a footpath leads past ivy-covered stone walls, gurgling watercourses and brightly coloured flowers cascading over narrow terraces. Patterns of light and shade are created by trellises of jasmine and wisteria, while palm and fruit trees jostle upwards, allowing only the occasional glimpse of the surrounding citrus groves. At the end of the path, the gardens' highlight is a verdant jungle of palm trees, bamboo and bullrushes tangling a tiny pool. It's an enchanting spot, especially on a hot summer's day, and an outdoor **bar** sells big glasses of freshly squeezed orange juice, a snip at 250ptas. A few paces away is the **house**, a rather mundane, verandaed *hacienda* whose handful of rooms house an eccentric mix of antiques and curios. Pride of place goes to a superb fourteenth-century **oak chair** adorned with delightful bas-relief scenes

honouring Mallorca's royals. The chair was ordered by the
uncrowned Jaume IV, though he never had a chance to sit on it:
after the Battle of Llucmajor in 1349, in which his father, Jaume
III, was killed by the Aragonese, he was captured and spent the
rest of his days in exile.

At the front of the house, the cobbled **courtyard** is shaded by a
giant plane tree and surrounded by pretty, rustic outbuildings;
beyond lies the **gatehouse**, an imposing structure sheltering a fine
coffered ceiling of Mudéjar design, with an inscription praising Allah.

Orient and the Castell d'Alaró

About 3km south of Alfabia along the C711, a country road forks east
past the plane trees and sun-bleached walls of the unassuming market town of **BUNYOLA**, before snaking across the forested foothills
of the Serra de Tramuntana. It's a beautiful drive (the tarmac's in
good nick too, though some of the bends are nerve-jangling) that
brings you, after about 13km, to **ORIENT**. This remote hamlet of
ancient houses is scattered along the eastern side of the lovely Vall
d'Orient, with hills rising all around olive and almond groves. There's
even somewhere to **stay** in the village, the simple, tiny *Hostal-residencia Muntanya* at c/Bordoy 6 (☎971 615373; ⑤), although this
is as nothing compared to the romantic *Hotel L'Hermitage* (mid-
Dec to Oct; ☎971 180303; ⑨), a luxuriously renovated medieval
manor house roughly 1km beyond Orient on the PM210. The hotel
gardens are lovely, the scenery gorgeous and the **restaurant**, with its
mammoth antique olive press, excellent, even if the decor is a little
twee. Needless to say, advance reservations are pretty much essential and, if you're paying this sort of money, try to get one of the four
rooms in the old manor house, rather than one of the twenty in the
modern annexe.

The Castell d'Alaró

Beyond *Hotel L'Hermitage*, the PM210 sticks to the ridge overlooking the narrow valley of the Torrent d'En Paragon for around 3km,
before veering south to slip between a pair of molar-like hills whose
bare rocky flanks tower above the surrounding forest and scrub. The
more westerly of the two sports the sparse ruins of the **Castell
d'Alaró**, originally a Moorish stronghold but rebuilt by Jaume I.
Visible for miles around, the castle looks impregnable on its lofty
perch, and it certainly impeded the Aragonese invasion of 1285.
Indeed, Alfonso III was so irritated by the effort involved in captur-
ing the place that he had the garrison's two commanders roasted
alive. Not that the men concerned helped their own cause. When an
Aragonese messenger suggested terms for surrender, they punned
on Alfonso's name in Catalan, calling him "fish-face" (*anfos* means
"perch"). Goodness knows what would have happened to them if
they had thought of something really rude.

Access to the castle is from the south: coming from Orient, watch for the signposted right turn just beyond the "Kilometre 18" stone marker. The first 3km of this narrow side road are well-surfaced, but the last 1.3km is gravel and dirt, with a tight series of hairpins negotiating a very steep hillside – after rain it's especially hazardous. The road emerges at an old ramshackle farmstead whose barn now holds the *Es Verger*, a **restaurant** with a car park. It's tempting to linger here: the views down over the plain are sumptuous and the food delicious, particularly the house speciality, oven-baked lamb. From the restaurant you can spy the ruins of the castle above, about an hour's walk away along a clearly marked track. The trail leads to the castle's stone gateway, beyond which lies an expansive wooded plateau accommodating the fragmentary ruins of the fortress, the tiny pilgrims' church of **Mare de Déu del Refugi**, and a simple restaurant and bar, where they serve traditional Mallorcan food – the *pa amb oli* is a snip at 500ptas.

Back on the PM210, about 1km south of the turn-off for the castle, **ALARÓ** itself is a sleepy little town of shuttered stone houses, just 5km from tedious Consell on the main Palma–Port d'Alcúdia highway.

Down the coast from Deià to Port d'Andratx

The southwesterly reaches of the **Serra de Tramuntana** rise out of the flatlands around Palma, with the range's forested foothills and sheltered valleys soon giving way to the craggy, wooded mountains that crimp most of the seashore. Several fast roads link Palma with the coast – the prettiest runs the 15km to Valldemossa – and a delightful network of country roads patterns the foothills, but the key sights (and the best scenery) are most readily reached along the main coastal road, the C710.

From Sóller, this main road skirts the broad and wooded slopes of the Puig d'es Teix to reach, after 10km, **Deià**, an ancient mountain village which perches precariously high above the seashore, clinging to the fame brought by Robert Graves. Moving on, the next 20km of coastline boasts three of the island's star attractions: **Son Marroig**, the well-appointed mansion of the Mallorca-loving archduke, Ludwig Salvator; the hilltop monastery of **Valldemossa**, complete with its gloomy cloisters and choice examples of modern art; and the old grandee's mansion and estate of **La Granja**. Allied to some of the island's finest coastal scenery, this captivating trio is hard to beat, although the tiered hamlets that decorate the coast further down the road are also instantly beguiling. Of these, both **Banyalbufar** and **Estellencs** occupy fine sites and are well worth at least a fleeting visit – or you can travel inland from La Granja, climbing the slopes of the

A fine walk connects Valldemossa with Deià; see p.125 for details.

leafy foothills and rambling through secluded valleys of almond, olive and carob trees, to reach the charming village of **Galilea**. Both the Galilea route and the C710 emerge from the Serra de Tramuntana at **Andratx**, a crossroads town with easy access to the tiny port of **Sant Elm** and the more commercialized harbour-cum-resort of **Port d'Andratx**.

Beach lovers have meagre pickings in this part of the island. There's a good sandy beach with safe swimming at Sant Elm, but further up the coast, shingle strips will have to suffice. The most impressive of these is **Cala de Deià**, set in the shadow of the mountains at the end of a narrow ravine. **Accommodation** can be hard to find, too. Each of the destinations mentioned above, with the exception of Galilea, has at least a couple of places to stay, but you're strongly advised to book well ahead from June to September or even October. With their clusters of hotels and *hostals*, Deià, Banyalbufar and Port d'Andratx represent the best bets for a last-minute vacancy, with Sant Elm the fourth favourite.

A **bus** service runs regularly from Palma to Valldemossa, Son Marroig and Deià, continuing on to Sóller and its port. There are also fast and frequent buses from Palma to Andratx and Port d'Andratx. Along the C710 between Andratx and Valldemossa, however, you're limited to a Monday–Saturday once-daily service, which originates in Peguera (see p.99). Distances between destinations are short, so **taxis** can work out a reasonable proposition if you're in a group – the fare for the twenty-kilometre trip from Port de Sóller to Valldemossa, for example, is 3200ptas, 2200ptas to Deià.

Deià

DEIÀ is beautiful. The mighty Puig d'es Teix meets the coast here, and, although its lower slopes are now gentrified by the villas of the well-to-do, the mountain retains a formidable, almost mysterious presence, especially in the shadows of a moonlit night. Doubling as the coastal highway, Deià's main street skirts the base of the Teix, showing off most of the village's hotels and restaurants. At times, this main street is too congested to be much fun, but the tiny heart of the village, tumbling over a high and narrow ridge on the seaward side of the road, still manages a surprising tranquillity. Labyrinthine alleys of old peasant houses curl up to a pretty country church, in the precincts of which is buried **Robert Graves** – the village's most famous resident – his headstone marked simply "Robert Graves: Poeta, E.P.D." (*En Paz Descanse*: "Rest In Peace"). From the graveyard, the views out over the coast and of the Teix are truly memorable, with banks of carefully terraced fields tumbling down from the mountain towards the sea.

The **church** itself is a dark and gloomy affair decked out with Baroque altar pieces. Next door, one of the church's outbuildings holds a tiny museum, the **Museu Parroquial** (100ptas donation),

Robert Graves in Deià

The English poet, novelist and classical scholar **Robert Graves** (1895–1985) had two spells of living in Deià, the first in the 1930s, and the second from the end of World War II until his death. During his earlier stay, he shared a house at the edge of the village with **Laura Riding**, an American poet and dabbler in the mystical. Riding had arrived in England in 1926 and, after she became Graves's secretary and collaborator, the two of them began an affair. The tumultuous course of their relationship created sufficient furore for them to decide to leave England, choosing to settle in Mallorca on the advice of Gertrude Stein in 1930. The fuss was not simply a matter of morality – many of their friends were indifferent to adultery – but more to do with the self-styled "Holy Circle" they had founded, a cabalistic and intensely self-preoccupied literary-mystic group. The last straw came when Riding, in her attempt to control the group, jumped out of a window exclaiming "Goodbye, chaps", and the besotted Graves leapt after her. No wonder his mate T. E. Lawrence wrote of "madhouse minds" and of Graves "drowning in a quagmire".

They both recovered, but the dottiness continued once they'd moved to Deià, with Graves acting as doting servant to Laura, who he reinvented as a sort of all-knowing matriarch and muse. Simultaneously, Graves thumped away at his prose: he had already produced **Goodbye to All That** (1929), his bleak and painful memoirs of army service in the World War I trenches, but now came his other best-remembered books, **I, Claudius** (1934) and its sequel **Claudius the God** (1935), historical novels detailing the life and times of the Roman emperor. To Graves however, these "pot-boilers", as he styled them, were secondary to his poetry, and indeed his verse works of this period, usually carefully crafted love poems of melancholic tenderness in praise of Riding, were well received by the critics.

At the onset of the Spanish Civil War, Graves and Riding left Mallorca, not out of sympathy for the Republicans – Graves was far too reactionary for that – but to keep contact with friends and family. During their exile, Laura ditched Graves, who subsequently took up with a mutual friend, **Beryl Hodge**. After Graves had returned to Deià in 1946, he worked on **The White Goddess**, a controversial study of prehistoric and classical myth which argued the existence of an all-pervasive, primordial religion based on the worship of a poet-goddess. In the midst of his labours (the book was published in 1948), Beryl joined him, and in 1950 they were married in Palma. However, they didn't live happily ever after. Graves had a predilection for young women, claiming the need for female muses to inspire his poetic vision; outwardly Beryl accepted this waywardness, but without much enthusiasm. While his novels became increasingly well-known and profitable, his poetry, with its preoccupation with romantic love, fell out of fashion, and his last anthology, *Poems 1965–1968*, was widely criticized by the literary establishment.

Nevertheless, Graves's international reputation as a writer attracted a steady stream of visitors to Deià from the ranks of the literati, with the occasional film star adding to the self-regarding stew. By the middle of the 1970s, however, he had begun to lose his mind, ending his days in sad senility.

where there's a folksy assortment of religious bric-a-brac and – on the stairs – a photo of Graves in his Deià study. Graves put Deià on the international map, and nowadays the village is the haunt of long-term expatriates, mostly ex-flower children and artists living on ample trust funds, judging from the sorts of monthly rents charged. These inhabitants congregate at the **Cala de Deià**, the nearest thing the village has to a beach – some 200m of shingle at the back of a handsome rocky cove of jagged cliffs, boulders and white-crested surf. It's a great place for a swim, the water clean, deep and cool, and there's a ramshackle beach bar, but the cove often gets crowded, especially when the day-trippers arrive by boat from Port de Sóller (usually on Fridays). It takes about twenty minutes to walk from the village to the *cala*, a delightful stroll down a wooded ravine – for directions, see the first part of the "A coastal walk from Deià to Port de Sóller" box on p.119. To drive there, head north along the main road out of Deià and watch for the sign.

Practicalities

The Palma–Valldemossa–Port de Sóller **bus** scoots through Deià five times daily in each direction, though there's a reduced service on Sundays from October to March. There's no tourist office, but the village's hotels and *hostals* will gladly provide local advice on walks and weather, and can fix you up with a **taxi** – or do it yourself with Taxi Deià on ☎971 633588, mobile ☎908 099947.

Accommodation

There's a good chance of a moderately priced **room** in high season at two lovely little places in the old village near the church. The first is the *Fonda Villa Verde* (usually April–Oct; ☎971 639037; ④), which has a charming shaded terrace overlooking the Teix, and the second is *S'Hotel d'es Puig* (March to mid-Nov; ☎971 639409, fax 971 639210; ⑥), a smart and tastefully furnished hotel with eight bedrooms in an elegantly converted, four-storey old stone house. Deià also possesses two of the most luxurious hotels on Mallorca, both overlooking the main road. At the west end of the village, *Es Moli* (April–Oct; ☎971 639000, fax 971 639333; ⑨) occupies a grand, lavishly refurbished mansion, surrounded by lovely gardens and equipped with a swimming pool. There are seventy air-conditioned bedrooms here, done out in dapper, modern style and most have balconies with sea views. About 1km to the northeast, opposite the old centre of the village, the *Hotel-residencia La Residencia* is also sited in a gracious old mansion (☎971 639011, fax 971 639370; ⑨), but its furnishings and fittings are more self-conscious, the whole place proud of its clean, modern lines superimposed on rooms with an antique appearance – big wooden bedsteads, timbered ceilings and the like. Finally, and perhaps most delightful of them all, the one-star *Costa d'Or* (April–Oct; ☎971 639025, fax 971 639347) occupies a

Down the coast from Deià to Port d'Andratx

simply wonderful coastal setting just a couple of kilometres from Deià at the hamlet of **Llucalcari**: take the main road north out of Deià, pass the turning for Cala Deià and after another 1.6km watch for the big "Hotel" sign (there's no name); turn left off the main road here and a zigzagging access road leads the 600m down to the hotel; the bus stops at the top of this side road too. The *Costa d'Or* overlooks an undeveloped slice of coast and is surrounded by pine groves and olive terraces. There's a shaded terrace bar and a splendid outdoor swimming pool. The rooms vary – the cheaper doubles (⑤) are in two buildings at the back of the complex, the more expensive (⑥) look directly over the ocean; all are spotlessly clean.

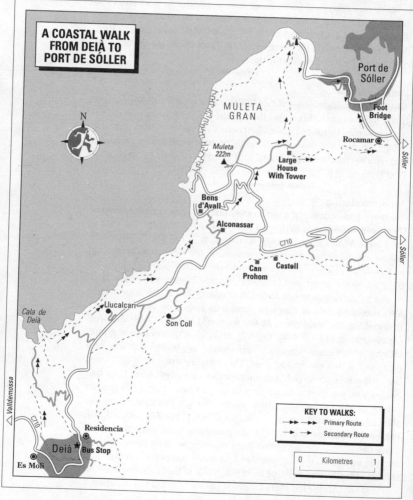

A COASTAL WALK
FROM DEIÀ TO
PORT DE SÓLLER

Port de Sóller

MULETA
GRAN

Foot
Bridge

Rocamar

△ Sóller

Muleta
222m

Large
House
With Tower

Bens
d'Avall

Alconassar

C710

△ Sóller

Can
Prohom

Castell

Cala de
Deià

Llucalcari

Son Coll

△ Valldemossa

C710

Residencia

Deià ★ Bus Stop

Es Molí

KEY TO WALKS:
➤➤ ➤➤ Primary Route
➤ ➤ Secondary Route

0   Kilometres   1

A coastal walk from Deià to Port de Sóller

12km, 4hr–4hr 30min.

Dotted with pine trees and abandoned olive terraces, the coast north of Deià slopes steeply down to the sea from the high massif of Sa Galera. On such steep terrain, run-off plays havoc with terrace walls and paths, so although this delightful walk is mainly easy, care is needed where erosion has taken place. All the way the views are superlative, from the panorama of the blue-green waters of Cala de Deià at the start, to the impressive 150-metre sea cliffs on the western edge of the Muleta Gran headland. The route, which sometimes drops almost to sea level and at other times rises to avoid difficult ground, is partially waymarked with red paint and cairns, although a certain amount of route-finding is required. There are stiles at all the boundary fences the path crosses. The walk starts in Deià village and ends at the *Rocamar* hotel in Port de Sóller; there's a fairly regular bus service between the two places which makes the round trip relatively straightforward, but he sure to confirm bus times beore you set out. The views from the bus are outstanding, too: notice especially the picturesque hamlet of Llucalcari, which cannot be seen from the coastal path below.

From the bus stop in Deià, walk in the Palma direction to a sharp right bend in the main road. Turn right down the shallow steps and continue downhill, past the Archeological Museum. After a few minutes take a right fork, where the road is marked with a "no through way" sign, and, where the lane ends, follow the signposted footpath which continues in the same direction. About 150m further, the footpath is marked by a green painted wooden arrow. After about 5min turn right (north) by a white "Cala" sign painted on a stone. Some 200m further on, the path joins a surfaced road, veering slightly to the left before reaching, after about 500m, tiny **Cala de Deià**, with its cluster of small boats and a beach bar serving meals in summer.

The **coastal path** begins up a flight of steps some 50m before the road end. There is another flight of steps closer to the beach, but this just leads to a squat square public toilet – the key is kept at the beach bar. After ascending the steps of the coastal path, ignore a left branch after about 5min, but 2min later turn left where the stepped path swings right, following the line of red painted stones. The path immediately turns right along a terrace, crosses a low wall and then turns sharp left downhill beside of the wall. One minute later it turns right again and leads to an attractive headland among pine trees, overlooking the sea and the white rocks of Cala de Deià.

Continue straight on along the path to the north, passing a *mirador* (viewpoint) with a private path descending to it from an unseen house above. Below the *mirador*, steps descend to a rocky inlet. Go halfway down these, then turn off right and ascend the earth path waymarked with red paint spots. Later, after crossing two stiles, there are notices saying "No picnic" next to a large circular table with surrounding seats – a useful landmark. Here the path forks left downhill, leading to another stile and, a few minutes later, passing below a stone enclosure and then past the left edge of a wall where the ground rises steeply inland. After the wall follow the direction of the red paint marks leading uphill to a headland with a few almond trees growing in bare red earth.

Round the corner beyond the headland there's an eroded gully, its edge protected with a wire fence. The path becomes less clear hereabouts. Go inland past a white house. Ascend to a terrace, which contours round the hillside to a 2–3 metre gap in the gully fence. At this point the stream, which created the gully, has been culverted. At the end of this terrace follow the lower path to reach the next stile and another terrace, quite low down near the sea. Next, go uphill by a fallen tree, cross a headland among boulders and heather, and then go fairly steeply upwards through terraces of olive trees. This part of the route is well marked and leads in about 15min to a path which contours left above a steep cliff to reach another stile.

The path then descends into and out of a stream bed and goes over a stile into a lane. Turn left and when the lane ends find the continuation of the footpath on the right. Five minutes later this reaches a concrete road near some houses. Follow it uphill and, after a few minutes of steep walking, cross another stream bed (normally dry) by means of the metal pegs in the enclosing dry-stone walls – an awkward manoeuvre which requires two free hands. Turn right along the wide road by the *Bens d'Avall restaurant* (closed in winter), and follow this uphill for 1.5km to reach the Muleta road junction. Turn left, then right, heading along a track towards a large farmhouse with a square tower. The most direct route to Port de Sóller from here is to turn right and go through the gate towards the house, following a path to the right between the buildings. Continue through a gate to the mule track which leads down to the *Rocamar* hotel. Turn left for the seafront and the stop for trams to Sóller town.

An alternative ending to the walk is to cross the Muleta Gran headland to the **lighthouse**, from where there are outstanding views of Port de Sóller's horsehoe-shaped harbour, and walk down the road to the port. To do this, turn left instead of right along the cross-track by the house with the tower, and climb over the wall on the right of the locked gate by means of inset metal bars. Follow the path ahead and after about 50m look for a blue arrow on the wall to the right. Cairns and more blue arrows show the way along a narrow path through abandoned terraces. The path descends a little, then rises across open ground strewn with wild flowers – look out for bright yellow hemispherical euphorbia bushes in spring. A track is met at the corner of a disused military building just before reaching the lighthouse.

Eating and drinking

As for **eating** in Deià, you're spoiled for choice. There's a concentration of cafés and restaurants along the main street towards the south end of the village. These include *Café La Fabrica*, which offers reasonably priced *tapas*, *bocadillos* and the traditional *pa amb oli* (bread rubbed with olive oil); and the *Bar-restaurante Deià*, where you'll pay a little more for a light meal (around 800ptas) but with the compensation of a terrace overlooking the valley. Further into the village, also on the main road, comes the excellent *Restaurante Jaime*, on the right-hand side, which specializes in traditional Mallorcan cuisine (dishes from around 1800ptas), and then *Las Palmeras*, a café with a shaded terrace much frequented by chess-playing expats; opposite is the *Restaurante Sa Dorada*, the best place in town for fish, with main courses from around 1800ptas. Both of Deià's deluxe hotels (see p.117) have excellent but expensive restaurants. At *Es Moli* it's the nearby *Restaurant Ca'n Quet*

(☎971 639196; closed Mon), with a *menú del día* for around 5500ptas, although even that's only half the price of a set meal at *El Olivo* (☎971 639011), adjoining *La Residencia*.

Son Marroig

Pressing on from Deià, the C710 snakes through the mountains for 3km to reach **Son Marroig**, an imposing L-shaped mansion perched high above the seashore (and just below the road). The house dates from late medieval times, but was refashioned in the nineteenth century to become the favourite residence of the Habsburg archduke **Ludwig Salvator** (1847–1915). Dynastically insignificant but extremely rich, the Austrian noble was a man in search of a hobby – and he found it in Mallorca. He first visited the island at the tender age of 19 and, falling head-over-heels in love with the place, returned to buy a chunk of the west coast between Deià and Valldemossa. In residence, Ludwig immersed himself in all things *Mallorquín*, learning the dialect and chronicling the island's topography, archeology, history and folklore in astounding detail. He churned out no fewer than seven volumes on the Balearics and, perhaps more importantly, played a leading role as a proto-environmentalist, conserving the coastline of his estates and, amongst many projects, paying for a team of geologists to chart the Coves del Drac (see p.180).

Son Marroig is open Mon–Sat 9.30am–2pm & 3–5/6pm; 350ptas.

The **house** boasts a handful of period rooms, whose antique furnishings and fittings are enlivened by an eclectic sample of Hispano-Arabic pottery. On display too are some of the archduke's manuscripts and pen drawings, as well as several interesting photographs of the man. It won't be long, however, before you're out in the **garden**, whose terraces are graced by a Neoclassical belvedere of Carrara marble. The views out along the jagged, forested coast are gorgeous, and down below is a slender promontory, known as **Sa Foradada**, "the rock pierced by a hole", where the archduke used to park his yacht – the hole in question is a strange circular affair, sited high up in the rock face at the end of the promontory. It takes about forty minutes to **walk** the three kilometres down to the tip, a largely straightforward excursion to a delightfully secluded and scenic spot. A sign on the gate at the beginning of the path (up the hill and to the left of the house) insists you need to get permission at Son Marroig before setting out – it's worth asking, but don't be too concerned if no one at the house seems bothered. There should be few problems with direction-finding on this short jaunt: about 100m beyond the gate, keep right at the fork in the track; and as you approach the end of the promontory, think carefully before deciding to attempt the precarious climb beyond the old jetties. On your return, you can slake your thirst at the café-bar *Son Marroig* overlooking the coast from beside the car park near the house.

Beyond Son Marroig, the C710 stays high above the coast, twisting through what was once the estate of the archduke en route to Valldemossa.

Valldemossa and around

The ancient and intriguing hill town of **VALLDEMOSSA** may at first appear disappointing if you're coming from Deià, as the C710 slices through the drab western outskirts to reach the centre. The best approach is from the south, where, with the mountains closing in, the road from Palma squeezes through a narrow, wooded defile before entering a lovely valley, whose tiered and terraced fields ascend to the town, a sloping jumble of rusticated houses and monastic buildings backclothed by the mountains. The origins of Valldemossa date to the early fourteenth century, when the asthmatic King Sancho built a royal palace here in the hills where the air was easier to breathe. Later, in 1399, the palace was gifted to Carthusian monks from Tarragona, who converted and extended the original buildings into a **monastery**, which is now the island's most visited building after Palma cathedral. Besides the monastery, however, there's not much to Valldemossa. The narrow cobbled lanes of the oldest part of town tumble prettily down the hillside beneath the monastery, but it only takes a few minutes' to explore them and there are only two specific sights: the dilapidated hulk of the church of **Sant Bartomeu** and – round the back along a narrow alley, c/Rectoria, at no. 5 – the humble birthplace of **Santa Catalina Thomàs**, a sixteenth-century nun revered for her piety. The interior has been turned into a glitzy little shrine.

The monastery

*The monastery
at Valldemossa
is open
March–Oct
Mon–Sat
9.30am–
1.20pm &
3–6pm, Sun
10am–1pm;
Nov–Feb
Mon–Sat
9.30am–
1.20pm &
3–5.30pm, Sun
10am–1pm;
1100ptas.*

Remodelled on several occasions, most of the present complex of the **Real Cartuja de Jesús de Nazaret** (Royal Carthusian Monastery of Jesus of Nazareth) is of seventeenth- and eighteenth-century construction. It owes its present notoriety almost entirely to the novelist and republican polemicist **George Sand**, who, with her companion, the composer **Frédéric Chopin**, lived here for four months in 1838–39. Just three years earlier the last monks had been evicted during the liberal-inspired suppression of the monasteries, so the pair were able to rent a commodious set of vacant cells. Their stay is commemorated in Sand's *A Winter in Majorca*, a stodgy, self-important book that is considerably overplayed hereabouts, being available in just about every European language. Reading the book today, what comes through strongly is the couple's mean-spirited contempt for their Spanish neighbours: Sand explains that their nickname for Mallorca, "Monkey Island", was coined for its "crafty, thieving and yet innocent" inhabitants, who, she asserts, are "heartless, selfish and impertinent". What the villagers made of Sand is unknown, but her trouser-wearing, cigar-smoking image – along with her "living in sin" – could hardly have made the woman popular.

There's an obvious, though limited curiosity in looking around Sand and Chopin's old quarters, but the monastery boasts far more interesting diversions, and it's easy to follow the multilingual signs around. A visit begins in the gloomy, aisleless **church**, a square and heavy construction with a kitsch high altar and barrel vaulting that's distinguished by its Late Baroque ceiling paintings and fanciful bishop's throne, though the lines of the nave are spoiled by the clumsy wooden stalls of the choir. Beyond the church lie the shadowy **cloisters**, where the first port of call is the **pharmacy**, which survived the expulsion of the monks to serve the town's medicinal needs well into the twentieth century. Its shelves are crammed with a host of beautifully decorated majolica jars, antique glass receptacles and painted wood boxes, each carefully inscribed with the name of a potion or drug.

The nearby **prior's cell** is, despite its name, a comfortable suite of bright, sizeable rooms, enhanced by access to a private garden with splendid views down the valley. The cell, together with the adjoining library, dining and audience rooms, are graced by a wide assortment of religious objets d'art. These include a handsome assortment of majolica and tin-glazed tiles and, displayed in the library, two fine but unattributed medieval triptychs: the *Adoration of the Magi*, a charmingly naive painting in the Flemish style, and an intricate three-panel marble sculpture celebrating the marriage of Pedro II of Aragon. This degree of luxury – the other cells are of similar proportions – was clearly not what the ascetic St Bruno had in mind when he founded the Carthusian order in the eleventh century, but it's hard to blame the monks at Valldemossa for lightening what must have been a very heavy burden of privations. Bruno's rigorous regime, inspired by his years as a hermit, had his monks in almost continuous isolation, gathering together only for certain church services and to eat in the refectory on Sundays. At other times, lay brothers fed the monks through hatches along the cloister corridors, though this was hardly an onerous task: three days a week the monks had only bread and water, and they never ate meat. The diet and the mountain air, however, seemed to suit: the Valldemossa monks' longevity was proverbial.

Along the corridor, **Cell No. 2** exhibits miscellaneous curios relating to Chopin and Sand, from portraits and a lock of hair to musical scores and letters (it was in this cell that the composer wrote the *"Raindrop" Prelude*). There's more of the same next door in **Cell No. 4**, plus Chopin's favourite piano, which only arrived after three months of unbelievable complications, just three weeks before the couple left for Paris. Considering the hype, these incidental mementos are something of an anticlimax. Neither do things improve much in the ground-floor galleries of the adjacent **Museu Municipal**, which feature local landscape painters and take a stab at tracing the diligent endeavours of Archduke Ludwig Salvator (see p.121). But don't give up: upstairs, another part of the museum (the "Museu Municipal Art Contemporani") has a small but outstanding collection of **modern art**, including work by Miró, Picasso, Francis Bacon and sketches by Henry Moore. There's also a substantial sample of the work of the Spanish modernist Juli Ramís (1909–1990), from geometric abstractions through to forceful, expressionistic paintings like *The Blue Lady* (*Dama Blava*).

Back beside the prior's cell, be sure to take the doorway which leads outside the cloisters to the **Palace of King Sancho**. It's not the original medieval palace at all – that disappeared long ago – but this fortified mansion is the oldest part of the complex and its imposing walls, mostly dating from the sixteenth century, accommodate a string of handsome period rooms cluttered with faded paintings and other curios. There's also an eccentric wooden drawbridge, linking two rooms above the original entrance, situated on the far side of the building, away from the cloisters. The "palace" was used as a political prison for much of its history, its most celebrated internee being the liberal reformer Gaspar de Jovellanos, a victim of the royal favourite Manuel de Godoy, who had him locked up here from 1801 to 1802. Nowadays, the palace has regular displays of folk dancing and there are hourly Chopin piano concerts.

Practicalities

There are several car parks along the modern bypass that skirts Valldemossa to the north; the biggest of these, at the west end of town, is where **buses** stop. Regular services arrive from Palma, 15km away, before continuing to Deià and Sóller; except on Sundays, one bus a day also comes from Peguera, Andratx and Estellencs. From the bus stop, it's just a couple of minutes' walk to the monastery – cross the bypass and keep going straight on. The town doesn't have a tourist office and maps of the place are impossible to come by, but orientation is easy – use the monastery, on the west side of the town centre, as your landmark.

Accommodation in Valldemossa itself is limited to the *Ca'n Mario*, c/Uetam 8 (☎971 612122; ④), an attractive little *hostal* where an elegant, antique-cluttered foyer leads to comfortably old-fashioned rooms; it's situated just a few seconds' walk from the monastery – from the pedestrianized area between the cloisters and the palace, go downhill and take the first turning on the right. The only other option nearby, off the C710 just over 2km south of town, is the solitary *Hotel Residencia Vistamar* (☎971 612300, fax 971 612583; ⑨), an opulently converted eighteenth-century *finca* (farmhouse) whose gardens and swimming pool abut a deep, green gully that plunges down towards the sea. It's a fancy place to stay, and the rooms are decorated in traditional style with dark wood and bright fabrics.

The centre of Valldemossa heaves with **restaurants and cafés**, mostly geared up for day-trippers – many offer dire fast food at inflated prices. Nonetheless, there are a couple of quality places amongst the dross, including *Ca'n Pedro* (closed Sun eve), a large café-restaurant beside the main car park, where tasty cheese omelettes start at 675ptas. There's also the popular *Ca'n Costa* (closed Tues), which occupies a *finca* about 2km out of town on the Deià road; the decor is over the top – old farm equipment and other rusticated touches – but the shaded terrace is lovely, and the Mallorcan cuisine is excellent and affordable, with main course from around 1500ptas.

From Valldemossa to Puig d'es Teix by the Archduke's Path

12.5km, 674m of ascent; 4hr 30min–5hr.

As elsewhere in Mallorca, the mountains around Valldemossa are criss-crossed with paths made by charcoal-burners, hunters and other local people, but this area is particularly richly endowed because of the work of the nineteenth-century Austrian archduke **Ludwig Salvator** (see p.121), who had some wonderful paths constructed so that he could ride on horseback to admire the scenery. Today walkers benefit from Salvator's efforts because his estate was acquired by ICONA (the island's organization for nature conservation) in 1967. The country between Valldemossa and Deià is mountainous and wild, abounding in steep cliffs and rocky summits. The lower slopes are wooded but the tops are almost devoid of vegetation, with numerous dramatic viewpoints, many of them overlooking the sea. The terrain is rough and even the paths are stony, but the following circular walk – which can be lengthened or shortened to suit – is a classic, showing the best of the area.

From the back of the small car park at the edge of Valldemossa, opposite the road which forks left into the town from the Palma road, head uphill to the school. Go up the steps at the left-hand side of the school, then turn right and almost immediately left. Descend slightly then turn left up an old path that leads into the woods, entered by a stile over a gate. The stony path rises moderately steeply in numerous bends to reach an opening in the wall at the edge of the wooded plain, the **Pla d'es Pouet** (a short cut near the top is waymarked, but it makes little difference which way you go). From the wall go straight on across the level ground to reach an old **well** (now polluted) in a large clearing with a rotten fallen tree. This well is a vital reference point in a confusing area and it is essential to take your bearings carefully. The option to lengthen the walk, taking in Veià, begins here and is described on p.127.

For the main walk be careful to take the path bearing slightly right, northeast at first and then north, which leads easily up to the **Coll de S'Estret de Son Gallard**. On the col is a barrier of brushwood set up by hunters who still practise the traditional *caza a coll* method, which you can observe: birds are lured into flying along artificial tunnels created by cutting passages through the trees, then captured in nets. From the nearby stone seats in the form of a "V", the path continues uphill to the right. **Cova de Ermita Guillem**, an interesting hermit's cave that offers excellent shelter if you are unlucky with the weather, can be visited to the south of the main path – look for a branch path on the right, which leads to the enclosure in front of the cave. The cave looks well cared for and contains icons and candles. To rejoin the uphill main path, retrace your steps for about 100m and then branch sharply off to the right. The most spectacular part of the walk begins here. It's a wide and easy walkway on the edge of cliffs with a simply breathtaking view.

As you approach Caragolí, a path branching off left towards the cliffs offers the possibility of an adventurous **descent to Deià** by a thrilling, but precarious cliff path. If you're tempted to try this, find the start by making for the largest of the holm oaks on the horizon, growing out of a pothole. A path from this holm oak descends into the woods below, then look out for a large *sitja* (charcoal-worker's shelter), with two

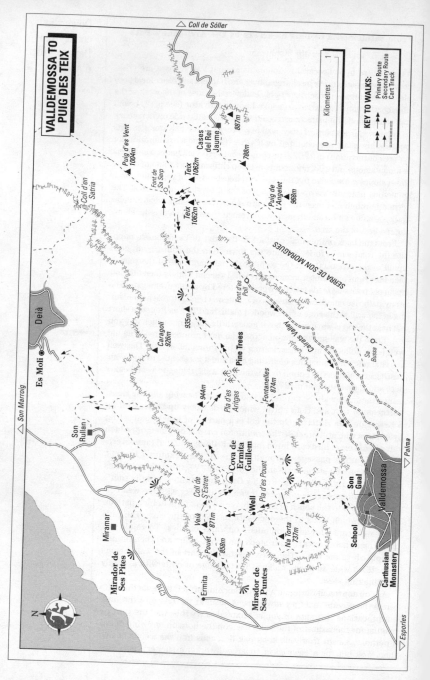

VALLDEMOSSA TO
PUIG DES TEIX

KEY TO WALKS:
Primary Route
Secondary Route
Cart Track

Kilometres
0   1

△ Coll de Sóller

▲ Puig d'es Vent
1004m

Font de
Sa Serp

Cases
del Rei
Jaume   ■   887m

▲ Teix
1062m

▲ Teix
1062m

▲ 788m

Puig de
L'Angelet
968m

SERRA DE SON MORAGUES

Coll d'en
Satria

Deià

○ Es Moli

△ Son Marroig

▲ 935m

Font d'es
Poll

Carrais Valley

○ Sa
Bassa

▲ Caragoli
926m

Pine Trees

Son
Rullan ■

▲ 944m

Pla d'es
Aritges

Fontanelles
874m

Cova de
Ermita
Guillem ●

Coll de
S'Estret

Pla d'es Pouet

● Well

Son
Gual

Valldemossa

▷ Palma

Miramar ■

Veià

Pouet
858m

871m

Na Torta
737m

School

Carthusian
Monastery

Mirador
de Ses Pites

Ermita

Mirador de
Ses Puntes

▷ Esporles

N

126

THE GUIDE: CHAPTER 2

stone shelters and a stone bread-oven: turn right here, join another track and turn left. Reaching a gate, double-back along terraces to a *caseta* (field-house), from where a path leads down to the *Es Moli* hotel in Deià

Following the main path, you can spy Port de Sóller down on the coast and the mountains Major, Teix and Galatzó rising high above the seashore. Then the path climbs southeast to 944m before descending gently over a sloping, arid plain, the **Pla d'es Aritges** (*aritge* is smilax, a plant with vicious backward curving thorns). A path junction at an isolated group of pine trees offers a short-cut back to Valldemossa via **Fontanelles**. To continue on the main route, take the left fork northeast, which brings you over a 935-metre top and, shortly after, to a viewpoint overlooking Deià. After this the path swings southeast and begins to descend to the Teix path junction.

The junction is marked by a metre-high conical cairn. Here, branch left, (northeast) on a path which scrambles up a little gully and then proceed over a wall positioned at right angles to the edge of a cliff. Stone steps take you to the top of the wall and an iron ladder down the far side. It's an easy walk to the **Pla de Sa Serp**, a plain where there is a spring, the Font de Sa Serp. A well-used path leads up to the col between the two tops and on to the main west summit of Teix (1062m), where the views are especially good to the northeast, looking over the Sóller valley to Mitx Dia, the western summit of Puig Major, with the tops of Cornadors, L'Ofre and the Alfabia ridge forming a fascinating skyline. Return to the Teix path junction by the same route (avoid the difficult-to-follow route southwest from Teix towards Sa Bassa) and turn left to follow the main track down the **Cairats valley**. First you'll come to an old "snowhouse" (a deep hole used for storing ice in winter), then a mountain hut and below that a spring and picnic site, the **Font d'es Poll** (Well of the Poplar). The wide track beyond is rather stony but there are no route-finding problems. On the way down you'll see reconstructions of a *sitja*, a charcoal-worker's shelter, signposted and labelled. Keep on the main track down the Cairats valley, going over a wall via stone steps to the left of a locked gate. Ignore two branches left, before joining a road which leads past a number of large new houses down to an old house with a square tower, Son Gual, from where there's a superb view over the old part of Valldemossa.

Extension of the walk to Mirador de Ses Puntes and Veià

1.5km, 116m of ascent; 45min.

From the well in the clearing on the Pla d'es Pouet, take the path which leads northwest at first, before zigzagging uphill and swinging west. Fork left shortly after passing an old bread-oven to reach the **Mirador de Ses Puntes**. From this superb viewpoint return to the fork and take the left branch, which rises through the trees to the top of **Pouet** (858m) and, after a little dip, **Veià** (871m). For much of the way the path is the wide bridleway built by Ludwig Salvator; from it you can look down on Sa Foradada, a rocky headland near his house, Son Marroig, pierced with an enormous hole. From the ruined shelter on Veià the path descends to the Coll de S'Estret de Son Gallard, where you rejoin the main path up from the well.

Port de Valldemossa

The closest spot to Valldemossa for a swim is **Port de
Valldemossa**, a hamlet set in the shadow of the mountains at the
mouth of a narrow, craggy cove. The beach here is small and
shingly, and prone to be battered by the surf, but the scenery is
stunning and the village sports a handful of **restaurants**. The pick
of the bunch is the busy *Es Port*, which has a well-deserved reputation for its superb seafood, with main courses from around
1900ptas. The drive down to the hamlet, once Valldemossa's gateway to the outside world, is stimulating: head south out of town
along the C710 and, after about 1.5km, turn right at the sign and
follow the twisty, six-kilometre-long side road through the mountains. There's no public transport.

La Granja and Esportes

*La Granja is
open daily
10am–6pm;
1500ptas.*

The *hacienda* of **La Granja** nestles in a tranquil wooded and terraced valley some 10km southwest from Valldemossa – follow the
C710 for about 8.5km and take the signposted left turn. The house
and its grounds are a popular day trip (Palma–Estellencs **buses**
stop by the entrance), but, despite the many visitors, the estate
maintains a languorous air of old patrician comfort. There's hardly anything new or modern on view, but neither does this seem
contrived. La Granja was occupied until very recently by the
Fortuny family, who took possession in the mid-fifteenth century
– from about the 1920s onwards it seems that modernization simply never crossed their minds.

From the entrance in front of the main forecourt, signs direct
you up round the back of the house, past an incidental collection
of well-weathered farming tackle and on into the tiny formal **gardens**. Next door, a small patio leads to the main **house**, a ramshackle sequence of apartments strewn with domestic clutter –
everything from childrens' games and mannequins, through old
costumes, musical instruments and a cabinet of fans, to a fully
equipped antique kitchen. There's also a delightful little theatre,
where plays were once performed for the household in a manner
common amongst Europe's nineteenth-century rural landowners.
Likewise, the dining room, with its faded paintings and heavy
drapes, has a real touch of country elegance, as does the graceful
first-floor loggia. Look out also for the finely crafted, green-tinted
Mallorcan chandeliers, and the beautiful majolica tile-panels that
embellish several walls.

Tagged onto the house, a series of **workrooms** recall the days
when La Granja was a profitable and almost entirely self-sufficient
concern. A wine press, almond and olive oil mills prepared the
estate's produce for export, whilst plumbers, carpenters, cobblers,
weavers and sail-makers all kept pace with domestic requirements
from their specialized workshops. The Fortunys were one of

Mallorca's more enlightened landowning families, and employees were well fed by the kitchen staff, who made cheeses, bread and preserves by hand. The main kitchen is in one of the **cellars**, where you'll also find a grain store and a "torture chamber", an entirely inappropriate recent addition. Moving on, you'll soon reach the family **chapel**, a dinky little affair with kitsch silver-winged angels, and then the expansive **forecourt**, shaded by plane trees and surrounded by antiquated workshops where costumed "artisans" practise traditional crafts such as wood-turning and candle-making. This part of the visit is a bit bogus, but good fun all the same – and the homemade pastries and doughnuts are lip-smacking. You may also coincide with a mildly diverting display of Mallorcan **folk dancing** (summer Wed & Fri 3.30–5pm).

Esporles

On the road from La Granja towards Palma, it's a couple of kilometres to **ESPORLES**, an amiable, leafy little town whose elongated main street follows the line of an ancient stone watercourse. This is Mallorca away from the tourist zone and although there's no special reason to stop, it's an attractive place to overnight. The only place to stay is the one-star *Hostal Central* (☎971 610202; ③), an unassuming *hostal* in an appealing old stone house, just off the main drag and by the church at Plaça Espanya 8. There's somewhere good to eat too, the *Restaurante Méson la Villa*, whose specialities are suckling pig and oven-roasted lamb; it's located a few metres from the church, across the street at c/Sant Pere 5 (daily 8–11pm).

Puigpunyent and Galilea

Heading southwest from La Granja, a narrow and difficult country road heads up a V-shaped valley before snaking through the foothills of the Serra de Tramuntana. After 10km you come to **PUIGPUNYENT**, a workaday farmers' village marginally enhanced by a seventeenth-century church with a squat bell tower.

Continuing southwest, the road threads along a benign valley of citrus groves and olive trees on its way to **GALILEA**, 4km away, an engaging scattering of whitewashed farmsteads built in sight of a stolid hilltop church. There's a rusty old café-bar beside the church, but the best place to soak up the bucolic atmosphere is at the *Bar Galilea*, below the church and beside the through road, where the views from the terrace are gorgeous and the Mallorcan **food** is both delicious and cheap, with filling snacks from just 500ptas.

Beyond Galilea, the road wriggles its way through to the unremarkable settlement of Capdellà, before squeezing through the mountains – the most beautiful, and nerve-jangling, part of the drive – for a further 8km to enter Andratx (see p.131) from the east.

Port d'es Canonge and Banyalbufar

Back on the C710, just beyond the turning for La Granja, a narrow side road forks down to the coast at **PORT D'ES CANONGE**. The five-kilometre journey down through thickly forested hills is splendid, but the settlement itself is disappointing, a scrawny, modern *urbanització* flanking a shingle beach. Far better, in fact, to stay on the main coast road for a further 6km, enjoying spectacular views on the way to the attractive village of **BANYALBUFAR**, whose terraced fields cling gingerly to the coastal cliffs. The land here has been cultivated since Moorish times, with a spring above the village providing a water supply that's still channelled down the hillside along slender watercourses into open storage cisterns, the unlikely-looking home for a few carp. The village itself is bisected by its main street, also the C710, with whitewashed houses and narrow cobbled lanes to either side. The cute main square perches above the C710, overlooked by a chunky parish church dating from the fifteenth century. It's a fine place to unwind and there's a rough and rocky **beach** fifteen minutes' walk away down the hill – ask locally for directions as the lanes that lead there are difficult to find.

Banyalbufar has two **hotels** and one **hostal**. The *Hotel Mar y Vent* has an enticing exterior but its rooms are spartan – although most have balconies with views of the sea, and there's a rooftop swimming pool too. It's on the main street towards the north end of the village (Feb–Nov; ☎971 618000, fax 971 618201; ⑤). There's probably more chance of a vacancy, however, at the rather more agreeable *Hostal Baronia*, at the south end of the main drag (April–Oct; ☎ & fax 971 618146; ④), an old-fashioned, laid-back sort of place with an outside pool and forty plain but perfectly adequate balconied bedrooms. At both the *Mar y Vent* and the *Baronia* the rooms are at the back in modern extensions which are attached to much older houses at the front. The *Hotel Sa Coma* (mid-March to Oct; ☎971 618034; ⑥), an unappealing concrete lump below the main street, is the third choice.

The village has a fair selection of **cafés** and **restaurants** strung along the main street. The *Café Bellavista* (closed Sun) serves salads, omelettes and light meals and has a seaview terrace, as does the best restaurant hereabouts, the *Son Tomas* (closed Tues), towards the south end of the village, where the steaks are great and the delicious "fish of the day" costs around 2100ptas.

Estellencs

About 2km southwest of Banyalbufar stands perhaps the most impressive of the lookout points that dot the coastal road, the **Mirador de Ses Animes**, a sixteenth-century watchtower built as a sentinel against pirate attack, which provides stunning views along the coast. **ESTELLENCS**, 6km further on, is similar to Banyalbufar, with steep coastal cliffs and tight terraced fields, though if anything it's a tad prettier. There's almost no sign of tourist development in the village, its narrow, winding alleys adorned with old stone houses and a trim, largely eighteenth-century parish church – peep inside for a look at the exquisite pinewood reredos. A steep, but driveable, two-kilometre lane leads down from the village, past olive and orange orchards, to **Cala Estellencs**, a rocky, surf-buffeted cove that shelters a beach (of sorts – you won't spot any sand) and a summertime bar.

Estellencs has one **hotel**, the routinely modern, two-star *Maristel*, with great views down over the coast (☎971 618529; ⑤). Amongst a handful of **cafés**, the low-price *Cafeteria Estallenchs*, opposite the *Maristel*, sells substantial and tasty snacks. The best **restaurant** is the *Montimar*, sited in a graceful old mansion near the church, which serves splendid traditional meals, including rabbit dishes for 1900ptas. Its principal rival is the *Son Llarg* next door, which also specializes in traditional Mallorcan cuisine.

Andratx

Heading southwest from Estellencs, the C710 threads along the littoral for 6km before slipping through a tunnel and, immediately beyond, passing the stone stairway up to the **Mirador de Ricardo Roca**. At 400m above the sea, this lookout point offers some fine coastal views, and you can wet your whistle at the *Es Grau* **restaurant** next door.

Beyond the *mirador*, the C710 turns inland, looping down through forested foothills to **ANDRATX**, a small and unaffected town 19km from Estellencs, where the main event is the Wednesday morning **market**, a tourist favourite. At other times there's not much to detain you, though the old houses and cobbled streets of the upper town form a harmonious ochre ensemble that culminates in the fortress-like walls of the thirteenth-century church of **Santa Maria**, built high and strong to deter raiding pirates.

*For informa-
tion about
Peguera, 7km
southeast of
Andratx, see
p.99.*

Sant Elm and Illa Dragonera

From Andratx there's a strenuous but enjoyable seven-kilometre **hike** along a narrow country road through the coastal hills and down to the low-key resort of **SANT ELM** (often signposted in Castilian: San Telmo). Directions couldn't be more straightforward: just follow the signs at the top of Andratx's main street and go west. After 3km you'll stumble across the hillside hamlet of S'Arracó, then into a pretty, orchard-covered landscape which buckles up into wooded hills and dipping valleys as it nears the coast.

Sant Elm is little more than one main street draped along the shore, with a sandy beach at one end and a harbour at the other. There are plans to expand the resort, but at present it's a quiet spot where there's a reasonable chance of a **room** in high season, either at the conspicuous *Hotel Aquamarín* (May–Oct; ☎971 239105, fax 971 239125;

④), a spectacularly unsuccessful concrete edifice built in the style of an old watchtower and equipped with spartan rooms; or, preferably, at the *Hostal Dragonera* (☎971 239086, fax 971 239013; ⑤), a simple modern building with clean and neat rooms, the best of which have balconies with sea views. For such a small place, there's a surprisingly wide choice of **cafés and restaurants** dotted along the main street. The *Bar-restaurante Flexas* serves tasty snacks at low prices, while the set meal at the *Hostal Dragonera* costs a very reasonable 1700ptas. Moving upmarket, the *Vistamar* has a mouthwatering paella for 1900ptas and, best of the lot, the *Na Caragola* specializes in seafood and has a charming terrace and ocean views – reckon on 6000ptas for a complete meal, including house wine.

If you've walked here, there's no need to trudge back. From May to October, **buses** ply between Sant Elm, Andratx and Peguera (see p.99) seven times a day Monday to Saturday (8.30am–5pm), three times on Sundays and once daily in winter. More enjoyably, you can leave Sant Elm by **boat** to Port d'Andratx (May–Sept 1 daily; 700ptas) – ring ☎971 470449 (mobile ☎939 617545) for timetable details or ask at the jetty.

Illa Dragonera

From Sant Elm's minuscule harbour, boats shuttle across to the austere offshore islet of **Illa Dragonera**. This uninhabited chunk of rock, some 4km long and 700m wide, lies at an oblique angle to the coast, with an imposing ridge of seacliffs dominating its northwestern shore. Behind the ridge, a rough track travels the length of the island, linking a pair of craggy capes and their lighthouses. Most people visit for the scenic solitude, but the island is also good for **birdlife** – ospreys, shags, gulls and other seabirds are plentiful and there may be chance sightings of several species of raptor.

There are two ways of getting to the island. Six times a day, four days a week, between May and September (usually Tues, Thurs, Sat & Sun), a **ferry** rattles across, dropping passengers about halfway up the east shore at a tiny cove-harbour. Arrangements for the return trip should be made on the way out; the return fare is 1100ptas. If, however, you're lukewarm about tramping the island, the better option is to take a two-hour **cruise**, which allows just thirty minutes on Dragonera and spends the rest of the time exploring the local coastline (twice daily on the other three days of the week, May–Sept only). This trip costs 1500ptas and reservations are a good idea, though not essential. For sailing times, ask at the harbour or telephone ☎971 470449 (mobile ☎939 617545).

Port d'Andratx

The picturesque port and fishing harbour of **PORT D'ANDRATX**, 5km southwest of Andratx, has been transformed by low-rise shopping complexes and apartment blocks. However, it's not quite a classic case of overdevelopment: there's still no denying the prettiness of the setting, with the port standing at the head of a long and slender inlet that's flanked by wooded hills; and the heart of the old town, which slopes up from the south side of the bay, more than hints at former virtues in its cramped network of ancient lanes. Sunsets show the place to best advantage, casting long shadows up the bay, and it's then that the old town's gaggle of harbourside restaurants crowd with holidaymakers and expatriates, a genteel and rather blimpish crew, occasionally irritated by raucous teenagers.

Practicalities

Port d'Andratx may be rather sedate (and the nearest sandy beach is over the hills at Camp de Mar – see p.100), but it's still an enjoyable place to spend a night or two, especially as it possesses several outstanding seafood restaurants, and it's easy to reach. There are summer **boat trips** along the coast to and from Sant Elm (see p.131), and regular **buses** from Andratx, Camp de Mar and Palma. Buses stop at the back of the bay, a brief walk from both the old town (on the left as you face the sea) and the big, modern marina (to the right). There's a taxi rank on the old harbourfront, or telephone Radio Taxi Andratx (☎971 136398).

Accommodation

There's a reasonably good chance of finding an **inexpensive room**. Try along the harbourfront of the old town where – at the east end – the no-frills *Hostal Las Palmeras*, at Avgda Mateo Bosch 12 (☎971 672078; ③), has bare and cheerless rooms, although you're much better off paying a little more to stay at the two-star *Hotel Brismar*, further down the quay at c/Almirante Riera Alemany 6 (☎971 671600, fax 971 671183; ⑤): it's a pleasant, old-fashioned kind of place with fifty spotless rooms, the pick of which have port-facing balconies (though these are to be avoided if you are a light sleeper). Better still, head one block up from the harbourfront to the quiet, relaxing *Hostal-residencia Catalina Vera*, c/Isaac Peral 63 (April–Oct; ☎971 671918; ③), a neatly shuttered and whitewashed building with frugal, tidy rooms, edged by a small orchard. **Upmarket accommodation** can be found at the *Villa Italia* (☎971 674011, fax 971 673350; ⑨), an opulent, 1920s twin-towered mansion set behind a steeply terraced garden. The hotel has luxuries such as a rooftop swimming pool, as well as gorgeous views out over the bay, and is a five-minute stroll west of the old part of town along Camí Sant Carles, an extension of c/Isaac Peral.

Eating and drinking

Most of the town's best and most expensive **restaurants** are along the harbourfront: at the far end of the quay, the *Layn* (closed Mon) serves a wide range of wonderful fish dishes, including a superb

Down the coast from Deià to Port d'Andratx

The first – eastern – part of Port d'Andratx's harbourfront is Avgda Mateo Bosch, which widens out below Plaça Almirante Oquendo before becoming c/Almirante Riera Alemany.

paella for 1700ptas per person, while the *Rocamar*, a few paces away, offers delicious seafood and a lovely waterside terrace. Nearby, back towards the head of the bay and just off the harbourfront, is Plaça Almirante Oquendo, a pleasant pedestrianized square crowded with restaurants including the extremely popular *La Piazzetta*, where you'll find less expensive seafood, as well as tasty pizzas and pastas from around 800ptas. There are several fine restaurants one block up from the waterside on c/Isaac Peral too – the bistro-style *Casa Galicia*, just up from Plaça Almirante Oquendo at c/Isaac Peral 52, is a superb Galician restaurant specializing in seafood, with main courses from 1800ptas, as does another Galician place, the less expensive *Cafeteria Galicia*, a few metres along the street at no. 37. Amongst a handful of harbourside **bars** on c/Almirante Riera Alemany, *Mitj & Mitj* is the liveliest and youngest, while *Tim's* next door is more laid-back and likable. For **coffee and cakes**, *La Consigna* is an enjoyably modern coffee house-cum-patisserie at Avgda Mateo Bosch 19.

Beyond Sóller: Cala Tuent to the Cap de Formentor

Beyond a doubt, the most interesting approach to the northernmost tip of the island, the Cap de Formentor, is the continuation of the **C710 beyond Sóller**, slipping through the highest and harshest section of the Serra de Tramuntana. For the most part, the mountains drop straight into the sea, precipitous and largely unapproachable cliffs with barely a cove in sight. The accessible exceptions are the comely beach at **Cala Tuent** and the horribly commercial hamlet of **Sa Calobra** next door. The best place to break your journey, however, is inland at the monastery and pilgrimage centre of **Lluc**, which offers a diverting museum, ready access to excellent hiking trails in the mountains, a campsite and a fairly reliable supply of inexpensive rooms.

There's more low-priced monastic accommodation at the hilltop **Ermita de Nostra Senyora del Puig**, just outside of **Pollença**, a beguiling old town of grandee mansions sitting at the foot of a beautiful calvary. Nearby, at the end of the C710 and just 60km from Sóller, is **Port de Pollença**, a low-key, medium-sized resort whose long sandy beach drapes around the Badia de Pollença. A popular summertime retreat for the inhabitants of Palma, the resort abounds in places to stay, and is within easy striking distance of the dramatic seacliffs of the **Península de Formentor**.

Long-distance **buses** link Palma with Pollença and its port, while twice every weekday from May to October a bus runs along the C710 from Port de Sóller to Port de Pollença, and on to Port d'Alcúdia. These services are supplemented by more localized routings, which are itemized in "Travel details" on p.159.

Cala Tuent, Sa Calobra and Escorca

Heading northeast from Sóller, the C710 zigzags up into the mountains. After 7km there's a last lingering look over the coast from the **Mirador de Ses Barques**, before the road snakes inland, tunnelling through the western flanks of **Puig Major**, the island's highest mountain at 1447m. Beyond the tunnel is the **Gorg Blau** (Blue Gorge), a bare and bleak ravine that was a well-known beauty spot until a hydroelectric scheme filled it with a trio of puddle-like reservoirs. And there's further bad news here: the dramatic trail which twists up Puig Major from the military base beside the main road remains off-limits because of the radar station on the summit. This makes **Puig de Massanella** (1367m), which looms over the gorge to the east, the highest mountain that can be climbed on Mallorca.

At the far end of the gorge the road tunnels into the mountains, to emerge just short of a left turn leading to Cala Tuent and Sa Calobra. An exhilarating, ear-popping detour to the seashore, this well-surfaced side road hairpins down the mountain slopes so severely that at one point it actually turns 270 degrees to run under itself. About 10km down the road, fork left over the hills for the four-kilometre journey to the **Ermita de Sant Llorenç**, a tiny medieval church perched high above the coast, and **CALA TUENT**, where a smattering of villas cling to the northern slopes of Puig Major as it tumbles down to the seashore. Ancient orchards temper the harshness of the mountain, and the gravel and sand beach is one of the quietest on the north coast. It's a lovely spot to while away a few hours and, provided you stay well inshore, the swimming is safe. There's nowhere to stay, but an excellent **restaurant** sits on the far side of the cove – the *Es Vergeret*, where lunch is the finest meal of the day, a wide range of fish and meat dishes from 1600ptas, best devoured at the terrace bar in sight of the ocean.

Puig de Massanella is best ascended from Lluc – see the recommended hike on p.138.

Sa Calobra

If you ignore the left fork to Cala Tuent, it's just 2km more to **SA CALOBRA**, a modern resort occupying a pint-sized cove in the shadow of the mountains. There's nothing wrong with the setting, but the place is an overvisited disaster. Almost every island operator deposits a busload of tourists here every day in summer and the crush is quite unbearable – as is the overpriced and overcooked food at the local cafés. The reason why so many people come here is to visit the impressive box canyon at the mouth of the **Torrent de Pareis** (River of the Twins). It takes about ten minutes to follow the partly tunnelled walkway round the coast from the resort to the mouth of the canyon. Here, with sheer cliffs rising on every side, the milky-green river trickles down to the narrow bank of shingle that bars its final approach to the sea – though the scene is transformed after heavy rainfall, when the river crashes down into the canyon and out into the sea.

Beyond
Sóller:
Cala Tuent
to the
Cap de
Formentor

Escorca

ESCORCA, a poorly defined scattering of houses along the C710, 4km northeast of the Sa Calobra turn-off, is the starting point for the descent of the Torrent de Pareis, a famous, though incredibly testing route, which requires rock-climbing skills, wetsuits and ropes. The river drops from here to Sa Calobra through an awesome, seven-kilometre-long limestone gorge, which takes about six hours to negotiate. The descent is not practicable in winter, spring, or after rainfall, when the river may be waist-high and the rocks dangerously slippery. A small danger sign marks the start of the trail across the road from the (conspicuous) *Restaurant Escorca*.

The Monestir de Lluc

Tucked away in a remote valley about 35km east of Sóller, the austere, high-sided dormitories and orange-flecked roof tiles of the **Monestir de Nostra Senyora de Lluc** (Monastery of Our Lady of Lluc) stand out against the greens and greys of the surrounding mountains. It's a magnificent setting for what has been Mallorca's most important place of pilgrimage since the middle of the thirteenth century. The religious significance of the place, however, goes back much further: the valley's animistic prehistoric inhabitants deified the local holm oak woods, and the Romans picked up on the theme, naming the place from *lucus*, the Latin for "sacred forest". After the Reconquest, however, the monks who settled here were keen both to coin a purely Christian etymology and to enhance their reputation. They invented the story of a shepherd boy named Lluc (Luke) stumbling across a tiny, brightly painted statue in the woods. Frightened by his discovery, the lad collared the nearest monk, and when the pair returned heavenly music filled their ears, bright lights dazzled their eyes, and celestial voices declared the statue an authentically heaven-sent image of the Virgin.

The monastery complex

The monastery, including the basilica, is open daily: April–Sept 10am–6.30pm; Oct–March 10am–5.30pm; free. The museum is open daily 10am–5.30pm; 300ptas.

Home to this much-venerated statue, Lluc's present monastic complex is an imposing and formal-looking affair mostly dating from the eighteenth and early nineteenth centuries. At its centre is the main shrine and architectural highlight, the **Basílica de la Mare de Déu de Lluc**, graced by an elegant Baroque facade. To reach it, pass through the monastery's stately double-doored entrance and keep straight on to the second – and final – courtyard, where a dreary statue of Bishop Campins, who overhauled Lluc in the early part of this century, does the basilica's good looks a disservice. Dark and gaudily decorated, the church is dominated by heavy jasper columns, whose stolidness is partly relieved by a dome over the crossing. On either side of the nave, stone steps extend the aisles round the back of the Baroque high altar to a small chapel. This is the holy of holies, built to display the statue of the Virgin, which has been commonly known as **La**

Beyond
Sóller:
Cala Tuent
to the
Cap de
Formentor

Moreneta ("the Dark-Skinned One") ever since the original paint-work peeled off in the fifteenth century to reveal brown stone under-neath. Just 61cm high, the Virgin looks innocuous, her face tweeked by a hint of a smile and haloed by a jewel-encrusted gold crown. In her left arm she cradles a bumptious baby Jesus, who holds the "Book of Life" open to reveal the letters alpha and omega. Every day, during the 11am mass, the **Escolania de Lluc**, a boys' choir founded in the early sixteenth century with the stipulation that it must be "composed of natives of Mallorca, of pure blood, sound in grammar and song", performs in the basilica. They're nicknamed *Los Blauets*, "The Blues", for the colour of their cassocks.

To the right of the basilica's main entrance, a small door leads into a covered passage, site of the monastery's information desk and a stairway which climbs up one floor to the enjoyable **Museu de Lluc**. After a modest section devoted to archeological finds from the Talayotic and Roman periods come cabinets of intricate old vest-ments, exquisite gold and silver sacred vessels, medieval religious paintings, and an intriguing assortment of votive offerings – folkloric bits and bobs brought here to honour La Moreneta. The museum also boasts an extensive collection of **majolica**, glazed earthenware whose characteristic shapes are two-handled drug jars and show dishes or plates, of which some two or three hundred are on display. The designs vary in sophistication – from broad and bold dashes of colour to carefully painted naturalistic designs – but the colours remain fairly constant, restricted by the available technology to iron red, copper green, cobalt blue, manganese purple and antimony yel-low. It was the Italians who first used the term "majolica", a bas-tardized version of Mallorca, where they picked up the manufactur-ing skills that had been pioneered by the Moors. The last, disap-pointing section of the museum displays the paintings and drawings of the early twentieth-century artist José Coll Bardolet.

Returning to the courtyard in front of the basilica's main facade, walk though the arch on the far side of the courtyard and you'll soon spot the large, rough-hewn column at the start of the **Camí dels Misteris del Rosari** (Way of the Mysteries of the Rosary), a broad pilgrims' footpath that winds its way up the rocky hillside directly behind the monastery. Dating from 1913, the solemn granite stations marking the way are of two types – simple stone pediments and, more intriguingly, rough trilobate columns of Gaudí-like design, each surmounted by a chunky crown and cross. The prettiest part of the walk is round the back of the hill where the path slips through the cool, green woods with rock overhangs on one side and views out over the bowl-shaped Albarca valley on the other. It takes about ten minutes to reach the crucifix at the top of the hill – and afterwards it's possible to stroll or drive down into the Albarca valley by follow-ing the country road that begins to the left of the monastery's main entrance. For a longer hike into the mountains, see p.138.

Beyond
Sóller:
Cala Tuent
to the
Cap de
Formentor

Practicalities

Buses to Lluc, which is situated 1.5km off the C710, stop right outside the monastery. In addition to the Port de Sóller–Port de Pollença–Port d'Alcúdia service, buses run to Lluc at least once a day from Palma via Inca – there's usually a departure at 9am or 10am, returning from Lluc at 5pm or 6pm, allowing you ample time to visit. For longer stays, **accommodation** at the monastery is highly organized, with simple, self-contained apartment-cells. In summer phone ahead if you want to be sure of space, but at other times simply book at the monastery's information office on arrival (☎971 517025, fax 971 517096; ②). Double rooms cost 3000ptas per night, but the price drops to 2500ptas for stays of three days and more; a room for four people for one night costs 3700ptas.

For **food**, there are several cafés and restaurants beside the car park, but far preferable, even though it has become a little pricey, is the monks' former dining room, a grandly restored old hall of wooden beams and wide stone arches. The food is traditional Spanish, with main courses from 1900ptas; the meat dishes are much better than the fish.

From Lluc to Massanella

14km, 887m of ascent; 5hr 30min– 6hr.

The large **Massanella massif** has eleven peaks over 1000m and is defended by many crags and steep rocky slopes. Since the construction of a military establishment put Puig Major out of bounds, it has become the best-loved high summit of the island. There are some well-defined paths and the classic ascent from Lluc monastery, with magnificent views, uses the best of these. Although quite strenuous, the route is not difficult and is deservedly popular. The top is all bare rock, although some small plants grow where moisture lingers in the crevices. Keep an eye open for black **vultures**, and for the friendly Alpine **accentors** who often appear on the summit or down by **Font de S'Avenc**, the spring on the southern flank.

From the front of the monastery, walk up through the vast car park to the **Font Cuberta restaurant**, turning left behind it to follow the road up to join the C710 at a junction on the Coll de Sa Batalla. Turn towards Inca and go past the service station, where walkers arriving by car may park. The ascent of Massanella from here takes about two and a quarter hours.

Cross the bridge and turn right through the iron gates onto a wide track. Follow the track for 250m past a spring and water trough. Ignoring the Camí Vell de Lluc, a restored footpath to Caimari which continues straight on, swing sharp right uphill following the red painted waymarks. Continue on the wide track through a gate into the area of the Coma Freda farm, whose owner charges 500ptas at this gate. Pause when you come to a wide opening into a field to look at the impressive **Es Fronto**, a high spur of Massanella with precipitous cliffs. At this point the track to the farm turns right and the path to Massanella goes straight on outside the wall enclosing the field. This path is well used and marked with paint signs and cairns. Rising through the woods, it joins a wide track by a **painted boulder**, a point of reference which you should note as it's of use in the descent.

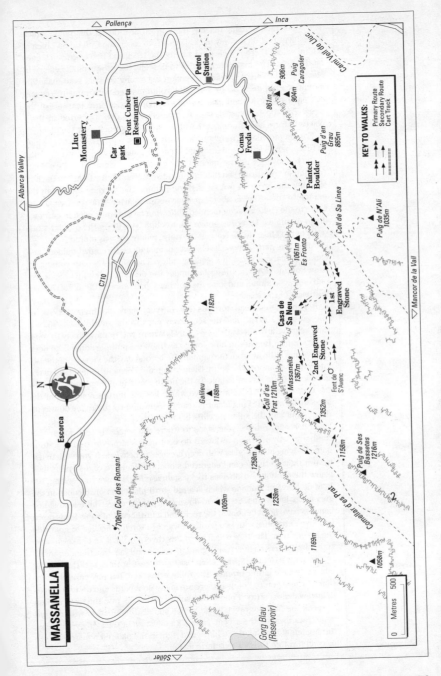

The wide track actually reaches the bottom of a dip at this point, which helps identify it on the way back. Turn left to reach the **Coll de Sa Linea** at 822m, where there is a clearing among the trees and two engraved stones on the right. The main track begins to descend here towards the village of Mancor de la Vall. A possible diversion for strong walkers is to make the ascent of **Puig de N'Ali** by a winding route marked with some cairns and red paint signs; it's not easy to follow, especially at first because of the trees. The top is unusual, with an immense boulder supported in three places to form a sheltering cave with a southern outlook over the plain.

For Massanella, turn right up a clearly defined path rising in big swings at first, then twisting and turning to reach a junction where the two paths to the top diverge. At the junction, there's a **stone** engraved "Puig y Font" (mountain and spring) on the right-hand side and "Font y Puig" on the left, showing the order of arrival at these points. The journey time from the garage to the stone is about an hour and a quarter. For the ascent, the route to the right is recommended, following an old track used to carry ice down on mules. Later on, above the treeline, you'll see the old dry-stone walls of the **Casa de Sa Neu** on the right, where ice was stored.

After the path almost levels out, it meanders through boulders and clumps of carritx grass in a shallow valley. The southerly path coming up from Font de S'Avenc (described under the descent below) passes a second engraved stone, and joins the northerly path about 100 to 200 metres northeast of the stone.

Beyond here, head towards the dip between the highest peak of **Massanella** (1367m) and the secondary peak to the southwest (1352m), then veer right to the main peak. This is where you're most likely to see a black vulture. Be careful how you go as there's a pothole some 20m deep not a stone's throw from the summit. On a good day the view from the top encompasses almost the entire island, from the Formentor headland in the northeast to the Bay of Palma. To the north, vertical cliffs plunge 150m to the **Coll d'es Prat** (1210m) above which lies the northern section of the Massanella massif. Puig Major is readily identified by the radar domes on the summit and the splendid cliffs below.

To descend, retrace your steps to where the southerly path joins. This southerly path offers an awkward descent over sharp cornered limestone boulders lying at all angles, with deep crevices in between. If you wish to use it, turn right to the second engraved stone, on the edge of a sloping shelf below the summit. An obvious rocky staircase leads down to a spring, the Font de S'Avenc, outside which is a red earth platform conspicuous in the grey rocky landscape. Steps lead down to an upper cave where a table and benches have been cut out of the rock, and a further set of steps leads down to a lower chamber with two basins of water (a torch is needed to go inside the lower cave). The flies which infest this cavern make it an unlikely picnic spot, but it offers shelter from lightning strikes and rain in a thunderstorm.

The path from the spring contours to the east at first, splitting briefly into two – take either branch. The route is marked, but pay careful attention to where you're going as there are many goat paths and natural ledges to lead walkers astray. Follow the marked path back into the trees and on to reach the first engraved stone, which signals the junction with the old mule track used on the ascent. Now it's a question of retracing your steps, turning left at the Coll de Sa Linea and right at the painted boulder, before passing through Coma Freda farm again.

Beyond
Sóller:
Cala Tuent
to the
Cap de
Formentor

> ### Alternative ascent via Coll d'es Prat
>
> With descent as above: 16km, 1022m of ascent, 6hr–6hr 30min.
>
> An alternative and longer ascent can be made by following the old track from Coma Freda up the valley on the north side of Massanella to the high Coll d'es Prat (1210m), then descending the Comellar d'es Prat valley for about 1km, until a way is found up to the 1158-metre col between Puig de Ses Bassetes (1216m) and Massanella by a short easy scramble. From this col, the direct ascent of the southwest ridge to a secondary peak of Massanella (1352m) is for rock-climbers only, but a walkers' route is found by a rising traverse, east at first, then looking out for the cairns which show the way up the steep and rocky ground. These cairns are difficult to see in the grey rocky wilderness and a descent by this route is not recommended.

Pollença and around

Founded in the thirteenth century, the tranquil little town of **POL-LENÇA** nestles among a trio of hillocks, where the Serra de Tramuntana fades into coastal flatland. Following standard Mallorcan practice, the town was established a few kilometres from the seashore to militate against sudden pirate attack, with its harbour, Port de Pollença (see p.147), left an unprotected outpost. For once the stratagem worked. Unlike most of Mallorca's old towns, Pollença successfully repelled a string of piratical onslaughts, the last and most threatening of which was in 1550, when the notorious Turkish corsair Dragut came within a hair's breadth of victory. In the festival of *Mare de Déu dels Àngels* on August 2, the townspeople celebrate their escape with enthusiastic street battles, the day's events named after the warning shouted by the hero of the resistance, a certain Joan Más: *Mare de Déu dels Àngels, assistiu-mos* (Our Lady of Angels, help us).

Pollença town

Although Pollença avoided being destroyed by Dragut, not much of the medieval town has survived, and the austere stone houses that now cramp the twisting lanes of the compact centre mostly date from the seventeenth and eighteenth centuries. In the middle, **Plaça Major**, the amiable main square, accommodates a cluster of laid-back cafés and is overseen by the severe facade of the church of **Nostra Senyora dels Àngels**, a sheer cliff-face of sun-bleached stone pierced by a rose window. Dating from the thirteenth century but extensively remodelled in the Baroque style five centuries later, the church's gloomy interior has a mildly diverting sequence of ceiling and wall paintings, as well as a whopping, tiered and towered high altarpiece. The original church was built for the Knights Templar, a rich and secretive organization founded as a military order in support of the Crusades, but suppressed by the pope in 1312 following trumped-up charges of heresy, sorcery and bestiality. As elsewhere, the Templars' Pollença possessions passed to the Hospitallers of St

Pollença's Plaça Major is the site of a lively fresh fruit and vegetable market on most Saturday and Sunday mornings

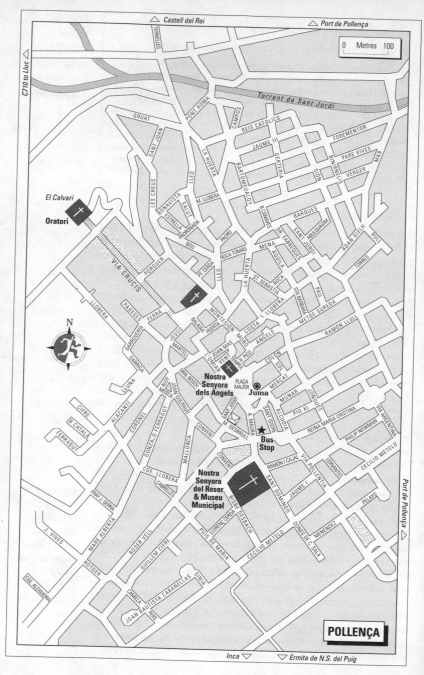

△ Castell del Rei   △ Port de Pollença

0   Metres   100

C710 to Lluc

Torrent de Sant Jordi

El Calvari

Oratori

VIA CRUCIS

N

Nostra Senyora dels Angels

PLAÇA MAJOR

Juma

Bus Stop

Nostra Senyora del Roser & Museu Municipal

Port de Pollença ▽

POLLENÇA

▽ Inca   ▽ Ermita de N.S. del Puig

John, a rival knightly order who struggled on until 1802 when the Spanish king appropriated all they owned.

Close by, along c/Antoni Maura – and behind a tiny square housing an antique water wheel and watchtower – stands the deconsecrated church of **Nostra Senyora del Roser**, outside which stands a curious piece of modern sculpture, chiselled in the shape of a bookcase. Inside, the church hosts contemporary art exhibitions which struggle to compete with the gaudiness of the church – from the barrel-vaulted ceiling through to the flamboyant Baroque high altar. In the adjoining cloisters of Santo Domingo is the **Museu Municipal**, which contains a modest collection of contemporary paintings and, amongst the ecclesiastical bric-a-brac, several good examples of Mallorcan Gothic art.

Pollença's pride and joy is its **Via Crucis** (Way of the Cross), a long, steep and beautiful stone stairway, graced by ancient cypress trees which ascends **El Calvari** (Calvary hill) to the north of the town centre. At the top, a much-revered thirteenth-century statue of **Mare de Déu del Peu de la Creu** (Mother of God at the Foot of the Cross) is lodged in a simple, courtyarded **oratori** (chapel), whose whitewashed walls sport some of the worst religious paintings imaginable. However, the views out over coast and town are sumptuous. On Good Friday, a figure of Jesus is slowly carried by torchlight down from the *oratori* to the church of Nostra Senyora dels Àngels, in the **Davallament** (Lowering), one of the most moving religious celebrations on the island.

There are further magnificent views from the **Ermita de Nostra Senyora del Puig**, a rambling, mostly eighteenth-century monastery perched on top of the Puig de Maria, a 320-metre-high hump facing the south end of town. The monastic complex, with its fortified walls, courtyard, chapel, refectory and cells, has had a chequered history, alternately abandoned and restored by both monks and nuns. It's now a working monastery again, with a handful of resident Benedictines supplementing their collective income by renting out cells to tourists (see "Practicalities", below). There are no specific sights, but the setting is extraordinarily serene and beautiful, with the mellow honey-coloured walls of the monastery surrounded by ancient carob and olive trees, a million miles away from the tourist resorts visible far below. To get to the monastery, take the signposted turning off the main Pollença–Inca/Palma road just south of town; head up this steep, 1500-metre-long lane until it fizzles out, to be replaced by a cobbled footpath which winds up to the monastery entrance. It's possible to drive to the top of the lane, but unless you've got nerves of steel, you're better off leaving your vehicle by the turning near the foot of the hill. Allow just over an hour each way if you're walking from the centre of town.

Practicalities

Regular **buses** from Palma, Inca and Port de Pollença halt immediately to the south of Plaça Major, at the foot of c/Antoni Maura. Alternatively, **taxis** can be a relatively inexpensive means of getting

In principle, if not always practice, the Museu Municipal and Nostra Senyora del Roser are open July–Sept Mon–Sat 10am–1pm & 5.30–8.30pm; Oct–June Mon–Sat 11am–1pm. Entry to the museum is 250ptas; the church is free.

Beyond
Sóller:
Cala Tuent
to the
Cap de
Formentor

*If you're dri-
ving into
Pollença, avoid
the baffling
one-way
streets of the
old part of
town and come
in from the
south, turning
off the main
Inca–Pollença
road along Via
Pollentia.*

around: telephone Radio Taxi Pollença (☎971 866213). The town doesn't have a tourist office and there's only one central place to stay – the first-rate *Hotel Juma*, a smart and tasteful conversion of an old stone merchant's house in the heart of things at Plaça Major 9 (☎971 535002, fax 971 534155; ⑥). The rooms are comfortable, air-conditioned and tidily furnished in modern style; those over-looking the square cost about 2000ptas more than the others. The nearest alternative accommodation is at the *Ermita de Nostra Senyora del Puig* (☎971 530235; ①), just over 2km south of town on the summit of Puig de Maria (see above for directions), where the original monks' cells have been renovated to provide simple accommodation including bedding, showers, meals if required and even barbecue facilities. Even in a monastery, however, there are degrees of frugality: as a rule of thumb, the most spartan rooms are rented to solitary travellers and those without reservations. Be warned also that it can get cold and windy at night, and the refecto-ry food is mediocre.

Pollença does very well for **restaurants**, supported by the villa owners who gather here every evening from the surrounding coun-tryside. One the best restaurants is *Il Giardino*, Plaça Major 11, a smart bistro-style place offering a superb range of French dishes from about 2000ptas, prepared with great flair. The neighbouring *Ca'n Olesa* is not so chic, but it's less expensive and the menu includes pastas and pizzas as well as delicious Mallorcan specialities. On c/Montesión, just north of Plaça Major, you'll find the fashionable *Restaurante Cantonet* (closed Tues), which offers top-notch inter-national cuisine from a limited menu – à la carte or a fixed menu at about 2400ptas; in the summer, you can sit out on the terrace of the large disused church a few metres away. On the same street, *La Font del Gall* also has an international rather than local menu; it's a justi-fiably popular spot, where you should allow 4000ptas for a full meal including wine. Much cheaper, and equally tasty, are the *tapas* sold by the *Hotel Juma* – a standard portion costs about 350ptas.

As for **bars**,*Café Espanyol*, on Plaça Major, is the liveliest spot in town – a good, old-fashioned place with dog-eared decor; round the corner, the comparable *Bar Centro*, c/Temple 3, is a good second choice. The ground floors of several old mansions in the vicinity of Plaça Major have been done out as bars; by and large, they don't work too well, but *Labaula*, c/Huerta 18, is agreeable enough.

The Castell del Rei

The battered ruins of the medieval **Castell del Rei** (Castle of the King) are glued to a remote and inhospitable crag, which rears high above the ocean about 7km north of Pollença. Founded by the Moors, this remote fastness was strengthened by Jaume I to guard the northerly approaches to Pollença against pirate attack. In this regard, however, it was something of a failure: the pirates simply ignored it, preferring to land at nearby Cala Sant Vicenç instead. More successfully, it held out for months against the Aragonese invasion of 1285 and was the last fortress to surrender to Pedro of Aragón, the supplanter of the Mallorcan king Jaume III, in 1343. Subsequently, the castle was used as a watchtower, finally being abandoned in 1715.

It takes about two hours to **walk** there, an undemanding hike along a country lane, and then a forest footpath leading through the pretty Ternelles valley. The problem, however, is getting in: the castle is on a vast private estate, whose owner allows visitors only limited access. Globespan (see p.147) or the tourist office in Port de Pollença are the best places to ask for information about current opening times.

If these restrictions don't deter you, directions are as follows: on the northern edge of Pollença, a signposted turning to "Ternelles" leads off the C710, twisting north past attractively renovated old *fincas* and olive and citrus groves. After 1.6km, you'll reach a guarded gate set in the narrow defile at the entrance to the Ternelles valley. If you're driving, you have to park here. An easy-to-follow, rough and dusty track leads to another set of gates, beyond which the path starts to rise, climbing through oak woods to a stretch of mixed woodland dominated by pines. Further on, the trees thin out and the castle ruins can be spied in the distance. About 100m after the start of a fenced-off area on the right-hand side, fork left off the main track – which continues down to the shingly beach at **Cala Castell** – for the climb up to the ruins.

Cala Sant Vicenç

The suburban modernity of **CALA SANT VICENÇ**, a small and well-heeled resort 6km northeast of Pollença, is largely camouflaged by its attractive setting, with sharp escarpments and steep hills back-dropping a narrow slice of rocky seashore. Nonetheless, it's the tediousness of the villas you'll probably remember, along with the overpowering *Hotel Don Pedro*, insensitively located on the minute headland that separates two small sandy beaches. The only real reason to visit is for a swim and here at least the resort scores highly – the water is crystal clear and the beach is sheltered from the wind.

Buses from Lluc, Pollença and Port de Pollença stop on Avinguda Temporal, a short walk from the **Oficina d'Informació Turistica** on Plaça Sant Vicenç (June–Aug Mon–Fri 9.30am–12.30pm & 4–6pm, Sat 9.30am–12.30pm; ☎971 533264): head along Avinguda Temporal towards the seashore, turn left down c/Cala Clara and then left again. Vacant **rooms** are extremely thin on the ground in summer, but you could try the *Hotel Niu*, a comfortably old-fashioned, low-rise place next to the beach (April–Oct; ☎971 530100, fax 971 531220; ④), or the more secluded *Hostal Los Pinos*, which has spick-and-span rooms and its own pool (May–Oct; ☎971 531210; ④). The best **restaurant** is the *Cavall Bernat* (May–Oct), which specializes in traditional Mallorcan dishes; the adjoining pizzeria is a less expensive option, serving delicious pizzas from 800ptas.

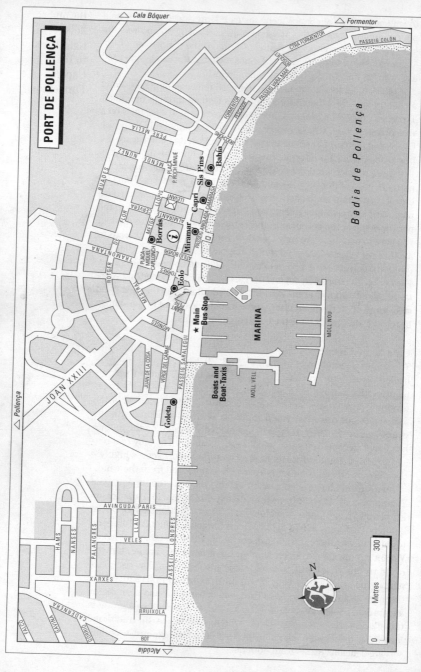

PORT DE POLLENÇA

△ Cala Bóquer △ Formentor

CTRA FORMENTOR

PASSEIG COLÓN

PASSE VARA MAR

FORMENTOR

PERE MELIA

MENDE NÚÑEZ

BUÁDES

FLOR

CERVERA

LLOMPART

PLAÇA P. ROCH MINUÉ

Sis Pins

Bahia

Badia de Pollença

METGE

BORRÀS

Borràs

LLEVANT

ALMIRANTE

Capri

Miramar

PASSEIG ANGLADA CAMARASA

ATILIO BOYER

DE FLOR

RAMONIANA

ROTGER

TRESFLRAL

PLAÇA MIQUEL CAPLLONCH

TORRES

Eolo

SANT PERE

MÒNGES

★ Main Bus Stop

MARINA

MOLL NOU

JOAN DE LA COSA

VERGE DEL CARME

PASSEIG SARALEGUI

Goleta

Boats and Boat-Taxis

MOLL VELL

△ Pollença

△ Alcúdia

JOAN XXIII

AVINGUDA PARIS

HAMS

NANSES

PALANGRES

LLAÜT

VÈLES

ONDRES

PASSEIG

XARXÈS

BRUIXOLA

BOT

GORRIÓ

CADERNERA

GAVINA

FALCÓ

N

Metres

0   300

Port de Pollença

Beyond Sóller: Cala Tuent to the Cap de Formentor

Over at **PORT DE POLLENÇA** things are a lot more lively, though still pleasantly low-key. With the mountains as a shimmering back-cloth, this family-oriented resort arches through the flatlands behind the Badia de Pollença, a deeply indented bay whose sheltered waters are ideal for swimming. The **beach** is the focus of attention, a narrow, elongated sliver of sand that's easily long enough to accommodate the crowds, though as a general rule you'll have more space the further south (towards Alcúdia) you walk. A rash of apartment buildings and hotels blights the edge of town, and the noisy main road to Alcúdia cuts through the centre, but there are no high-rises to speak of and the resort is dotted with attractive whitewashed and stone-trimmed villas. All in all it's quite delightful, especially to the north of the marina, where a portion of the old beachside road – along Passeig Anglada Camarasa – has been pedestrianized.

For a change of scene, **boat-taxis** shuttle between the marina and the Platja de Formentor, one of Mallorca's most attractive beaches (June–Oct 5 daily; 30min; 800ptas each way), whilst **boat trips** cruise the bay (June to mid-Oct Mon–Fri 1 daily; 2hr; 1500ptas), or work their way along to Cap de Formentor (June to mid-Oct Mon & Fri 1 daily; 2hr 30min; 1600ptas). There's also the option of making a delightful three-kilometre **hike** across the neck of the Península de Formentor to **Cala Bóquer** (see box on p.149).

For more on the Platja de Formentor and Cap de Formentor, see p.151.

Practicalities

Buses to Port de Pollença from Pollença, Palma, Alcúdia, Port d'Alcúdia and Port de Sóller stop by the marina right in the town centre. A couple of minutes' walk away is the **Oficina d'Informació Turística**, one block behind the seafront at Carretera Formentor 31 (May–Oct Mon–Fri 9am–1pm & 4–7pm, Sat 9am–1pm; ☎971 865467), which has loads of local information and accommodation lists. The flatlands edging the Badia de Pollença and stretching inland as far as Pollença and along the bay to Alcúdia make for easy, scenic cycling. **Mountain bikes** can be rented from March, c/Joan XXIII, 89 (☎971 864784), as can **mopeds** and **motorcycles. Car** rental companies include La Parra, c/Joan XXIII, 20 (☎971 866721), and Avis, along the street at no.80 (☎971 865394). On the same street at no. 9, Viajes Iberia (☎971 866262) are the **American Express** agents for this part of Mallorca. The walking holiday specialists Globespan also have an office here in Port de Pollença, on the waterfront at Passeig Saralegui 114 (☎971 864711), where you can pay to join one of their day-long guided walks (around 2000ptas per person). The office will provide all the details – you should book a minimum of 24 hours beforehand.

Accommodation

Port de Pollença has around a dozen **hotels** and not quite as many **hostals**. Needless to say, most of the rooms are block-booked by the tour operators, but there's a fairly good chance of finding a vacancy

Beyond
Sóller:
Cala Tuent
to the
Cap de
Formentor

in the places listed below – especially in the shoulder season. Prices are generally quite reasonable.

Hostal Bahía, Passeig Vara Mar s/n (May–Oct; ☎971 866562, fax 971 865630; ⑤). In a lovely location, a few minutes' walk north of the marina along the seashore, this pleasant, unassuming one-star *hostal* offers 30 rooms in one of the port's older villas.

Hostal-residencia Borrás, Plaça Miquel Capllonch 16 (☎971 531474; ③). Agreeable two-star *hostal*. Most of the rooms are comfortably spacious and you can eat breakfast in the pretty little courtyard. Overlooks the old town's tiny main square, a couple of minutes' walk from the beach.

Hotel Capri, Passeig Anglada Camarasa 69 (May–Oct; ☎971 531600, fax 971 533322; ⑤). Standard-issue, modern hotel just north of the marina with 30 pleasant rooms. Overlooks the beach where it's flanked by the pedestrianized walkway – the prettiest part of town.

Hostal-residencia Eolo, Carretera Formentor 10 (☎971 866550, fax 971 866301; ④). Straightforward, middle-sized *hostal* metres from the marina. Rooms are a bit spartan, but perfectly OK. A hikers' favourite.

Hostal-residencia Goleta, Passeig Saralegui 118 (mid-March to Oct; ☎971 865902, fax 971 866002; ④). Simple, workaday one-star *hostal* with 16 rooms on the traffic-heavy seafront south of the marina.

Hotel Miramar, Passeig Anglada Camarasa 39 (April–Oct; ☎971 867211, fax 971 864075; ⑤). Attractive three-star hotel in an elegant building – all iron grilles and stone lintels. Every room has its own balcony, but try to get a room at the front with a sea view, otherwise you might be plonked at the back looking out over Carretera Formentor.

Hotel-residencia Sis Pins, Passeig Anglada Camarasa 77 (April–Oct; ☎971 867050, fax 971 534013; ⑤). This medium-sized, three-star hotel occupies a handsome whitewashed and balconied villa on the waterfront. Very comfortable.

Eating

Port de Pollença heaves with **restaurants**. Some offer run-of-the-mill tourist fodder and there's a plethora of pizza places, but others serve the freshest of seafood and skilfully blend Catalan and Castilian cuisines.

Pizzeria Eolo, Carretera Formentor 10. There's nothing gourmet about the *Eolo*, but the pizzas are tasty, filling and inexpensive. Beneath the *hostal* of the same name (see above).

El Pozo, c/Joan XXIII, 25. Less expensive than its seafront rivals, this informal, laid-back restaurant specializes in seafood and serves a delicious paella (1600ptas). A couple of minutes' walk from the marina.

Restaurant Simbad, Passeig Saralegui 116. Excellent family-run restaurant offering delicious Spanish-Catalan cuisine. A full meal with house wine for two costs around 5000ptas.

Restaurant Stay, on the marina's Moll Nou jetty. This chic little place features superb seafood dishes and charges about 5500ptas for a full à la carte meal – and the romantic seashore setting.

Restaurante Tribeca, Carretera Formentor 43 at junction with c/Llevant. Small and intimate bistro-style restaurant offering the best of Spanish and Catalan dishes. Smart but competitively priced, with dishes from about 2000ptas.

Beyond
Sóller:
Cala Tuent
to the
Cap de
Formentor

A valley walk from Port de Pollença to the coast at Cala Bóquer

6km, 101m of ascent; 1hr 30min.

The walk through the sheltered **Vall de Bóquer** is an attractive, easy stroll over gently undulating ground, coast to coast across the neck of the Península de Formentor. Return is by the same route, about 3km each way. The walk is popular with family groups, being suitable for most ages and abilities, and is also favoured by ornithologists for the variety of resident and migrant **bird life**.

Start by walking along the seafront north of Port de Pollença's marina and turn left up Avinguda Bocchoris. When this ends, keep straight along a wide footpath fringed with pine trees and tamarisk. At a sign saying "Predio Bóquer Propriedad Privada Camin Particular" take the wide path north with the ridge of Serra del Cavall Bernat straight ahead. After 150m the path swings to the northeast past olive trees. On the right is a striking example of the lentisk or mastic tree, a dark evergreen with a resinous smell which grows to 3m. Its flowers vary in colour from red to brown and are succeeded by fruits which are first red then black. The other trees with long pods are carobs.

Seventy-five metres further on, the path veers left at the car park and, after about 250m, passes through an iron gate. The **Bóquer farmhouse** is just ahead on the right, while on the left, opposite the farmhouse, is an interesting but neglected **terraced garden** shaped like a ship with its prow facing out to sea – the terraces were watered from stone irrigation channels fed from holding tanks, all now dry. There's a splendid view of the Badia de Pollença from here and, at the far end of the garden, some fine examples of the *Agave americana*, a succulent whose flower spikes reach heights of three metres. On the farmhouse side of the path there's an equally impressive two-metre-high opuntia cactus.

Beyond the farmhouse, the path turns round to the right, heading north through a small iron gate, then ascends steadily for about 500m, passing between large rocks. Niches in the rocks are occupied by clumps of dwarf fan palms, and you will probably see the blue rock thrushes which inhabit the area. Here and further along the walk, you may also spot wheatears, black-eared wheatears, black redstarts, rock sparrows and wryneck, as well as buzzards, peregrines, kestrels, booted eagles, the occasional osprey, Elconora's falcons in spring and summer, stone chats and goldfinches. Various warblers pass through this area on migration too, but the big ornithological sight here is the **black vulture**, with a wingspan of around two metres, which glides the air currents of the northwest coast. There's a fairly good chance of spotting one from the Vall de Bóquer, and if you're really lucky you'll get a close view, its large, black body contrasting with a brownish head, beak and ruff.

Beyond the boulders the path descends, becoming less rocky, then passes through a gap in a dry-stone wall before ascending gently for about 150m – a scattering of pine trees 50m to the left offers a shady spot for a picnic. This area has been heavily grazed by the valley's semi-wild goats, leaving the vegetation sparse and scrubby. The most noticeable plant is *Asphodelus microcarpus*, which grows up to 2m high, bearing tall spikes of white flowers with a reddish brown vein on each petal. Not even the goats like it. Other common shrubs are the *Hypericum balearicum*, a St John's wort whose yellow flowers are at their best in spring and early summer, and the narrow-leaved cistus and spurges, whose hemispherical bushes bear bright yellow glands. Other spring flowers include a yellow-centred blue gentian and the scarlet pimpernel.

At the top of the next incline the path passes through another wall. On the left there's a large hole in the ridge of the **Serra del Cavall Bernat** – a feature which can only have been created by the action of waves bearing sand and pebbles, meaning that it used to be at sea level. About 50m off to the right of the junction of wall and path, more or less due south, is a 1.5m-high **tunnel**, inside which is a spring. Be careful, however, if you venture in, as it's popular with goats, who like the water and shade. They'll sometimes panic and charge out if they see you coming.

To descend to the sea take the path which bears to the left and then runs down alongside a dried-up watercourse amidst the cries of sea birds and the whispering of the tall carritx grass. Patches of aromatic blue-flowered rosemary line the path. The **beach** at the end of the walk at Cala Bóquer is disappointing. It's predominantly shingle, with at most only a couple of metres of sand, and can be dirty. Nevertheless, the *cala* offers good swimming in clean water.

Return to Port de Pollença via the same route.

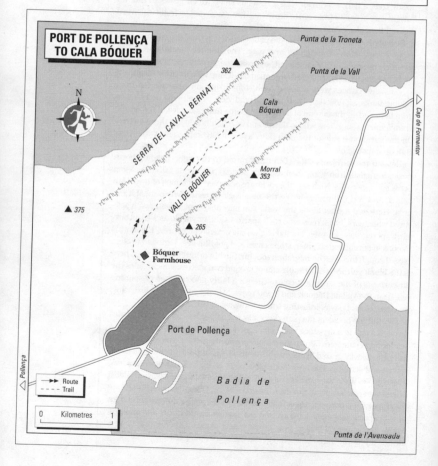

The Península de Formentor

Beyond
Sóller:
Cala Tuent
to the
Cap de
Formentor

Heading northeast out of Port de Pollença, the road clears the military zone at the far end of the resort, before weaving up into the hills at the start of the twenty-kilometre-long **Península de Formentor**, the final spur of the Serra de Tramuntana. At first, the road (which suffers a surfeit of tourists from mid-morning to mid-afternoon) travels inland, out of sight of the true grandeur of the scenery, but after about 4km the **Mirador de Mal Pas** rectifies matters with a string of lookout points perched on the edge of plunging, north-facing sea-cliffs. There are further stunning views, in this case over the south shore, from the **Talaia de Albercutx** watchtower viewpoint, but you'll have to be prepared to tackle the rough side road that climbs the ridge opposite the Mirador de Mal Pas.

Continuing along the main road, it's another couple of kilometres to the roadside parking lot (600ptas) for the **Platja de Formentor**, a pine-clad beach of golden sand in a pretty cove. From the car park, it's a ten-minute walk to the beach through the woods. It's a beautiful spot, with views over to the mountains on the far side of the bay, though it can get a little crowded. In summer, except on Sundays, you can get here from Palma and Port de Pollença on a once-daily **bus** service, or there's also a twice-daily bus, Monday to Saturday, from Alcúdia and Port d'Alcúdia.

At the far end of the beach, and with its own access road from near the parking lot, stands the **Hotel Formentor** (☎971 899100, fax 971 865155; ⑨). Opened in 1930, this wonderful hotel – arguably the island's best – lies low against the forested hillside, its *hacienda*-style architecture enhanced by Neoclassical and Art Deco features and exquisite terraced gardens. The place was once the haunt of the rich and fashionable – Charlie Chaplin and Scott Fitzgerald both stayed here – and although these socialite days are long gone, the hotel preserves an air of understated elegance. The hotel has every facility, and dinner is served on an outside terrace perfumed by the flowers of the gardens; breakfast is taken on the splendid first-floor loggia with spectacular views over the bay. The rooms are not quite as grand as you might imagine, but they are still charming. Stay here if you can afford it – there's a surprisingly good chance of a vacant room, even in high summer.

Beyond the turn-off for the hotel, the main peninsula road runs along a wooded ridge, before tunnelling through Mont Fumat to emerge on the rocky mass of **Cap de Formentor**. This tapered promontory of bleak seacliffs and scrub-covered hills offers magnificent views and is a fruitful area for **birdwatching**, especially from the silver-domed lighthouse stuck on the windswept tip. The lighthouse itself is out of bounds, but you can wander round its rocky environs, where the sparse vegetation is a perfect habitat for lizards and small birds, especially the deep-blue feathered rock thrush and the white-rumped rock dove. From the lighthouse you can also view the steep,

**Beyond
Sóller:
Cala Tuent
to the
Cap de
Formentor**

eastward-facing seacliffs, which shelter colonies of nesting Eleonora's falcons from April to October, whilst circling overhead there are often ravens, martins and swifts. During the spring and summer migrations, thousands of seabirds fly over the cape, Manx and Cory's shearwaters in particular. If you're ready for a snack before heading back from the cape, pop into the **coffee bar** next to the lighthouse.

Alcúdia and around

Moving south from Port de Pollença, it's just 10km round the bay to the compact old town of **Alcúdia**, whose main claims to fame are its imitation medieval walls and the battered remains of the old Roman settlement of Pollentia. Within easy striking distance lies the mega-resort of **Port d'Alcúdia**, where glistening sky-rises sweep around the Badia d'Alcúdia's glorious sandy beach. In summer the place is eminently missable – it's far too crowded to be much fun – but the shoulder seasons are more relaxing and the beach comparatively uncrowded. In the wintertime you'll barely see a soul, but almost all the hotels and restaurants are closed.

The resort stretches for 10km round the bay to the end of the beach at Ca'n Picafort. Most of the swampland that used to extend behind this coastal strip has been drained, but a small area of marsh has been left to form the **Parc Natural de S'Albufera**, a real bird-watchers' delight. Further behind the coast lies a tract of fertile farm-land dotted with country towns, amongst which **Muro**, with its imposing church and old grandee mansions, is the most diverting.

Accommodation is concentrated in Port d'Alcúdia, but in the sum-mertime it's nearly all reserved for package tourists. As a possible alternative, both of Mallorca's official **campsites** border the Badia d'Alcúdia – one on the edge of Ca'n Picafort, the other outside Colònia de Sant Pere (see p.172) – the first is much the better, though in both cases advance reservations are advised.

Transport connections, particularly from May to October, are very good. Frequent **buses** link Port de Pollença, Pollença, Alcúdia, Port d'Alcúdia and Ca'n Picafort. There are also regular services to Alcúdia and its port from Palma, and reasonable summertime con-nections from Port de Sóller and Sóller.

Palma to Alcúdia

Alcúdia is best seen in conjunction with a visit to Pollença and the Serra de Tramuntana, but if you're in a hurry to get there from Palma, there's a more direct, though far less memorable route over the island's central plain. Between five and fifteen **buses** a day make the trip from the capital to Alcúdia, and a **rail line** covers about half the distance, shunting through the wine-producing centre of Binissalem to arrive at its terminus in **INCA**. This industrialized town is heavily promoted for its distilleries, leather factories and Thursday market, but it's an ugly place that's best avoided unless you're a devotee of leather goods (available at several huge factory shops on the bypass). Beyond Inca, the C713 pushes on towards Alcúdia, cutting between Campanet, home to an uninspiring cave complex, and the rural town of Sa Pobla, where one of the island's better markets is held on Sunday mornings. Beyond Inca there's a more attractive look to the landscape – arable land liberally scattered with broken-down windmills – and Muro, 5km southeast of Sa Pobla but easily accessible from Ca'n Picafort, is one of Mallorca's more appealing country towns.

Alcúdia

To pull in the day-trippers, pint-sized ALCÚDIA wears its history on its sleeve. The crenellated wall that encircles much of the town centre is mostly a modern imitation of the medieval original, and, although the sixteenth- to eighteenth-century houses behind it are genuine enough, the whole place is overly spick and span. In fact, little can be seen today which reflects the town's true historical importance. Situated on a neck of land separating two large, sheltered bays, the site's strategic value was first recognized by the Phoenicians, who settled here in around 700 BC and used the place as a staging post for sea trade between northwest Africa and Spain. A few Phoenician trinkets have been unearthed here – most notably examples of their delicate, coloured glass jewellery – but their town disappeared when the Romans built their island capital, Pollentia, on top of the earlier settlement. In 426, the place was destroyed by the Vandals and lay neglected until the Moors built a fortress in about 800, naming it Al Kudia (On the Hill). After the Reconquest, Alcúdia prospered as a major trading centre for the western Mediterranean, a role it performed well into the nineteenth century, when the town slipped into a long and gentle decline – until tourism refloated the economy.

It only takes an hour or so to walk around the antique lanes of Alcúdia's compact centre, and to explore the town walls and their fortified gates. This pleasant stroll can be extended by a visit to four specific sights, though none of them is compelling. Perhaps the most diverting is the **Museu Monogràfic**, at c/Sant Jaume 2, where a single room is stuffed with archeological bits and bobs, primarily Roman artefacts from Pollentia, including amulets, miniature devotional objects and tiny oil-burning lamps. A few paces away, dominating the southwest corner of the old town is the heavyweight and heavily reworked Gothic church of **Sant Jaume**, which holds a modest religious museum. The third sight is on the other side of the ring road just beyond the church, and comprises the broken pillars and mashed-up walls that make up the meagre remains of Roman **Pollentia** (open access; free). Nearly all the stone has been looted by the townsfolk over the centuries, so it's no longer possible to discern the layout of the former capital, which is disappointing. However,

The C713 runs from Palma to Alcúdia via Inca; there's also a newer, faster road – an autopista – running parallel to the old road, but at present it ends at Inca, where it joins the C713.

The Museu Monogràfic is open Tues–Fri 10am–1.30pm & 5–7pm (Oct–March 10am–1.30pm & 4–6pm), Sat & Sun 10.30am–1pm; 200ptas.

Sant Jaume is open, in theory at least, on Tues, Wed, Thurs & Fri 10am– 1pm, Sun 10am–noon; 100ptas.

Pollentia's other Roman remains, the **Teatre Romà** (open access; free), an open-air theatre, are much less skimpy. To get there on foot, a five- to ten-minute stroll, take c/Santa Anna south from the ring road a couple of hundred metres east of the remains of Pollentia; to drive there (c/Santa Anna is one-way into town), take the Port d'Alcúdia road from the ring road and watch for the sign. Dating from the first century BC, this is the smallest of the twenty Roman theatres to have survived in Spain. Despite its modest proportions, however, the builders were able to stick to the standard type of lay-out: eight tiers of seats were carved out of the rocky hillside, divided by two gangways. Inevitably, the stage area, which was constructed of earth and timber, has disappeared.

Buses to Alcúdia halt beside the town walls on Plaça Carles V; there's no tourist office. The only **rooms** in town are above a café at the no-frills *Hostal C'an Llabres* (☎971 545000; ③), on Plaça Constitució, right in the middle of the old town. There are several good places to eat, beginning with the smart *Restaurante Sa Plaça*, also on Plaça Constitució, where they offer traditional Mallorcan cuisine with dishes at around 1800ptas. A less expensive choice is the cosy café-bar of *Ca's Capella*, just east of Sant Jaume at the far end of c/Rectoria.

The Santuari de la Victòria

The northwest shore of the promontory beyond Alcúdia offers fine views of the Badia de Pollença, but first you have to clear the villas of Bonaire, a sprawling development of precious little interest. Beyond, about 4km from Alcúdia, you'll pass the barracks-like *Albergue Juvenil de Alcúdia* (mid-June to Aug; ☎ & fax 971 545395; ①), a 120-bed **youth hostel** where vacant beds are a rarity – school parties predominate – so turning up on the off-chance is pretty pointless and reservations need to be made well in advance; there's no public transport.

About 1km further along the headland, a turning on the right climbs 500m up the wooded hillside to the **Santuari de la Victòria**, a fortress-like church in a lovely spot, sheltering a crude but much-venerated statue of the Virgin. The adjacent **restaurant** (closed Mon), a cavernous affair named after the sanctuary, has splendid views from its terrace bar and serves first-rate food – guinea fowl and chicken are the specialities.

Port d'Alcúdia

PORT D'ALCÚDIA, 2km south of Alcúdia, is easily the biggest and busiest of the resorts on the north coast, its myriad restaurants and café-bars attracting crowds from a seemingly interminable string of high-rise hotels and apartment buildings. This is not, however, to equate this resort with some of its seamier rivals, for the tower blocks are relatively well distributed, the streets are neat and tidy and

there's a prosperous and easy-going air, with families particularly well catered for. Predictably, the daytime focus is the **beach**, a superb arc of pine-studded golden sand, which stretches south for 10km from the two purpose-built jetties of Port d'Alcúdia's combined marina, cruise boat and fishing harbour. About half a kilometre east of the marina along the headland lies the **commercial port**, Mallorca's second largest container terminal after Palma.

A tourist **"train"** (on wheels, with clearly marked roadside stops) runs up and down the length of the resort at hourly intervals, transporting sunbaked bodies from one part of the beach to another. Not that there's very much to distinguish anywhere from anywhere else – the palm-thatched *balnearios* (beach-bars) are a great help in actually remembering where you are. A walkway runs along the back of the beach, which is usually more crowded to the north. A kilometre or so inland, reached along Avinguda del Tucan, the much-vaunted **Hidropark** is a gigantic pool complex with all sorts of flumes and chutes (May–Oct daily 10am–6pm; 1900ptas).

Practicalities

Port d'Alcúdia acts as northern Mallorca's summertime transport hub, with **bus** services to and from Palma, Port de Sóller, Artà, Cala Millor and Cala Rajada, as well as neighbouring towns and resorts. Most local and long-distance bus services travel the length of **Carretera d'Artà**, the main drag, which slices right through the resort, running broadly parallel to the bay and punctuated by a series of clearly signed bus stops (there is no bus station). The main

Alcúdia and around

Oficina d'Informació Turística (Mon–Sat 9am–7pm; ☎971 892615) is situated on Carretera d'Artà about 2km southwest of the marina. The office can supply all sorts of information, most usefully free maps marked with all the resort's hotels and apartments.

In season, vacant rooms are few and far between, but there's a vague chance amongst the low-priced **hostals** clustered behind the marina in the oldest (and tattiest) part of the resort. The least expensive rooms here – basic, no-frills affairs – are provided by the mundanely modern *Puerto*, c/Teodor Canet 47 (April–Oct; ☎971 545447; ③), and the *Vista Alegre*, which at least has the advantage of being on the seafront, at Passeig Marítim 10 (☎971 546977; ③). In winter almost all the hotels and *hostals* close down, but in the shoulder seasons it's sometimes possible to get a good deal at one of the plusher **hotels**. Try along the seafront at the *Hotel Platja d'Or*, an attractive 230-bedroom complex about 3km south of the marina, with its own swimming pools and balconied bedrooms looking out to sea (April–Oct; ☎971 890052; ⑦), or at the *Hotel Condesa*, a few metres further along the beach, a huge L-shaped complex with all the facilities you can think of, from bike rental to a children's playground (April–Oct; ☎971 890120, fax 971 890049; ⑤).

There's also the possibility of **camping**, at *Sun Club Picafort*, 9km southeast of Port d'Alcúdia, an all-year site with a great location, just a stone's throw from the beach (☎971 537863, fax 971 537511). It has 500 pitches, as well as its own swimming pool, tennis courts, supermarket, nightclub and restaurant. Watersports equipment can be rented, as can mobile homes, though these usually need to be booked well in advance. In high season (mid-June to mid-Sept) campers pay 575ptas each, plus 1530–2625ptas for a site, depending on size; cars (525ptas) and IVA (7 percent) further add to the bill and there are small supplementary charges for electrical hook-ups and hot water. Off-season rates are around 25 percent less.

There are dozens of cafés and restaurants in Port d'Alcúdia, although most are identikit pizzerias and tourist-style restaurants serving mediocre versions of Spanish food. There are, however, exceptions, in particular the *Miramar*, Passeig Marítim 2, which serves delicious seafood, and the well-established *Restaurante Lovento*, along the waterfront at c/Gabriel Roca 33, with fish dishes from about 1800ptas. Alternatively, *Pizzeria Roma Restaurante*, opposite the main tourist office on Carretera d'Artà, serves great crepes, steaks and pizzas at very reasonable prices – pizzas cost from 650ptas.

There's a superabundance of **car, moped and bicycle rental** companies strung out along Carretera d'Artà. Mountain bikes work out at about 1500ptas per day, 3000ptas for three days; cars 4200ptas and 9900ptas respectively. Summer **boat trips**, leaving from the marina at the north end of the beach, explore the rocky, mountainous coastline to the northeast of Port d'Alcúdia: the shorter excursion travels as far as the tip of the headland, the Cap des Pinar, without venturing into the Badia de Pollença (March–Oct 3 daily; 3hr; 1600ptas); the longer version continues round this headland and across the bay to the Platja de Formentor (May–Oct: 1 daily; 4hr; 2000ptas).

The Parc Natural de S'Albufera

Port d'Alcúdia lies at the beginning of an intensively developed tourist zone, which takes advantage of a great swath of pine-studded sandy beach around the Badia d'Alcúdia. Some lessons have been learnt from earlier developments – there are more recreational facilities and at least some of the coast has been left unscathed – but first impressions are primarily of concrete and glass. The beach and the sky-rises end on the outskirts of **Ca'n Picafort**, once an important fishing port – the old town still preserves vestiges of its earlier function – but today an uninteresting suburban sprawl.

The Parc Natural de S'Albufera is open daily: April–Sept 9am–7pm; Oct–March 9am–5pm; free. The reception centre is open daily 9am–1pm & 2–5.30pm (7pm April–Sept).

In this unpromising environment, the 2000-acre **Parc Natural de S'Albufera**, a segment of pristine wetland on the west side of Ca'n Picafort, makes a wonderful change. Swampland once extended round much of the bay, but large-scale reclamation began in the nineteenth century, when a British company dug a network of channels and installed a steam engine to pump the water out. These endeavours were prompted by a desire to eradicate malaria – then the scourge of the local population – as much as by the need for more farmland. Further drainage schemes accompanied the frantic tourist boom of the 1960s, and only in the last decade has the Balearic government recognized the ecological importance of the wetland and organized a park to protect what little remains.

Access to the park is straightforward, but if you're driving you'll need to be alert: heading southeast from Port d'Alcúdia on the C712, watch for the large *Hotel Playa Esperanza* on the left after about 6km; the park's signposted entrance is on the right about 200m further on, a sharp turn just after a small bridge. **Buses** from Port d'Alcúdia to Ca'n Picafort and points southeast stop by the entrance. From here, a country lane leads to the reception centre, **Sa Roca**, just over 1km away, where you can pick up a free map, a permit and a list of birds you might see. There's a small wildlife display here too and an adjacent building houses a second flora and fauna identity parade.

Footpaths and cycle trails leave the reception area to explore the reedy, watery tract beyond. It's a superb habitat, where ten well-appointed hides allow excellent **birdwatching**. Over 200 species have been spotted, resident wetland-loving birds such as the crake, warbler, tern and hoopoe; autumn and/or springtime migrants, like the heron, crane, plover and godwit; and wintering species such as the egret, sandpiper and wagtail. Such rich pickings attract birds of prey in their scores, especially kestrels, marsh harriers and ospreys. The open ground edging the reed beds supports many different wild flowers, the most striking of which are the orchids that bloom during April and May.

Muro

From the west side of Ca'n Picafort, a gentle country road crosses a pancake-flat, windmill-studded hinterland before reaching the hill-top town of **MURO**, a sleepy little place, dotted with big old town houses built by wealthy landowners. There's a big bash here on January 16 for the Revetla de Sant Antoni Abat (Eve of St Antony's Day), when locals gather round bonfires to drink and dance, tucking into specialities like sausages and eel pies (*espinagades*) made with eels from the marshes of S'Albufera. Quite what St Antony (251–356) – an Egyptian hermit who spent most of his long life resisting temptation in the desert – would have made of these high jinks it's hard to say, even if for the rest of the year he would have been quite safe in Muro.

In the main square, Plaça Constitució, the domineering church of **St Joan** is a real hotchpotch of architectural styles, its monumental Gothic lines uneasily modified by the sweeping sixteenth-century arcades above the aisles. A slender arch connects the church to the adjacent **belfry**, an imposing seven-storey construction partly designed as a watchtower; sometimes it's possible to go to the top, where the views out over the coast are superb. The church's cavernous interior has a mighty vaulted roof and an immense altarpiece, a flashy extravaganza of columns, parapets and tiers in a folksy Baroque style.

The main square itself is an attractive open area flanked by old stone houses. From here it's a couple of minutes' walk to the **Museu Etnològic**, c/Major 15, surely one of the least visited museums on the island – the custodians seem positively amazed when a visitor shows up. The museum occupies a rambling old mansion and showcases a motley assortment of local bygones, from old agricultural implements, pottery and apothecary jars through to Mallorcan bagpipes and traditional costumes. Amongst the agricultural equipment there's a broken-down example of a mule- or donkey-driven water wheel, a *noria*. Introduced by the Moors, these were a common feature of the Mallorcan landscape for hundreds of years, though there are few of them left today. Among the pottery, look out for the *siurels*, miniature green- and red-painted figurines created in a naive style. Now debased as a mass-produced tourist trinket, they were originally made as whistles – hence the spout with the hole – shaped in the form of animals, humans, and mythological or imaginary figures.

The Museu Etnològic is open Tues–Sat 10am–2pm & 4–7pm, Sun 10am–2pm; 300ptas.

That's just about it for Muro, though on a hot summer's day you'll be glad of a drink at one of the **cafés** around the main square – the *Ca'n Costitx*, opposite the church, is as good a place as any. Local **buses**, arriving by the main square, link Muro with Ca'n Picafort and Palma.

Travel details

Buses

From **Alcúdia** to: Ca'n Picafort (May–Oct every 15min; Nov–April 3 daily; 45min); Lluc (May–Oct Mon–Sat 2 daily; 1hr 10min); Palma (May–Oct Mon–Sat hourly, 5 on Sun; Nov–April 5 daily; 1hr); Platja de Formentor (May–Oct Mon–Sat 2 daily; 35min); Pollença (May–Oct every 15min; Nov–April 3 daily; 30min); Port d'Alcúdia (May–Oct every 15min; Nov–April 5 daily; 15min); Port de Pollença (May–Oct every 15min; Nov–April 3 daily; 15min); Port de Sóller (May–Oct Mon–Sat 2 daily; 2hr 15min); Sóller (May–Oct Mon–Sat 2 daily; 2hr).

From **Andratx** to: Camp de Mar (May–Oct hourly; Nov–April every 2hr; 10min); Palma (May–Oct hourly; Nov–April every 2hr; 35min); Peguera (May–Oct Mon–Sat 7 daily, 3 on Sun; Nov–April 1 daily; 10min); Port d'Andratx (May–Oct hourly; Nov–April every 2hr; 10min); Sant Elm (May–Oct Mon–Sat 7 daily, 3 on Sun; Nov–April 1 daily; 10min); Valldemossa (Mon–Sat 1 daily; 1hr).

From **Cala Sant Vicenç** to: Lluc (May–Oct Mon–Sat 2 daily; 35min); Pollença (3–5 daily; 15min); Port de Pollença (3–5 daily; 20min).

From **Ca'n Picafort** to: Alcúdia (May–Oct every 15min; Nov–April 3 daily; 45min); Cala Millor (May–Oct Mon–Sat 7 daily; 1hr); Cala Rajada (May–Oct Mon–Sat 9 daily; 35min); Lluc (May–Oct Mon–Sat 2 daily; 1hr 45min); Muro (May–Oct 2–3 daily; 10min); Palma (2–3 daily; 1hr); Pollença (3–5 daily; 50min); Port d'Alcúdia (May–Oct every 15min; Nov–April 3 daily; 30min); Port de Pollença (3–5 daily; 1hr); Port de Sóller (May–Oct Mon–Sat 2 daily; 3hr); Porto Cristo (May–Oct Mon–Sat 3 daily; 1hr); Sóller (May–Oct Mon–Sat 2 daily; 2hr 50min).

From **Deià** to: Palma (5 daily; 45min); Port de Sóller (5 daily; 25min); Sóller (5 daily; 20min); Valldemossa (5 daily; 15min).

From **Lluc** to: Alcúdia (May–Oct Mon–Sat 2 daily; 1hr 10min); Cala Sant Vicenç (May–Oct Mon–Sat 2 daily; 35min); C'an Picafort (May–Oct Mon–Sat 2 daily; 1hr 45min); Palma (1–2 daily; 1hr); Pollença (May–Oct Mon–Sat 2 daily; 25min); Port d'Alcúdia (May–Oct Mon–Sat 2 daily; 50min); Port de Pollença (May–Oct Mon–Sat 2 daily; 1hr 15min); Port de Sóller (May–Oct Mon–Sat 2 daily; 1hr 15min); Sóller (May–Oct Mon–Sat 2 daily; 1hr 10min).

From **Muro** to: Ca'n Picafort (May–Oct 2–3 daily; 10min); Palma (2–4 daily; 50min).

From **Peguera** to: Andratx (May–Oct Mon–Sat 7 daily, 3 on Sun; Nov–April 1 daily; 10min); Port d'Andratx (May–Oct Mon–Sat 8 daily, 3 on Sun; Nov–April 1 daily; 10min); Sant Elm (May–Oct Mon–Sat 7 daily, 3 on Sun; Nov–April 1 daily; 20min); Valldemossa (Mon–Sat 1 daily; 1hr 10min).

From **Platja de Formentor** to: Alcúdia (May–Oct Mon–Sat 2 daily; 35min); Palma (May–Oct Mon–Sat 1 daily; 1hr 15min); Port d'Alcúdia (May–Oct Mon–Sat 2 daily; 25min); Port de Pollença (May–Oct Mon–Sat 1 daily; 20min).

From **Pollença** to: Alcúdia (May–Oct every 15min; Nov–April 3 daily; 30min); Cala Sant Vicenç (3–5 daily; 15min); Ca'n Picafort (3–5 daily; 50min); Lluc (May–Oct Mon–Sat 2 daily; 25min); Palma (3–5 daily; 1hr); Port d'Alcúdia (3–5 daily; 20min); Port de Pollença (6–16 daily; 10min); Port de Sóller (May–Oct Mon–Sat 2 daily; 1hr 45min); Sóller (May–Oct Mon–Sat 2 daily; 1hr 30min).

Travel Details

From **Port d'Alcúdia** to: Alcúdia (May–Oct every 15min; Nov–April 5 daily; 15min); Artà (May–Oct Mon–Sat 5 daily; 30min); Cala Millor (May–Oct Mon–Sat 3 daily; 1hr); Cala Rajada (May–Oct Mon–Sat 2 daily; 40min); Ca'n Picafort (May–Oct every 15min; Nov–April 3 daily; 30min); Lluc (May–Oct Mon–Sat 2 daily; 1hr 15min); Palma (May–Oct Mon–Sat hourly, 5 on Sun; Nov–April 5 daily; 1hr 10min); Platja de Formentor (May–Oct Mon–Sat 2 daily; 25min); Pollença (3–5 daily; 20min); Port de Pollença (May–Oct every 15min; Nov–April 3 daily; 15min); Port de Sóller (May–Oct Mon–Sat 2 daily; 2hr 30min); Sóller (May–Oct Mon–Sat 2 daily; 2hr 15min).

From **Port d'Andratx** to: Andratx (May–Oct hourly; Nov–April every 2hr; 10min); Camp de Mar (May–Oct hourly; Nov–April every 2hr; 20min); Palma (May–Oct hourly; Nov–April every 2hr; 45min); Peguera (May–Oct Mon–Sat 8 daily, 3 on Sun; Nov–April 1 daily; 10min).

From **Port de Pollença** to: Alcúdia (May–Oct every 15min; Nov–April 3 daily; 15min); Cala Sant Vicenç (3–5 daily; 20min); Ca'n Picafort (3–5 daily; 1hr); Lluc (May–Oct Mon–Sat 2 daily; 50min); Palma (3–5 daily; 1hr 10min); Platja de Formentor (May–Oct Mon–Sat 1 daily; 20min); Pollença (6–16 daily; 10min); Port d'Alcúdia (May–Oct every 15min; Nov–April 3 daily; 15min); Port de Sóller (May–Oct Mon–Sat 2 daily; 2hr); Sóller (May–Oct Mon–Sat 2 daily; 1hr 50min).

From **Port de Sóller** to: Alcúdia (May–Oct Mon–Sat 2 daily; 2hr 15min); C'an Picafort (May–Oct Mon–Sat 2 daily; 3hr); Deià (5 daily; 25min); Lluc (May–Oct Mon–Sat 2 daily; 1hr 15min); Palma (5 daily; 35min); Pollença (May–Oct Mon–Sat 2 daily; 1hr 45min); Port d'Alcúdia (May–Oct Mon–Sat 2 daily; 2hr 30min); Port de Pollença (May–Oct Mon–Sat 2 daily; 2hr); Sóller (7 daily; 5min); Valldemossa (5 daily; 30min).

From **Sant Elm** to: Andratx (May–Oct Mon–Sat 7 daily, 3 on Sun; Nov–April 1 daily; 10min); Peguera (May–Oct Mon–Sat 7 daily, 3 on Sun 3; Nov–April 1 daily; 20min).

From **Sóller** to: Alcúdia (May–Oct Mon–Sat 2 daily; 2hr); C'an Picafort (May–Oct Mon–Sat 2 daily; 2hr 50min); Deià (5 daily; 20min); Lluc (May–Oct Mon–Sat 2 daily; 1hr 10min); Palma (5 daily; 30min); Pollença (May–Oct Mon–Sat 2 daily; 1hr 30min); Port d'Alcúdia (May–Oct Mon–Sat 2 daily; 2hr 15min); Port de Pollença (May–Oct Mon–Sat 2 daily; 1hr 50min); Port de Sóller (7 daily; 5min); Valldemossa (5 daily; 25min).

From **Valldemossa** to: Andratx (Mon–Sat 1 daily; 1hr); Banyalbufar (Mon–Sat 1 daily; 30min); Deià (5 daily; 15min); Estellencs (Mon–Sat 1 daily; 45min); Palma (5 daily; 30min); Peguera (Mon–Sat 1 daily; 1hr 10min); Port de Sóller (5 daily; 35min); Sóller (5 daily; 30min).

Chapter 3

Southeast Mallorca

For most visitors, the hinterland of southeast Mallorca is simply a monotonous interlude between airport and resort. However, it was this fertile central plain – Es Pla as it's known to the islanders, stretching from the Serra de Tramuntana in the west to the Serres de Llevant, the hilly range which shadows the east coast – that defined Mallorca until the twentieth century. The majority of the island's inhabitants lived here, it produced enough food to meet almost every domestic requirement, and Palma's gentry were reliant on Es Pla estates for their income. To defend "The Plain" from marauding pirates, Mallorca's medieval kings constructed hilltop fortresses along the Serres de Llevant, leaving the eastern shoreline an unprotected area fit only for a smattering of insignificant fishing villages and tiny ports. And so matters remained until the tourist boom stood everything on its head: from the 1960s onwards, the developers simply bypassed Es Pla to focus on the picturesque coves of the east coast, where they constructed a long string of brash resorts.

In truth, the towns of Es Pla do not put themselves out to attract visitors. There's hardly anywhere to stay, and restaurants are thin on the ground, while tourist offices simply don't exist. As a consequence, visiting the region is mostly a matter of day trips. The softly hued landscape, patterned with olive orchards, chunky farmhouses and country towns of low, whitewashed houses huddled beneath outsized churches, is appealing, though there's precious little to distin-

---

Accommodation price codes

All the accommodation prices in this book have been coded using the symbols below, corresponding to the least expensive double room in each establishment in high season, excluding special offers. For a full explanation see p.34.

① Under 3000ptas   ④ 6000–8000ptas   ⑦ 14,000–20,000ptas
② 3000–4000ptas   ⑤ 8000–10,000ptas   ⑧ 20,000–25,000ptas
③ 4000–6000ptas   ⑥ 10,000–14,000ptas   ⑨ Over 25,000ptas

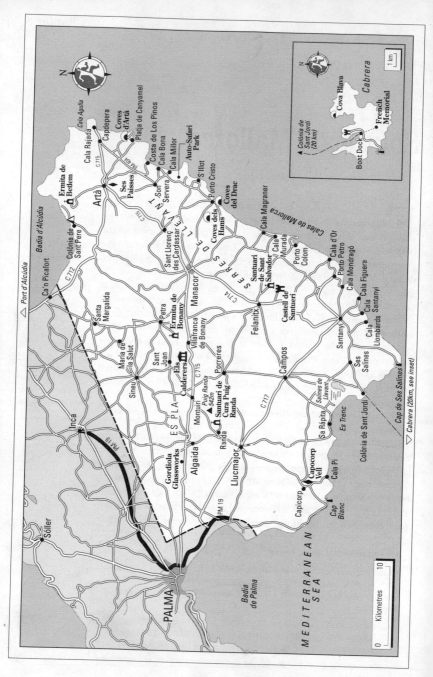

Castell de Santueri

Taula, Menorca

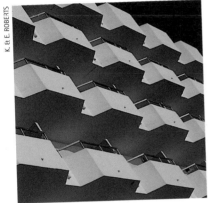

Holiday apartments, Cala Millor

Windsurfers, Fornells

Cala San Vicenç

Traditional farm gate, Menorca

Maó

Port de Pollença

Deià

Península de Formentor

Ermita de Nostra Senyora de Bonany, Petra

Cap de Formentor

guish one settlement from another, with the notable exception of Sineu, which has a particularly imposing parish church. Other sights worth making a beeline for are the impressive monastery perched on the summit of **Puig Randa** and, in the Serres de Llevant, the hilltop shrine at **Artà** and the delightful medieval castle at **Capdepera**. All these destinations are accessible from the C715, which runs the 70km from Palma to Artà.

The ancient fishing villages of the **east coast** have mostly been transformed into mega-resorts, but there are a couple of enjoyable seaside towns which have avoided the worst excesses of concrete and glass: **Cala Rajada**, a lively holiday spot bordered by fine beaches and a beautiful pine-shrouded coastline, and **Cala Figuera**, which surrounds a lovely, steep-sided cove. This coast also boasts the cave systems of **Coves d'Artà** and **Coves del Drac**, justifiably famous for their extravagant stalactites and stalagmites. On the **south coast**, the scenery changes again with hills and coves giving way to sparse flat-lands, whose only star turn is the port-cum-resort of **Colònia de Sant Jordi**, from where boat trips leave for the scrubby remoteness of the fauna-rich island of **Cabrera**.

Given the general dearth of **accommodation** in the interior, and the difficulty of finding a room in the coastal package resorts, it's well worth bearing in mind the monastery on Puig Randa, which offers simple accommodation, as does the Ermita de Sant Salvador, outside Felanitx, and the Ermita de Nostra Senyora de Bonany, near Petra – especially as there's usually space and the rates are low.

Travelling by **bus** presents problems. Palma has direct links with almost every resort and town, but services between the towns of Es Pla are virtually non-existent while those along the coast are patchy. Broadly speaking, you'll manage to get around most easily in the north between Cala Rajada, Artà and Cala Millor, and to the south between Cala d'Or, Cala Figuera and Colònia de Sant Jordi. Elsewhere, you'll be struggling without a car.

East from Palma to Artà

Whisking through the agricultural landscape to the east of Palma, the C715 is lined with roadside tourist attractions. The most successful of these are the **Gordiola Glassworks**, which houses a superb muse-um, and **Els Calderers**, a big old country house which was once the focus of a prosperous estate but is now a museum illustrating *hacienda* life in the nineteenth century. The third choice, the pearl-making factory of **Perlas Majorica**, at Manacor, lags some way behind. By far the most interesting detours from the highway are to the monastery surmounting **Puig Randa**, and to **Sineu**, once the site of a royal palace and now the prettiest town on the plain. Neither should **Artà**, tucked away amongst the Serres de Llevant, be over-looked, not only for its delightful location, but also for its proximity to the fascinating Talayotic settlement of **Ses Paisses** and the laid-back mini-resort of **Colònia de Sant Pere**.

Buses from Palma to Petra, Manacor and Artà are fast and frequent, but there are no services to Sineu. Apart from the spartan rooms at the monasteries on Puig Randa and at the Ermita de Bonany near Petra, the only places to stay on or near the C715 are at Artà and Sineu.

Gordiola Glassworks

The Gordiola Glassworks is open May– Sept daily 9am–8pm; Oct–April Mon–Sat 9am–1.30pm & 3–7pm, Sun 9am–1pm; free.

Some 19km east of Palma along the C715, the **Gordiola Glassworks** (Ca'n Gordiola) occupies a conspicuous castle-like building whose crenellated walls and clumsy loggias date from the 1960s. Don't be put off by its appearance, however – or by the herd of tourist coaches parked outside. For a start, you can watch highly skilled glass-blowers in action, practising their precise art in a gloomy hall, designed to resemble a medieval church and illuminated by glowing furnaces. Guides explain the techniques involved – the fusion of silica, soda and lime at a temperature of 1100°C – and you can hang around for as long as you like. It is, of course, all part of a public relations exercise intended to push you towards the adjacent gift shops. Here, amongst a massive assortment of glass and ceramic items, you'll find everything from the most abysmal tourist tat to works of great delicacy, notably green-tinted chandeliers of traditional Mallorcan design priced at around 190,000ptas.

The gift shops are one thing, but the **museum**, tucked away on the top floor, is quite another. The owners of the glassworks, the Gordiola family, have been in business in Mallorca since the early eighteenth century, when the first of the line, Gordiola Rigal, arrived from the Spanish mainland. Since then, seven successive generations have accumulated an extraordinary collection of glassware: each of the museum's fifty-odd cabinets is devoted to a particular theme or country and each is labelled, though if you've more than a general interest it's worth investing in a guidebook from the gift shop (950ptas).

On display are examples of the earliest Gordiola work, green-coloured jugs and jars of a frothy consistency, where both the shade and the trapped air bubbles were entirely unwanted. Heated by wood and coal, the original hoop-shaped furnaces had tiny windows through which works-in-progress could be rotated. With such limited technology, however, it was impossible to maintain a consistently high temperature, so the glass could neither be clarified nor cleared of its last air bubbles. Aware of these deficiencies, the next of the line, Bernardo Gordiola, spent years in Venice cultivating the leading glassmakers of the day, and the results of what he learnt can be seen in the same display case. He developed a style of Mallorcan-made jugs decorated with *laticinos*, glass strips wrapped round the object in the Venetian manner, and, in general, improved the quality of the glass. Amongst later Gordiola work, kitchen- and tableware predominate – bottles, vases, jugs and glasses – in a variety of shades, of which green remains the most distinctive. There's also a tendency to extrapolate functional designs into imaginative, ornamental pieces, ranging from hideous fish-shaped receptacles designed for someone's mantlepiece to the most poetic of vases.

Yet Gordiola glassware is just a fraction of the collection. Other cabinets feature pieces from every corner of the globe, beginning with finds from Classical Greece, the Nile and the Euphrates. There's also an exquisite sample of early Islamic glassware, Spanish and Chinese opalescents, and superb Venetian vases dating to the seventeenth and eighteenth centuries. More modern stuff includes goblets from Germany and Austria, devotional pieces from Poland, traditional Caithness crystal from Scotland, and a striking melange of Norwegian Art Nouveau glasswork. The museum also exhibits decorative items from cultures where glass was unknown: an eclectic ensemble of pre-Columbian pieces worked in clay, quartz and obsidian, along with the zoomorphic and anthropomorphic basalt figures characteristic of the Sahara.

Algaida and around

ALGAIDA, just off the main highway 2km east of the glassworks, is typical of the small agricultural towns that sprinkle Mallorca's central plain – low, whitewashed houses fanning out from an old Gothic-Baroque church. It's hardly inspiring, but if you're travelling the C715 you'll need to pass through here to reach **Puig Randa**, the highest of a slim band of hills on the north side of Llucmajor. Beginning around 3km south of Algaida, the road to the 542-metre summit – a well-surfaced but serpentine affair, some 5km long – starts by climbing through the hamlet of **RANDA**, a pretty little place of old stone houses harbouring a comfortable three-star hotel, *Es Reco de Randa* (☎971 660997, fax 971 662558; ⑦). The hotel, with only fourteen rooms and an outdoor swimming pool, is usually booked up months in advance, but it's a good spot to take a break – the terraced restaurant serves delicious food, especially roast lamb and suckling pig.

The top of the hill is flat enough to accommodate a substantial walled complex, the **Santuari de Nostra Senyora de Cura** ("Hermitage of Our Lady of Cura" – Cura is the name of the upper part of Puig Randa). Entry is through a seventeenth-century portal, but most of the buildings beyond are plain and modern, the work of the present incumbents, Franciscan monks who arrived in 1913 after the site had lain abandoned for decades. The original hermitage was founded by the scholar and missionary Ramon Llull in the thirteenth century, and it was here that he prepared his acolytes for their missions to Asia and Africa. Succeeding generations of Franciscans turned the site into a centre of religious learning, and the scholastic tradition was maintained by a grammar school, which finally fizzled

*For more on
Ramon Llull,
see p.246.*

out in 1826. The Llull connection makes the monastery an important place of pilgrimage, especially for the Bendición de los Frutos (Blessing of the Crops) held on the fourth Sunday after Easter.

Nothing remains of Llull's foundation and the oldest surviving building is the quaintly gabled **chapel**, parts of which date from the 1660s. Situated to the right of the entrance, the chapel is homely and familiar inside, its narrow, truncated nave spanned by a barrel-vaulted roof. Next door, in the old school, there's a modest **museum** (donation requested) with a collection of ecclesiastical bric-a-brac and a few interesting old photos taken by the Franciscans before they rebuilt the place. It only takes a few minutes to look around and soon you'll be moving on to the nearby terrace **café**, which offers average food and superb views out across the island. There are a couple of other belvederes on the hilltop, plus an information office by the main entrance where you can get free maps and fix yourself up with a **room** in the guest quarters – a self-contained, modern block of basic bedrooms (advance bookings on ☎971 660994; ①).

The sanctuaries of Sant Honorat and Gràcia

There are two other, less significant sanctuaries on the lower slopes of Puig Randa. Heading back down the hill, past the radio masts, it's a couple of kilometres to the easily missable sharp left turn for the **Santuari de Sant Honorat**, which comprises a tiny church and a few conventual buildings of medieval provenance. Back on the main summit road, a further 1.2km down the hill, is the more appealing third and final monastery, the **Santuari de Gràcia**, which is approached through a signposted gateway on the left and along a short asphalt road. Founded in the fifteenth century, the white-washed walls of this tiny sanctuary are tucked underneath a severe cliff face, which throngs with nesting birds. The simple barrel-vaulted church boasts some handsome majolica tiles, but it's the panoramic view of Es Pla's rolling farmland that holds the eye.

East of Algaida

Travelling east of Algaida on the C715, you'll soon reach the new, giant-sized Munper leather shop and then the **Perlas Orquidea factory**, where artificial pearls are made up from glass globules, an industry for which Mallorca is internationally famous. The sales rooms are extensive and you can glimpse aspects of the production process. Similar pearl plants can be found at Manacor, further east on the main road (see p.169), though it's more enjoyable to detour north to Sineu and Petra via **MONTUIRI**, a gentle sweep of pastel-shaded stone houses on a low hill immediately north of the main road. In the heart of town, it's worth taking a peek at the Baroque retables of the largely Gothic church of **Sant Bartomeu**, an imposing pile next to the small main square.

Sineu

SINEU, 12km north of Montuiri, is undoubtedly the most interesting
of the ancient agricultural towns of Es Pla. Glued to a hill at the geographical centre of the island, the town had obvious strategic advantages for the independent kings of fourteenth-century Mallorca.
Jaume II built a royal palace here; his asthmatic successor, Sancho,
came to take the upland air; and the last of the dynasty, Jaume III,
slept in Sineu the night before he was defeated and killed at the battle of Llucmajor by Pedro of Aragon. The new Aragonese monarchs
had no need of the Sineu palace, which disappeared long ago, but
former pretensions survive in the massive stone facade of **Nostra
Senyora de los Angeles**, the grandest parish church on the island.
Built in the thirteenth century, the church was extensively remodelled three hundred years later, but the majestic simplicity of the
original Gothic design is still plain to see – though it's in a poor state
of repair. At the side a single-span arch connects with the colossal
freestanding bell tower, and at the front, at the top of the steps, a big,
modern and aggressive statue of a winged lion – the emblem of the
town's patron, St Mark – stands guard, courtesy of Franco's cronies.

Beside the church is the unassuming main square, Sa Plaça. Here
you'll find the first of two excellent, traditional Mallorcan **restaurants**. The *Celler Ca'n Font*, whose cavernous interior doubles as a
wine vault, hence the enormous wooden barrels, has inexpensive
Mallorcan snacks from 600ptas. The nearby *Celler Es Grop*, c/Major
18, has similar decor but a more welcoming atmosphere, and the
food, if anything, is even better, with main courses at around
1000ptas. Both restaurants are at their busiest on Wednesdays,
when the town fizzes with one of Mallorca's biggest fresh produce
markets. Sineu also has (and this is something of a surprise) a very
good **hotel**, the German-run *Leon de Sineu*, c/Bous 129 (☎971
520211, fax 971 855058; ⑨), set in an attractively refurbished mansion five minutes' stroll from Sa Plaça: walk down the hill from the
square, turn first right and keep going.

Petra

Nothing very exciting happens in **PETRA**, 11km east of Sineu, but it
was the birthplace of Junipero Serra, the eighteenth-century
Franciscan friar who played an important role in the settlement of
Spanish North America. Serra's missionary endeavours began in
1749 when he landed at Veracruz on the Gulf of Mexico. Despite a
particularly unpleasant voyage, he and his band of monks promptly
walked 500km to Mexico City, thereby completing the first of many
mind-boggling treks. For eighteen years Serra thrashed around the
remoter parts of Mexico until, entirely by chance, political machina-
tions back in Europe saved him from obscurity. In 1768, Carlos III
claimed the west coast of the North American continent for Spain

and, to substantiate his claim, dispatched a small expeditionary force of soldiers and monks north. Serra happened to be in the right place at the right time, and was assigned to lead the priests. Even by Serra's standards, the walk from Mexico City to California was a hell of a trek, but almost all the force survived to reach the Pacific Ocean somewhere near the present US–Mexico border in early 1769. Over the next decade, Serra and his small party of priests set about converting the Native Americans of coastal California to the Catholic faith, and established a string of nine missions along the Pacific coast, including San Diego and San Francisco. Serra was beatified by Pope Paul II in 1988.

Petra makes a reasonable hand of its connection with Serra. In the upper part of town, on c/Major, is the chunky church of **Sant Bernat**, beside which – down a narrow side street – lies a modest sequence of majolica panels honouring Serra's life and missionary work. This simple tribute is backed up by a self-effacing **museum** (donation requested) in a pleasant old house at the end of the side street, with several rooms devoted to Serra's cult: the honours paid to him, the books written about him, and the paintings of him. Another room focuses on Serra's work in California, with photos and models of his foundations. Three doors up the street, at no. 6, is the humble white-washed stone and brick dwelling **house** where he was born. Both can be visited between 9am and 8pm, Monday to Friday, but sometimes you have to collect the key from the custodian – follow the instructions posted outside.

Other than that, there's little reason to hang around – intriguing Els Calderers is just 10km away to the south off the C715 (see below) – though the hilltop **Ermita de Nostra Senyora de Bonany**, immediately to the south of Petra, does offer extensive views. To get there, take the Felanitx road out of Petra and, on the edge of the village, watch for the sign. The monastery is at the end of a bumpy, four-kilometre country lane and offers simple **rooms** (reservations on ☎971 561101; ①), but there's no hot water, food, cooking utensils or bed linen for guests.

Els Calderers

*Els Calderers
is open daily:
April–Sept
10am–6pm;
Oct–March
10am–5pm;
900ptas.*

Dating mostly from the eighteenth century, **Els Calderers** is a charming country house which bears witness to the wealth and influence the island's landed gentry once enjoyed. The house is tucked away at the end of a country lane 2km north of – and clearly sign-posted from – the C715 between Montuiri and Villafranca de Bonany. It was built for the Veri family as the focus of a large estate which produced a mixed bag of agricultural produce. The main cash crop was originally grapes, though this changed in the 1870s when *phylloxera*, a greenfly-like aphid, destroyed the island's vineyards. The Veris switched to cereals, and at the beginning of the twentieth century were at the forefront of efforts to modernize Mallorcan agriculture – much to the consternation of some of their more stick-in-the-mud neighbours, and to the horror of a workforce unused to the clanking of metal and the swivelling of fast-moving parts.

Flanked by a pair of crumpled-looking lions, the entrance to the house leads to a sequence of handsome rooms surrounding a cool courtyard with a freshwater well. All are kitted out with antique furniture, objets d'art and family portraits, and each has a clearly defined function, from the dainty music room to the hunting room, with assorted stuffed animal heads, and the master's office, with big armchairs and a much-polished desk. You can also see the family's tiny chapel (like every landed family on the island, the Veris had a live-in priest) and there's more religious material upstairs in the assorted prints that line the walls. They're neither original nor of good quality, but they give the flavour of the mawkish piety that characterized the island's landed class in the late nineteenth century. Attached to (but separate from) the family house are the living quarters of the *amo* (farm manager), the barn and the farmworkers' kitchen and eating area. To complete your visit, take a stroll round the animal pens, though don't expect to see much farmyard activity in the heat of the day. The animals are breeds traditionally used on Mallorcan farms, though they're here to illustrate the past rather than to be of any practical use.

It takes an hour or so to wander round the house and the adjacent animal pens, more if you stop at the simple little **café**, where they serve traditional Mallorcan snacks – the *pa amb oli* (bread rubbed with olives with ham and cheese) is delicious.

Manacor

MANACOR declares its business long before you arrive: vast roadside hoardings promote its furniture and artificial pearl factories. On the strength of these, the city has risen to become the second urban centre of Mallorca, far smaller than Palma but large enough to have sprawling suburbs on all sides. It's far from compelling, but Manacor does have an industrial independence distinctly lacking elsewhere.

The town also musters several modern attractions, situated beside the C715 on the west side of town, to catch the passing tourist trade. The first, the **Olive Wood Shop and Museum**, is more shop than museum, churning out thousands of household ornaments – oversized ashtrays and the like – stained a sticky-looking brown. Sometimes it verges on the kitsch, but mostly it's just ugly – and the plastic, life-size dinosaurs outside don't make things any better.

Next door is the first of the town's several Perlas Majorica **artificial pearl shops**, but skip it in favour of the company's factory, 1km further east along the main road and well signposted. At this main complex, you can go on a **free factory tour**, a somewhat perfunctory cruise giving just a general insight into the manufacturing process. The core of the imitation pearl is a glass globule on to which are

*The Perlas
Majorica fac-
tory is open
Mon–Fri
9am–1pm &
3–7pm, Sat &
Sun 10am–
1pm.*

painted many layers of a glutinous liquid primarily composed of fish scales. The finished item – anywhere between soft yellow and metallic grey – is gently polished and then included within many different types of jewellery. Artificial pearls last longer than, and are virtually indistinguishable from, the real thing, but consequently they're expensive – as you'll discover at the end of the tour when you're shepherded into the adjacent showroom and gift shop.

If you decide to take a peek at Manacor's busy centre, then head for the lively main square and be sure to try the local speciality, spicy, black pork sausage (*sobrasada de cerdo negro*).

Artà and around

Beyond Manacor the C715 veers northwest to run parallel to the coast, with the flatlands soon left behind for the peaks of the Serres de Llevant. The top end of this mountain range bunches to fill out Mallorca's northeast corner, providing a dramatic backdrop to ARTÀ, an ancient hill town of sun-bleached roofs clustered beneath a castellated chapel-shrine. It's a delightful scene, though at close quarters the town is something of an anticlimax – the cobweb of cramped and twisted alleys doesn't quite match the setting. Nonetheless, the ten-minute trek to the **Santuari de Sant Salvador**, the panoramic shrine at the top of Artà, is a must. It's almost impossible to get lost – just keep going upwards. From the main street, c/Ciutat, proceed to the main square, Plaça Conqueridor, and then head on to Plaça Espanya, site of the town hall, before a short stroll through streets of gently decaying grandee mansions brings you to the gargantuan parish church of Sant Salvador. From this unremarkable pile, steep stone steps and cypress trees lead up the Via Crucis (Way of the Cross) to the *santuari*, which, in its present form, dates from the early nineteenth century, though the hilltop has been a place of pilgrimage for much longer. The Catalan soldiers of the Reconquest demolished the Moorish fort that once stood here and replaced it with a shrine accommodating an image of the Virgin Mary which they had imported with them. This edifice was, in its turn, knocked down in 1820 in a superstitious attempt to stop the spread of an epidemic that was decimating the region's population. Built a few years later, the interior of the present chapel is hardly awe-inspiring – the paintings are mediocre and the curious seventeenth-century statue behind the high altar has Jesus smiling like an imbecile – but the views out over eastern Mallorca more than compensate.

Practicalities

Buses to Artà from several directions, including Palma, Cala Rajada and Ca'n Picafort, stop on the edge of the town centre, beside the C715. From the bus stop, it's a couple of hundred metres east to the short main street, c/Ciutat. If you've driven here, finding somewhere handy to **park** can be a bit awkward: try along c/Ciutat and the adjoining Plaça Conqueridor. There are several cafés along c/Ciutat, the best being *Café Parisien*, at no.18, a trendy little place with an outside terrace, modernist decor and tasty *tapas* and salads at reasonable prices. The *Ca'n Balague*, at no.19, is a more traditional café-bar also serving light meals. Artà has one hotel, the *Casal d'Artà*, a comfortable and central spot footsteps from the Sant Salvator church at c/Rafael Blanes 19 (☎971 829163; ⑥).

Ses Paisses

One kilometre to the south of Artà lie the substantial and elegiacally rustic remains of the Talayotic village of Ses Paisses. To get there, walk to the bottom of c/Ciutat, turn left along the main through-road (the C715) and watch for the signposted (and well-surfaced) country lane on the right. A clear footpath explores every nook and cranny of the site, and its numbered markers are thoroughly explained in the English language guidebook available at the entrance (300ptas).

Tucked away in a grove of olive, carob and holm-oak trees, the village is entered through a monolithic gateway, whose heavyweight jambs and lintel interrupt the Cyclopean walls that still encircle the site. These outer remains date from the second phase of the Talayotic culture (c. 1000–800 BC), when the emphasis was on consolidation and defence; in places, the walls still stand at their original size, around 3.5m high and 3m thick. Beside the gate, there's also a modern monolith erected in honour of Miquel Llobera, a local writer who penned romantic verses about the place. Beyond the gateway, the central **talayot** is from the first Talayotic phase (c. 1300–1000 BC), its shattered ruins flanked by the foundations of several rooms of later date and uncertain purpose. Experts believe the horseshoe-shaped room was used, at least towards the end of the Talayotic period, for cremations, whilst the three rectangular rooms were probably living quarters. In the rooms, archeologists discovered various items such as iron objects and ceramics imported from elsewhere in the Mediterranean, some of which were perhaps brought back from the Punic Wars (264–146 BC) by mercenaries – the skills of Balearic stone slingers were highly prized by the Carthaginians, and it's known that several hundred accompanied Hannibal and his elephants over the Alps in 218 BC.

Ses Paisses is open April–Sept daily 9am–1pm & 3–7pm; Oct–March Mon–Sat 9am–1pm & 2.30–5pm; 200ptas. For more information on Talayotic culture, see p.241.

The Ermita de Betlem

A longer excursion from Artà will bring you to the **Ermita de Betlem**, a remote and minuscule hermitage hidden away in the hills 10km northwest of town. The road begins near Plaça Espanya in the centre of Artà, though the start is poorly signed and tricky to find, while its rough surface and snaking course make for a difficult drive, so it's far better to **walk** the route (2–3hr one way). The first portion is an easy stroll up along the wooded valley of the Torrent d'es Cocones. After about 3km, the road squeezes through the narrowest of defiles, with the hills rising steeply on either side, and beyond begins to climb into the foothills of the Serra de Llevant (here classified as the Massís d'Artà). A signposted left turn about 3km beyond the defile signals the start of the strenuous part of the journey, as the track wriggles up the steep hillside, finally reaching the Ermita de Betlem after a further 4km. The buildings, which date from the hermitage's foundation in 1805, are quite unassuming – although, if you've come this far, you'll undoubtedly want to peep into the tiny church, where the walls are decorated with crude religious frescoes – but the views over the Badia d'Alcúdia are magnificent. The hermitage doesn't offer accommodation or food, just picnic tables, which does seem a bit cruel if you've hiked all the way here.

Colònia de Sant Pere

West of Artà the C712 weaves through the hills and past the turning for **COLÒNIA DE SANT PERE**, a downbeat resort and one-time fishing village nestling beside the Badia d'Alcúdia, with the stern escarpments of the Massís d'Artà for a backdrop. New villa complexes have sprouted along the foreshore, but mercifully the developers have pretty much left the village alone – not that there's much to the place. Founded in 1881, Colònia de Sant Pere is no more than a few blocks across, its plain, low-rise, modern buildings set behind a small sandy beach. It's all very low-key and laid-back, and this, along with the setting, is the place's charm.

Colònia de Sant Pere has just one convenient **hostal**, the agreeable *Rocamar*, c/Sant Mateu 9 (☎ & fax 971 589312; ④), an unassuming whitewashed and blue-shuttered building right in the centre three blocks back from the seashore, with a restaurant on the ground floor and a handful of simple rooms up above. About 1.5km east of the village is one of Mallorca's few **campsites**, the unkempt *Camping Club San Pedro* (June to mid–Sept; ☎971 589023), which occupies a bleak and unappetizing location overlooking the bay. It can hold 500 campers, and has a swimming pool, bar, restaurant and sports facilities. Pitch prices start at 1400ptas, added to which is a charge per person of 600ptas, and per car of 700ptas. You can eat well in Colònia de Sant Pere at the cosy *Acuàrium*, a restaurant serving the freshest of fish and a tasty *menú del día* (800ptas); it's on c/Sant Mateu, opposite the *Rocamar*. There are several seafront cafés too.

The east coast

Mallorca's **east coast**, stretching for about 60km south from Cala Rajada to Cala Llombards, is fretted by narrow coves, the remnants of prehistoric river valleys created when the level of the Mediterranean was much lower. All of these inlets have accrued at least some tourist development, ranging from a mild scattering of second homes to intensive chains of tower blocks. An attractive

minor road links the resorts, running, for the most part, a few kilometres inland along the edge of the Serres de Llevant, a slim band of
grassy hills which rises to over 500m at its two extremities – south
outside Felanitx and north around Artà. If you have your own transport, this coastal route enables you to pick and choose destinations
with the greatest of ease, dodging the crassest examples of overdevelopment – principally Cala Millor, Cales de Mallorca and Cala d'Or
– altogether. Amongst the larger resorts, boisterous **Cala Rajada** is
easily the most enticing, and is also within easy reach of excellent
sandy beaches and the lovely medieval fortress of **Capdepera**. For a
quiet day on the beach, however, you'll have to head much further
south to the relatively untouched beaches of **Cala Mondragó** and
Cala Llombards. In between these last two is scenic **Cala Figuera**, a
lively, medium-sized resort that possesses some fine restaurants and
a top-notch diving centre. The east coast is also famous for its limestone cave systems: the most impressive formations are to be found
at the **Coves d'Artà** in the north, closely followed by the **Coves del
Drac** at Porto Cristo.

It would be lovely to work your way down the coast, stopping for
a couple of nights here and there, but the problem is **accommodation**. In the height of the season, locating a vacant room in one of the
more attractive resorts can be a real tribulation – if you do find somewhere reasonable, you'll probably want to stay put. An alternative is
to select a less popular spot, such as workaday **Porto Cristo** or
dishevelled **Porto Colom**, where there's far more chance of a bed.
Naturally, things ease up in the shoulder season, but in winter many
hotels and *hostals* close down.

To explore the east coast thoroughly you'll need your own **transport**. All the major resorts have regular bus links with Palma and, in
summer, there are good connections to Port d'Alcúdia from Porto
Cristo and points north, but services up and down the coast are generally inadequate.

Capdepera

Spied across the valley from the west, the crenellated walls dominating **CAPDEPERA**, a tiny village 8km east of Artà and 3km west of
Cala Rajada, look too pristine to be true. Yet the triangular fortifications are genuine enough, built in the fourteenth century by the
Mallorcan king Sancho to protect the coast from pirates. Snuggling
below the walls, the village contains a pleasant medley of old houses,
its slender main square – Plaça de L'Orient – acting as a prelude to
the steep steps up to the **Castell de Capdepera**. The steps are the
nicest way to reach the castle, but you can also follow the signs and
drive up narrow c/Major. Flowering cactuses give the fortress a special allure in late May and June, but it's a beguiling place at any time,
with over 400m of wall equipped with a parapet walkway and sheltering neat terraced gardens. At the top of the fortress, **Nostra**

*The Castell de
Capdepera is
open daily:
April–Oct
10am–8pm;
Nov–March
10am–5pm;
200ptas.*

Senyora de la Esperança (Our Lady of Good Hope) is the quaintest of Gothic churches: its aisle-less, vaulted frame is furnished with outside steps leading up, behind the bell gable, to a flat roof, from where the views are superb.

There are several mundane **cafés** on the main square – the best is probably *L'Orient* – and a very good bar-restaurant close by, the German-run *Cassandra* (from 7pm every evening, closed Thurs), one of whose specialities is charcoal-grilled meat – it's on c/Centre, which runs west from the castle end of Plaça de L'Orient. There's nowhere to stay in Capdepera, but it's easy enough to visit by bus from Artà, Cala Rajada, Cala Millor or even Palma.

Cala Rajada

Awash with cafés, bars and hotels, vibrant **CALA RAJADA** lies on the southerly side of a stubby headland in the northeast corner of Mallorca. The town centre, an unassuming patchwork of low-rise modern buildings, is hardly prepossessing, but all around is a wild and rocky coastline, backed by pine-clad hills and sheltering a series of delightful beaches. The resort was once a fishing village, but there's little evidence of this today, and the old **harbour**, at the far end of the main drag, c/Elíonor Servera, is now used by pleasure boats and overlooked by restaurants. From the harbour, walkways extend along the headland's south coast. To the southwest, past the busiest part of town, it takes about five minutes to stroll round to **Platja Son Moll**, a slender arc of sand overlooked by Goliath-like hotels. More rewarding is the ten-minute stroll east to **Cala Gat**, a narrow cove beach tucked tight up against the steep, wooded coastline. The beach is far from undiscovered – there's a beach bar and at times it gets decidedly crowded – but it's an attractive spot all the same.

Up above the footpath to Cala Gat you can glimpse some of the modern sculptures that embellish the gardens of the **Palau Joan March**, a lavish mansion built for the eponymous tobacco merchant, the richest man in Franco's Spain. The house isn't open to the public, but the gardens are. Here, amongst the pine woods, you'll find over seventy sculptures, mostly Spanish pieces but also including a bronze by Rodin and examples of the work of three British sculptors: Henry Moore, Barbara Hepworth and Anthony Caro. The entrance is on c/Joan March, a turning off c/Elíonor Servera just beyond the harbour. Opening times are at the discretion of the family (Wednesday mornings are your best bet), and visits – at 500ptas per person – can only be arranged via the town's Oficina d'Informació Turística (see opposite). Beyond the gardens, continuing east along c/Elíonor Servera, the road twists steeply up through the pine woods to reach, after about 1km, the bony headlands and lighthouse of the **Cap de Capdepera**, Mallorca's most easterly point: the views out along the coast are a treat.

*For more
about the
Joan March
see p.80.*

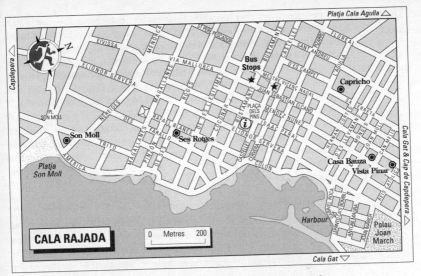

On the northern side of Cala Rajada, c/L'Agulla crosses the promontory to hit the north coast at **Platja Cala Agulla**. The approach road – some 2km of tourist tackiness – is of little appeal, but the beach, a vast curve of bright golden sand, is big enough to accommodate hundreds of bronzing pectorals with plenty of space to spare. The further you walk – and there are signed and shaded footpaths through the pine woods to assist you – the more isolation you'll get.

Practicalities

Most **buses** to Cala Rajada stop right in the town centre, a couple of minutes' walk west of the main square, Plaça dels Pins, where you'll find the **Oficina d'Informació Turística** (March–Oct Mon–Fri 9.30am–1.30pm & 4–7pm, Sat 9.30am–1.30pm; Nov–Feb Mon–Fri 9.30am–1.30pm & 2.30–5pm; ☎971 563033). The office can supply an excellent range of local information including restaurant lists, bus schedules, details of car and bicycle rental firms, and free town maps marked with all the accommodation. They also have a popular, though not very detailed, pamphlet on hiking tours (500ptas), and sell tickets for the Palau Joan March gardens. The town centre is easy to explore on foot, but for the outlying beaches you'll probably want a **local bus**. Among several summertime services from the bus stops along c/Castellet – a few metres to the north of Plaça dels Pins – the most useful are to Cala Agulla, Platja de Canyamel and the Coves d'Artà; note that there are no Sunday services.

The only real problem with Cala Rajada is **accommodation**. The town is a favourite German package resort and in high season you'll be lucky to find a room. The best place to try is among the *hostals* and hotels dotted around the pleasant residential streets just up from the harbour. Reasonable bets here are the *Vista Pinar*, at c/Reis Catòlics 11, a large, comfortable two-star hotel with its own swimming pool (April–Oct; ☎971 563751, fax 971 565721; ④); the two-star *Hostal Casa Bauza*, at c/Méndez Núñez 61, which has simply furnished, spick-and-span rooms as well as a pool (April–Oct; ☎971 563844, fax 971 818091; ③); and the three-star *Hotel Capricho*, off c/L'Agulla at c/Sa Serreta 5 (April–Oct; ☎971 563500, fax 971 565186; ⑦), a modern, air-conditioned place with a pool and sports facilities. In the shoulder season, it's probably worth trying one of Cala Rajada's popular seafront hotels. A particularly good-value choice is the unassuming *Cala Gat* (April–Oct; ☎971 563166, fax 971 564637; ⑤), which offers a secluded location in the pine woods above Cala Gat. A more workaday option, the *Son Moll*, overlooking the Platja Son Moll at c/Tritó 25 (April–Oct; ☎971 563100, fax 971 563581; ⑥), has light and airy rooms, most with balconies, and magnificent views out to sea. Finally, the three-star *Ses Rotges*, c/Rafael Blanes 21 (April–Oct; ☎971 563108, fax 971 564345; ⑥) is a delightful place in an elegantly restored antique villa just out of earshot of the main square.

The *Hotel Ses Rotges* boasts the best **restaurant** in town, but it's pricey and there are scores of less expensive rivals. It's hard to make specific recommendations as there are so many good places to eat, serving everything from sauerkraut and sausages through to traditional Spanish cuisine, but several of the restaurants down on the harbour offer especially good seafood. Squeezed together on c/Gabriel Roca you'll find the *Restaurante Escorcat*, a chic and attractive spot with seafood main courses from 1800ptas, and the comparable *Restaurant El Puerto*. Here too is *Pizzeria Negresio*, a popular and cheerful cafeteria with low-price pizzas, sandwiches, steaks and spaghetti.

Boats leave the harbour for regular summer excursions down the east coast and back. Destinations include Porto Cristo (1 daily except Sun; 900ptas) and Platja de Canyamel (3 daily; 1400ptas); for the Coves d'Artà, see below. There's also a new passenger-only **hydrofoil** service over to Ciutadella on Menorca operated by Cape Balear de Cruceros, whose offices are in the centre of Cala Rajada at c/Pizarro 49 ☎971 818668 (for details see p.33). The trip takes 75 minutes and there are between one and three sailings daily; a return costs 7500ptas in summer, 6000ptas in winter. Be warned, however, that ferry operations between the two islands have been plagued by financial problems – time alone will tell if this company makes it pay.

The Coves d'Artà

The succession of coves, caves and beaches notching the seashore between Cala Rajada and Cala Millor begins promisingly with the **Coves d'Artà** (often signposted in Castilian: Cuevas de Artà), reached along the first turning off the main coastal road (the PM404) south of Capdepera. The entrance to the caves is stunning, with a majestic stairway straight out of a Hammer Horror movie leading up to the yawning hole, which beckons like the mouth of Hell, high in the cliffs above the bay. This is the pick of the numerous cave systems of eastern Mallorca, its sequence of cavernous chambers, studded with stalagmites and stalactites, extending 450m into the rock face. Artificial lighting exaggerates the bizarre shapes of the caverns and their concretions, especially in the **Hall of Flags**, where stalactites up to 50m long hang in the shape of partly unfurled flags. Visiting the caves for their scientific interest became fashionable amongst the rich and famous – including Jules Verne – at the end of the nineteenth century, and nowadays they feature prominently on package-tour itineraries. It wasn't, however, much of a treat to be here during the Reconquest, when a thousand Moors – refugees from Artà – hid inside the caves until they were literally smoked out to be slaughtered by the Catalan soldiers waiting outside.

Guided tours of the Coves d'Artà run daily: April–Oct 10am–7pm; Nov–March 10am–5pm; 1000ptas.

Tours leave every thirty minutes and the guides give a complete geological description in tedious detail and in several languages (including English) as you wander the illuminated abyss. Allow about an hour for the visit – more if there's a queue, as there sometimes is. The caves are linked by **bus** with Artà and Cala Rajada four times daily in summer except on Sundays.

Platja de Canyamel

PLATJA DE CANYAMEL is a recently developed cove resort, with smart modern villas draped around a pine-backed sandy beach in sight of a pair of rocky headlands. It's situated about 1km south of the Coves d'Artà, and you can also get there from the main coastal road, a few kilometres inland – just follow the signs, but don't confuse Platja de Canyamel with the tedious Costa de Canyamel *urbanització*, immediately to the south. Platja de Canyamel makes an agreeable spot for a few hours sunbathing, though it can get a little crowded, and there are a couple of good **restaurants**. In the centre, a short walk up from the beach, is the *Isabel*, where the seafood is fresh and well prepared, or you can sample traditional Mallorcan cuisine at the excellent *Porxada de Sa Torre* (closed Mon & Nov–April; ☎971 563044), which occupies a tastefully converted old watchtower about 3km to the west along the main access road.

There are several **hotels** in Platja de Canyamel, but the only one you've any chance of finding a room in is the appealing, white-washed *Laguna* (May–Oct; ☎971 841150, fax 971 841049; ④), plonked right on the beach, though even here you'll be lucky to find a vacancy – it's almost always block-booked by German package tour operators. Local **buses** from Cala Rajada and Artà stop outside the *Laguna*.

Cala Millor and around

Continuing south along the main coast road, you'll soon reach the turning for the well-heeled villas of **COSTA DE LOS PINOS**, the most northerly and prosperous portion of a gigantic resort conurbation centred on **CALA BONA** and **CALA MILLOR**. This is development gone quite mad, a swath of apartment buildings, sky-rise hotels and villa-villages overwhelming the contours of the coast as far as the eye can see. The only redeeming feature – and the reason for all this frantic construction in the first place – is the beach, a magnificent two-kilometre stretch of sand fringed by what remains of the old pine woods. The principal **Oficina d'Informació Turística**, at Parc de la Mar 2, just behind the beach at the south end of Cala Millor (Mon–Fri 9am–1pm & 3–7pm, Sat 9am–1pm; ☎971 585409), has all the usual information, including free maps.

South of Cala Millor, the main coastal road passes by the **Auto-Safari Park**, where a motley assortment of African animals roams open countryside. Beyond, there are yet more acres of concrete and glass at **S'ILLOT**, though the main road, set back from the coast, cuts a rustic route through vineyards and almond groves, before reaching the multicoloured billboards which announce the cave systems of Porto Cristo.

The Auto-Safari Park is open daily: April–Sept 9am–7pm; Oct–March 9am–5pm; 1500ptas.

Porto Cristo

Although **PORTO CRISTO** prospered in the early days of the tourist boom, sprouting a string of hotels and *hostals*, it's fared badly since mega-resorts such as Cala Millor and Cala d'Or were constructed. Don't be deceived by the jam of tourist buses clogging the town's streets on their way to the nearby caves – few of their occupants will actually be staying here. Consequently, this is one of the very few places on the east coast where you're likely to find a room in July and August – and it's not too bad a spot to spend a night either, having benefited from a recent clean-up.

Porto Cristo's origins are uncertain, but it was definitely in existence by the thirteenth century, serving as the fishing harbour and seaport of the inland town of Manacor. Nothing remains of the medieval settlement, and today the centre, which climbs the hill behind the harbour, consists of high-sided terraced buildings, mostly dating from the late nineteenth and early twentieth centuries. At the bottom of the hill, right in front of the main square-cum-promenade, is the **beach**, a small sliver of sand, poor for sunbathing, which cannot compete with the long, flat strands of the new mega-resorts. The beach is tucked inside the harbour, a narrow V-shaped channel entered between a pair of humpy promontories. Beyond the beach, the harbour accommodates a large marina and then meets the oily-green Es Rivet river, which forms the town centre's southern perimeter. Long a naval base,

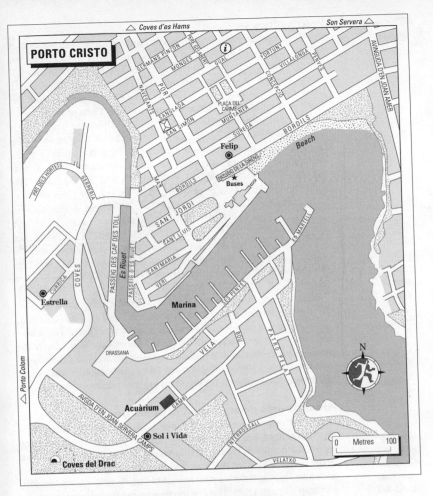

PORTO CRISTO

GERMANS PINZÓN
MONGES
PORT GELABERT
GUAL
FORTUNY
VILLALONGA
PENYES
AVINGUDA D'EN JOAN AMER

ℹ️

PORT
NAVEGANTS
SANGLADA
SAN SIMÓN
PLAÇA DEL CARMENER
MUNTANER
SUREDA
BORDILS
CONCEPCIÓ

Felip ●

Beach

PAS DES HORTETS
GERRERIA
BORDILS
SANT JORDI
SANT LLUÍS
PASSEIG DE LA SIRENA
★ Buses
ES MARTEL

PASSEIG DES CAP DES TOLL
PASSEIG D'ES RIUET
Es Riuet
SANT JORDI
SANTAMARIA
VERI

COVES
CURRICA
● Estrella

Marina

SES PENYES

VELA
BOU
PATRÓ PELAT

DRASSANA

N

AVGDA D'EN JOAN SERVERA CAMPS

Acuàrium
GAMBI

● Sol i Vida

ENTEROSSALL

△ Porto Colom

◖ **Coves del Drac**

VELATXO

0   Metres   100

the harbour is one of the most sheltered on Mallorca's east coast and was the site of the **Republican landing** in August 1936 to try to capture the island from the Falangists. The campaign was a fiasco: the Republicans disembarked over 7000 men and quickly established a long and deep bridgehead, but their commanders, completely surprised by their initial success, quite literally didn't know what to do next. The Nationalists did. They counterattacked and, supported by the Italian air force, soon had the Republicans dashing back to the coast. Barcelona radio put on a brave face, announcing, "The heroic Catalan columns have returned from Mallorca after a magnificent action. Not a single man suffered from the effects of the embarkation."

Practicalities

The main coastal road passes along Porto Cristo's seafront, and a healthy number of long-distance buses, principally from Palma and Port d'Alcúdia, terminate in the centre beside the harbour and the beach. The town's **Oficina d'Informació Turistica** is at c/En Gual 31 (Mon–Fri 8am–3pm; ☎971 820931): take c/Concepció up from the beach and make the fifth turning on the left. They provide useful maps of the town and neighbouring resorts. There are half a dozen **hotels and hostals** in Porto Cristo. By and large, they're an undistinguished lot, though the one-star *Hotel Felip* does have a great location, in a big old balconied building overlooking the beach at c/Bordils 67 (Feb–Oct; ☎971 820750, fax 971 820594; ③). The hotel has recently been revamped and the rooms are plain but perfectly adequate – ask for a harbour view. Other less sightly options include the one-star *Hotel Estrella*, which occupies an old and slightly frayed house at c/Curricà 16 (May–Oct; ☎971 820833, fax 971 820892; ④) – follow the main road south over the river and it's the third turning on the right; and the *Sol i Vida*, a small and tidy two-star hotel a few metres from the Acuàrium at Avgda Joan Servera Camps 11 (☎ & fax 971 821074; ③).

With most of Porto Cristo's **restaurants and cafés** geared up for the passing tourist trade, getting a decent meal is none too easy. There are only a couple of places of any quality: *Sa Carrotja*, a low-key family-run restaurant at the first intersection north from the beach along c/Bordils at Avgda Joan Amer 45; and the rather more polished *Siroco*, whose cosy terrace abuts the harbour a few metres south from the beach on c/Veri. Both are inexpensive.

Around Porto Cristo – the Coves del Drac

Hourly guided tours of the Coves del Drac run daily: April–Oct 10am–5pm; Nov–March 10.30am–3.30pm; 900ptas. For more on Ludwig Salvator, see p.121.

Across the river, about fifteen minutes' walk south of the centre along the coastal road, lies Porto Cristo's pride and joy, the **Coves del Drac** (often signposted in Castilian: Cuevas del Drach). Locals had known of the "Dragon's Caves" for hundreds of years, but it was the Austrian archduke Ludwig Salvator who recruited French geologists to explore and map them in 1896. The French discovered four whopping chambers that penetrated the coast's limestone cliffs for a distance of around 2km. In the last cavern they found one of the largest subterranean lakes in the world, some 177m long, 40m wide and 30m deep. The eccentric shapes of the myriad stalactites and stalagmites adorning each chamber immediately invited comparison with more familiar objects. As the leader of the French team, Edouard Martel, wrote, "On all sides, everywhere, in front and behind, as far as the eye can see, marble cascades, organ pipes, lace draperies, pendants of multifaceted gems hang suspended from the walls and roof".

Since the French exploration, the caves have been thoroughly commercialized. The present complex accommodates a giant car park, ticket office and restaurant, behind which lurk the gardens that lead to the flight of steps down to the caves – you may come to know each step well, as, especially on the weekend, you can wait in line for ages. Inside, the myriad concretions of calcium carbonate, formed by the dissolution of the soft limestone by rainwater, are shrewdly illuminated. Shunting you through the hour-long, multilingual tour, the guides invite you to gawp and gush at formations such as "the Buddha", "the Pagoda" and "the Snowy Mountain", and magnificent icicle-like stalactites, some of which are snowy white, while others pick up hints of orange and red from the rocks they pass through. The *tour de force* is the larger of the two subterranean lakes, whose translucent waters flicker with reflected colours, the effects further enhanced by musicians drifting about in boats playing harmoniums (performances begin on the hour). At the end of the tour, most visitors leave on foot, but there's also the option of a brief and disappointing boat ride across part of the lake.

Leaving the caves, it's a short walk across the car park to the well-stocked Acuàrium, where the glass tanks magnify such exotic horrors as electric eels, piranhas and stinging fish – kids love it. Though you'd hardly want to visit both, there's another cave system situated 2km west of Porto Cristo on the road to Manacor. The Coves d'es Hams (in Castilian: Cuevas del Hams) follow the same format as their rival, with a sequence of (somewhat smaller) caverns lit to emphasize the beauty of the stalagmites and stalactites. As at the Coves del Drac, musicians play from boats on an underground lake (every 20min till 4.30pm).

*The Acuàrium
is open daily:
April–Oct
10.30am–5pm;
Nov–March
11am–3pm;
700ptas.
Guided tours
(about every
thirty min-
utes) of the
Coves d'es
Hams run
daily
10.30am–
5.30pm;
1300ptas.*

South to Porto Colom

The modern resorts swarming the pint-sized coves to the south of Porto Cristo reach a crescendo at the CALES DE MALLORCA, the collective name for a band of tourist settlements extending from Cala Magraner in the north to Cala Murada in the south. This part of the shoreline didn't have much charm in the first place – the coves are mostly scrawny and shadeless – and it's even less compelling now. Inland, however, the main coast road gives few hints of these scenic disasters as it wends its pastoral way past honey-coloured dry-stone walls and a smattering of ancient farmhouses in the lee of the Serres de Llevant.

PORTO COLOM straggles round a long and irregular bay some 20km south of Porto Cristo. Originally a fishing village supplying the needs of the neighbouring town of Felanitx, the port boomed throughout most of the nineteenth century from the export trade in wine to France. The good times, however, came to an abrupt end when, in the 1870s, *phylloxera* wiped out the island's vines. The villagers returned to fishing, which still makes up a significant part of the local economy – the boats they use, as well as some old boat sheds, litter the kilometre-long quay on the southwest side of the bay. The quayside, along with the modest settlement immediately behind it, constitutes the heart of the present village and although there's little to grab your attention, it's still an amiable, downbeat spot. The oldest part of the village is about 300m from the west end of the quay, round the back of the harbour, and comprises a small parcel of pastel-shaded cottages shadowing a dinky little square. Elsewhere, the headlands overlooking the entrance to the bay house a lighthouse and a scrawny mix of villas and hotels, while over the hill behind the village (about 1km to the south) is **Cala Marsal**, a crowded, shadeless wedge of sand overlooked by the concrete flanks of the eponymous hotel.

Practicalities

Bus services to Porto Colom, principally from Palma, arrive at the quayside. The resort has a smattering of inexpensive and resolutely mundane **hostals** including the *Hostal-residencia César*, c/Llaud (April–Oct; ☎971 825302; ③), and the equally undistinguished *Hostal Bahía Azul*, Ronda Creuer Baleares 88 (☎971 825280, fax 971 824452; ③), both situated amongst the scrubland at the far (east) end of the quay. For something rather more comfortable, especially in the shoulder season, try the three-star *Hotel Cala Marsal* (April–Oct; ☎971 825225, fax 971 825250; ⑤) in Cala Marsal, a package-tour favourite with sea-facing rooms and all the usual facilities from swimming pools to tennis courts.

Dotted along the quayside are several quality **restaurants**. The cream of the crop is the *Celler Sa Sínia* at the west end of the quay (closed Mon), whose fish dishes are both reasonably priced and very tasty. At the other end of the quay, just along Ronda Creuer Baleares, the smart *Celler Ses Portadores* is a good alternative; it's a bit pricier, but the fish is just as fresh and there's a wider selection.

Felanitx and around

FELANITX, the main town of the southeastern corner of the island and 13km inland from Porto Colom, is an industrious place, producing wine, ceramics and pearls. It's short on specific sights, though the honey-gold, Baroque facade of the church of **Sant Miquel** gives an elegant air to the mostly modern main square. Nor are there many facilities – no tourist office, accommodation or noteworthy restaurant – but strolling the old streets and alleys is an agreeable way to pass the odd hour, and you can sample local wines at the *Celler Ca'ntia*, near the church at c/Pou de la Vila 5. Buses, linking the town with Palma and Porto Colom, stop by the main square.

The Santuari de Sant Salvador and the Castell de Santueri

From Felanitx the Serres de Llevant are within easy striking distance. The best approach is to head back along the road to Porto Colom for about 2km and take the signposted, four-kilometre tarmac byroad that wriggles up the mountain to the **Santuari de Sant Salvador**, recognizable from miles around by its conspicuous stone cross and enormous statue of Christ. Long an important place of pilgrimage, the monastery occupies a splendid position near the summit of the highest mountain in these parts, the 510-metre Puig Sant Salvador, with sumptuous views out over the east coast. The sanctuary was founded in the mid-fourteenth century, but the original buildings were razed by raiding pirates and most of today's complex is Baroque. The heavy gatehouse is its most conspicuous feature while, inside the compound, the eighteenth-century church shelters a much-venerated image of the Virgin Mary. You can usually get a meal at the monastery, and rent simple rooms (☎971 827282; ①) where bedding is provided. With a car, the sanctuary can make an unusual base for exploring the locality – and it's certainly very quiet.

The custodians should be able to point you towards the footpath to the **Castell de Santueri**, about 4km away across the hills to the south, which is also accessible by car along a five-kilometre country lane starting on the Felanitx–Santanyí road – watch for the sign a couple of kilometres south of Felanitx. The hiking route is fairly easy to follow and the going isn't difficult, although it's still advisable to have a walking map and stout shoes. The path meanders through a pretty landscape of dry-stone walls, flowering shrubs and copses of almond and carob trees, bringing you to the castle after about an hour and a half. Glued to a rocky hilltop, the battered ramparts date from the fourteenth century, though it was the Moors who built the first stronghold here. Getting inside the ruins is pot luck – sometimes you can, when a small entry fee is levied at the main gate, and sometimes you can't.

Cala d'Or and around

Down the coast from Porto Colom, the pretty little fishing villages that once studded the discrete coves between Cala Serena and Porto Petro have been blasted by development. The interconnected resorts that now stand in their place are largely indistinguishable, a homogenously designed strip of whitewashed, low-rise villas, hotels, restaurants and bars in a sort of *pueblo* style. Confusingly, this long string of resorts is now usually lumped together under the name **CALA D'OR**, though in fact this particular cove is one of the smallest. For simplicity's sake, the "Cala d'Or" we refer to in this account is the original cove and not the whole development.

To be fair, the pseudo-Mexican style of the new resorts blends well with the ritzy *haciendas* left by a previous generation of sun-seekers, the latter largely concentrated on the humpy, pint-sized headland which separates Cala d'Or from its northerly neighbour **CALA GRAN**. These two fetching little coves, tucked between the cliffs and edged by narrow golden beaches, are the highlights of the area. The beaches are jam-packed throughout the season, but the swimming is perfect and the wooded coastline here is far preferable to the more concentrated development all around. A ten-minute walk north beyond Cala Gran are the densely packed villas of uninspiring **CALA ESMERALDA**. In the opposite direction, the headland on the south side of Cala d'Or is genteel and leafy, but this is a flattering and brief preamble to the massive marina and endless villas of **CALA LLONGA**.

Practicalities

Buses to Cala d'Or stop on the crowded and charmless main drag, Avinguda Fernando Tarrago, two minutes' walk from the beach. Under various designations, this same street links the main cove resorts, from Cala Esmeralda in the north to Cala Llonga in the south, about a twenty-minute walk. The area's Oficina d'Informació Turística is situated a few metres up from the Cala Llonga waterside (May–Dec Mon–Fri 8.15am–2pm; Jan–April Tues & Wed 8.15am–2pm; ☎971 657463). They provide free maps marked with all the hotels and *hostals*, though finding a room is well-nigh impossible in the summer – a better bet is to try the *Hotel Nereida* at Porto Petro (see below). The most luxurious place to stay – and where you'll almost certainly need an advance reservation – is the luxurious, four-star *Hotel Cala d'Or*, right above Cala d'Or's beach on Avinguda Belgica (April–Oct; ☎971 657249; ⑧). The hotel has seventy balconied bedrooms, each furnished in an attractive modern style with fine sea views, while the equally appealing public areas include a bar, restaurant and an outside swimming pool. Cala Gran also has a good upmarket hotel, the *Cala Gran* (April–Oct; ☎971 657100; ⑦), a bigger and brisker affair at the back of the beach, where the modern bedrooms have balconies and sea views, and there's every convenience including a swimming pool. There are myriad **cafés and restaurants** around Cala d'Or and Cala Llonga, especially on the main street, Avinguda Fernando Tarrago. One that's worth going out of your way for is the popular *Ca'n Trompé*, Avgda Belgica 4 (closed Dec–Feb), which serves delicious, though pricey, meals, with the emphasis on Mallorcan mainstays.

Porto Petro

Only recently swallowed into the Cala d'Or conurbation, **PORTO PETRO** rambles round a twin-pronged cove a couple of kilometres south of Cala Llonga. There's no beach here, so the development has been fairly restrained. The old fishing harbour has been turned into a marina, and villas dot the gentle wooded hillsides edging the coast, but it remains a quiet and tranquil spot – the only real activity is the promenade round the crystal-watered cove. The minuscule centre of the village perches on the headland above the marina. Here you'll have a reasonable chance of getting a **room** at the two-star *Hotel Nereida* (April–Oct; ☎971 657223, fax 971 659235; ⑤), a comfortable and neat little place with its own pool and rooftop sun ter-

A tourist "train" on wheels, the mini tren, shuttles up and down the coast from Cala Serena in the north to Porto Petro and Cala Mondragó in the south, with stops along the main street and beside all the beaches (6 daily in each direction; 400ptas per trip).

races. If you do find a room here, the village has all the amenities to make for a good base: there's car and cycle rental; daily **boat trips** around the neighbouring coast; and regular *mini tren* connections up and down the coast to all the resorts between Cala Serena and Cala Mondragó. There are also a couple of fine harbourside **restaurants**: the *Ca'n Martina*, at the head of the marina, boasts a paella to die for and a sweet outside terrace, whilst the nearby *Restaurant Porto Petro* serves delicious and reasonably priced seafood from first-floor premises overlooking the bay.

Cala Mondragó

The *mini tren* shuffles to its terminus at **CALA MONDRAGÓ**, about 4km south of Porto Petro. There's some development here, but it's not so intensive as to destroy the cove's pelagic beauty: low, pine-clad cliffs frame a pair of sandy beaches, which are linked along a concrete footpath. However, the cove's "unspoilt" reputation and safe bathing acts as a magnet for sun-lovers from miles around. To escape the crowds, come early in the morning, or else stay the night (if there's space), either at the beachside *Hostal Playa Mondragó*, a straightforward, modern concrete block with forty plain but adequate rooms (April–Oct; ☎ & fax 971 657752; ③), or at the rather more enticing *Hostal Condemar*, about 300m from the beach, where most of the rooms have balconies (May–Oct; ☎ & fax 971 657756; ③).

Santanyí and around

The crossroads town of **SANTANYÍ**, 18km from Porto Colom, was once an important medieval stronghold guarding the island's southeastern approaches. It was ransacked by corsairs on several occasions, but one of the old town gates, **Sa Porta**, has survived along with the occasional chunk of masonry extant from the old city walls. However, it's Santanyí's narrow alleys, squeezed between high-sided stone houses, that are the town's main appeal. Several pavement cafés edge the main square, but these should not detain you long, whether you're making the fast, fifty-kilometre journey west along the C717 to Palma or heading east to the coast.

Cala Figuera and Cala Santanyí

Travelling southeast from Santanyí, a five-kilometre side road cuts a pretty, rustic route through to **CALA FIGUERA**, whose antique harbour sits beside a fjord-like inlet below the steepest of coastal cliffs. Local fishermen still land their catches and mend their nets here, but nowadays it's to the accompaniment of scores of photo-snapping tourists. Up above, the pine-covered shoreline heaves with villas, hotels and *hostals*, although, the absence of high-rise buildings means the development is never overbearing.

Cala Figuera is extremely popular, and there are few vacant **rooms** at its dozen or so establishments, even in the shoulder seasons. If you do chance your arm, the obvious place to start is on the steep pedestrianized ramp – c/Verge del Carmen – which leads up from the harbour. In this prime location, at no. 50, is the unassuming *Hostal Cala*, whose twenty rooms are stashed above a restaurant (April–Oct; ☎971 645018; ⑤). Close by at no. 58, the all-year *Hostal Ca'n Jordi* has just six simple bedrooms, also over a restaurant (☎ & fax 971 645035; ③). Up the hill, overlooking the cove from a wide ridge, stands the modern and comfortable *Hotel Rocamar* (April–Oct; ☎971 645125, fax 971 645182; ⑤). In dire emergencies, try the unprepossessing *Hostal Oliver*, stuck at the back of the resort, which has a few spartan rooms that aren't booked by package operators in summer (May–Sept; ☎971 645127, fax 971 645325; ③). Of Cala Figuera's many restaurants, the most distinguished are the seafood eateries lining c/Verge del Carmen. It's difficult to select – and hard to go wrong – but *La Marina*, *Ca'n Jordi* and *Cala* are all excellent and not too pricey.

In terms of amenities, the resort has car and cycle rental outlets, and, down by the harbour, a diving school which hires out a wide range of sub-aqua gear to experienced divers, and arranges novice courses – three days of tuition for around 45,000ptas. The resort also has several lively music bars and discos dotted along its main street.

What you won't get is a beach. The nearest is 4km away at CALA SANTANYÍ, a busy little resort with a medium-sized (and frequently crowded) beach at the end of a steep-sided, heavily wooded gulch. To get there, head back towards Santanyí for about 2km and follow the signs.

Cala Llombards

The next bay down from Cala Santanyí is little-developed CALA LLOMBARDS, a beautiful pine-forested cove of gleaming sand, turquoise sea and sheer cliffs. There's a scrawny villa-village behind, not visible from the beach, a beach-bar and a dirt car park, but otherwise it's pristine stuff. As you'd expect, you won't have the beach to yourself, but it's rarely crowded; a handful of campers often sleep rough in the woods behind, to the chagrin of many locals. Cala Llombards is only accessible from the Santanyí–Colònia de Sant Jordi road; buses from Colònia de Sant Jordi, Santanyí and Cala Figuera drop passengers at the village of Llombards on the main road, leaving a signposted four-kilometre walk to the beach.

The south coast

Mallorca's south coast, stretching from the rim of the Bay of Palma to the island's most southerly point, Cap de Ses Salines, has hardly been developed at all, but the reasons behind this lack of interest are pretty obvious when you come here. Most of the shoreline is unenticingly spartan, a long and low rocky shelf that meets the sea almost as an afterthought – with barely a decent beach in sight. Behind is a flat, sparsely populated hinterland of little shade or variety. Villages are few and far between, and in places the land has an eerie sense of desolation – especially at the wind-buffeted **Cap de Ses Salines** – which some assert as its fascination.

A smattering of modern resorts gamely make the most of these disheartening surroundings. The pick of the crop is undoubtedly **Colònia de Sant Jordi**, a curious amalgamation of plush tourist settlement and old seaport which thoroughly deserves an overnight visit, not least because it offers boat trips to the remote islet of Cabrera and is near the wildlife-rich saltflats that back onto the region's longest beach, **Es Trenc**. The other resort you might consider is **Cala Pi**, where a deep ravine frames a sandy beach, but only if you're dropping in on the substantial remains of prehistoric **Capocorp Vell** just up the road. East of Cala Pi, through the grim and untidy resorts of Valgornera, S'Estanyol and Sa Rapita, clumps of mundane second homes decorate the treeless shoreline.

Planning an itinerary is straightforward. The best advice is to use the C717, which runs from Santanyí to the Bay of Palma's Ca'n Pastilla, as your baseline, branching off as you wish. The following account is written east to west, but it doesn't make much difference in which direction you're travelling. As ever, **accommodation** is at a premium. Throughout the season, your best chance, by a long chalk, is in Colònia de Sant Jordi, but from November to March nearly everything is closed and you'll almost certainly have to visit on a day trip. **Bus** services are adequate if you're heading somewhere specific from Palma, or between Colònia de Sant Jordi and Cala d'Or, but are dreadful when you attempt to move between other resorts.

Colònia de Sant Jordi and around

Heading southwest from Santanyí, a fast and easy country road drifts through a landscape of old dry-stone walls and straggling fields towards Colònia de Sant Jordi. After about 4km, you pass the turning for Cala Llombards (see p.186) and shortly afterwards the byroad that leads 10km down through coastal pine woods to the lighthouse on **Cap de Ses Salines**, a bleak, brush-covered headland that is Mallorca's most southerly point. The lighthouse itself is closed to the public, but there are fine views out to sea. Thekla larks and stone curlews are often to be seen on the cape, whilst gulls, terns and shearwaters glide about offshore, benefiting from the winds which, when they're up, can make the place intolerable.

Back on the road to Colònia de Sant Jordi, billboards welcome you to **Botanicactus**, a huge botanical garden mostly devoted to indigenous and imported species of cactus. A surprise here is the artificial lake, which encourages the growth of wetland plants – a welcome splash in arid surroundings – but otherwise the place has all the atmosphere of a garden centre and is definitely missable.

Botanicactus is open daily: April–Sept 9am–7pm; Oct–March 9am–5pm; 700ptas.

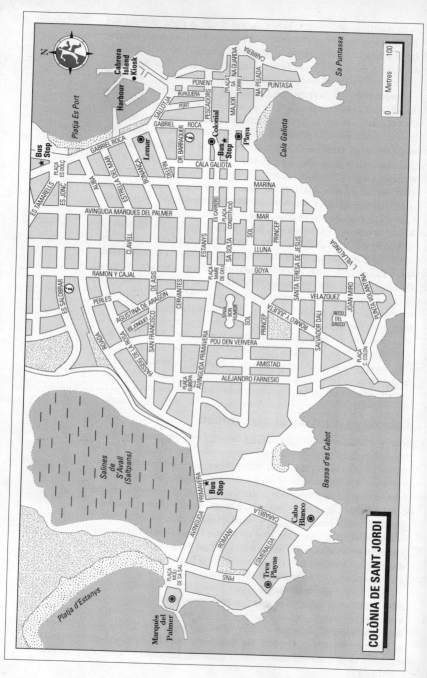

COLÒNIA DE SANT JORDI

Beyond, just 13km from Santanyí, is **COLÒNIA DE SANT JORDI**, whose wide streets pattern a substantial and irregularly shaped headland. It's a confusing place, at least at first, and you'll need to get your bearings. The main approach road is the Avinguda Marqués del Palmer, at the end of which – roughly in the middle of the headland – lies the principal square, the innocuous **Plaça Constitució**. From here, c/Sa Solta and then, across another square, Avinguda Primavera lead west, with the surprisingly pleasant main tourist zone appearing on the left, the domineering lines of its flashy hotels broken by low-rise villas and landscaped side streets. To the right are the **Salines de S'Avall**, saltpans which once provided the town with its principal source of income. At the end of the avenue, the polished *Hotel Marqués del Palmer* sits tight against the **Platja d'Estanys**, whose gleaming sands curve round a dune-edged cove.

East from Plaça Constitució along c/Major, and then left down c/Gabriel Roca, is the old **harbour**, the most diverting part of town. Framed by an attractive, early twentieth-century ensemble of balconied mansions, the port makes the most of a handsome, horseshoe-shaped bay. There's nothing special to look at, but it's a relaxing spot with a handful of restaurants, fishing smacks, a pocket-sized beach and a marina.

Practicalities

Buses to Colònia de Sant Jordi from places such as Palma, Cala d'Or and Cala Figuera stop at several downtown locations, and there's a bus stop close to the harbour. A toytown mini-train shuttles around town during the season every hour or two. The **Oficina d'Informació Turística** is on the first floor of the town hall at c/Doctor Barraquer 5 (May–Oct Mon–Fri 9am–1pm & 5–7.30pm, Sat 9am–1pm; ☎971 656073); follow c/Gabriel Roca from the harbour and take the first road on the right. Staff have free town maps to hand out and information about local **bike rental** shops (cycling in the flatlands around the resort is a popular and enjoyable pastime), as well as details of local **accommodation**. In the budget range, there's a handful of hotels and *hostals* beside and behind the harbour – these are your best chance if you're looking for a last-minute room in high season. Try the clean and frugal, one-star *Hostal Colonial*, c/Gabriel Roca 9 (March–Oct; ☎971 655278; ③); or the smarter, two-star *Hotel Lemar*, a whitewashed and balconied old building overlooking the harbour at c/Bonança 1 (May–Oct; ☎971 655178, fax 971 655162; ⑥) – ask for a room at the front. There's also the charming two-star *Hostal Playa*, about five minutes' walk from the harbour at c/Major 25 (April–Oct; ☎971 655256; ④). This cosy and well-cared-for little *hostal*, with just eight rooms, has folksy bygones in its public areas, and you're served breakfast on a pretty patio terrace with views along the seashore.

Moving upmarket, Colònia de Sant Jordi boasts some of the flashiest hotels in southeast Mallorca, glistening towers of air-conditioned, balconied bedrooms with ocean panoramas, all concentrated in the main resort area at the west end of Avinguda Primavera. This is, however, very much package-holiday territory and rooms are well nigh impossible to come by on spec, except perhaps in the shoulder seasons. The cream of the crop are the opulent *Tres Playas*, which looms over the seashore on c/Esmeralda and has lovely gardens and outside pools among many other facilities (April–Oct; ☎971 655151, fax 971 655644; ⑧), and the nearby *Cabo Blanco*, c/Carabela 2, a polished three-star which also has pools and attractive gardens (April–Oct; ☎971 655075, fax 971 656318; ⑥). The *Marqués del Palmer*, right at the end of Avinguda Primavera, isn't quite as new and glitzy, but it's still a good-quality, comfortable hotel and right beside the town's best beach (May–Oct; ☎971 655100, fax 971 656369; ⑤).

There's a cluster of first-rate **restaurants** beside the harbour. On the south side, *La Mar* serves delicious seafood from around 1600ptas for a main course, while the nearby *El Puerto* divides into two: a café-bar offering bargain-basement pizzas and spaghetti, and a restaurant specializing in seafood. On the north side of the harbour is another good seafood place, the *Pep Serra*, c/Gabriel Roca 87, which has a seashore terrace and serves a local delicacy, perch caught off Cabrera island.

Cabrera island

Beside Colònia de Sant Jordi harbour a tiny kiosk (daily 8am–1pm & 5–9pm; ☎971 649034) has information on, and takes reservations for, boat trips to the island of **Cabrera** (late April–Oct 1 daily; 8hr; 3300ptas, plus optional 800ptas for food). Easily the largest of a clustered archipelago, Cabrera ("Goat Island") is a bumpy, scrub-covered chunk lying 20km offshore. Bare, almost entirely uninhabited, and no more than 7km wide and 5km long, the only significant hint of its eventful past is the protective castle above its supremely sheltered harbour. Pliny claimed the island to have been the birthplace of Hannibal; medieval pirates hunkered down on it to plan future raids; and, during the Napoleonic Wars, the Spanish stuck nine thousand French prisoners of war out here and tried to forget about them – during their three-year captivity, two thirds of Napoleon's men died from hunger and disease. More recently, it was colonized by Franco's armed forces but now they've departed, no one is quite sure what to do with it: at the moment it's protected as a national park, but there's pressure to develop it into a resort.

The day trip starts with a fifty-minute voyage to the island followed by a speedy circumnavigation, weather (and winds) permitting. On the final stretch, the boat nudges round a hostile-looking headland to enter the harbour – **Es Port** – a narrow finger of calm water, edged by hills and equipped with a tiny jetty. From here, you're shepherded up the path to the ruins of the fourteenth-century castle high above. Perched on the island's west coast, the views from the fortress back across to Mallorca are magnificent, and all sorts of birds can be viewed gliding round the seacliffs, including Manx and Cory's shearwaters, herring gulls and the far rarer Audouin's gulls, as well as peregrine falcons and shags. It is, however, the blue-underbellied Lilfords wall lizard that really takes the naturalists' biscuit: after you've completed the walk to the castle and back (which takes about twenty minutes each way), there's time to have a drink down by the jetty, where you can tempt the Lilfords lizards out from the scrub with pieces of fruit. You can also head off into the interior to view the sombre memorial to the dead French prisoners of war, but you can't wander the island willy-nilly – at present, there's still a real danger from discarded, unexploded armaments left here by the military. On the return journey, the boat bobs across the bay to visit the **Cova Blava** (Blue Grotto), sailing right into the cave, through the fifty-metre-wide entrance and on into the yawning chamber beyond. The grotto reaches a height of 160m and is suffused by bluish light, from which it gets its name; you can swim in the grotto too.

*For more on
Mallorca's
flora and
fauna, see
p.255.*

Es Trenc

One of Colònia de Sant Jordi's attractions is its proximity to **Es Trenc**, a 4km strip of sandy beach that extends as far as the eye can see. It's neither unknown, nor unspoilt, but the crowds are easily absorbed and the development only scratches away at the edges. To get there, head north from Colònia de Sant Jordi and, about 1km out of town, turn left towards Campos; 2.8km along this road take the signed left turn and follow the country lanes leading across the salt flats to the car park at the east end of the beach – a total distance of around 7km. This end of the beach is far more appealing than the other, which is splotched by the scrawny holiday hamlet of Ses Covetes.

The saltpans backing onto the beach – the **Salines de Llevant** – along with the surrounding farmland and scrubland support a wide variety of **birdlife**. Resident birds such as marsh harriers, kestrels, spotted cranes, fan-tailed warblers and hoopoes make a visit enjoyable at any time of year, but the best time to come is in the spring when hundreds of migrants arrive from Africa. Commonly seen in the springtime are avocets, little-ringed plovers, little egrets, common sandpipers, little stints, redshanks, black-tailed godwits, collared pratincoles and black terns. Several footpaths lead from Es Trenc beach into the saltpans, but it's not a good area to explore on foot – the scenery is boring, it's smelly and for much of the year insects are a menace. It's much better to drive (or maybe cycle) round, using the maze-like network of narrow country lanes that traverse the saltpans and stopping anywhere that looks promising.

The south
coast

For informa-
tion on Puig
Randa, 9km
north of
Llucmajor,
see p.165.

Capocorp Vell
is open daily
except Thurs
10am–5pm;
250ptas. For
more informa-
tion on talay-
ots, see p.241.

Campos, Llucmajor, Capocorp Vell and Cala Pi

On the C717, 13km northwest of Santanyí, the unassuming town of
CAMPOS will hardly fire the imagination, though the immaculately
restored sixteenth-century town hall does merit a quick gander for its
fine facade. Neither will LLUCMAJOR, the next settlement along,
delay your progress, despite its medieval origins as a market town and
its long association with the island's shoemakers. It was here, just outside the old city walls, that Jaume III, the last of the independent kings
of Mallorca, was defeated and killed by Pedro IV of Aragon.

Llucmajor is just 12km from the teeming hotel strip at S'Arenal
(see p.94); it's also at the head of the byroad leading south to Cap
Blanc and Cala Pi. About 13km along this road lies Capocorp Vell
(often signposted in Castilian: Capicorp Vey), whose extensive
remains date from around 1000 BC. Surrounded by arid scrubland
and enclosed within a modern dry-stone wall, this prehistoric village
incorporates the battered ruins of five *talayots* and 28 dwellings. A
footpath weaves round the haphazard remains, but most of what you
see is hardly inspiring and gives little idea of how the village was
arranged. The most impressive features are the Cyclopean walls,
which reach a height of 4m in places. To make more sense of what
you see, pick up the free leaflet, in English, at the entrance.

A short distance further south, just beyond the village of Capicorp,
there's a choice of routes: straight on for Cap Blanc, a desultory
cape with a lighthouse, or left for the four-kilometre trip to CALA PI.
Spreading over a bleak headland, this resort is the remote setting for
the glitzy *Club Cala Pi*, a self-contained resort complex that's a
favourite with French tourists. In the cove, there's a lovely beach, a
tiny finger of sand wedged between high, pine-studded cliffs and
fringed by ramshackle fishing huts. You won't find anywhere to stay
on spec, but you can refresh your palate at the *Miguel* restaurant,
where the grilled fish is very tasty, or snack at the bar next door.

Travel details

Buses

From Artà to: Cala Rajada (Mon–Sat 9 daily, 1–2 on Sun; 10min); Coves d'Artà
(May–Oct Mon–Sat 4 daily; 15min); Palma (Mon–Sat 4 daily, 1–2 on Sun; 1hr
25min); Platja de Canyamel (May–Oct Mon–Sat 4 daily; 10min); Port d'Alcúdia
(May–Oct Mon–Sat 5 daily; 30min).

From Cala d'Or to: Colònia de Sant Jordi (Mon–Sat 1 daily; 45min); Palma
(2–4 daily; 1hr 10min); Santanyí (2–4 daily; 15min).

From Cala Figuera to: Cala Santanyí (May–Oct Mon–Sat 2 daily; Nov–April
Mon–Sat 1 daily; 5min); Colònia de Sant Jordi (Mon–Sat 2 daily; 40min);
Palma (Mon–Sat 1–2 daily; 1hr 20min); Santanyí (Mon–Sat 2 daily; 15min).

From Cala Millor to: Cala Rajada (May–Oct Mon–Sat 11 daily; Nov–April
Mon–Sat 1 daily; 25min); Palma (Mon–Sat 5–7 daily, 1–2 on Sun; 1hr 15min);
Port d'Alcúdia (May–Oct Mon–Sat 3 daily; 1hr).

From **Cala Pi** to: Palma (May–Oct 1 daily except Thurs; 45min).

From **Cala Rajada** to: Artà (Mon–Sat 9 daily, 1–2 on Sun; 10min); Cala Agulla
(May–Oct Mon–Sat 4 daily; 5min); Cala de Sa Font (May–Oct Mon–Sat 4 daily;
10min); Cala Millor (May–Oct Mon–Sat 11 daily; Nov–April Mon–Sat 1 daily;
25min); Ca'n Picafort (May–Oct Mon–Sat 9 daily; 35min); Capdepera (Mon–Sat
9 daily, 1–2 on Sun; 5min); Coves d'Artà (May–Oct Mon–Sat 4 daily; 25min);
Palma (Mon–Sat 4 daily, 1–2 on Sun; 1hr 30min); Platja de Canyamel (May–Oct
Mon–Sat 3 daily; 20min); Port d'Alcúdia (May–Oct Mon–Sat 2 daily; 45min).

From **Capdepera** to: Cala Rajada (Mon–Sat 9 daily, 1–2 on Sun; 5min); Palma
(Mon–Sat 4 daily, 1–2 on Sun; 1hr 30min).

From **Colònia de Sant Jordi** to: Cala d'Or (Mon–Sat 1 daily; 45min); Cala
Figuera (Mon–Sat 2 daily; 40min); Palma (2–5 daily; 1hr); Santanyí (2–4 daily;
25min).

From **Coves d'Artà** to: Artà (May–Oct Mon–Sat 4 daily; 15min); Cala Rajada
(May–Oct Mon–Sat 4 daily; 25min).

From **Coves del Drac** to: Palma (Mon–Sat 2–5 daily, 1 on Sun; 1hr).

From **Felanitx** to: Palma (3–4 daily; 50min); Porto Colom (2–3 daily; 15min).

From **Manacor** to: Palma (Mon–Sat 8 daily, 3 on Sun; 45min); Porto Cristo
(Mon–Sat 8 daily, 3 on Sun; 25min).

From **Montuiri** to: Petra (2–3 daily; 10min); Palma (2–3 daily; 40min).

From **Palma** to: Algaida (3–5 daily; 20min); Artà (Mon–Sat 4 daily, 1–2 on Sun;
1hr 25min); Cala d'Or (2–4 daily; 1hr 10min); Cala Figuera (Mon–Sat 1–2 daily;
1hr 20min); Cala Millor (Mon–Sat 5–7 daily, 1–2 on Sun; 1hr 15min); Cala Pi
(May–Oct 1 daily except Thurs; 45min); Cala Rajada (Mon–Sat 4 daily, 1–2 on
Sun; 1hr 30min); Cales de Mallorca (May–Oct Mon–Sat 2 daily; 1hr); Colònia de
Sant Jordi (2–5 daily; 1hr); Coves del Drac (Mon–Sat 2–5 daily, 1 on Sun; 1hr);
Felanitx (3–4 daily; 50min); Inca (Mon–Fri 8 daily, 4 on Sat, 3 on Sun; 30min);
Manacor (Mon–Sat 8 daily, 3 on Sun; 45min); Petra (2–3 daily; 50min); Montuiri
(2–3 daily; 40min); Porto Colom (1–3 daily; 1hr); Porto Cristo (Mon–Sat 8 daily,
3 on Sun; 1hr 10min); Porto Petro (2 daily; 1hr 10min); Santanyí (2–4 daily; 1hr);
Ses Covetes (for Es Trenc beach; May–Oct 1 daily; 1hr).

From **Petra** to: Montiuri (2–3 daily; 10min); Palma (2–3 daily; 50min).

From **Porto Colom** to: Palma (1–3 daily; 1hr).

From **Porto Cristo** to: Ca'n Picafort (May–Oct Mon–Sat 3 daily; 1hr); Palma
via Manacor (Mon–Sat 7 daily, 2 on Sun; 1hr 10min); Port d'Alcúdia (May–Oct
Mon–Sat 3 daily; 1hr).

From **Santanyí** to: Cala Santanyí (May–Oct Mon–Sat 2 daily; Nov–April 1 daily;
10min).

Chapter 4

Menorca

Second largest of the Balearics, boomerang-shaped MENORCA stretches from the enormous natural harbour of Maó in the east to the smaller port of Ciutadella in the west, a distance of just 45km. These two towns, boasting over sixty percent of the population, are the only points of arrival (Menorca's airport lies on the outskirts of Maó). Each has preserved much of its eighteenth- and early nineteenth-century appearance, though Ciutadella's labyrinthine centre, with its grandee mansions and Gothic cathedral, has the aesthetic edge over Maó's plainer, more mercantile architecture. Running through the little-developed interior between the two, the main C721 highway forms the island's backbone, linking a trio of pocket-sized market towns – Alaior, Es Mercadal and Ferreries – and succouring what little industry Menorca enjoys, a few shoe factories and cheese-making plants. Branching off the highway, a sequence of asphalted side roads lead to the resorts that notch the north and south coasts. Mercifully, however, the tourist development is largely confined to individual coves and bays, and only amongst the sprawling villa-villages of the southeast and on the west coast has it become overpowering. What's more, there are still many remote cove beaches with not a speck of concrete in sight, though access to them is usually along rough and dusty lanes.

The main highway also acts as a rough dividing line between Menorca's two distinct geological areas. In the north, sandstone predominates, giving a red tint to the low hills which roll out towards the

---

Accommodation price codes

All the accommodation prices in this book have been coded using the symbols below, corresponding to the least expensive double room in each establishment in high season, excluding special offers. For a full explanation see p.34.

① Under 3000ptas	④ 6000–8000ptas	⑦ 14,000–20,000ptas
② 3000–4000ptas	⑤ 8000–10,000ptas	⑧ 20,000–25,000ptas
③ 4000–6000ptas	⑥ 10,000–14,000ptas	⑨ Over 25,000ptas

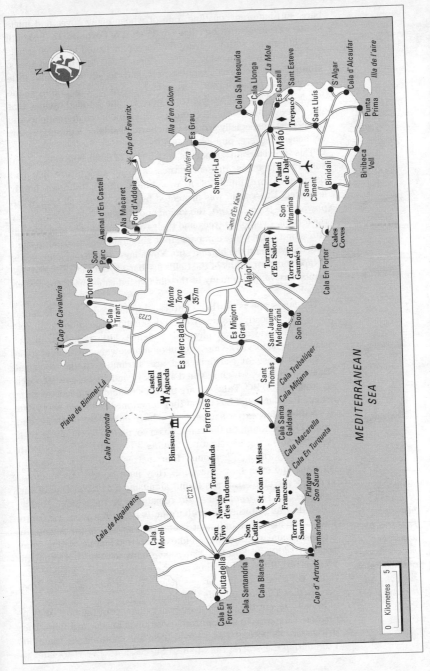

bare, surf-battered coastline, one of whose many coves and inlets shelters the lovely fishing village and resort of **Fornells**. To the south all is limestone, with low-lying flatlands punctuated by bulging hills and fringed by a cove-studded coastline. Straddling the two zones, **Monte Toro**, Menorca's highest peak and the site of a quaint little convent, offers panoramic views which reveal the topography of the whole island. Clearly visible from here are the wooded ravines that gash the southern zone, becoming deeper and more dramatic as you travel west – especially around **Cala Santa Galdana**, a popular resort set beneath severe, pine-clad seacliffs.

This varied terrain supports a smattering of minuscule villages and solitary farmsteads, present witnesses to an **agriculture** that had become, before much of it was killed off by tourism, highly advanced. Every field was protected by a dry-stone wall (*tanca*) to prevent the *tramóntana*, the vicious north wind, from tearing away the topsoil. Even olive trees had their roots individually protected in little stone wells, while compact stone ziggurats sheltered cattle from both the wind and the blazing sun. Nowadays, apart from a few acres of rape and corn, many of the fields are barren, but the walls and ziggurats survive, as do many of the old twisted gates made from olive branches.

The landscape is further cluttered by hundreds of crude stone memorials, mostly dating from the second millennium BC. Yet, despite this widespread physical evidence, little is known of the island's prehistory. The most common monuments are thought to be linked to those of Sardinia and are attributed to the so-called Talayotic culture, which reached a peak of activity here in Menorca in around 1000 BC. **Talayots** are the rock mounds found all over the island. Popular belief has it that they functioned as watchtowers, but it's a theory few experts accept: they have no interior stairway, and only a few are found on the coast. Even so, no one has come up with a more convincing explanation. **Taulas** – huge stones topped with another to form a "T", around four metres high – are unique to Menorca and even more puzzling. They have no obvious function, and they are almost always found alongside a *talayot*. One of the best-preserved *talayot* and *taula* remains is on the edge of Maó at **Talatí de Dalt**; another, **Torrellafuda**, is near Ciutadella. The third kind of prehistoric monument found on Menorca is the **naveta**, a stone-slab construction shaped like an inverted loaf tin, dating from between 1400 and 800 BC. Many have false ceilings, and although you can stand up inside, they were clearly not living spaces, but rather communal tombs, or ossuaries. The prime example is the **Naveta d'es Tudons**, outside Ciutadella.

All of Menorca's prehistoric sights have free, open access. For more information on Talayotic culture, see p.241.

In more recent times, the deep-water channel of the port of Maó promoted Menorca to an important position in European affairs. The **British** saw its potential as a **naval base** and captured the island in 1708 during the War of the Spanish Succession – five years later it was ceded to them under the Treaty of Utrecht. Spain regained possession in 1783, but with the threat of Napoleon in the Mediterranean, a new British base was temporarily established under admirals Nelson and Collingwood until Britain finally relinquished all claims to the island in 1802. The British influence on Menorca, especially its architecture, is still manifest: the sash windows so popular in Georgian design are even now sometimes referred to as *winderes*, locals often part with a fond *bye-bye*, and there's a substantial expatriate community. The British also introduced the art of distilling juniper berries, and Menorcan gin (Xoriguer, Beltran or Nelson) is now world-renowned.

Maó and around

Despite its status as island capital, **MAÓ** (in Castilian, **Mahón**) has a comfortable, small-town feel, and wandering around the ancient centre, with its long-established cafés and old-fashioned shops, is a relaxing and enjoyable way to pass a few hours. Nowadays most visitors approach Maó from its landward side, but this gives the wrong impression. The town has always been a **port** and it's only from the water that the logic of the place becomes apparent, with its centre crowding a steeply inclined ridge set tight against the south side of the harbour – which, in turn, marks the westerly limit of a narrow five-kilometre-long inlet that stretches to the Mediterranean. From this angle Maó is extraordinarily beautiful, its well-worn, pastel-shaded houses tumbling down the hillside, interrupted by bits and pieces of the old city walls and the occasional church. It's the general flavour that really appeals rather than individual sights, particularly the town's striking and unusual hybrid architecture, with tall, monumental Spanish mansions alongside classical Georgian sash-windowed town houses, reminders of the British occupation.

Port it may be, but there's no seamy side to Maó, and the harbourfront is home to a string of excellent **restaurants and cafés** that attract tourists in their droves. Few, however, stay the night, preferring the purpose-built resorts and villa complexes which fill much of Menorca's southeast corner. As a result, Maó has surprisingly few *hostals* and hotels, which means that you can base yourself here and – if you avoid the waterfront – escape the tourist throngs with the greatest of ease. Nonetheless, rooms are still in short supply in July and August, when reserving in advance is strongly recommended.

Arrival, orientation and information

Menorca's **airport** (☎971 360150), just 5km west of Maó, is a modest affair with just a handful of car rental outlets and a **tourist information desk**, which has a good selection of free literature (May–Oct

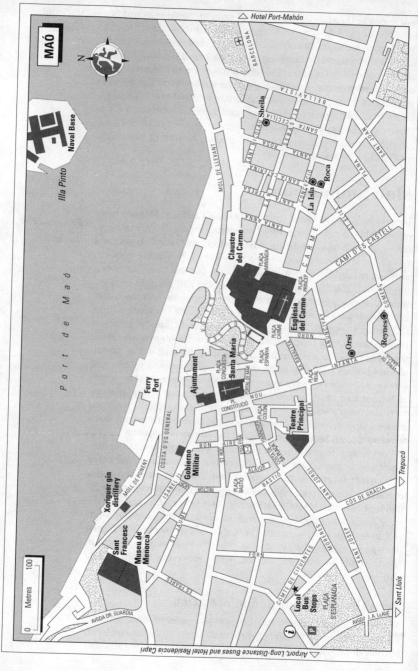

MAÓ

N

Port de Maó

Illa Pinto

Naval Base

Hotel Port-Mahón

BARCELONA

BELLAVISTA

Sheila

SANTA CECÍLIA

SANT NICOLAU

SANTA TERESA

ROSA

SANTA CATERINA

SANT JOAN

PLANA

Roca

La Isla

COSTA PINES

SANTA VINYES

CONCEPCIÓ

LLUC

CARME

CAMÍ D'ES CASTELL

SANTA ANNA

SANTA ANNA

Claustre
del Carme

PLAÇA
MIRANDA

MOLL DE LLEVANT

PLAÇA
PRÍNCEP

Església
del Carme

PLAÇA
CARME

NORD

Orsi

ANUNCIVAY

Reynés

COMERÇ

VERGE DE GRÀCIA

INFANTA

Santa Maria

PLAÇA
CONQUESTA

PLAÇA
ESPANYA

PLAÇA
REAL

Ajuntament

Ferry
Port

VIVES

PORTA DE MAR

PLAÇA
NOU

SA RAVALETA

COSTA D'ES GENERAL

PL.
CONSTITUCIÓ

PLAÇA
COLÓN

CÒNSUL

Teatre
Principal

DE LA

MOLL DE PONENT

BON AIRE

ST. ROC

ESGLÉSIA

SES VOLTES

Xoriguer gin
distillery

ISABEL II

NOU

RECTOR

SANTA EULÀLIA

ALAIOR

BASTIÓ

Gobierno
Militar

PLAÇA
BASTIÓ

SANT JORDI

Sant
Francesc

Museu de
Menorca

ST. JAUME

LES FRARES

FORN

CÒS DE GRÀCIA

MORERES

SANT JOSEP

Trepucó

AVGDA DR. GUÀRDIA

COMTE DE CIFUENTES

Local
Bus
Stops

PLAÇA
S'ESPLANADA

AVGDA J. A. LLAVE

Sant Lluís

Airport, Long-Distance Buses and Hotel Residencia Capri

Metres   100

0

daily 8.30am–11pm; ☎971 157115). There are no buses into town,
but the taxi fare will only set you back about 1000ptas. **Ferries** from
Barcelona and Palma sail right up the inlet to Maó harbour, mooring
next to the Trasmediterranea offices (☎971 366050) directly
beneath the town centre. From behind the ferry dock, it's a brief walk
up the wide stone stairway of Costa de Ses Voltes to **Plaça Espanya**.
The oldest part of Maó runs east and west of this small square, rolling
along the clifftop above the harbour for roughly 1km. Behind, to the
south, the predominantly nineteenth-century town climbs up the hill.
Its complicated pattern of tiny squares and short lanes is bisected by
the principal shopping street and pedestrianized main drag, which
goes under various names, with **Costa de Sa Plaça** and **c/Moreres**
being the longest individual strips. A fairly steep five- to ten-minute
walk from one end to the other, this street leads directly to **Plaça
S'Esplanada**, the plain main square with its underground car park
and local bus terminus.

Exploring Maó on foot doesn't require much effort, but driving in
the centre is well-nigh impossible and you're better off **parking** on
the periphery. The obvious – and easiest – spot is the underground
car park below Plaça S'Esplanada, but this is quite expensive at
175ptas per hour up to a maximum of 1750ptas – which is also what
you have to pay if you lose your ticket. On-street parking (when you
can find a place) is free except during shopping hours (Mon–Fri
9am–2pm & 4.30–7.30pm, mid-June to mid-Sept 8.30pm, Sat
9am–2pm) when you should take a ticket from a meter – the maximum stay of two hours costs 200ptas. Note that if the time allowed
overlaps into a free period, your ticket is still valid when the next
restricted time begins.

*Further infor-
mation about
Menorca's bus
services can be
found on
p.237.*

The **Oficina d'Informació Turística** in Plaça S'Esplanada
(Mon–Fri 8.30am–7.30pm, Sat 9am–2pm; ☎971 363790) provide
maps of the island and free leaflets giving the lowdown on almost
everything you can think of, from archeological sites and beaches to
bus timetables, car rental, accommodation and banks. **Local buses**,
which shuttle up and down the southeast coast, stop on the square,
just across from the tourist office. **Island-wide buses** arrive at the
stands along Avinguda J. M. Quadrado, just to the west of the tourist
office.

*Details of fer-
ries and flights
to Maó are
given on p.33.*

Accommodation

Maó has a limited supply of accommodation and excessive demand
tends to inflate prices at the height of the season. However, along
with Ciutadella, it remains the best Menorcan bet for bargain lodgings, with a small concentration of **hostals** (and one hotel) among
the workaday streets beyond Plaça Princep, a few minutes' walk
east of the town centre. None of these places is especially inspiring,
but they're reasonable enough and convenient – unlike Maó's two
quality hotels, which are stuck out on the edge of town.

Hostals

Hostal La Isla, c/Santa Caterina 4, at the corner of c/Concepció ☎971 366492. Recently refurbished, comfortable one-star with 22 rooms, all with showers, and its own bar and restaurant. ③.

Hostal-residencia Orsi, c/Infanta 19 ☎ & fax 971 364751. The most agreeable *hostal* in town, English-owned and a couple of minutes' walk from Plaça Reial. Pleasant, spick-and-span old rooms with large windows and green shutters; mostly shared showers. ③.

Hostal Reynes, c/Comerç 26, just off c/Infanta ☎971 364059. One-star *hostal* with basic rooms five minutes' walk from Plaça Reial occupying an undistinguished modern block in a quiet residential area. ③.

Hostal-residencia Roca, c/Carme 37, at the corner of c/Santa Caterina ☎971 351539. Fourteen no-frills rooms in a plain but quite cheerful modern block with a ground-floor café. ③.

Hotels

Hotel del Almirante, Carretera de Maó, nearly 2km east of Maó beside the coastal road to Es Castell ☎971 362700, fax 971 362704. Once the residence of British admiral Lord Collingwood, this maroon-and-cream Georgian house has a delightful, antique-crammed interior, though some of the bedrooms are modern affairs overlooking the swimming pool round the back. The package-tour operators Thomson use the place, but there are often vacancies. To get there, take a bus or taxi towards Es Castell and ask to be dropped off. Open May to October. ⑤.

Hotel-residencia Capri, c/Sant Esteve 8 ☎971 361400, fax 971 350853. Routine, modern, three-star hotel with plain but perfectly adequate rooms in the centre of Maó, a brief walk west of the tourist office – head down Avgda J. M. Quadrado and take the first turn on the left. ⑥.

Hotel Port-Mahón, Avgda Fort de L'Eau s/n ☎971 362600, fax 971 351050. Elegant colonial-style hotel of columns, pediments and circular windows in a superb location overlooking the Maó inlet. There's a swimming pool and a smart patio café, and each of the seventy-odd rooms has air conditioning. The hotel has recently been refurbished in a crisp modern style with Art Deco garnishings. Room prices vary enormously, with the top whack a hefty 30,000ptas. It's situated a twenty-minute walk east of the town centre via c/Carme or c/Barcelona at the corner of Avgda Fort de L'Eau and Avgda Port de Maó. ⑤.

Hotel Sheila, c/Santa Cecília 41, at the corner of c/Sant Nicolau ☎971 364855. This old terraced house has been intelligently refurbished in ultra-modern style to hold eleven spick-and-span rooms. There's car parking space and a café here too. ⑤.

The Town

Maó's setting and architecture are delightful, but it musters few sights of specific interest. The highlights are the exquisite Churrigueresque chapel in the church of **St Francesc** and, next door, the prehistoric and classical artefacts of the **Museu de Menorca**. These two attractions are in the town centre above the **harbour**, where you can sample as much of the island's liquors as you like at the enjoyable **Xoriguer gin distillery**.

Plaça Espanya and Plaça Carme

From just behind the ferry terminal, a graceful stone stairway and a narrow, twisting street – the Costa de Ses Voltes – tangle together as they climb up the hill to emerge in the old town at the compact **Plaça Espanya**. On the north side of the square, plonked on top of a mighty bastion that was once part of the Renaissance city wall, is a sociable little fish market, beside which a narrow alley offers fine views back down over the port. Immediately to the east, **Plaça Carme** is over-shadowed by the massive facade of the **Església del Carme**, a Carmelite church whose cavernous interior is almost entirely devoid of embellishment. The adjoining cloisters, the **Claustre del Carme**, have recently been refurbished to house the town's fresh meat, fruit and vegetable market, with the market stalls set against sculpted angels and religious carvings.

Plaça Conquesta and Plaça Constitució

North of Plaça Espanya lies **Plaça Conquesta**, whose full-length but poorly crafted statue of Alfonso III, the Aragonese king who expelled the Menorcan Moors, was donated by Franco. The narrow confines of the adjacent **Plaça Constitució** are dominated by the church of **St Maria**, founded in 1287 by Alfonso III to celebrate the island's recon-quest, but thoroughly remodelled in the late eighteenth century to create the broadly Neoclassical structure of today. The interior boasts a hangar-like, aisle-less nave with an eye-catching high altar, whose larger-than-life Baroque excesses shoot up to the roof flanked by spiral columns. Several side chapels exhibit similar Baroque flour-ishes, but the church's pride and joy is its **organ**, a monumental piece of woodwork filling out the elevated gallery above the south entrance. The organ, with its trumpeting angels, four keyboards and three thousand pipes, was made in Austria in 1810 and lugged across half of Europe at the height of the Napoleonic wars. Britain's Admiral Collingwood helped with the move, probably as a crafty piece of appeasement: defiance of their new Protestant masters had played a large part in the locals' decision to rebuild the church during the British occupation.

Next door, the genteel arcades, bulls'-eye upper windows and wrought-iron grilles of the **Ajuntament** (town hall) also date from a late eighteenth-century refurbishment. There's another example of British goodwill here too, for the clock was presented to the town by the island's first British governor, Sir Richard Kane.

*For a brief
biography of
Richard Kane,
see p.217.*

Carrer Isabel II

Georgian doors and fanlights, sash windows and fancy ironwork dis-tinguish **Carrer Isabel II** as it runs west from Plaça Constitució. This narrow, elongated street, lined by a string of fine patrician mansions backing onto the cliffs above the harbour, once lay at the heart of the British administration. Halfway along, the present **Gobierno Militar** (military governor's house) is the most distinctive building today, with its elaborate paintwork and shaded, colonial-style arcades.

The Església de St Francesc

There's a useful shortcut down to the harbour from c/Isabel II: Costa d'es General, an alley at the foot of c/Rector Mort, which tunnels through the old city wall before snaking its way down the cliff to the waterside below.

At the end of c/Isabel II the Baroque facade of the **Església de St Francesc** appears as a cliff-face of pale golden stone set above the rounded, Romanesque-style arches of its doorway. The church was a long time in the making, its construction spread over the seventeenth and eighteenth centuries, following the razing of the town by Barbarossa in 1535 – a random piece of piracy during the protracted struggle for control of the Mediterranean between the Ottomans and the Habsburgs which lasted until the destruction of the Turkish fleet at Battle of Lepanto in 1571. Inside, the mighty nave, with its lofty arching roof, encloses a crude but flamboyant high altar with panels of biblical scenes designed to edify the (illiterate) congregation. The nave is poorly lit, but it's still possible to pick out the pinkish tint in much of the stone and the unusual spiral decoration of the pillars. In contrast, the **Chapel of the Immaculate Conception**, tucked away off the north side of the nave, is flooded with light: an octagonal wonderland of garlanded vines and roses in the Churrigueresque style. The chapel is attributed to Francesc Herrara, the painter, engraver and architect who trained in Rome and worked in Menorca before moving on to Palma's church of St Miquel.

The Museu de Menorca

The Museu de Menorca is open Tues–Sat 10am–2pm & 5–8pm, Sun 10am–2pm; free.

The adjacent monastic buildings now house the **Museu de Menorca**, easily the island's biggest and best museum, with multilingual labels to explain most of the exhibits. Entry to the collection is through the cloister, whose sturdy pillars and vaulted aisles illustrate the high point of the Menorcan Baroque.

The first floor holds a wide sampling of prehistoric artefacts, beginning with bits and pieces left by the neolithic pastoralists who were well established here by about 4000 BC. There's also an extensive range of material from the **Talayotic period**. The early stuff, household objects and the like, is pretty crude, but the displays ably illustrate the increasing sophistication of the Talayotic people, both in their home-made goods and in their use of imported items. In particular, look out for the dainty, rather quizzical-looking bronze bull, probably of Phoenician manufacture, found at the Torralba d'En Salort Talayotic site. Other imported items include several enormous amphorae and a few pieces of charming, multicoloured Punic jewellery. These reflect the final flourishing of Talayotic culture when Menorca became a major port of call for ships sailing between Italy and Spain.

The Torralba d'En Salort Talayotic site is described on p.219

On the second floor, the collection deteriorates. A series of skimpy displays gallop through the Moorish period and continue to 1900, but without much conviction. The only interest is in the folkloric

wooden figurines carved by the **Monjo Brothers**: whimsical repre-
sentations of various *Menorquín* characters dating from the late
nineteenth century.

Plaça Bastió and Plaça S'Esplanada

Leaving the museum, it's a brief walk southeast along narrow side
streets to **Plaça Bastió**, the site of Maó's one remaining medieval
gateway. A few metres further southeast is **Costa de Sa Plaça**, a
steeply sloping street whose old-fashioned shops and tiny piazzas
form the town's commercial centre. There are more shops up the hill
along c/Moreres, which brings you to the flowerbeds and pine trees
of the principal square, **Plaça S'Esplanada**. The square's large military barracks is edged by an unpleasant reminder of Fascist days, a
monumental Civil War memorial endowed with Francoist insignia
and inscribed with the old fable, *Honor todos los que dieron su vida
por Espanya* (Honour to all those who gave their life for Spain). The
main excitement here is at the weekend, when the square becomes a
social hub, with crowds converging on its icecream vendors, and
street entertainers playing to the strolling multitudes.

The quayside

Below the town, Maó's ferry port is situated in the middle of the two-
kilometre-long **quayside**. To the west, a partly abandoned industrial
area overlooks the murky waters at the head of the inlet. To the east,
fishing jetties precede the town's elongated marina, where flashy
chrome yachts face a string of restaurants, bars and cafés. By day,
the half-hour stroll along the quayside is tame verging on boring; at
night, with tourists converging on the restaurants, it's slightly more
animated, but not much. There is, however, one enjoyable attraction
a couple of minutes' walk west of the ferry dock. This is the showroom of the **Xoriguer gin distillery**, where you can help yourself to
free samples of gin, various liqueurs and other spirits. Multilingual
labels give details of all the different types, and there are some pretty
obscure examples, such as *calent*, a sweet, brown liqueur with
aniseed, wine, saffron and cinnamon, and *palo*, a liquorice-tasting
spirit supposedly of Phoenician provenance. The lime-green *hier-
bas*, a favourite local tipple, is a sweet and sticky liqueur, partly
made from camomile collected on the headlands of La Mola outside
Maó. In all its guises, it is, however, gin which remains the main
product, and *pomada*, a gin cocktail with lemonade, is now as near
as damn it Menorca's national drink. Gin was first brought to the
island by British sailors in the late eighteenth century, but a local
businessman, a certain Beltran, obtained the recipe in obscure cir-
cumstances and started making the stuff himself. Nowadays,
Xoriguer is the most popular island brand, mostly sold in modern
versions of the earthenware bottles once used by British sailors,
which are known locally as *canecas*.

*The Xoriguer
distillery is
open Mon–Fri
8am–7pm, Sat
9am–1pm;
free. They also
run boat trips
– see p.208.*

Eating, drinking and nightlife

Maó has a place in culinary history as the eighteenth-century birth-place of mayonnaise (*mahonesa*). Various legends, all of them involving the French, claim to identify its inventor: take your pick from the chef of the French commander besieging Maó; a peasant woman dressing a salad for another French general; or a housekeeper disguising rancid meat from the taste buds of a French officer. The French also changed the way the Menorcans bake their bread, while the British started the dairy industry and encouraged the roasting of meat. Traditional Balearic food is, however, not very much in evidence these days, as most of Maó's restaurants specialize in Spanish, Catalan or Italian dishes. These tourist-oriented establishments are mainly spread out along the quayside – the Moll de Ponent west of the main stairway, the Moll de Llevant to the east. There's also a smattering of cheaper restaurants and coffee bars in the centre of town, though surprisingly few *tapas* bars. Almost all the town's cafés and restaurants open daily during the season, though restaurants usually take a siesta between 4pm and 8pm. Out of season, many places shut completely; others open only at weekends. Nightlife is not Maó's forte, but some fairly lively bars dot the harbourfront, staying open till around 2am on summer weekends. There's a cluster near the ferry dock and another towards the east end of the harbour on Moll de Llevant.

Cafés and tapas bars

Cafeteria La Bombilla, c/St Roc 31. Unenticing decor, but this modest little café in the town centre beside Plaça Bastió offers a good range of *tapas*, averaging about 400ptas per portion.

Cafeteria Consey, Plaça S'Esplanada 72. Amongst the string of mundane cafés on the main square, this is probably the best option for its above-average and reasonably priced snacks.

La Farinera, Moll de Llevant 84. Spruce and modern café-bar offering tasty snacks near the ferry port. Usually open from 6am.

Mirador Café, Plaça Espanya s/n. Tasty meals and great views over the harbour from this little café-bar with a terrace. Footsteps from the fish market, at the top of the main stairway leading from the harbour to the town centre.

Restaurants

L'Arpó, Moll de Llevant 124. Cosy and intimate restaurant featuring a superb selection of fish dishes from 1800ptas.

Ca'n Pau, Moll de Llevant 200. Pint-sized French restaurant with delicious daily specials from as little as 1500ptas.

Gregal, Moll de Llevant 43. Chic little establishment towards the east end of the harbourfront serving the best of Greek cuisine as well as excellent seafood, with main courses at around 2300ptas.

Pilar, c/Forn 61. A very intimate and cosy family-run place featuring traditional Menorcan cuisine, with main courses costing around 1700ptas. It's near Plaça

S'Esplanada: leave the square along c/Moreres, take the first left and then the first right. Closed Nov–April and on Sun & Mon.

Il Porto, Moll de Llevant 225. Enjoyable place to eat with a fountain and an arcaded terrace. The cooks perform in full view, turning out tasty fish and meat dishes from a wide-ranging menu.

Roma, Moll de Llevant 295. Popular, fast-service eatery specializing in well-prepared Italian food at bargain prices, with pasta and pizzas from 800ptas. The decor is a tad old-fashioned, but that seems to suit the *Daily Express*-reading clientele.

Bars and nightclubs

Bar Akelarre, Moll de Ponent 41. Relaxed, fashionable bar set in an imaginatively refurbished old stone vault, close to the ferry terminal.

Café Baixamar, Moll de Ponent 17. Modernist decor, great atmosphere and music to suit most tastes.

Café Blues, c/Santiago Ramon i Cajal 3. Trendy basement bar with jazz through to R&B, and a favourite with local twenty-somethings. It's a couple of minutes' walk south of Plaça Reial, along c/Infanta then first right up to the end of c/Verge de Gràcia.

Nou Bar, c/Nou 1, at the corner of c/Hannover. The café here, with its ancient armchairs and gloomy lighting, is a dog-eared old place much favoured by locals.

Salsa Bar, Moll de Ponent 29. Lively bar playing mostly Latin sounds.

Si, c/Verge de Gràcia 16. Low-key nightspot south of Plaça Reial. Usually open from 11.30pm to around 3am.

Listings

Airport information Central switchboard ☎971 157000.

American Express At Viajes Iberia, c/Nou 35 (☎971 362848).

Banks Banco de Credito Balear, Plaça S'Esplanada 2; Banca March, c/Sa Ravaleta 7; Banco de Santander, c/Moreres 46.

Bicycle rental Just Bicicletas, c/Infanta 19 (☎971 364751), rents mountain bikes at reasonable rates.

Car rental Avis (☎971 361838) and Atesa (☎971 366213) have branches at the airport, while downtown there's another Avis outlet at Plaça S'Esplanada 53 (☎971 364778), plus many smaller concerns – the tourist office has an exhaustive list.

Emergencies Creu Roja (Red Cross) for an ambulance ☎361180; firefighters ☎092; police (Policía Municipal) ☎092.

Ferries Schedules, tariffs and tickets are available direct from the operator, Trasmediterranea (☎971 366050), at the ferry port.

Hospital There's a private hospital, the Virgen de Gràcia, on the west edge of the city centre at the junction of Camí Sta Maria and Avgda Vives Llull. The public Virgen de Monte Toro is on the opposite side of the centre at the junction of c/Bellavista and c/Barcelona.

Maps and books Librería Católica, facing Plaça Colón at c/Hannover 14, has a fair selection of guidebooks and general maps of Menorca, as well as a reasonable, though far from exhaustive, assortment of IGN island walking maps.

Mopeds Motos Gelabert, Avgda J. A. Clavé 12 (☎971 360614).

Pharmacies Among several downtown pharmacies, there's one at c/Sa Ravaleta 5 and another at c/Moreres 30.

Post office The central *correu* is at c/Bon Aire 15, near Plaça Bastió (Mon–Fri 9am–5pm, Sat 9am–1pm).

Taxis There's a taxi rank on Plaça S'Esplanada. Alternatively, telephone Radio Taxis ☎971 367111.

Travel agencies There's a full list in the yellow pages under *"viajes agencias"*. Viajes Iberia, c/Nou 35 (☎971 362908) is one of the more reliable.

Trepucó and Talatí de Dalt

Two notable prehistoric sites are located close to Maó, both with open access and no entry charge. One of them, **Trepucó**, is on the southern edge of town near the ring road, the other – the more appealing **Talatí de Dalt** – is about 4km to the west of Maó beside the C721.

Trepucó

It takes about twenty minutes to walk to **Trepucó** from the Plaça S'Esplanada: follow c/Cós de Gràcia and then go straight on down c/Verge de Gràcia to the ring road, cross the traffic island and follow the twisting lane directly ahead that leads past the cemetery. Surrounded by olive trees and dry-stone walls, the tiny site's focal point is a 4.2-metre-high and 2.75-metre-wide **taula**, one of the largest and best-preserved of these T-shaped monoliths on the island. The

---

Menorca's Talayotic sites

Menorca's **Talayotic sites** conform to a common pattern, though there are of course differences in the condition in which each has been preserved. The tallest structure on each site is generally the **talayot**, a cone-shaped tower between 5m and 10m high. These are positioned a few metres from the **taula**, a T-shaped structure up to 4.5m high. Some sites may contain several *talayots*, but there's only ever one *taula*, and this almost always sits in the middle of a circular enclosure whose perimeter is (or was) marked by a low wall. Archeologists have unearthed objects in these enclosures and the remains of firepits have been found against the perimeter wall, both of which seem to imply a religious function, though this is only conjecture – there's certainly insufficient evidence to justify referring to these enclosures as "shrines", as they've sometimes been called. There's general agreement, however, that the *taula* and its enclosure formed the public part of the settlement, and on many sites they are surrounded by the remains of circular family dwellings.

Archeologists divide the Talayotic period into several different periods, but as far as the non-specialist is concerned, the only significant difference between the various phases is the encircling **wall**, a dry-stone affair often several metres high and made up of large stones. These walls were for defence and probably reflect an increase in piracy across the western Mediterranean: the earlier settlements don't have them; the later ones – from around 1000 BC – do.

---

taula stands beside a circular compound which is edged by the scant remains of several broadly circular buildings. These were thoroughly excavated by a team of archeologists from Cambridge University in the late 1920s, but even they couldn't work out how the complex was structured. There are two cone-shaped **talayots** close by, though the lines of the larger one were mucked up by the French – during the invasion of 1781, they increased the width of the walls and mounted their guns on them. (By all accounts, the detachment posted here was in a state of chaos. The commander became so exasperated with the drunkenness of his soldiers that he announced, rather strangely, that only sober soldiers would be allowed to participate in the hazardous assault on Maó. The reaction of his men is not recorded.)

Talatí de Dalt

Another illuminating Talayotic remnant, **Talatí de Dalt**, lies 4km from Maó, just south of the main C721 highway: if you're driving, take the short and signposted country lane on the left; by public transport, take any Alaior bus, though it's best to check first that the driver is prepared to let you off. Much larger than Trepucó, the site is partly enclosed by a Cyclopean wall and features an imposing *taula* set within a circular precinct. The *taula* here appears to be propped up by a T-shaped pillar, though it's generally agreed that this is the result of an accidental fall, rather than by prehistoric design. Next to the *taula* are the heaped stones of the main *talayot* and all around are the meagre remains of prehistoric dwellings. The exact functions of these are not known, but there's no doubt that the *taula* was the village centrepiece, and probably the focus of religious ceremonies. The rustic setting is charming – olive and carob trees abound and a tribe of hogs roots around the undergrowth.

Port de Maó

Port de Maó, as Menorcans term the whole of the extended inlet that links Maó with the Mediterranean, is one of the finest natural harbours in the world. No less than 5.4km long and a maximum of 900m wide, the channel also boasts the narrowest of deep-sea entrances, strategic blessings that have long made it an object of nautical desire. The high admiral of the Holy Roman Emperor Charles V opined that "June, July, August and Mahon are the best ports in the Mediterranean", and after Barbarossa's destruction of Maó in 1535, his master finally took the point and had the harbour fortified. Later, the British eyed up the port as both a forward base for Gibraltar and a lookout against the French naval squadron in Toulon. Using the War of the Spanish Succession as their excuse, they occupied Menorca in 1708 and, give or take occasional French and Spanish interventions, stayed in control until 1802, pouring vast resources into the harbour defences. Since the departure of the Brits, the fortifications have been repeatedly reinforced by the Spanish.

Nowadays, both shores, and a trio of mid-channel islets, carry the
marks of all this military interest. Sights include the garrison town of
Es Castell, purpose-built by the English in the 1770s, and a string of
mostly ruined **fortifications**, thick-walled affairs hugging the contours of the coast to counteract the effects of hostile artillery fire. To
explore the harbour thoroughly you'll need your own transport,
though there is a frequent bus service from Maó to Es Castell. **Boat
trips** leave both these places for hour-long harbour tours, costing
800ptas. In Maó, the boats leave six to eight times daily from the
Xoriguer gin distillery, where tickets can be bought (see p.203). The
excursion comprises a dash down to La Mola headland and back,
with guides pointing out the sights in several languages. The boats
from Es Castell leave four times daily, with tickets available at the
kiosk on the quayside. Es Castell is halfway down the inlet, so the
cruises are more circular than those departing from Maó, but they
still cover all the sights from Maó to La Mola.

The north shore

Port de Maó's remaining fortifications are at their most impressive
on the north shore. Here, a narrow byroad leaves the west end of the
inlet to twist up across the coastal hills, passing after 3km the farmstead of **St Antoni**, also known as the **Golden Farm** (no entry), a fine
old, pastel-painted mansion that was at one time the headquarters of
Admiral Nelson. He barely visited it, however, being more concerned
with his mistress Emma Hamilton, who was ensconced at Naples,
than with the possibility of a French attack on his Menorcan base.

East of Golden Farm, the road skirts the wealthy suburb of Cala
Llonga and offers fine panoramas of both the harbour and its smaller
islands – **Illa del Rei**, whose buildings once accommodated a military
hospital, and **Illa Plana**, also known as Illa Quarentena, a pancake-flat
islet that's variously been a quarantine station, a US and now a
Spanish naval base. At the end of the promontory stands the formidable headland fastness of **La Mola**, still in use by the military, so visitors can't get in. The view from the road, however, is daunting, tier
upon tier of complementary gun emplacements designed to resist
prolonged bombardment. To the right lies the island of Latzareto (no
access), a former leper colony which was made more secure when it
was cut off from the peninsula by a canal in 1900. Lazareto's massive
walls are a tribute to superstition rather than military necessity: the
Menorcans were convinced that contagion could be carried into town
by the wind, so they built the walls to keep the germs inside.

Returning from La Mola, a signposted turning (west of Golden
Farm) wriggles north for 2km to **SA MESQUIDA**, which possesses
the nearest beach to Maó. Flanked by a rough and rocky shoreline,
the beach is a popular strip of dark red sand, but all in all it's not an
endearing spot – the village is a tatty affair which sprawls along the
coast in the shadow of a ruined fortress.

Es Castell and the south shore

Tucked in tight against the shore just 3km from Maó, the gridiron streets of **ES CASTELL** (also known as Villa Carlos) have a militaristic and very English air. Originally called Georgetown, the town is ranged around Plaça S'Esplanada, the old parade ground-cum-plaza. This expansive square bears witness to the British in its Georgian-style town hall, graced by a soaring clock tower, and the elongated facades of its barracks. Elsewhere, sash windows, doors with glass fanlights, and wrought-iron work adorn many of the older houses, though nowadays the centre looks rather bedraggled. As a garrison town, the fortunes of Es Castell have always been tied to those of the military; with Franco gone, the army no longer has the same prestige, and this is reflected in the town's general demeanour.

Nevertheless, Es Castell is still worth a brief wander, beginning in the main square, where one of the barracks houses a modest military museum, equipped with a motley collection of old rifles and uniforms (Sat & Sun 11am–1pm; free). From the plaza, it's a couple of minutes' walk east down c/Stuart to the harbour, a pretty spot occupying the thumb-shaped cove of Cales Fonts. The waterside is lined with a string of restaurants, two of the best being the *Vell Parrander* at Moll de Cales Fonts 52, and the *Siroco* at no. 40; both serve tasty seafood at reasonable prices. Walking round the Cales Fonts harbour, you'll come to the slight remains of the town's fortifications at the foot of c/Bellavista, which leads back towards the main square – hang a left at either c/Sant Ignasi or c/Victori. Buses from Maó stop on c/Gran, footsteps away from the main square along c/Victori.

Beyond Es Castell, the coastal road runs down towards the mouth of the harbour, where the *zona militar* (no access) incorporates the site of Fort Sant Felip. Once the island's greatest fortification, the fort was levelled by the Spanish in 1807, and nothing survives except ruins – though rumours persist of secret tunnels. To extend the excursion, you can follow the road round from just before the military zone and proceed to **SANT ESTEVE**, a pretty little village strung out along a narrow cove – and close enough to the harbour entrance to be extensively fortified. The fortifications have mostly rotted away, but on the south side of the cove near the telephone box a tunnel burrows into the hillside to enter what was once Fort Marlborough, a subterranean stronghold whose passages and galleries were dug out by the British in the eighteenth century. Proceed with caution – though there are plans to develop the whole complex as a tourist attraction.

Southeast Menorca

The **southeastern corner** of Menorca, delineated by the road between Maó and Cala En Porter, consists of a low-lying limestone plateau fringed by a rocky shoreline with a string of craggy coves. In recent years this stretch of coast has been extensively developed and

For information about boat tours of Port de Maó from Es Castell and Maó, see p.208.

From Sant Esteve, it's possible to drive on down country lanes to Sant Lluís, described on p.210.

today thousands of villas cover what was once empty scrubland. The result is not pretty and, although many prefer this low-rise architecture to the high-rise hotels of the 1960s, it's difficult to be enthusiastic, especially in **Cala En Porter**, the biggest and perhaps the ugliest *urbanització* of the lot. That said, the coast itself can be beautiful and the resort of **Cala d'Alcaufar**, one of the earliest developments, fringes a particularly picturesque cove. Inland lies an agricultural landscape crisscrossed by country lanes and dotted with tiny villages, plus one town – unassuming **Sant Lluís**.

Most of the district is devoted to villa-style accommodation, but there is a smattering of **hotels** and **hostals** open from April or May to October. As a consequence, advance reservations are pretty much essential. It's best to stay in Cala d'Alcaufar, but Punta Prima, a plain modern resort with a wide, windy beach in the southeast corner of the island, is a reasonable second choice.

Getting around without your own transport is fairly easy. There are hourly **buses** from Maó to Sant Lluís and Punta Prima, as well as regular services to Cala En Porter and Cala d'Alcaufar. Bear in mind, however, that with the exception of compact Cala d'Alcaufar, all of these resorts spread for miles, and if you've hired a villa you could be facing a very long, hot and confusing trek from the nearest bus stop – it's best to ring for a taxi from Maó's Radio Taxis on ☎971 367111.

Sant Lluís and Cala d'Alcaufar

Heading south from Maó along the main road, it's just 4km to **SANT LLUÍS**, a trim, one-square, one-church town of brightly whitewashed terraced houses. As at Es Castell, the town's grid plan betrays its colonial origins. A French commander, the Duc de Richelieu, built Sant Lluís to house his Breton sailors in the 1750s, naming the new settlement after the thirteenth-century King Louis IX, who was beatified for his part in the Crusades. The French connection is further recalled by the trio of coats of arms carved on the west front of the church – those of the royal household and two French governors. **Buses** from Maó stop at the north end of town beside Plaça Nova; there are no *hostals*.

Beyond Sant Lluís the road runs 5km to the east coast. Here you reach either **S'ALGAR**, where rank upon rank of suburban-looking villas sprawl along the coast, or – a far better option – the neighbouring resort of **CALA D'ALCAUFAR**. The development here is restrained, a smattering of holiday homes and old fishermen's cottages set beside a handsome inlet of flat-topped limestone cliffs and a turquoise sea. You can stroll out across the surrounding headlands, one of which has a Martello tower, or enjoy the sandy beach, which is linked to an expensive bridge that, oddly enough, has been waiting for a connecting road for years. The main footpath down to the beach runs through the *Hostal Xuroy* (May–Sept; ☎ & fax 971 151820; ⑤), a pleasant two-star establishment with forty modern rooms – though most of them are booked up months in advance for Thomson package tours.

Punta Prima to Binidali

Directly south of Sant Lluís lies **PUNTA PRIMA**, a large, standard-issue resort whose villas and supermarkets back onto a wide, sandy beach at the island's southeastern tip. Just offshore is the **Illa de l'Aire**, an inaccessible and uninhabited chunk of rock equipped with an automatic lighthouse. The sea, funnelled between the island and the shore, can make swimming dangerous from the beach – watch for the green or red flags. Windsurfing and sailing equipment is available for rent, as are pedaloes and sunbeds. Of the two hotels, the comfortable *Xaloc* is a one-star establishment with its own swimming pool (May–Oct; ☎ & fax 971 150106; ⑤), while the nearby 500-room *Pueblo de Menorca* also has its own pools, plus sports facilities and disco, though it's rather too large for many tastes (April–Oct; ☎971 159070, fax 971 159211; ⑥).

Travelling Menorca's south coast from Punta Prima to Binidali, a distance of around 10km, is a depressing experience: poorly signposted roads drift across the coastal scrubland encountering patches of undistinguished tourist development. On the map, it looks as if there are about half a dozen resorts, but on the ground it's impossible to determine where one settlement ends and another begins. The only vague light in the architectural gloom is **BINIBECA VELL**, a purpose-built settlement of second homes which, with its narrow whitewashed alleyways, wooden balconies and twisting flights of steps, was designed to resemble an old Mediterranean fishing village. At the end of the coastal road is scrawny **BINIDALI**, from where you can head inland to Sant Climent, on the main road between Maó and Cala En Porter.

Cales Coves and Cala En Porter

It's hard to understand why anyone thought the projected villa complex of **SON VITAMINA**, off the main road 4km west of Sant Climent, would prosper – it's simply too far from the sea. Nonetheless, ambitious plans were laid and a wide access road was constructed. But the plot buyers failed to materialize and now it's the most forlorn of places, an untidy smattering of villas surrounded by waste ground. It's only of use if you fancy the 2.5-kilometre hike down to the coast to see the remote prehistoric caves of **Cales Coves** (or Ses Coves). The walk starts on the square at the entrance to Son Vitamina: take the lane that exits diagonally to the right – it's too rough to drive in an ordinary car – and proceed down through the scrubland to the seashore, where a pair of pebbly beaches edge an attractive forked inlet; a sketchy footpath climbs the rocks to link the two. The surrounding cliffs are punctured by over one hundred man-made caves, the earliest of which date to Neolithic times when they served as both funerary chambers and troglodytic dwellings, equipped with circular living quarters. Later, in the Talayotic period, the caves were used exclusively as burial chambers and, though the necropolis was abandoned as a burial site long before the end of the Iron Age, several engraved stones discovered here indicate a continued interest well into Roman times, when the caves were visited during pagan festivals. It's easy and fun to explore the caves by clambering around the cliffs, though there's nothing specific to see once you're inside.

Returning to the main road, it's a short haul west to **CALA EN PORTER**, a shabby, sprawling *urbanització* which has engulfed a bumpy plateau with hundreds of villas of such similar appearance and proportions that it soon becomes disorienting. Neither is there any focus to the development, which is limited in the west by a steep, marshy ravine and to the south by steep cliffs towering above a wide strip of pale gold sand. Access to the beach is either by road along the ravine or by flights of steps running down the cliffside. Restaurants and bars back onto the beach, and the bathing is safe. The resort does boast one popular attraction, the **Cova d'En Xoroi**, a large cave stuck in the cliff-face high above the beach. A stairway from the entrance on the cliff-top wriggles down to the cave, offering stirring views along the coast. You can also visit at night, as a local businessman has installed a bar and disco in the cave, which warms the place up from about midnight onwards.

The Cova d'En Xoroi is open daily 11am–1pm & 4–9pm; 400ptas. The bar-disco is open nightly from 10pm until around dawn, with entry about 1000ptas.

Fornells and the northeast coast

North of Maó, the 25km minor road to Fornells takes in some of Menorca's finest scenery, running alongside cultivated fields protected by great stands of trees with the low hills that form the backbone of this part of the island bumping away into the distance. There's little to stop for along the way, but at regular intervals you can turn off towards beachside communities on what is, generally speaking, a harsh and rocky shoreline. Renowned for the excellence of its restaurants, **Fornells** itself boasts a delightful bayside location, and is, with its measured development, one of the most appealing resorts on the island. None of the village's three *hostals* is block-booked by package-tour operators, so there's also a reasonable chance of a room, and, although there's no beach at Fornells itself, it's a good base for visiting some of the remote cove beaches of the north coast – providing you're up to tackling the access roads, which require sturdy cars and steady nerves.

Buses leave Maó for Fornells and the bigger resorts of the northeast coast twice a day from Monday to Saturday, and once on Sunday.

Es Grau and Cap de Favaritx

Just outside Maó, the first turning off the Fornells road leads to **ES GRAU**, a tidy hamlet overlooking a horseshoe-shaped bay that's fringed by dunes and an unenticing arc of greyish sand. The shallow

waters here are ideal for children, and on weekends the handful of
bars and **restaurants** – the best of them is the waterside
Tamarindos – are crowded with holidaying *Mahonese*. Also popular is the quick boat trip over to the **Illa d'En Colom** (Pigeon Island),
a rocky, one-kilometre-square islet with jagged cliffs and a couple of
beaches, the more scenic of which is Arenal d'en Moro on the sheltered west side of the island. You can get off the boat at either beach,
and there are sailings roughly every hour – either wait around at the
jetty, a tiny little thing at the end of the village just along the shore
from the beach, or ask at the beachside *Ca'n Bernat* bar for precise
departure times. The return fare will set you back 700ptas.

The scrub-covered dunes behind Es Grau's beach form the periphery of an expanse of wetland that encircles the freshwater lake of
S'Albufera. The marshland is rich in migrant birdlife – all sorts of
waders and terns are especially common in the springtime – and has,
as a consequence, recently been designated a nature reserve. This has
come a little too late, however, for the protection of the lake's southern shore, now blighted by the villas of Shangri-La, but at least the
northern shoreline is undeveloped and offers viewpoints across the
lake and wetlands. The footpaths hereabouts are neither clear nor
well-maintained; the bridle path from Es Grau to Cap de Favaritx runs
through the dunes behind the beach and a couple of informal tracks
lead from it across to the low-lying hillocks overlooking the lake.

Back on the Maó–Fornells road and heading west, it's just over
1km to the left turn that leads down the **Camí d'En Kane** (see p.217)
and a further 4.5km to the right turn that weaves its way north to **Cap
de Favaritx**. This side road cuts along a slender valley and slips
through dumpy little hills to reach, after 6km, an unsigned fork
where you turn right for the final leg of the journey. The further you
go, the barer the landscape becomes – grass gives way to succulents,
but even they can't survive on the wind-stripped headland where the
solitary lighthouse shines out over a bare lunar-like landscape of
tightly layered slate.

Port d'Addaia to Son Parc

"I shall ever think of Adaia, and of the company I enjoyed at that
charming little Retirement, with the utmost Complacency and
Satisfaction," wrote John Armstrong, an engineer in the British army,
in the 1740s. If he could only see it now. The old **PORT D'ADDAIA**,
at the mouth of a long, wooded inlet, has mushroomed dreary holiday
homes, supermarkets and a marina, and as if that wasn't bad enough,
the neighbouring headlands now heave with the villas and apartment
buildings of two oversized resorts, low-key **NA MACARET** and the
more boisterous **ARENAL D'EN CASTELL**. A redeeming feature is
the latter's wide and sandy beach, set within a circular, cliff-edged
cove, but otherwise you'll probably be keen to move on – by returning along the access road that's shared by all three resorts.

The next turning along the main road leads to **SON PARC**, a workaday grid of holiday homes surrounding a golf course. One of the more upmarket resorts, Son Parc is fringed by thick pine woods and has a wide, pink-tinged sandy beach, equipped with a restaurant and beach bar. For a tad more isolation, walk the 1km north to **Cala Pudent**, a peaceful sandy strip set beside a narrow inlet. A stony track connecting the two beaches runs just behind the seashore.

Fornells

FORNELLS, a low-rise, classically pretty fishing village at the mouth of a long and chubby bay, has been popular with tourists for years, above all for its **seafood restaurants**, whose speciality, *caldereta de llagosta* (*langosta* in Castilian), is a fabulously tasty – and wincingly expensive – lobster stew. Nevertheless, there's been comparatively little development, just a slim trail of holiday homes extending north from the village in a suitably unobtrusive style. Behind the village and across the bay lie rockily austere headlands where winter storms and ocean spray keep vegetation to a minimum. This bleak terrain envelops a quartet of ruined **fortifications**, evidence of the harbour's past importance, of which two are easy to reach: an old watchtower peering out over the coast on the headland beyond Fornells and a shattered fort in the village itself. Built to protect the inlet from Arab and Turkish corsairs in the late seventeenth century, the forts were refurbished by the British, who constructed another on an island in the middle of the bay and posted a garrison. In a controversial piece of early tourist development, one of the commanders turned a local chapel into a tavern, incurring the disapproval of fellow officer John Armstrong: "In the Temple of Bacchus, no bounds are set to their [the soldiers'] Debauches and such a quantity of Wine is daily swallowed down, as would stagger Credulity itself."

Practicalities

Nowadays, with the British garrison long gone, nightlife is confined to the expensive **restaurants** that edge the waterfront on either side of the minuscule main square, Plaça S'Algaret. Such is their reputation that King Juan Carlos has been known to drop by on his yacht, and many people phone up days in advance with their orders. The royal favourite is the harbourside *Es Pla* (☎971 376655), whose sedately bourgeois dining room offers a superb paella for two for 7000ptas as well as the traditional lobster stew. More relaxed alternatives include *Sibaris*, Plaça S'Algaret 1, and *El Pescador*, next door, which concentrates on a magnificent *caldereta de llagosta* – as does the *Es Port*, a couple of doors down at c/Rosario 17. Also consider *Es Cranc*, Escoles 29, a smooth and polished restaurant offering a wide variety of fish dishes a couple of minutes' walk north of Plaça S'Algaret. As a general rule, reckon on about 2000–2500ptas for a seafood main course, twice that for paella or lobster stew.

Fornells has three reasonably priced and comfortable hostals. The two-star *S'Algaret* is a neat little place, with slightly old-fashioned furnishings and plain but cheerful rooms, at Plaça S'Algaret 7 (May–Oct; ☎971 376674, fax 971 376666; ⑤); the *Hostal-residencia La Palma* a few doors along is similar (April–Oct; ☎ & fax 971 376634; ④). The three-star *Hostal Fornells*, c/Major 17 (☎971 376676, fax 971 376688; ⑥), is slightly smarter: a spruce modern three-star with swimming pool.

Fornells' sweeping inlet provides ideal conditions for windsurfers; Windsurf Fornells (☎971 376400), situated beside the main road on the southern edge of the village, offers tuition to both novices and more experienced hands and teaches sailing skills too. Lessons include the use of their wetsuits, boards or boats. The town has no beach to speak of, but there is a strip of sand 1.5km back down the access road beside the unenticing apartment complex of Ses Salines (more interesting beaches in the area are detailed below). If you need a bike or car, try Roca-Roselló, in Fornells at c/Major 57 ☎971 376540. Buses stop beside the main square, Plaça S'Algaret.

Beyond Fornells

The wild and rocky coastline west of Fornells boasts several **cove beaches** of outstanding beauty. Getting to them, however, can be a problem: this portion of the island has barely been touched by the developers so the coast is often poorly signposted and the access roads are of very variable quality: some are gravel or dirt tracks, particularly slippery after rain, others are asphalted but sometimes extremely narrow, and others are a mixture of all three. These byroads branch off from the narrow but metalled country lanes which cross the lovely pastoral hinterland. Public transport around here is, as you might expect, non-existent.

Cala Tirant

From Fornells, the obvious starting point for a coastal excursion is the stepped crossroads about 3km south of the village, where the roads from Maó and Es Mercadal meet. At the junction, a signposted turning leads west down a country lane to pass, after 1.4km, the clearly marked turning to Cala Tirant. This side road is unmade, so it's a rough and dusty two-kilometre drive down to the cove, where a thick arc of ochre-coloured sand lies trapped between bumpy headlands, with grassy dunes and marshland to the rear. It's an attractive spot, but not a perfect one – there are villa developments on both sides of the cove and the beach is exposed to the north wind. To serve the villa residents, facilities include a beach bar and windsurfing.

Cap de Cavalleria

West of the Cala Tirant turn-off, the country lane continues through a charming landscape of old stone walls and scattered

*The Ecomuseu
Cap de
Cavalleria is
open daily:
April–June &
Oct 10am–
7pm; July–
Sept 10am–
8pm; 350ptas.*

farmsteads. After about 1km, keep straight on at the intersection and proceed for another 1km or so to the signposted right turning that leads north (along an asphalted byroad) towards Cap de Cavalleria. This is easy driving and 4km later, halfway to the cape, you stumble across the **Ecomuseu Cap de Cavalleria**, an odd little museum occupying an old farmstead perched on a hillock with wide views of the cape. The Romans settled on the sheltered side of this headland in 123 AD and it was here they built the town and port of **Sanisera** on the ruins of an earlier Phoenician settlement, though almost nothing survives from either period. This ancient history convinced the European Union to fund the Ecomuseu, though it's hard not to think it was more of a job creation scheme – an impression the museum's paltry if gallant collection of Roman and Talayotic bits and pieces does little to dispel.

Beyond the museum, the road becomes bumpy and narrow as it threads its way to **Cap de Cavalleria**, Menorca's most northerly point, a bleak and wind-buffeted hunk of rock with mighty seacliffs and a lonely lighthouse (no access).

Platja de Binimel-Là

Back on the country lane, it's a further 1.6km west to the signposted turning for **Platja de Binimel-Là**. At first the dirt access road is wide and fairly easy to negotiate but, after 1.5km, you hang a left and the last bit of road deteriorates – 500m of bone-jangling motoring. Once you've arrived, you'll spy a tiny freshwater lake set behind a narrow band of dark red dunes which in turn gives onto a beautiful sand and pebble beach. This is a popular spot, though there are several more secluded and much smaller beaches on the east side of the cove, reached by clambering along the seashore. In the summer, there's usually an ad hoc beach bar and it's possible to rent **pedaloes and windsurfing boards**. The beach lacks trees and shade, so you may be confronted with the odd sight of bathers protecting themselves from the sun by plastering themselves in mud from the stream running across the beach.

One significant problem at Binimel-Là is the seaweed and detritus that sometimes get driven onto the beach by a northerly wind. If this has happened, and if you've come equipped with reasonably stout shoes and a hiking map, move on to **Cala Pregonda**, a splendid, seastack-studded bay with pine woods and a sandy beach, thirty minutes' walk away to the west. The terrain isn't difficult, though there's no clear route except at the start: climb the little hill above the west end of Binimel-Là beach, clamber over a wall just to the right of a large stone inscribed "1915" and follow the wide track beyond, though this soon fizzles out as it approaches an expanse of salt flats.

Central Menorca

Richard Kane, Menorca's first British governor, devoted much time and energy to improving the island's communications, and his principal achievement was the construction of a highway between Maó and Ciutadella – funded by a tax on alcohol. The only surviving stretch of this original road makes a lovely alternative route for those with their own transport travelling from Maó to Alaior and central Menorca. To reach it, take the Fornells road out of Maó and, 1.2km after the Es Grau turning, watch for the **Camí d'En Kane** sign on the left. The old road follows the agricultural contours of the island, passing ancient *haciendas* and dry-stone walls to approach Alaior from the north.

Most of Kane's original road, however, has disappeared beneath the modern highway, the C721. Between Maó and Alaior this runs across a flattish agricultural district that's liberally sprinkled with prehistoric remains: the Talayotic complex of Talatí de Dalt, 4km from Maó, is easily the most diverting, though you could also drop by the twin *navetas* of **Rafal Rubí Nou**, 3km further on. Pushing on

Talatí de Dalt is described on p.207.

Richard Kane

Born in Ulster in 1666, Richard Kane was the quintessential military man. His long career in the British army included service in Canada and campaigns with the Duke of Marlborough, experiences which he crystallized in a much-lauded pamphlet on infantry tactics. In 1713, following the Treaty of Utrecht, Kane was appointed Lieutenant-Governor of Menorca. He was transferred in 1720, but returned a decade later for a second stint, staying until 1736, the year of his death.

When Kane arrived in Menorca, he found a dispirited and impoverished population, governed from Ciutadella by a reactionary oligarchy. Kane's initial preoccupation was with the island's food supply, which was woefully inadequate. He promptly set about draining swampland near Maó and introduced new and improved strains of seed corn. The governor also had livestock imported from England – hence the Friesian cattle that remain the mainstay of the island's cheese-making industry. Meanwhile, a tax on alcohol provided the cash to develop Menorca's infrastructure, resulting in improved port facilities at Maó and the construction of the first road right across the island.

These were innovations not at all to the taste of the Menorcan aristocracy, who, holed up in Ciutadella, were further offended when Kane arranged for the capital to be moved to Maó. They bombarded London with complaints, eventually inducing a formal governmental response in an open letter to the islanders entitled *A Vindication of Colonel Kane*. Most Menorcans, however, seem to have welcomed Kane's benevolent administration – though not in the matter of religion. Here, the governor created genuine offence by holding Protestant services for his troops in Catholic churches. That apart, there's little doubt that, by the time of his death, Kane was a widely respected figure, whose endeavours were ill served by the colonial indifference of some of his successors.

west, the hilltop town of **Alaior** has a pretty little centre of mazy cobbled streets and ancient whitewashed houses, and is home to a couple of cheese-making factories where you can sample local brands. Alaior also signals a change in scenery, from the plains of the southeast to the limestone hills of central Menorca. These culminate, just outside the antique village of **Es Mercadal**, in the highest peak of the lot, **Monte Toro**, home to both a military lookout point and a convent. The road to the summit is excellent and the views are superb, making this an essential detour – unlike the excursions south to the seaside resorts of **Son Bou** and **Sant Tomàs**, grimly modern affairs only redeemed by their sandy beaches. Back on the main road, you'll soon reach the third and last market town on the C721, **Ferreries**, a partly industrialized shoemaking centre. From here, a short excursion south leads to **Cala Santa Galdana**, an attractive resort of manageable proportions that's within easy hiking distance of several superb and isolated cove beaches.

Getting around is no problem: **buses** along the C721 are fast and frequent, and from Monday to Saturday, there's one service a day from Maó to Sant Tomàs, five to Son Bou, and two to Cala Santa Galdana; in the opposite direction, one bus a day from Monday to Friday links Ciutadella with Sant Tomàs and Cala Santa Galdana. **Accommodation**, on the other hand, is difficult for independent travellers. The resorts are dominated by the package-tourist industry, though you can, of course, try pot luck. Of the three inland towns, only Es Mercadal has a recommendable *hostal* – and even here there's only one.

Alaior

Cheese is the main reason to stop at **ALAIOR**, an old market town 12km from Maó which has long been the nucleus of the island's dairy industry. There are two major companies, La Payesa and Coinga, both of which have factory shops near to – and clearly signposted from – the old main road as it cuts through the southern periphery of town. From the new bypass, which swings round the town to the south, the easiest option is to come off at the most easterly of the three Alaior exits. From this direction, the first shop you reach is owned by La Payesa (Mon–Fri 9am–1pm & 4–7pm), while the second is the bigger and better outlet of Coinga (Mon–Fri 9am–1pm & 5–8pm, Sat 9am–1pm). Both companies sell a similar product, known generically as *Queso Mahon*, after the port, Maó, from which it was traditionally exported. It's a richly textured, white, semi-fat cheese made from pasteurized cow's milk with a touch of ewe's milk added for extra flavour. The cheese is sold at four different stages of maturity, either *tierno* (young), *semi-curado* (semi-mature), *curado* (mature) or *añejo* (very mature). Both shops have the full range and, although quite expensive, their prices are the most competitive you'll see.

Both these shops (and the old main road) are in the lower part of Alaior; the medieval centre, a tangle of narrow streets and bright white houses, climbs the steep hillside above. It's a quick two-minute drive or a strenuous walk to the top, where the imposing parish church of **Santa Eulalia**, a magnificent edifice of fortress-like proportions built between 1674 and 1690, has recently been restored. The main doorway is a Baroque extravagance, its exuberant scrollwork dripping with fruits and fronds, whilst the facade above accommodates a rose window and a pair of balustrades. Beyond the church – just up the hill to the north-west along the L-shaped c/Moli de l'Angel – is a mini-watchtower from where you can look out over the countryside. From the end of c/Moli de l'Angel, it's a few metres north to the old town's main square, **Plaça Nova**, an attractive piazza flanked by pastel-painted civic buildings of considerable age.

There's nowhere to stay in Alaior, but for food, *The Cobblers Garden*, in an old town house at c/Sant Macari 6 – just east of Santa Eulalia along c/Pare Diego Saura and right onto c/Verge Sa Muntanyeta – has tasty snacks and light meals at reasonable prices. Buses stop at the foot of town, a stiff 1km walk from Santa Eulalia. Apart from a bite to eat and a quick gambol round the town, however, there's not much reason to hang around – unless you happen to be here in the second weekend of August. This is when Alaior lets loose for the **Festa de Sant Llorenç**, a drunken celebration and display of horsemanship. As its highlight, with the town square packed, a procession of horses tears through the crowd, bucking and rearing, with their riders clinging on for dear life. Although no one seems to get hurt, you'd probably do best to witness the spectacle from the safety of an overlooking balcony.

Around Alaior: the Torralba d'En Salort

One of the more extensive Talayotic settlements, **Torralba d'En Salort**, lies about 3km southeast of Alaior beside the road to Cala En Porter. The site is muddled by the old (and disused) Cala En Porter road, which slices right through the site, and by the modern stone walls built alongside both the old and new roads. Nevertheless, it doesn't take too long to figure things out. From the car park, signs direct you round the Talayotic remains, beginning with the *taula*, one of the best preserved on the island; the rectangular shrine surrounding it is also in good condition, and has been the subject of minute examination and much conjecture by archeologists. They discovered that several of the recesses contained large fire pits, which may well have been used for the ritual slaughter of animals. It was, however, the unearthing of a tiny bronze bull that really got the experts going, the suggestion being that, just as the bull was venerated by other prehistoric Mediterranean peoples, so it was worshipped here in Menorca, with the *taula* a stylized representation of a bull's head. The argument continues to this day. Beyond the *taula*, the signed trail circumnavigates the remainder of the site, which contains a confusion of stone remains, none of them especially revealing. The most noteworthy are the battered remains of a *talayot* just across from the *taula* and, about 30m further to the north, an underground chamber roofed with stone slabs.

Torre d'En Gaumés and Son Bou

West of Alaior on the C721, take the Son Bou turning for the beaches of the south coast and, if you still have the enthusiasm, the rambling Talayotic settlement of **Torre d'En Gaumés**. The drive to both is easy enough – for the coast keep straight, for the ruins go left at the signposted fork 2.5km south of the C721 and follow the asphalted lane for another 2km. The site possesses no less than three *talayots*, the largest of which is next to a broken-down *taula* in the centre of a badly ruined circular enclosure. Together these remains form what is presumed to have been the public part of the village and it was here in the enclosure that the archeologists unearthed a little bronze figure of the Egyptian god of knowledge, Imhotep, a discovery which reinforced the theory that these enclosures possessed religious significance. It's impossible to interpret precisely the remains surrounding the outside of the enclosure, as the site was inhabited – and continually modified – well into Roman times. That said, you can pick out the broadly circular outlines of a sequence of private dwellings dating from as early as 1500 BC.

At **SON BOU**, 8km south of Alaior, the antiquarian interest is maintained by an extensive cave complex, cut into the cliff-face above the final part of the approach road, and the foundations of an early Christian basilica, set behind the beach at the east end of the resort. They're hardly popular attractions, however, when compared with the beach, a whopping pale-gold strand some 3km long and 40m wide. This is Menorca's longest beach, and behind it has mushroomed a massive tourist complex of skyscraper hotels and villa-villages that spreads west into the twin resort of **SANT JAUME MEDITERRANI**. The sand shelves gently into the sea, but the bathing isn't quite as safe as it appears: ocean currents are hazardous, particularly when the wind picks up, and you should watch for the green or red flags. The beach accommodates several beach bars, and watersports equipment is widely available – everything from jet-skis, snorkels and windsurfing boards to sunbeds and pedaloes. The development is at its crassest – and the crowds at their worst – towards the east end of the beach, where the foreshore is dominated by several huge sky-rise hotels, including the *Club Sol Milanos* (April–Oct; ☎971 371200, fax 971 371226; ⑦) and the *Club Sol Pinguinos* (same details). These two hotels, with their spruce, modern, balconied bedrooms, share facilities, including sun terraces, outside pools, bars and restaurants. A little to the west, a strip of dune-fringed, marshy scrubland runs behind the beach. This has provided the shoreline with some much needed protection, pushing the villa developments a kilometre or so inland. As a result, the bathing along this stretch of coast is far more secluded.

Es Mercadal and Monte Toro

Nine kilometres northwest of Alaior you arrive at **ES MERCADAL**, squatting amongst the hills at the very centre of the island. Another old market town, it's an amiable little place of whitewashed houses and trim allotments whose antique centre straddles a quaint watercourse. Tucked down c/Major is a Ruritanian town hall, and the minuscule main square, a few paces away, has a couple of sleepy cafés. The town also boasts one top-notch **restaurant**, popular with tourists, the *Ca N'Aguedet*, c/Lepanto 30, which serves up excellent traditional Menorcan cuisine – suckling pig, for instance, costs around 1800ptas. Es Mercadal also has a one-star hostal-residencia, the spick-and-span *Jeni*, in a modern building at Miranda del Toro 81 (☎971 375059, fax 971 375124; ④). The thirty rooms here are comfortable, with attractive modern furnishings, there's a rooftop swimming pool, and the bar, though a little glum, is a pleasant enough spot to nurse a drink. To get there, walk south from the main square – Sa Plaça – along c/Nou and take the first left and then the first right. Buses from Maó, Ciutadella and Sant Tomàs stop just off the C721 on Avinguda Metge Camps, which leads on to c/Nou.

Monte Toro

From Es Mercadal you can set off on the ascent of **Monte Toro**, a steep 3.4km climb along a serpentine road. At 357m, the summit is the island's highest point and offers wonderful vistas: on a good day you can see almost the whole island, on a bad one to Fornells, at least. From this lofty vantage point, Menorca's geological division becomes apparent: to the north, Devonian rock (mostly reddish sandstone) supports a rolling, sparsely populated landscape edged by a ragged coastline; to the south, limestone predominates in a bumpy plain that boasts the island's best farmland and, as it approaches the south coast, its deepest valleys.

It's likely that the name of the hill is derived from the Moorish *El Tor* (the height), but Christians have invented an alternative etymology, involving villagers spotting a mysterious light on the mountain, and, on closer investigation, being confronted by a bull (*toro*) who, lo and behold, leads them to a miracle-making statue of the Virgin. Whatever the truth, Monte Toro has been a place of pilgrimage since medieval times, the highlight of the year being the first Sunday in May when the local bishop blesses the land.

The Augustinians plonked a monastery on the summit in the seventeenth century and bits of the original construction survive in the convent, which shares the site today with an army outpost bristling with all sorts of aerials and radar dishes, and a monumentally ugly statue of Christ. Much of the convent is out of bounds, but the public part, approached across a handsome courtyard, encompasses a couple of gift shops, a delightful terrace café and a charming Neoclassical church, whose simple porch contains an ancient well girt with bright flowers and deep green shrubs. Inside, the truncated nave features a Baroque high altar with a much-venerated image of the Virgin.

Es Migjorn Gran and Sant Tomàs

Es Mercadal is an important crossroads: the road north meanders through gentle wooded hills and red-soiled fields to reach the coast at Fornells, while the road south weaves a rustic route to unassuming **ES MIGJORN GRAN**, an elongated hillside village flanked by intricate terraced fields. Beyond the village, these scenic pleasures continue with the wooded ravine that leads on towards the south coast, where they end abruptly in the crass hotel and apartment buildings of **SANT TOMÀS**. The three-kilometre-long sandy beach, however, is superb, very similar to that of Son Bou, a couple of headlands away to the east – though all is not quite as it seems. A thunderous storm stripped the existing sand away in 1989, and what you see has been imported. The beach looks very inviting as it slopes gently into the ocean, but there are sometimes dangerous undercurrents so you should observe the green or red flags. The access road reaches the shore halfway along the beach, which is called Platja Sant Adeodat to the west and Platja Sant Tomàs to the east. The latter is easily the more congested and it's here you'll find the high-rise hotels, amongst which the air-conditioned, ultra-modern *Santo Tomàs* is the most lavish (May–Oct; ☎971 370025, fax 971 370204; ⑨), whilst the less expensive *Sol Cóndores* will do almost as well, though there's no air conditioning (☎971 370050, fax 971 370348; ⑦). Both have pools, restaurants, night-time entertainment and many types of sports facility. Windsurfers, jet-skis and pedaloes can all be rented on the beach nearby.

Ferreries

Tucked into a hollow beneath a steep hill, the narrow, sloping streets of **FERRERIES**, 8km from Es Mercadal on the C721 and 7km from Es Migjorn Gran on a minor road, are framed by terraced fields. A surprise here is the pagoda-like piece of modern sculpture in the main square, the Plaça Espanya, whilst, just up the hill, the old town centre is marked by the neatly shuttered town hall, primly facing the old parish church. There's not much to detain you, though you could spare time either to watch or to buy from one of the self-employed shoemakers who ply their craft from tiny workshops in the town centre – despite competition from the Jaime

Mascaró shoe factory and factory shop, a kilometre or so back along the C721. The factory shoes are less expensive, but the quality is nowhere near as high.

One definite plus in town is the *Vimpi* café-bar, beside the main road on Plaça Joan Carles, which serves some of the tastiest *tapas* on the island. You wouldn't choose to stay in Ferreries – it's just too quiet – which is just as well because there's no accommodation. Buses to Ferreries stop in front of the *Vimpi*, which is a couple of minutes' walk from Plaça Espanya, straight up Avinguda Verge de Monte Toro.

Binisues and Castell Santa Agueda

A lattice of rough country roads covers the sparsely inhabited hills and farmland in between Ferreries and the north coast. The district's main attractions are the rural manor house of Binisues and the nearby Castell Santa Agueda, whose modest remains perch atop the peak of the same name, Menorca's second highest at 268m. To get to the mansion and the castle, take the C721 west out of Ferreries. At about 3km, turn right down the well-surfaced (and signposted) lane and after about 700m you'll spy the pastel-painted stonework of **Binisues** (April–Oct daily 11am–7pm; 500ptas) on a gentle ridge to the left. The house occupies a grand setting, overlooking the valleys and hills of central Menorca: its elegant symmetries reflect the self-confidence of the island's nineteenth-century aristocracy, but the interior is a yawn. Presumably, the intention is to re-create the mansion's old aristocratic air, but the accumulated knick-knacks look as if they've been thrown in haphazardly. Even worse, if you persevere beyond the family rooms, you'll find an assortment of old agricultural implements on the second floor and a collection of mounted butterflies above – you're much better off sipping coffee at the restaurant and admiring the view.

Returning to the lane below Binisues, it's about 2km more to the deserted schoolhouse (and parking space) on the right-hand side which marks the start of the hour-long hike up rocky and lightly wooded mountainside to the **Castell Santa Agueda**. The Romans were the first to recognize the hill's strategic value, fortifying the summit in the second century BC, but it was the Moors who developed the stronghold, and it was here that they made their final stand against Alfonso III's invasion in 1287. Fresh from their defeat at Maó, the demoralized Moors didn't put up much of a fight – though they would certainly have been more determined if they had known of their ultimate fate. After the surrender, the Catalans demanded a heavy ransom for every captive. Those who couldn't pay were enslaved and those who weren't fit to work as slaves were shoved onto ships, taken out to sea and thrown overboard. Nowadays, little remains of the Moorish castle bar a few crumbling turrets and walls, but the views are spectacular.

Cala Santa Galdana

South from Ferreries, an excellent eight-kilometre road leads
through a picturesque pastoral landscape down to **CALA SANTA
GALDANA**. Once a much-loved beauty spot, the bay has experienced a rash of development since the building of the road and is
now cluttered with high-rises. But, despite the concrete, there's no
denying the beauty of the setting, the curving sandy beach framed
by pine-studded, limestone cliffs and intercepted by a rocky
promontory adjacent to a narrow river. Early in the morning or out
of season is the best time to appreciate the scene – or you can
escape the crowds by hiking round the headland beside the *Hotel
Audax* at the west end of the bay. Alternatively, it's possible to hire
out all sorts of watersports equipment – from pedaloes and water
scooters to windsurfing boards and snorkelling tackle; and small
boats ply regularly to other more secluded beaches (see below).

Among the resort's three high-rise **hotels**, you're most likely to
find a vacant room at the luxurious, four-star *Audax* (Feb–Oct;
☎971 154646, fax 971 154647; ⑧), though if you're prepared to
pay this much, make sure you get a sea-facing balcony. The three-
star *Cala Galdana*, set just back from the beach (April–Oct; ☎ &
fax 971 154500; ⑥) and the massive *Sol Gavilanes* (April–Oct;
☎971 154545, fax 971 154546; ⑦) both have spick-and-span modern rooms, but lack style or special interest. At the other end of the
market, the simple *S'Atalaia* **campsite** is located about 3km back
down the road towards Ferreries (open all year; ☎971 373095, fax
971 374232). Pine trees shade much of the site, which has an outdoor swimming pool and a restaurant-bar. It can accommodate about
100 guests but advance reservations are strongly advised. Charges
are 525ptas for a site, 450ptas for a vehicle, and 575ptas per person.

Back in the resort, there's a good-quality seafood **restaurant**, *El
Mirador*, built into the promontory that pokes out from the beach,
though you do pay over the odds for the setting. Among several less
expensive choices stuck behind the *Hotel Audax*, *Sa Lluna* offers
reasonably priced Italan food, with pizzas for around 850ptas.
There's an Avis **car rental** outlet (☎971 154532) close by.

Around Cala Santa Galdana

Several exquisite cove beaches lie within easy reach of Cala Santa
Galdana, the most obvious choice being **Cala Mitjana**, just 1km to the
east. The footpath to the cove begins beside the *Hotel Sol Gavilanes*
at the Plaça Na Gran, where a gate at the back of the parking lot leads
onto an easy-to-follow path through coastal pine woods. At the first
fork veer right and after a few minutes you'll reach a clearing which
you should cross diagonally to the left. Beyond the clearing, the path
soon descends to the beach. Once you get there you'll be rewarded
with a broad strip of sand set beneath wooded cliffs at the end of a
beguiling bay – though sometimes there's an unpleasant smell from

an accumulation of seaweed. A favourite sport here is jumping into the crystal-clear water from the surrounding cliffs.

Equally beautiful but also afflicted with periodic seaweed problems is **Cala Trebalúger**, a further 2.5km east and best reached by boat from Cala Santa Galdana (1–2 daily). Cala Trebalúger boasts a beautiful arc of sand flanked by steep cliffs and crossed by a stream which emerges from the gorge behind. There are no beach facilities, so take your own food and drink.

Walking west from Cala Santa Galdana on the footpath starting opposite the *Hotel Audax* (at the top of the small flight of steps beside the telephone boxes) it takes about forty minutes to reach **Cala Macarella**. Here, severe, partly wooded limestone cliffs surround a band of white sand that shelves gently into the Med. It's a beautiful spot, with ideal conditions for swimming – and unlike the other beaches around Cala Santa Galdana, seaweed is never a problem. There's a touch of development in the form of a summertime beach bar, and sunbeds and pedaloes for hire, but it's nothing excessive.

Ciutadella and around

Like Maó, **CIUTADELLA** sits high above its harbour. Here, though, navigation is far more difficult, up a narrow channel too slender for all but the smallest of cargo ships. Despite this nautical inconvenience, Ciutadella has been at the centre of affairs as the island's capital for most of its history. The Romans chose it, the Moors adopted it as Medina Minurka, and the Catalans of the *Reconquista* flattened the place and began all over again. In 1558, the Catalan-built town was, in its turn, razed by Turkish corsairs. Several thousand captives were carted off to the slave markets of Istanbul, but the survivors determinedly rebuilt Ciutadella in grand style, its compact, fortified centre brimming with the mansions of the rich. To the colonial powers of the eighteenth century, however, Ciutadella's feeble port had no appeal when compared with Maó's magnificent inlet. In 1722 the British moved the capital to Maó, which has flourished as a trading centre ever since, whilst Ciutadella has stagnated – a long-lasting economic reverie that has, by coincidence, preserved its old and beautiful centre as if in aspic.

The story of the Turkish raid of 1558 is told on p.247.

The bulk of the Menorcan aristocracy remained in Ciutadella, where the island's foreign rulers pretty much left them to stew – an increasingly redundant, landowning class far from the wheels of mercantile power. Consequently, there's very little British or French influence in Ciutadella's **architecture**; instead, the narrow, cobbled streets boast fine old palaces, hidden away behind high walls, and a set of Baroque and Gothic churches very much in the Spanish tradition. Essentially, it's the whole ensemble, centred on stately **Plaça d'es Born**, that gives Ciutadella its appeal rather than any specific sight, though the mostly Gothic **cathedral** is a delight, as is the

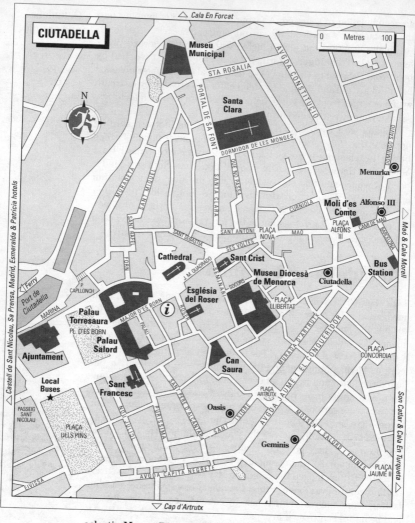

eclectic **Museu Diocesà de Menorca**. An ambitious renovation programme has further enhanced the town, restoring most of the old stone facades to their honey-coloured best. Added to this are some excellent restaurants, especially on the harbourfront, and a reasonably adequate supply of *hostals* and hotels. It's a lovely place to stay, and nothing else on Menorca rivals the evening *passeig* (promenade), when the townsfolk amble the narrow streets of the centre, dropping in on pavement cafés as the sun sets. Allow at least a couple of days, more if you seek out one of the beguiling cove beaches within easy striking distance of town: **Cala En Turqueta** is the pick of the bunch.

Arrival, information and orientation

Ciutadella's compact centre could hardly be more convenient. **Buses** from Maó and points east arrive at the station on c/Barcelona, just south off the end of the Camí de Maó, an extension of the main island highway, the C721. **Local buses** shuttle up and down the west coast from Plaça dels Pins, on the west side of the town centre next to the main square, Plaça d'es Born. **Hydrofoils** from Cala Rajada on Mallorca, dock in the harbour right below the Plaça d'es Born. If you're **driving** in, there's no missing the ring road which, under various names – principally Avinguda Jaume I El Conqueridor and Avinguda Capità Negrete – encircles the old town. Approaching from the east, turn left when you hit it and keep going until you reach its conclusion beside the Plaça dels Pins; if you can't find a parking spot actually on this square, turn left at the top near the bus stops and drive down Passeig Sant Nicolau, where there's always space.

The seasonal **Oficina d'Informació Turística** (May–Oct Mon–Fri 9am–1.30pm & 6–8pm, Sat 9am–1pm ☎971 382693) has a good range of information on Menorca as a whole and Ciutadella in particular, including bus timetables, ferry schedules, lists of *hostals* and hotels, and free maps. It's opposite the cathedral on Plaça Catedral, bang in the middle of the old town, which can only be explored on foot. Keeping your bearings here is straightforward – the main square and harbour are on the west side of the centre, the ring road on the east.

Accommodation

There's hardly a plethora of accommodation in Ciutadella, but the town does have three quality hotels that aren't booked up by package-tour operators – the *Patricia*, *Sant Ignasi* and *Geminis* – and a handful of fairly comfortable and reasonably priced *hostals* dotted in and around the centre.

Inexpensive

Hostal-residencia Oasis, c/Sant Isidre 33 ☎971 382197. Footsteps away from Plaça Artrutx, an attractive one-star with nine simple rooms set around a gaudily decorated courtyard-restaurant. ③.

Hostal Sa Prensa, Plaça Madrid s/n ☎971 382698. Recently refurbished, villa-like, one-star *hostal* with six spartan bedrooms above a café-bar. It's a 15-min walk west of the centre, close to the rocky seashore at the end of c/Madrid: follow Passeig Sant Nicolau from the Plaça dels Pins, take the fifth turning on the left (c/Joan Ramis i Ramis) and you'll hit c/Madrid at the first major intersection – Plaça Madrid is 100m away on the left. ③.

Moderate

Hotel Alfonso III, Camí de Maó 53 ☎971 380150, fax 971 481529. Brashly modern but well-maintained hotel with 50 simple one-star rooms. Located beside the main road from Maó, a couple of minutes' walk from the ring road; try to get a room at the back away from the noisy road. ④.

Hostal-residencia Ciutadella, c/Sant Eloi 10 ☎ & fax 971 383462. Unassuming yet comfortable two-star, in an old terraced house down a narrow side street off Plaça Alfons III. ⑤.

Hotel-residencia Geminis, c/Josepa Rossinyol 4 ☎971 384644, fax 971 383683. Painted bright pink and white with blue awnings, this well-tended, very comfortable one-star certainly hits the eye. To get there on foot, walk a few paces down c/Mossèn J. Salord i Farnés from the ring road and watch for the archway on the right; proceed through the arch and the hotel's on the right at the bottom of a prosperous, suburban street. Closed Jan. ④.

Hotel Madrid, c/Madrid 60 ☎971 380328. Fourteen quite comfortable rooms in a well-maintained, villa-style building with its own ground-floor café-bar. Located near the waterfront a 15-min walk west of the town centre, halfway along c/Madrid (directions as for *Hostal Sa Prensa* overleaf). Open May–Oct. ④.

Hostal-residencia Menurka, c/Domingo Savio 6 ☎971 381415, fax 971 381282. Tidy two-star establishment of 21 rooms, some with balconies, though they overlook a mundane side street. C/Domingo Savio is just east of the town centre and one block up from Camí de Maó. ⑤.

Expensive

Hotel Esmeralda, Passeig Sant Nicolau 171 ☎971 380250, fax 971 380258. The sweeping curves of this four-storey hotel are a classic example of 1960s design, with a swimming pool and private gardens out front. Most of the bedrooms have wide and expansive balconies and face out to sea, but the majority are booked up by package-tour operators. At the west end of the street, a 15 min walk from the centre. Open April–Oct. ⑥.

Hotel-residencia Patricia, Passeig Sant Nicolau 90 ☎971 385511, fax 971 481120. The smartest hotel in town, popular with business folk and handy for the centre. Extremely comfortable, ultra-modern rooms with all facilities, the only downer being the lack of a sea view – though the best rooms have rooftop balconies with panoramic vistas. Open March to October. ⑦

Hotel Sant Ignasi, Carretera Cala Morell s/n ☎971 359393, fax 971 359006. This elegant nineteenth-century manor house has been tastefully converted into an immaculate, excellent-value hotel. Each of the twenty bedrooms is individually decorated in a style that blends with the original building, and there are gardens and an outside pool too. It's in the middle of the countryside, though the surrounding farmland is flat and dull. The hotel is about 4km northeast of the centre of Ciutadella, clearly signposted (down a very narrow 1.5km-long lane) from the road to Cala Morell. ⑥.

The Town

Ciutadella's centre crowds around the fortified cliff shadowing the south side of the harbour. The main plazas and points of interest are within a few strides of each other, on and around the expansive Plaça d'es Born.

Plaça d'es Born

Primarily a nineteenth-century creation, **Plaça d'es Born** is easily the finest main square in the Balearic islands. In the middle is a soaring **obelisk** commemorating the futile defence against the Turks in 1558, a brutal episode that was actually something of an accident. The Ottomans had dispatched 15,000 soldiers and 150 warships west to assist their French allies against the Habsburgs. With no particular place to go, the Turks rolled around the Mediterranean for a few weeks and, after deciding Maó wasn't worth the candle, they happened on Ciutadella, where the garrison numbered just a few hundred. For the Menorcans, the results were cataclysmic. The one-sided siege ended with the destruction of the town and the enslavement of its population – there was so much damage that when the new Spanish governor arrived, he was forced to live in a cave. The obelisk's Latin inscription, penned by the nineteenth-century historian Josep Quadrado, reads, "Here we fought until death for our religion and our country in the year 1558".

On the western side of the square stands the **Ajuntament**, whose nineteenth-century arches and crenellations mimic Moorish style, purposely recalling the time when the site was occupied by the Wali's *alcázar* (palace). Opposite, tucked away in the southeast corner of the square, is the church of **St Francesc**, a clean-lined, airy structure of Gothic design, though the chancel and the dome were added later. Most of the town's churches were looted during the Civil War, but this one survived pretty much intact, preserving its chintzy carved wood altars, embossed ceiling and polychromatic saints. In the square's northeast corner, the massive **Palau Torresaura**, built in the nineteenth century but looking far older, is the grandest of several aristocratic mansions edging the plaza. Embellished by self-important loggias, its frontage proclaims the family coat of arms above a large wooden door leading into a spacious coutryard. The antique interior, however, is off limits – like most of its neighbours, the house is still owner-occupied. An exception is the adjacent **Palau Salord**, which is entered round the corner on c/Major d'es Born. Dating from 1813, this rambling mansion has seen more illustrious days, but it's still of some mild interest for its sequence of high-ceilinged rooms redolent of nineteenth-century aristocratic life.

The cathedral

Beyond Palau Salord, c/Major d'es Born leads to the **cathedral**, built by Alfonso III at the end of the thirteenth century on the site of the chief mosque. Constructed so soon after the Reconquest, its design is fortress-like – with windows set high above the ground – though the effect is somewhat disturbed by the flashy columns of the Neoclassical west doorway, the principal entrance. Inside, light from the narrow, lofty windows bathes the high altar in an ethereal glow, the hallmark of the Gothic style. There's also a wonderfully kitschy, pointed altar arch, and a sequence of glitzy Baroque side chapels. Most of the church's original furnishings and fittings, however, were destroyed in a frenzy of anticlericalism when the Republicans took control of Menorca during the Civil War. Despite losing its status as

Just to the north of Plaça d'es Born, steep steps lead down to the harbour, where yachts and fishing smacks bob up and down in front of a series of waterside restaurants (see p.233), with the old city walls forming a scenic back-ground.

The Palau Salord is open Mon–Sat 10am–2pm; 400ptas.

the island capital, Ciutadella had remained Menorca's ecclesiastical centre. Its resident Catholic hierarchy were, by and large, rich and reactionary in equal measure, and they enthusiastically proclaimed their support for the officers of Maó garrison when the latter declared for Franco in July 1936. This insurrectionary gesture was, however, a miserable failure: the bulk of the garrison stayed loyal to the Republic and, allied with local left-wing groups, they captured the rebels, shot their leaders and ransacked Ciutadella's main churches as retribution.

The Museu Diocesà de Menorca and around

Cutting south down c/Roser from the cathedral, you'll pass the tiny **Església del Roser**, whose striking Churrigueresque facade, dating from the seventeenth century, boasts a quartet of pillars festooned with intricate tracery. The church was the subject of bitter controversy when the British commandeered it for Church of England services – not at all to the liking of the Dominican friars who owned the place.

At the end of c/Roser, turn left past the palatial, seventeenth-century mansion of **Can Saura**, now an antique shop, and then left again for c/Seminari and the **Museu Diocesà de Menorca** (Diocesan Museum), housed in an old and dignified convent. Before you go in, take a look at the elongated perimeter wall, a sober affair cheered by the delicate flutings of a Neoclassical **portal** with a bizarre sculpted cameo stuck on top. This is certainly the town's most unusual sight, depicting the Virgin Mary, armed with a cudgel, standing menacingly over a cringing, cat-like dragon-devil. Inside, the conventual buildings surround an immaculately preserved Baroque cloister, whose vaulted aisles sport coats of arms and religious motifs. The museum's collection is distributed chronologically amongst the tiny rooms edging the cloister; the labelling – where it exists – is in Spanish. The first three rooms hold a hotchpotch of Talayotic and early classical archeological finds, notably a superbly crafted, miniature bull and a similarly exquisite little mermaid (*sirena*), almost certainly Greek bronzes dating from the fifth century BC. Room 4 is devoted to the workaday paintings of a local artist, Pere Daura, and Room 5 has scale models of old Menorcan buildings made by one of the priests. Moving on, Rooms 6–8 occupy parts of the old refectory and display some dreadful religious paintings as well as all sorts of ecclesiastical tackle – elaborate monstrances, communion cups, reliquaries, croziers and suchlike. It's the general glitter that impresses, rather than any individual piece.

*The Museu
Diocesà is
open May–Oct
Tues–Sun
10am–1.30pm;
restricted
hours are in
operation during the rest of
the year;
300ptas.*

Plaça Llibertat and the Capella del Sant Crist

Just north of the museum along c/Seminari, turn right down c/Socors to make the quick detour east to the market (*mercat*) on **Plaça Llibertat**. This is another delightful corner of the old town, where fresh fruit, vegetable and fish stalls mingle with lively and inexpensive cafés selling the freshest of *ensaimadas*.

Retracing your steps to c/Seminari, turn right past the flamboyant facade of the **Capella del Sant Crist**, a Baroque extravaganza with garlands of fruit and a pair of gargoyle-like faces, and continue the few metres north to the narrow, pedestrianized main street that runs through the old town – here c/ J. M. Quadrado. Look to the left and you'll spy a tiny bronze lamb, symbolizing the Lamb of God, stuck on a column. The lamb carries a flag bearing the cross of St John the Baptist and is a reminder of Ciutadella's biggest shindig, the Festa de Sant Joan, held from June 23 to 25.

There's a choice of routes from here: you can either go north to the Museu Municipal or east to Plaça Alfons III

For more on the Festa de Sant Joan, see p.50.

North to the Museu Municipal

Directly opposite the top of c/Seminari, a long, straight street – c/Santa Clara – shoots off north hemmed in by the walls of old aristocratic palaces. At the top is the convent of **Santa Clara**, a mundanely modern incarnation of a centuries-old foundation. In 1749, this was the site of a scandal that had tongues clacking from Ciutadella to Maó. During the night, three young women hopped over the convent wall and placed themselves under the protection of their British boyfriends. Even worse, as far as the local clergy were concerned, they wanted to turn Protestant and marry their men. In this delicate situation, Governor Blakeney had the room where the women were staying sealed up by a priest every night. But he refused to send them back to the convent and allowed the weddings to go ahead, thereby compounding a religious animosity – Catholic subject against Protestant master – which had begun in the days of Richard Kane.

Beyond, at the end of c/Portal de Sa Font, the **Museu Municipal** occupies part of the old city fortifications, a massive honeysuckle-clad bastion overlooking a slender ravine that once had, until it was redirected, a river running along its base and into the harbour. Inside the museum, a long vaulted chamber is given over to a wide range of archeological artefacts, amongst which there's a substantial collection of Talayotic remains, featuring finds garnered from all over the island and covering the several phases of Talayotic civilization. The earlier pieces, dating from around 1400 to 700 BC, include many examples of crudely crafted beakers and tumblers. Later work – down to around 120 BC – reveals a far greater degree of sophistication, both in terms of kitchenware, with bowls and tumblers particularly common, and bronze weaponry, notably several finely chiselled arrow-heads. From this later period comes most of the (imported) jewellery, whose fine detail and miniature size suggests a Carthaginian origin. A leaflet detailing the exhibits in English is available free at reception. Temporary exhibitions take place downstairs.

From the Museu Municipal, it's a five-minute walk back to Plaça d'es Born along c/Muradeta with pleasant views down the ravine to the harbour.

The Museu Municipal is open May–Oct Tues–Sat 10am–4pm; Nov–April Tues–Fri 11am–1pm & Sat 10am–1pm; 200ptas. Note that opening times change frequently.

East to Plaça Alfons III

From the top of c/Seminari, the pedestrianized main street of the old town runs east as c/J. M. Quadrado. The first stretch is cramped by a block of whitewashed, vaulted arches, **Ses Voltes**, distinctly Moorish in inspiration and a suitable setting for several attractive shops and busy cafés. C/J. M. Quadrado then leads into **Plaça Nova**, an attractive little square edged by some of the most popular pavement-cafés in town. Nearby, off c/Sant Antoni, a narrow archway cuts through what was once the city wall, which explains the name of the alley beyond, Qui no Passa (The one that doesn't go through). Returning to Plaça Nova, c/Maó leads east to leave the cramped alleys of the old town at Plaça Alfons III, where the big old windmill, the **Moli d'es Comte**, looks as if it should be in the countryside, its forlorn appearance not helped by its partial conversion into a bar.

The Castell de Sant Nicolau

The Castell de Sant Nicolau is open Mon–Sat 7.30–9.30pm; free.

West from Plaça d'es Born, Passeig Sant Nicolau runs along the northern edge of Plaça S'Esplanada and reaches, after about fifteen minutes' walk, the **Castell de Sant Nicolau**. This seventeenth-century watchtower is a dinky little thing, equipped with a drawbridge, oil holes and turrets, all stuck on unwelcoming rocks. The interior, however, is disappointingly bare and is, indeed, only open in the evening, when people come here to watch the sun set out beyond Mallorca.

Beside the castle is a statue honouring **David Glasgow Farragut**, who is shown with telescope in hand and wind in his hair. The son of a Ciutadellan who emigrated to America in 1776, Farragut entered the US navy in 1810, the start of a long naval career distinguished by several brave attacks on Confederate strongholds in the Civil War. Most famously, Farragut forced the surrender of New Orleans in 1862 and as a result of this and other actions was made an admiral of the US fleet four years later.

Eating, drinking and nightlife

For an early breakfast make your way to the *mercat* on Plaça Llibertat, where a couple of simple cafés serve coffee and fresh pastries. Later in the day, aim for c/J. M. Quadrado and Plaça Nova, which are jam-packed with tiny café-bars offering reasonably priced snacks and light meals. More ambitious and expensive food is available at a string of excellent restaurants down by the harbourside, or at a couple of good places tucked away near Plaça d'es Born.

People don't come to Ciutadella for the nightlife. There are a few late-night bars, mostly down by the harbour, though this is very much a tourist zone. If you want the flavour of the town, you're better off nursing a drink and watching the early-evening crowds on, or in the vicinity of, Plaça Nova.

Cafés and bars

Aladdino, c/Pere Capllonch s/n. Ciutadella's busiest nightspot, this late-night tourist bar tunnels into the cliffside beside the harbour at the foot of the steps near the bridge.

Café Central, Plaça Catedral. Busy little place next to the cathedral's main entrance, serving traditional Menorcan *tapas*, including various sausages and cheeses.

Bar Sa Llesca, Plaça Nova 4. One of several pleasant, and largely indistinguishable, café-bars on this tiny square.

Pastisseria Mol, c/Roser 2. Delicious takeaway pizza slices, filled bread rolls and mouthwatering cakes from this little pastry shop off Plaça Catedral.

Bar Es Moli, Camí de Maó 1. Noisy and gritty café-bar, with a young Menorcan crowd, in the old windmill across the street from Plaça Alfons III. Open till 1am.

La Torre de Papel, Camí de Maó 46. The most urbane coffee house in town, all polished wood floors, with a bookshop at the front, and a tiny terrace café at the back. Open Mon–Fri 10am–1pm & 5–8pm.

Bar Ulises, Plaça Llibertat. No-frills café-bar next to the market. Their *ensaimadas*, a snip at 200ptas each, are probably the best in town.

Cafeteria Ses Voltes, c/J. M. Quadrado 22. Reasonably tasty and inexpensive snacks and light meals, at a down-to-earth eatery in the town centre.

Restaurants

Café Balear, c/Marina s/n. Popular and attractive café-restaurant down on the harbourside by the bridge. Delicious shellfish, pasta and *tapas* all at reasonable prices.

El Bribón, c/Marina 115. Superb harbourside restaurant specializing in seafood, often prepared in traditional Menorcan style. Reckon on around 1700ptas for the *menú del día*, 2000–2500ptas for a main course. Next door to *Casa Manolo*.

Casa Manolo, c/Marina 117. Fabulous seafood, with main courses averaging around 2500ptas, at the end of the long line of restaurants flanking the south side of the harbour.

Ca's Quintu, Plaça Alfons III, 3. Open all day for both *tapas* and full meals, with the emphasis on Menorcan cuisine. Next to the ring road on the eastern edge of the old town.

El Horno, c/Forn 10. French-style basement restaurant, with good and reasonably priced food. Near the northeast corner of Plaça d'es Born. Evenings only.

La Payesa, c/Marina 65. Popular tourist restaurant where the menu is wide-ranging and the seafood is usually good.

Listings

Banks Banca March, Plaça d'es Born 10; Sa Nostra, c/Maó 2, on Plaça Nova.

Bicycle and moped rental Bicicletas Tolo, c/Sant Isidre 28, off Plaça Artrutx (☎971 381576).

Car rental Ciutadella has about five car rental companies. Amongst them, there's an Avis outlet on the ring road at Avgda Jaume I El Conqueridor 81 (☎971 381174) and a Betacar along the street at no. 59 (☎971 382998).

Emergencies Creu Roja (Red Cross) for an ambulance ☎361180; firefighters ☎092; police (Policia Municipal) ☎092.

Hydrofoils and ferries The main operator of ferry and hydrofoils between Mallorca and Ciutadella, Flebasa, has suspended these services until further notice. In the meantime, Cape Balear de Cruceros (☎971 818668) are operating passenger-only hydrofoils to Ciutadella from Cala Rajada. They don't have offices in Ciutadella, but the tourist office should have details of sailings – if not ask down at the harbour – and you can buy tickets on the boat. There's supposed to be at least one sailing per day, the journey time is 1hr 15min and the return fare is 7500ptas, dropping to 6000ptas in winter.

Maps and books Both Punt i Apart, c/Roser 14, and Libreria Pau, c/Nou de Juliol 23, have a reasonably good selection of travel books, general maps and Menorcan walking maps from the IGN series.

Pharmacies Amongst several downtown options, there's one at Plaça Nova 2.

Post office The main *correu* is just beyond the ring road off Camí d'es Degollador at c/Pius VI, 4–6 (Mon–Fri 8.30am–2.30pm, Sat 9.30am–1pm).

Taxis There are taxi ranks on Plaça dels Pins and Avgda Constitució, round the corner from Plaça Alfons III. Alternatively, telephone Auto Taxi (☎971 384179).

Around Ciutadella

The pristine cove beaches southeast of Ciutadella make delightful day trips, particularly beautiful **Cala En Turqueta**, though you do have to negotiate some rough country tracks to get there. East of town, on the road to Maó, you could also consider the quick excursion to two enjoyable prehistoric sites, the **Naveta d'es Tudons**, the most complete monument of its type on the island, and **Torrellafuda**, with its *taula* and *talayot*. Alternatively, you could drop by the smart villa-village of **Cala Morell**, which occupies a singularly bleak and barren cove northeast of town. Entirely different is the intensively developed west coast, where long lines of villas carpet the flat and treeless seashore on either side of Ciutadella, from **Cala En Forcat** in the north to the **Cap d'Artrutx**, 14km away to the south. By and large, this is all pretty dreadful – especially to the north of town in the dreary *urbanitzacions* of Cala En Blanes, Los Delfines and Cala En Forcat, and in the far south where interminable Tamarinda is ugly and dull in equal measure. Here and there, however, the villas bunch round a narrow cove to form reasonably pleasant resorts, easily the pick being **Cala Blanca**, which also possesses a recommendable hotel where there's a reasonable chance of a room in high season.

Buses leave Plaça dels Pins in Ciutadella for the tourist settlements of the west coast hourly. There are no services from town northeast towards Cala Morell or southeast towards Cala En Turqueta; buses to Maó pass by the Naveta d'es Tudons and Torrellafuda regularly, but check the driver is prepared to stop near either sight before you depart.

Southeast of Ciutadella

The cross-country routes running southeast from Ciutadella to the remote coves of the south coast begin in town at Plaça Jaume II, just off the ring road along c/Mossén J. Salord i Farnés. From this square, head southeast out into the countryside along Camí Sant Joan de Missa. After about 3km, you reach the clearly marked farmhouse of **Son Vivó**, where the road branches into two with each (signposted) fork leading to several south coast beaches, all about 8km away. On both roads, it's easy driving to begin with, but the going gets rougher, and the routes harder to discern, as you approach the coast; if you've hired a moped be prepared for a bumpy ride and watch out for the dust and muck churned up by passing cars.

The prime objective along the more easterly road is **Cala En Turqueta**, a lovely cove backed by wooded limestone cliffs. The beach, a sheltered horseshoe of white sand, slopes gently into the sea, making ideal conditions for bathing, and because there are no facilities it's most unusual to find a crowd. To get there, push on from the Son Vivó fork, go past the hermitage of St Joan de Missa, and, with the road now becoming a track, keep going until you round the farmhouse of Sant Francesc. If the gate here is locked, park and follow the track for the last 1km down to the beach; if it's open you can drive down – but only just.

Back at the Son Vivó fork, it's 3km along the more westerly road to **Son Catlar**, the largest prehistoric settlement on Menorca and one which was still expanding when the Romans arrived in force in 123 BC. The most impressive feature of this Talayotic village is its extraordinary stone wall, originally three-metres high and made of massive blocks – the square towers were added later. Inside the walls, however, all is confusion. The widely scattered remains are largely incomprehensible and only the *taula* compound and the five battered *talayots* make any sense.

Pushing on south from Son Catlar, the asphalt peters out around 1.5km further down the road, just before you reach the fortified farmhouse of Torre Saura. At the farmhouse you have to turn left to follow the rough, unsurfaced and well-worn track that leads east. Some 700m further on, keep right at the junction and press on to the coast, opening and closing the gates as you proceed. From the end of the track it's a short walk to the twin beaches of **Platges Son Saura**, a beautiful and – except on summer weekends – sparsely populated spot, whose bright white sands fringe a pine-clad, semicircular cove. If it's windy, head for the eastern, more protected part of the beach.

East of Ciutadella

The best-preserved *naveta* on the island, the **Naveta d'es Tudons**, can be found in a field to the east of Ciutadella, approximately 6km along the C721, then five minutes' walk from the roadside car park –

but be aware that the sign is easy to miss. Seven metres high and fourteen long, the *naveta* is made of massive stone blocks slotted together using a sophisticated dry-stone technique. The narrow entrance on the west side leads into a small antechamber, which was once sealed off by a stone slab; beyond lies the main chamber where the bones of the dead were stashed away after the flesh had been removed. Folkloric memories of the *navetas*' original purpose survived into modern times, for the Menorcans were loathe to go near these odd-looking and solitary monuments until well into the eighteenth century.

If your enthusiasm for prehistory has been fired, you should also take in **Torrellafuda**, where a broken *taula* stands in the shadow of olive trees abutting a particularly well-preserved *talayot*. There are Cyclopean walls here too, but it's the setting that appeals as much as the remains, with the site encircled by fertile farmland – a perfect spot for a picnic. To get here, look out for the sign on the C721 about 3km east of Naveta d'es Tudons. Turn down the lane, bump the 800m to the car park, and it's a couple of minutes' walk.

Northeast of Ciutadella

To the northeast of Ciutadella, and signposted from the ring road, a well-surfaced country lane carves across a pastoral landscape on its way to **CALA MORELL**, on the island's north coast just 8km from Ciutadella. This small tourist settlement is one of the more refined *urbanitzacions*, its streets – named in Latin after the constellations – hugging a narrow and rocky bay. Besides swimming off the gritty beach, you can visit some of the man-made caves for which Cala Morell is noted, visible beside the road as you approach the village. Dating from the late Bronze and Iron Ages, the caves form one of the largest prehistoric necropolises known in Europe, and are surprisingly sophisticated, with central pillars supporting the roofs, and, in some instances, windows cut into the rock and classical designs carved in relief. No one owns the caves, so there's unlimited access – just scramble up from the road. The sight of one or two is sufficient for most visitors, but if you're after more than a glimpse, bring a torch.

Backtracking along the country lane from Cala Morell, it's about 3km to the signed intersection where a narrow side road forks east across farmland to reach – after 2.5km – a guarded gate, where the landowner levies 700ptas for the one-kilometre onward drive down to **Cala de Algaiarens**. Backed by attractive dunes and pine forests, the two sandy cove beaches here offer excellent swimming in sheltered waters.

South along the coast from Ciutadella

After a couple of kilometres the main road running south from Ciutadella skirts sprawling Cala Santandría and then proceeds to swing round **CALA BLANCA**, the prettiest of the resorts hereabouts with low limestone seacliffs framing a narrow cove and a small beach. The swimming is safe and pedaloes and sunbeds can be rented. For somewhere to stay, there's little to choose between several sky-rise hotels, but the *Riu Mediterrani* probably has the edge, with spacious balconied and air-conditioned rooms just footsteps away from the beach (☎971 384203, fax 971 386162; ⑦). Most visitors eat wherever they stay, but it's worth trying the *Grill Es Caliu*, beside the main road in between Cala Blanca and Cala Santandría, a big, popular place which serves delicious charcoal-grilled meats.

From Cala Blanca, the main road continues south for 6km to reach the dreary villaland of Tamarinda which backs onto the Cap d'Artrutx.

Travel details

Details of flights and ferries to Menorca are given in *Basics*.

Buses

From **Ciutadella** to: Alaior (Mon–Sat 6 daily, 4 on Sun; 40min); Cala En Forcat (hourly, 20min), Es Mercadal (Mon Sat 6 daily, 4 on Sun; 30min); Ferreries (Mon–Sat 8 daily, 5 on Sun; 20min); Maó (Mon–Sat 6 daily, 4 on Sun; 1hr); Sant Tomàs (Mon–Fri 1 daily; 40min); Santandría (hourly; 10min); Tamarinda (hourly; 15min).

From **Ferreries** to: Alaior (Mon–Sat 6 daily, 4 on Sun; 20min); Cala Santa Galdana (6 daily; 35min); Ciutadella (Mon–Sat 8 daily, 5 on Sun; 20min); Es Mercadal (Mon–Sat 6 daily, 4 on Sun; 10min); Maó (Mon–Sat 6 daily, 4 on Sun; 40min).

From **Fornells** to: Es Mercadal (Mon–Fri 1 daily; 15min); Maó (1–2 daily; 35min).

From **Maó** to: Alaior (Mon–Sat 11 daily, 9 on Sun; 20min); Arenal d'En Castell (1–2 daily; 20min); Cala d'Alcaufar (6 daily; 25min); Cala En Porter (7 daily; 25min); Cala Santa Galdana (1–2 daily; 1hr); Ciutadella (Mon–Sat 6 daily, 4 on Sun; 1hr); Es Castell (every 30min; 10min); Es Mercadal (Mon–Sat 6 daily, 4 on Sun; 30min); Ferreries (Mon–Sat 6 daily, 4 on Sun; 40min); Fornells (1–2 daily; 35min); Punta Prima (hourly; 20min); Sant Lluís (hourly; 10min); Sant Tomàs (Mon–Sat 1 daily; 35min); Son Bou (5 daily; 35min); Son Parc (1–2 daily; 35min).

Part 3

Contexts

A history of Mallorca and Menorca   241

A chronology of Spanish history   251

Flora and fauna   255

Books   259

Language   262

Glossary   267

A history of Mallorca and Menorca

Earliest peoples

The earliest inhabitants of the Balearics seem to have reached the islands from the Iberian peninsula, and carbon-dating of remains from both Menorca and Mallorca indicates that human occupation was well established by 4000 BC. The discovery of pottery, flints and animal horns fashioned into tools suggests that these early people were **Neolithic pastoralists**, who supplemented their food supplies by hunting, particularly the now-extinct *Myotragus balearicus*, a species of mountain goat. Hundreds of these animals' skulls have been discovered and several are exhibited in each of the islands' major museums.

Why, or how, these peoples moved to the islands is unknown. Indeed, the first landfall may have been accidental, made by early seafarers travelling along the shores of the Mediterranean – part of the wave of migration that is known to have taken place in the Neolithic period. Many of the oldest archeological finds have been discovered in natural **caves**, where it seems likely these early settlers first sought shelter and protection. Later, cave complexes were dug out of the soft limestone that occurs on both islands, comprising living quarters, usually circular and sometimes with a domed ceiling, as well as longer, straighter funerary chambers; the best example is at **Cales Coves**, near Cala En Porter, on Menorca, a complex which contains no less than 145 excavated chambers.

These Balearic cave dwellers soon came into regular contact with other cultures – the Mediterranean Sea, with its relatively calm and tide-free waters, has always acted as a conduit of civilization. The discovery of Beaker ware at Deià, in Mallorca, indicates one of the earliest of these cultural influences. The **Beaker People**, whose artefacts have been found right across Western Europe, are named after their practice of burying their dead with pottery beakers. They had knowledge of the use of bronze, an alloy of copper and tin, a skill which they introduced to the islanders. The introduction of bronze-working by the Beaker People in around 1400 BC marked the end of the Balearic Cave Culture and the beginning of the Talayotic period, which was also distinguished by the establishment of stone-and-earth villages across the interior of both islands.

The Talayotic period

The megalithic remains of the **Talayotic period**, which extended almost to the Christian era, are strewn all over Mallorca and more particularly Menorca – though, surprisingly, there's no evidence of them on Ibiza. The structure which gives its name to the period is the **talayot** (from *atalaya*, Arabic for "watchtower"), a cone-shaped tower with a circular base, between five and ten metres in height, built without mortar or cement. There are literally hundreds of *talayots* on Mallorca and Menorca and the detail of their design varies from site to site: some are solid, others contain one or more chambers; most are found in settlements, but there are solitary examples too. This diversity has helped to generate considerable debate about their original purpose, with scholars suggesting variously that they were built for defence, as dwellings for chieftains, as burial sites or as storehouses. The mystery of the *talayots* is compounded by their unusualness. The only Mediterranean structures they resemble are the Nuragh towers found on Sardinia. A Sardinian connection would support the view that this phase in the Balearics' development resulted from contact with other cultures, though Egypt, Crete and Greece have also been touted as possible influences. Whatever the origins, it is clear that by 1000 BC a relatively sophisticated, largely pastoral society had developed on Mallorca and Menorca, with at least some of the islanders occupying walled settlements, like **Capocorp Vell**, south of Llucmajor on Mallorca, where you can still inspect four *talayots* and the remains of up to thirty houses, and **Ses Paisses**, a settlement of comparable proportions outside Artà.

Talayotic culture reached its highest level of development on Menorca, and here you'll find the most enigmatic remains of the period. These are the **taulas** ("tables" in Catalan), T-shaped structures standing as high as four metres and consisting of two massive dressed stones. Their purpose is unknown, though many theories have been advanced. One early nineteenth-century writer suggested that they were altars for human sacrifice. Unfortunately for this lurid theory, however, the height of most *taulas* makes it very unlikely. Other writers have noted that many *taulas* are surrounded by enclosures and have argued that the "T" formed the centre of a roofed structure, thatched in some way. Another theory is that the "T" was a stylized head of a bull, an animal that was venerated in many parts of the ancient Mediterranean, most notably in Crete. That these enclosures had a religious purpose is supported by Professor Fernandez Mirando's excavations of the *taula* enclosure of **Torralba d'En Salort**. There he found animal remains and pottery in side recesses of fireplaces, and concluded that these must have been ritual offerings. He also found a bronze sculpture of a bull, suggesting that cattle were, indeed, worshipped.

The other distinctive structure to be found on Menorca is the **naveta**. Referring to its resemblance to the upturned hull of a boat, the name was first given to the **Naveta d'es Tudons**, near Ciutadella, which was built at the beginning of the Talayotic period. Like the other thirty-five *navetas* on the island it was a collective tomb, or, more correctly, an ossuary. The bones of the dead, once the flesh had been removed, were placed in the *navetas* along with some personal possessions such as jewellery, pottery and bone buttons. Several other Talayotic settlements have also survived in relatively good condition, primarily Menorca's **Talatí de Dalt**, which incorporates a *talayot*, a *taula* and several columned chambers or hypostyles. Partly dug out of the ground

and roofed with massive slabs of stone, these hypostyles must have taken considerable effort to build, and may have been used for important gatherings, possibly of communal leaders. Dating from around 1400 BC, Talatí de Dalt, like other Menorcan settlements of this time, was occupied well into the Roman period.

Phoenicians, Greeks and Carthaginians

Fearful of attack from the sea, the Talayotic peoples of Mallorca and Menorca built their walled settlements a few kilometres inland. This pattern was, however, modified during the first millennium BC when the islands became a staging post for the **Phoenicians**, maritime traders from the eastern Mediterranean whose long voyages reached as far as Cornwall. According to the Roman historian Pliny, the Phoenicians established the settlement of Sanisera on Menorca's north coast, and archeologists have discovered Phoenician artefacts at **Alcúdia** on Mallorca. In general, however, very few Phoenician remains have been found on the Balearics – just a handful of bronze items, jewellery and pieces of coloured glass.

The Phoenicians were displaced by **Greeks** from around 800 BC, as several city-states explored the western Mediterranean in search of trade and potential colonies. Like the Phoenicians, the Greeks appear to have used the Balearics primarily as a staging post, for no Greek buildings have survived either on Mallorca or on Menorca – which the Greeks called Meloussa, "Cattle Island", an indication of the preoccupations of its inhabitants. The absence of metal apparently made the islands unsuitable for long-term colonization, and the belligerence of the native population may have played a part too: the Greeks coined another name for the islands, the **Balearics**, which they derived from *ballein*, meaning "to throw from a sling". The islanders were adept at this form of warfare, and many early visitors were repelled with showers of polished sling-stones. Some historians dispute this theory, claiming rather that the name comes from the Baleri tribe of Sardinia.

The Greeks were also discouraged from colonization by the growth of the **Carthaginian** empire across the western Mediterranean. The Phoenicians had established Carthage, on the North African coast, under the leadership of the princess Elissa, better known as Dido, the tragic hero of Virgil's *Aeneid*. According to the Greek historian Diodurus Siculus, the Carthaginians began to colonize the Balearics in the early seventh century BC, and certainly by the beginning of the third century BC, the islands were firmly under their control. Little is known of the Carthaginian occupation except that they established several new settlements, including Jamma (Ciutadella) and Maghen (Maó). It is also claimed that the famous Carthaginian general, Hannibal, was born on Mallorca, though Ibiza and Malta claim this honour too.

In the third century BC, the expansion of the Carthaginian empire across the Mediterranean and up into the Iberian Peninsula precipitated the first two **Punic Wars** with Rome. In both of these wars the Balearics proved extremely valuable, first as stepping stones from the North African coast to the European mainland and second as a source of mercenaries. Balearic slingers were highly valued and accompanied Hannibal and his elephants across the Alps in the Second Punic War, when (for reasons that remain obscure) the islanders refused gold and demanded payment in wine and women instead. After Hannibal's defeat by the Romans at the battle of Zama in 202 BC, Carthaginian power began to wane and they withdrew from Mallorca and Menorca, although they continued to have some influence over Ibiza for at least another seventy years.

Romans, Vandals and Byzantines

As the Carthaginians retreated so the **Romans** advanced, incorporating Ibiza within their empire after the final victory over Carthage in 146 BC. On Mallorca and Menorca, the islanders took advantage of the prolonged military chaos to profit from piracy, until finally, in 123 BC, the Romans, led by the consul Quintus Metellus, restored maritime order by occupying both islands. These victories earnt Metellus the title "Balearico" from the Roman senate and the islands were given new names, Balearis Major (Mallorca) and Balearis Minor (Menorca).

For the next five hundred years the Balearics were part of the **Roman Empire**. Amongst many developments, Roman colonists introduced viticulture, turning the Balearics into a wine-exporting area, and initiated olive oil production from newly planted groves. As was their custom, the Romans consolidated their control of the islands by building roads and establishing towns: on Mallorca they founded Pollentia (Alcúdia) in the northeast and Palmaria on the south coast, near the site of modern Palma; on Menorca, Port Magonum (Maó) was developed as an administrative centre and Sanisera – previously the site of a Phoenician trading post – became an important port. Initially, the Balearics were part of the Roman province of Tarraconensis (Tarragona), but in 404 AD the islands became a province in their own right with the name Balearica.

By this time, however, the Roman Empire was in decline, its defences unable to resist the westward-moving tribes of central Asia. One of these tribes, the **Vandals**, swept across the Balearics in around 425 AD, thereby ending Roman rule. So thoroughgoing was the destruction they wrought that very few signs of the Romans have survived – the only significant remains are those of Pollentia.

Christianity had taken root in the Balearics during the Roman occupation. The Vandals had themselves been Christianized long before they reached the Mediterranean, but they were followers of what was denounced as the **Arian** heresy. This interpretation of Christianity, founded by Arius, an Alexandrian priest, insisted that Christ the Son and God the Father were two distinct figures, not elements of the Trinity, along with the Holy Ghost. To orthodox Christians this seemed dangerously close to the pagan belief in a multiplicity of gods. Arianism had largely been eliminated within the Roman Empire by the end of the fourth century AD, but Arian missionaries had enjoyed considerable success converting the Germanic peoples outside the empire. Armed with their "heretical" beliefs, the Vandals subjected the orthodox islanders to severe persecution and destroyed their churches. As a consequence, only a handful of Christian remains from this period have survived, such as the ruins of the basilica at **Son Bou**, Menorca.

In 533 the Vandals were defeated in North Africa by the Byzantine general, Count Belisarius (who was the subject of a novel by one of Mallorca's adopted sons, Robert Graves). This brought the Balearics under **Byzantine** rule and, for a time, restored prosperity and stability. However, the islands were too far removed from Constantinople to be of much imperial importance and, when the empire was threatened from the east at the end of the seventh century, they were abandoned in all but name.

The Moors

As the influence of Byzantium receded, so militant Islam moved in from the south and east to fill the power vacuum. In 707–8 the **Moors** of North Africa conducted an extended raid against Mallorca, destroying its entire fleet and carrying away slaves and booty. By 716 the Balearics' position had become even more vulnerable with the completion of the Moorish conquest of Spain. In 798 the Balearics were again sacked by the Moors – who were still more interested in plunder than settlement – and in desperation the islanders appealed for help to **Charlemagne**, the Frankish Holy Roman Emperor. As emperor, Charlemagne was the military – the Pope the spiritual – leader of Western Christendom, so the appeal signified the final severance of the Balearics' links with Byzantium.

Charlemagne's attempt to protect the islands from the Moors met with some success, but the respite was only temporary. By the middle of the ninth century, the Christian position had deteriorated so badly that the Balearics were compelled to enter a non-aggression pact with the Moors, and, to add to the islanders' woes, the Balearics suffered a full-scale Viking raid in 859. Finally, at the beginning of the tenth century, the **Emir of Cordoba** conquered both Menorca and Mallorca. Moorish rule lasted over three hundred years, though internal political divisions among the Muslims meant that the islands experienced several different regimes. In the early eleventh century, the emirate of Cordoba collapsed and control passed to the Wali (governor) of Denia, on the Spanish mainland. This administration allowed the Christians – who were known as **Mozarabs** – to practise their faith, and the islands prospered from their position at the heart of the trade routes between North Africa and Islamic Spain.

In 1085 the Balearics became an independent emirate with a new dynasty of *walis*, from **Amortadha** in North Africa, who pursued a more aggressive foreign and domestic policy, raiding the towns of the mainland and persecuting their Christian citizens. These actions blighted trade and thereby enraged the emergent city-states of Italy at a time when Christendom was fired by crusading zeal. Anticipating retaliation, the Amortadhas fortified Palma, which was known at this time as Medina Mayurka, and other principal towns. The Christian attack came in 1114 when a grand Italian fleet – led by the ships of Pisa and

supported by the pope as a mini-crusade – landed an army of 70,000 Catalan and Italian soldiers on Ibiza. The island was soon captured, but Mallorca, the crusaders' next target, proved a much more difficult proposition. Medina Mayurka's landward lines of defence had to be overcome separately in a number of bloody engagements, the coastal defences proving impregnable. When the city finally fell, most of the surviving Muslim population was slaughtered. Despite their victory, however, the Christians had neither the will nor the resources to consolidate their position and, loading their vessels with freed slaves and loot, they returned home.

It took the Moors just two years to re-establish themselves on the islands, this time under the leadership of the **Almoravids**, a North African Berber tribe who had previously controlled southern Spain. The Almoravids proved to be tolerant and progressive rulers, and the Balearics prospered under them: agriculture improved, particularly through the development of irrigation, and trade expanded as commercial agreements were struck with the Italian cities of Genoa and Pisa. The Pisans, Crusaders earlier in the century, defied a papal ban on trade with Muslims to finalize the deal – consciences could, it seems, be flexible even in the "devout" Middle Ages when access to the precious goods of the east (silks, carpets and spices) was the prize.

Jaume I and the Reconquest

In 1203 the Almoravids were supplanted by the **Almohad** dynasty, who forcibly converted the islands' Christian population to Islam and started raiding the mainland. This was an extraordinary miscalculation as the kingdoms of Aragón and Catalunya had only recently been united, strengthening the Christian position in this part of Spain. This unification was a major step in the changing balance of power – with their forces combined, the Christians were able to launch the *Reconquista*, which was eventually to drive the Moors from all of the peninsula. In the meantime, in 1228, the Emir of Mallorca antagonized the young **King Jaume I** of Aragón and Catalunya by seizing a couple of his ships. The king's advisers, with their eyes firmly fixed on the wealth of the Balearics, determined to capitalize on the offence. They organized the first Balearic publicity evening, a feast at which the king was presented with a multitude of Mallorcan delicacies and Catalan sailors told of the islands' prosperity. And so, insulted by the emir and persuaded by his nobility, Jaume I committed himself to the invasion that was to end Moorish rule in the Balearics.

Jaume's expedition of 150 ships, 16,000 men and 1500 horses set sail for Mallorca in September 1229. The king had originally planned to land at Pollença, in the northeast, but adverse weather conditions forced the fleet further south, and it eventually anchored off Sant Elm. The following day, the Catalans defeated the Moorish forces sent to oppose the landing and Jaume promptly pushed on, laying siege to Medina Mayurka. It took three months to breach the walls, but on December 31 the city finally fell and Jaume was hailed as "**El Conqueridor**".

The cost of launching an invasion on this scale placed an enormous strain on the resources of a medieval monarch. With this in mind, Jaume subcontracted the capture of Ibiza, entering into an agreement, in 1231, with the Crown Prince of Portugal, Don Pedro, and the Count of Roussillon. In return for the capture of the island, the count and the prince were to be allowed to divide Ibiza between themselves, provided they acknowledged the suzerainty of Jaume. This project initially faltered, but was revived with the addition of the Archbishop of Tarragona. The three allies captured Ibiza in 1235 and divided the spoils, although Don Pedro waived his rights and his share passed to Jaume.

In the meantime, Jaume had acquired the overlordship of Menorca. Unable to afford another fullscale invasion, the king devised a clever ruse. In 1232 he returned to Mallorca with just three galleys, which he dispatched to Menorca carrying envoys, while he camped out in the mountains above Capdepera, on Mallorca. As night fell and his envoys negotiated with the enemy, Jaume ordered the lighting of as many bonfires as possible to illuminate the sky and give the impression of a vast army. The ruse worked and the next day, mindful of the bloodbath of the invasion of Mallorca, the Menorcan Moors capitulated, informing the envoys – according to the king's own account – that "they gave great thanks to God and to me for the message I had sent them for they knew well they could not long defend themselves against me". The terms of submission were generous: the Moors handed over Ciutadella and a number of other strongpoints, but Jaume acknowledged the Muslims as his subjects and appointed one of their leaders as his *rais* (governor).

This retention of Moorish government, albeit under the suzerainty of the king, was in marked contrast to events on Mallorca. Here, the land was divided into eight blocks, with four passing to the king and the rest to his most trusted followers, who leased their holdings in the feudal fashion, granting land to tenants in return for military service. In 1230 Jaume issued the **Carta de Població** (People's Charter), guaranteeing equality before the law, a very progressive precept for the period. Mallorca was exempted from taxation to encourage Catalan immigration, and special rights were given to Jews resident on the island, a measure designed to stimulate trade. Twenty years later, Jaume also initiated a distinctive form of government for Mallorca, with a governing body of six **jurats** (adjudicators) – one from the nobility, two knights, two merchants and one peasant. At the end of each year the *jurats* elected their successors. This form of government remained in place until the sixteenth century.

From a modern perspective, the downside of the Reconquest in Mallorca was the wholesale demolition of almost all Moorish buildings, with mosques systematically replaced by churches (at a later date the same policy was followed on Menorca). The main compensation is the architectural magnificence of **Palma Cathedral**, which was consecrated in 1269. Shortly afterwards, Jaume I died at Valencia. In his will he divided his kingdom between his two sons: Pedro received Catalunya, Aragón and Valencia, whilst Jaume II was bequeathed Montpellier, Roussillon and the Balearics. Jaume II was crowned in Mallorca on September 12, 1276.

The Kingdom of Mallorca

Jaume I's division of his kingdom infuriated **Pedro**, as Mallorca stood astride the shipping route between Barcelona and Sicily, where his wife was queen. He forced his brother to become his vassal, but in response Jaume II secretly schemed with the French. When Pedro discovered this treachery, he promptly attacked his brother's territories, but died before the planned assault on Mallorca could be launched. Pedro's son, **Alfonso III**, carried out the invasion plans and, late in 1285, his army speedily captured Palma. Other strongholds, especially Alaró, held out for longer; when he finally managed to take them, Alfonso brutally vented his frustation on their defenders. For his atrocities, the king was excommunicated by the pope but only for a brief period.

With Mallorca secured and Jaume deposed, Alfonso turned his attention to Menorca where he suspected the loyalty of the Moorish governor: rumour had it that the *rais* was in conspiratorial contact with the Moors of North Africa. Alfonso's army landed on Menorca in January 1287 and decisively defeated the Moors just outside Maó. The Moors retreated to the hilltop fortress of Santa Agueda, but their resistance didn't amount to much and the whole island was Alfonso's within a few days. The king's treatment of the vanquished islanders was savage: those Muslims who were unable to buy their freedom were enslaved, and those who couldn't work as slaves – the old, the sick and the very young – were taken to sea and thrown overboard by the boatload. Alfonso rewarded the nobles who had accompanied him with grants of land and brought in hundreds of Catalan settlers. The capital, Medina Minurka, was renamed **Ciutadella**, and the island's mosques were converted to Christian usage, before being demolished and replaced.

Alfonso's brutal career was cut short by his death in 1291 at the age of 25. He was succeeded by his brother, Jaume, who was king of Sicily. A more temperate man, Jaume conducted negotiations through the papacy that eventually led, in 1298, to the restoration of the partition envisaged by Jaume I: he himself presided over Catalunya, Aragón and Valencia, while his exiled uncle, **Jaume II**, ruled as king of Mallorca. Restored to the crown, Jaume II devoted a great deal of time to improving the commerce and administration of the Balearics. To stimulate trade, he established a weekly market in Palma, reissued the currency in gold and silver, and founded eleven towns in inland Mallorca, including Manacor, Felanitx, Llucmajor and Binissalem. Jaume II attended to God as well as Mammon, and this period saw the building of many churches and monasteries. The king patronized the Mallorcan poet, scholar and Franciscan friar, **Ramon Llull** (see p.165), providing him with the finance to establish a monastic school near Valldemossa. Jaume also established new settlements on Menorca – most notably Alaior – and divided the island into seven parishes, ordering the construction of churches for each of them. Perhaps his most important act, though, was to grant Menorca its own Carta de Població, which bestowed the same legal rights as the Mallorcans enjoyed.

On his death in 1311 Jaume was succeeded by his son, **Sancho**, who spent most of his time in the mountains – he is thought to have been asthmatic – in the palace of Valldemossa. The new monarch continued with the successful economic policies of his father, whilst, internationally, he worked hard to avoid entanglement in the antagonism between Aragón and France. He also built up his fleet to protect the islands from North African pirates. Sancho died without issue in 1324 and, theoretically, the islands should have passed to the crown of Aragón. The Balearic nobility, however, crowned Sancho's ten-year-old nephew as **Jaume III** and, to forestall Aragonese hostility, had him rapidly betrothed to the king of Aragón's five-year-old daughter.

In the long term this marriage did Jaume III little good. After he came of age, his relations with his brother-in-law, Pedro IV of Aragón, quickly deteriorated, and Pedro successfully invaded the Balearics in response to an alleged plot that was hatching against him. Jaume fled to his mainland possessions and sold Montpellier to the French to raise money for an invasion. He landed on Mallorca in 1349, but was no match for Pedro and was defeated and killed; his son was also captured, outside Llucmajor. Although the uncrowned Jaume IV eventually escaped from prison, he was never able to drum up sufficient support to retake his throne from the Aragonese monarchy.

Unification with Spain

For a diversity of reasons the **unification** of the Balearics with Aragón – and their subsequent incorporation within Spain – proved a disaster. The mainland connection meant that the islands' nobility tended to gravitate towards the Aragonese court, regarding their local estates as little more than sources of income to sustain their expensive lifestyles. The neglect and exploitation inherent in this arrangement led to an uprising on Mallorca in 1391. Crowds marched on Palma and massacred most of the Jewish population, mainly because many landowners had delegated their authority to Jewish agents. In Menorca, the discontent of the period was manifested in terms of rivalry between Ciutadella and Maó: for a decade from 1426 to 1436 there was intermittent warfare between the two, reflecting the mainland conflict between the Aragonese king, supported by Ciutadella, and his nobles, favoured by Maó.

Discontent was also fuelled by economic trends. After the fall of Constantinople to the Islamic Turks in 1453, the lucrative overland trade routes from the eastern Mediterranean to the Far East were blocked. Worse still as far as the Balearics were concerned, the Portuguese discovered the way around the Cape of Good Hope to the Indies and, in 1492, Columbus reached the Americas. As a consequence, the focus of European trade moved from the Mediterranean to the Atlantic seaboard. Meanwhile, **Fernando V of Aragón** married **Isabella I of Castile** in 1479, thereby uniting the two largest kingdoms in Spain. This increased the tendency towards centralization, rendering the islands a remote provincial backwater – a trend compounded by a royal decree that forbade Catalunya and the Balearics from trading with the New World. By the start of the sixteenth century, the Balearics were starved of foreign currency and the islands' merchants had begun to leave, signalling a period of long-term **economic decline**.

These problems led to an **armed uprising** of Mallorcan peasants and artisans in 1521. Organized in a *germania*, or armed brotherhood, they seized control of Palma when their complaints about the neglectful nobility and the high rate of taxation fell on deaf ears. Resident nobles tried either to flee the island or to beat a hasty retreat to the safety of the Bellver or Alcúdia citadels; those who didn't move fast enough were slaughtered on the streets. A massacre of blue bloods also followed the fall of the Castell de Bellver three months later, though Alcúdia held out until relieved. It was a long wait: only in 1523 did the forces of authority return under the command of **Emperor Charles V**, king of Spain (he was the grandson of Fernando and Isabella) and Habsburg Holy Roman Emperor – a powerful union of crowns that was to last until 1713. Charles negotiated generous terms for the surrender of Palma, but once in possession of the city, promptly broke the agreement and ordered the execution of five hundred of the rebels, who were duly drawn and quartered.

Mallorca witnessed other sixteenth-century horrors with the arrival of the **Holy Office of the Inquisition**. The Inquisitors focused their attention on the Jewish community, which had earlier been confined within the Palma ghetto, El Call. Many Mallorcan Jews chose the course of least resistance and converted to Christianity, but scores of others were burnt to death. As late as the 1970s, the descendants of the converts still formed a distinct group of gold- and silversmiths in Palma.

The Balearics were also troubled by the renewal of large-scale maritime raids from North Africa This development was partly stimulated by the final expulsion of the Moors from Spain in 1492, and partly by the emergence of the Ottoman Turks as a Mediterranean superpower. Muslim raiders ransacked Pollença (1531 and 1550), Alcúdia (1551), Valldemossa (1552), Andratx (1553) and Sóller (1561), attacks which are still commemorated each year by these communities. In 1535 the Ottoman admiral Khair-ed-din, better known as **Barbarossa**, landed on Menorca, taking Maó after a three-day seige. Hundreds of Menorcans were enslaved and carted away, prompting Charles V to construct the fort of Sant Felip to guard the Maó harbour. Two decades later, the Turks returned and sacked Ciutadella, taking a further three thousand prisoners. Muslim incursions continued until the seventeenth century, but declined in frequency and intensity after the Turkish fleet was destroyed by a combined Italian and Spanish force at Lepanto in 1571.

British and French occupation

The Balearics' woes continued throughout the seventeenth century. Trade remained stagnant and the population declined, a sorry state of affairs that was exacerbated by internal tensions. In Palma, the Canavall and Canavant factions engaged in a long-running vendetta, while on Menorca there remained friction between the rival towns of Maó and Ciutadella. By the 1630s the population problem had become so critical that Philip IV exempted the islands from the levies that raised men for Spain's armies – though this gain was offset by the loss of 15,000 Mallorcans to the plague in 1652.

A new development was the regular appearance of **British** vessels in the Mediterranean, a corollary of Britain's increasing share of the region's seaborne trade and the Royal Navy's commitment to protect their country's merchantmen from Algerian pirates. The British first put into Maó harbour to take on water in 1621 and were impressed by this secure, deep-water anchorage. In 1664 Charles II of England formalized matters by instructing his ambassador to Spain to "request immediate permission for British ships to use Balearic ports and particularly

Port Mahon". The Spanish king granted the request, and the advantages of using Port Mahon (Maó) were noted by a poetic British seaman, a certain John Baltharpe:

> Good this same is upon Minork
> For shipping very useful 'gainst the Turk.
> The King of Spain doth to our King it lend,
> As in the line above to that same end.

For a time the British were simply content to "borrow" Maó, but their expanding commercial interests prompted a yearning for a more permanent arrangement. It was the dynastic **War of the Spanish Succession**, fought over the vacant throne of Spain, which gave them their opportunity. A British force invaded Menorca in 1708 and, meeting tepid resistance, captured the island in a fortnight. Apart from the benefits of Maó harbour, Menorca was also an ideal spot from which to blockade the French naval base at Toulon, thereby preventing the union of the French Atlantic and Mediterranean fleets. Indeed, so useful was Menorca to the British that they negotiated its retention at the **Treaty of Utrecht**, which rounded off the War of the Spanish Succession in 1713.

The island's first British governor, **Sir Richard Kane**, was an energetic and capable man who strengthened Menorca as a military base, and worked hard at improving the administration of the island, civilian facilities and the local economy. He built the first road across the island from Maó to Ciutadella and introduced improved strains of seed and livestock. During the first forty years of British occupation, the production of wine, vegetables and chickens increased by 500 percent. Relations between the occupying power and the islanders were generally good – though the Catholic clergy no doubt found it difficult to stomach the instruction to "pray for His Britannic Majesty".

The first phase of British domination ended when the island was captured by the **French** in 1756 at the start of the **Seven Years War**. Admiral Byng was dispatched to assist the beleaguered British force but, after a lacklustre encounter with a French squadron, he withdrew, leaving Menorca to its fate. Byng's indifferent performance cost him his life: he was court-martialled and executed for cowardice, prompting Voltaire's famous aphorism that the English shoot their admirals "pour encourager les autres". The new French governor built the township of

Sant Lluís to house his Breton sailors and, once again, the Menorcans adjusted to the occupying power without too much difficulty. In 1763, Britain regained Menorca in exchange for the Philippines and Cuba, which it had captured from France during the Seven Years War.

The **second period of British occupation** proved far less successful than the first. The governor from 1763 to 1782, General Johnston, was an authoritarian and unpopular figure who undermined the Menorcans' trust in the British. The crunch came in 1781 when, with Britain at war with both Spain and France, the Duc de Crillon landed on the island with a force of 8000 men. With a total of only 2692 men, the new British governor, General John Murray, withdrew to the fort of Sant Felip, where he was besieged for eight months. Succoured by the Menorcans, the Franco-Spanish army finally starved the British into submission; Murray's men were badly stricken with scurvy, and only 1120 survived. The **third and final period of British rule** ran from 1798 to 1802, when the island was occupied for its value as a naval base in the Napoleonic Wars. The British finally relinquished all claims to Menorca in favour of Spain under the terms of the Treaty of Amiens in 1802.

Meanwhile, Mallorca, lacking a harbour of any strategic importance, was having a far quieter time. The Mallorcans chose the wrong side in the War of the Spanish Succession – most of Spain favoured the French candidate, Philip of Anjou, but Catalunya and Mallorca preferred the Austrian archduke Charles, who was supported by Britain and the Netherlands. After Philip had won the war, the Mallorcans paid for their choice: the new king stripped the island of its title of kingdom and many of its historic rights were removed. For the rest of the eighteenth century, however, Mallorca was left untouched by the European conflicts that rippled around it, though there was one major change imposed by Madrid: Castilian replaced the local dialect of Catalan as the official language.

The nineteenth century and the Spanish Civil War

For both Menorca and Mallorca, the nineteenth century brought difficult times. Neglected outposts, the islands were extremely poor and subject to droughts, famines, and epidemics of cholera, bubonic plague and yellow fever. The islanders were preoccupied with the art of survival rather than politics, and generally stayed out of the Carlist wars between the liberals and the conservatives which so bitterly divided the Spanish mainland. Many islanders emigrated, some to Algeria after it was acquired by the French in 1830, others to Florida and California. However, the use of Maó as a training base by the American navy between 1815 and 1826 brought the Menorcans some measure of economic relief.

Matters began to improve towards the end of the nineteenth century, when agriculture, particularly Mallorcan almond cultivation, boomed. Meanwhile, Menorca developed a thriving export industry in footwear, largely as a result of the efforts of Don Jeronimo Cabrisas, a Menorcan who had made his fortune in Cuba, and later supplied many of the boots worn by troops in World War I. Modern services, like gas and electricity, began to be installed and a regular steam packet link was established between the islands and the mainland. Around this time too, a **revival of Catalan culture**, led by the middle class of Barcelona, stirred the Mallorcan bourgeoisie. In Palma, Catalonian novelists and poets were lauded, Catalan political groupings were formed, and the town was adorned with a series of magnificent *Modernista* buildings.

During the **Spanish Civil War** (1936–39), Mallorca and Menorca supported opposing sides. General Goded made Mallorca an important base for the Fascists, but when General Bosch attempted to do the same on Menorca, his NCOs and men mutinied and, with the support of the civilian population, declared their support for the Republic. In the event – apart from a few bombing raids and an attempted Republican landing at Mallorca's Porto Cristo – the Balearics saw very little actual fighting. Nevertheless, the Menorcans were dangerously exposed towards the end of the war, when they were marooned as the last Republican stronghold. A peaceful conclusion was reached largely through the intervention of the British, who brokered the surrender of the island aboard HMS *Devonshire*. Franco's troops occupied Menorca in April 1939 and the *Devonshire* left with 450 Menorcan refugees.

Recent times

Since World War II the most significant development has been the emergence of **mass tourism** as the principal economic activity, though the islands' charms had been discovered by the privileged long before. Frédéric Chopin and George Sand spent the winter of 1838 at Valldemossa, and Edward VII and the German Kaiser regularly cruised the Balearics before World War I. The high-water mark of this elitist tourist trade was reached in the 1930s when the Argentinian poet Adan Diehl opened the *Hotel Formentor*, overlooking the bay of Pollença. Diehl advertised the hotel in lights on the Eiffel Tower and attracted guests such as Edward VIII, the Aga Khan and Winston Churchill. From such small and privileged beginnings, the Balearics' tourist industry has mushroomed in the latter part of this century. In 1950 Mallorca had just one hundred registered hotels and boarding houses; by 1972 the total had risen to 1509. Menorca experienced a similar rate of growth: in 1961 the total number of tourists was only 1500, but by 1973 it had reached over half a million each year.

The pace of development accelerated after the death of Franco in 1975, thereby further strengthening the economies of Mallorca and Menorca. The Balearics now have one of the highest per capita incomes in Spain, twice that of Extremadura for instance, and in 1995 received nearly five million holiday-makers, compared to a resident population of just 700,000. For as long as the islands remain popular holiday destinations, their economic future seems secure, though the Balearic government isn't resting on its laurels: aware of its somewhat tacky image, Mallorca, in particular, is doing its best to move upmarket, greening its resorts, imposing strict building controls and spending millions of pesetas refurbishing the older parts of Palma.

The Balearics have also benefited from the recent political restructuring of Spain. In 1978, just three years after Franco's death, the Spanish parliament, the Cortes, passed a new constitution, which reorganized the country on a more federal basis and allowed for the establishment of Autonomous Communities in the regions. In practice however, the demarcation of responsibilities between central and regional governments has proved problematic, leading to interminable wrangling, not least because the Socialists, who were in power from 1983 to 1996, waivered in their commitment to decentralization. Nonetheless, the Balearics, constituted as the **Comunidad Autónoma de las Islas Baleares** in 1983, have used their new-found independence to assert the primacy of their native Catalan language – now the main language of education – and to exercise a tighter local control of their economy. Since 1996, this trend towards decentralization has continued under a Conservative government which was only able to secure a majority in the Cortes with the support of several regionally based nationalist parties, including Basque, Catalan and Balearic groupings. Consequently, these regional groups have been in a more powerful position than their numbers would otherwise justify, and have been able to keep the momentum of decentralization going despite the innate centralist tendencies of the Conservatives in Madrid. In particular, most government expenditure is now controlled by the regions and the Balearic administration have used their control of these resources to upgrade a string of holiday resorts, build new roads and upgrade the old stone houses and towns, especially Palma.

A chronology of Spanish history

C11th–5th BC Phoenicians, Greeks and Celts invade Spain and intermingle with the native (Iberian) population.

C3rd BC Carthaginians conquer southeast Spain, incorporating the region within their Mediterranean empire.

C3rd–2nd BC Carthage and Rome wrestle for control of the Iberian Peninsula in the three Punic Wars. Rome wins all three and their final act is the destruction of Carthage (in present-day Tunisia) in 146 BC.

C2nd BC Spain becomes part of the Roman Empire, its administrative capital established at Córdoba in 151 BC. The region's mines and granaries bring unprecedented prosperity, and roads, bridges and aqueducts are built to network the peninsula.

C1st AD Christianity makes rapid progress across Roman Spain.

264–76 Barbarian tribes, the Franks and the Suevi, ravage the peninsula.

414 The Visigoths reach Spain and become the dominant military force, with their capital at Toledo.

711 Islamic Moors (Arabs and Berbers from North Africa) invade and conquer the Visigoths' kingdom in a whirlwind campaign that lasts just seven years. However, a Christian victory at the battle of Covadonga (722) halts the Moorish advance and leads to the creation of the kingdom of the Asturias – a Christian toehold on the northwest corner of the Iberian peninsula.

756 Abd ar-Rahman I proclaims the Emirate of Córdoba, confirming Moorish control over almost all of Spain.

778 The Holy Roman Emperor Charlemagne invades Spain from France, but is defeated. In the dash back across the Pyrenees, the Christian rearguard – led by Roland – is hacked to pieces at Roncesvalles, inspiring the epic poem the *Chanson de Roland*. Charlemagne's subsequent endeavours meet with more success and undermine Moorish control of Navarra and Catalunya.

C9th The Christian kingdoms of Catalunya and Navarra are founded.

C10th–early 11th The Emirate of Córdoba flourishes, its capital becoming the most prosperous and civilized city in Europe. Abd ar-Rahman III breaks with Baghdad to declare himself Caliph of an independent western Islamic empire.

C11th The Caliphate disintegrates into squabbling *taifas*, or petty fiefdoms. A local chieftain, El Cid, leads Christian forces against the Moors of Valencia, but his victories have no lasting effect. Independent Catalunya expands.

1037	Fernando I unites the kingdoms of Castile and León-Asturias.
1162	Alfonso II unites the kingdoms of Aragón and Catalunya.
C13th	The pace of the Christian Reconquest accelerates after the kings of Navarra, Castile and Aragón combine to defeat the Muslims at the crucial battle of Las Navas de Tolosa in 1212. Subsequent Christian victories include the capture of the Balearics (1229), Córdoba (1236), Valencia (1238) and Sevilla (1248). The reconquered territories are mostly distributed amongst the Christian nobility in great estates, the *latifundia*. Men from the ranks also receive land, forming a lower, larger landowning class, the *hidalgos*.
1479	Castile and Aragón, the two pre-eminent Christian kingdoms, are united under Isabella I and Fernando V, the so-called Catholic Monarchs (Los Reyes Católicos). Subsequent emergence of Spain as a single political entity, with the Inquisition acting as a unifying force. The Inquisitors concentrate their attention on the Jews, expelling around 400,000 from Spain for refusing Christian baptism.
1492	The fall of Granada, the last Moorish kingdom. Columbus reaches the Americas.
1494	At the Treaty of Tordesillas, under the approving eye of the pope, Spain and Portugal divide the New World between them. Portugal gets Brazil and Spain takes the rest of modern-day Latin America.
1516–56	On the death of Fernando, his grandson Carlos I succeeds to the Spanish throne. Three years later Carlos also becomes Holy Roman Emperor – as Charles V – adding Germany, Austria and the Low Countries to his kingdom. Throughout his reign, he wages almost incessant war against his many enemies, principally the French, the Protestants and the Muslims of North Africa. He funds his campaigns with the gold and silver bullion that is pouring into Spain from the New World, where Spanish adventurers have conquered, colonized and exploited a vast new empire.
1519	Cortés lands in Mexico, seizing its capital two years later.
1532	Pizarro "discovers" Peru, capturing Cuzco the next year.
1539	Hernando de Soto stakes out Florida.
1541	Pedro de Valdivia founds Santiago, Chile.
1555	Charles V finally accepts he is unable to suppress the German Reformation and agrees to a compromise peace with the Protestants at the Treaty of Augsburg.
1556	Charles V abdicates. His son, Felipe II, becomes king of Spain and its colonies, Naples, Milan and the Low Countries. His brother, Ferdinand I, becomes Holy Roman Emperor, ruling Germany and Austria. An ardent and autocratic Catholic, Felipe continues the militaristic policy of his father, but concentrates his efforts against the Protestants.
1567	The Protestants of the Low Countries rise against Felipe II, beginning a protracted conflict that will drain Spanish resources and exhaust the Low Countries.

1571	Spain wins control of the Mediterranean after defeating the Turkish fleet at Lepanto.
1581	Spain annexes Portugal.
1588	The English defeat Felipe II's Armada, thereby eliminating Spain as a major sea power.
1598	Felipe II dies. His legacy is an enormous but bankrupt empire: Spain's great wealth, so ruthlessly extracted from its colonies, has been squandered in over seventy years of continuous warfare.
C17th	The decline. Spain's international credibility is undermined by the loss of Portugal (1640) and the Netherlands (1648), emphasizing her military degeneration. Domestically, the poverty and suffering of the mass of the population − as compared with the opulence of the royal court − fuels regional discontent and insurrection. Cervantes publishes *Don Quixote* in 1605.
1701–14	Europe's nation states slug it out in the War of the Spanish Succession. The Bourbon (French) claimant − as opposed to that of the Holy Roman Emperor − wins out to become Felipe V. The British pick up Gibraltar and Menorca. As Spain declines, so it moves into the French sphere of influence.
1804	Napoleon crowned Emperor of France. Spain assists him in his war against England.
1805	The British navy, under Nelson, destroys the Franco-Spanish fleet at the Battle of Trafalgar.
1808	Napoleon arrests the Spanish king and replaces him with his brother, Joseph. This starts the War of Independence (otherwise known as the Peninsular War) in which the Spaniards fight the French army of occupation with the help of their new-found allies, the British.
1811 onwards	The South American colonies take advantage of the situation to assert their independence, detaching themselves from Spain one by one.
1815	The end of the Napoleonic Wars.
C19th	Further Spanish decline. The nineteenth century is dominated by the struggle between the forces of monarchist reaction and those of liberal constitutional reform. There are three bitter Carlist wars − "Carlist" after one of the claimants to the throne. The progressives finally triumph in the 1870s, but the new government's authority is brittle and Spanish society remains deeply divided. Elsewhere, Puerto Rico, the Philippines and Cuba shake off Spanish control with the help of the US. Spain's American empire is at an end.
1900–31	Liberals and conservatives fail to reach a secure constitutional consensus, keeping the country on a knife's edge. Working-class political movements − of anarchist, Marxist and socialist inclination − grow in strength and stir industrial and political discontent. Spain stays neutral in World War I, but the success of the Russian Bolsheviks terrifies King Alfonso XIII and the bourgeoisie, who support the right-wing military coup engineered by General Primo de Rivera in 1923. Rivera dies in 1930 and the king abdicates in 1931 when anti-monarchist parties win the municipal elections.

1932–36 The new Republican government introduces radical left-of-centre reforms, but separatists (in Catalunya, Galicia and the Basque country), revolutionaries and rightists undermine its authority. Spain polarizes to the political left and right. Chaos and confusion prevail.

1936–39 The Spanish Civil War. General Francisco Franco leads a right-wing military rebellion against the Republican government. His Nationalists receive massive support from Hitler and Mussolini. The Republicans get sporadic help from the Soviet Union and attract thousands of volunteers, organized in the International Brigades. The Civil War is vicious and bloody, ending in 1939 with a Fascist victory. Franco becomes head of state and massive reprisals follow. Pope Pius XII congratulates the dictator on his "Catholic victory".

1939–75 Franco establishes a one-party state, backed up by stringent censorship and a vigorous secret police. By staying neutral during World War II, he survives the fall of Nazi Germany. In 1969, Franco nominates the grandson of Alfonso XIII, Juan Carlos, as his successor, but retains his vice-like grip on the country until his death in 1975.

1976–82 Juan Carlos recognizes the need for political reform and helps steer the country towards a parliamentary system. He reinforces his democratic credentials by opposing the attempted coup of 1981, when Colonel Tejero of the Guardia Civil storms the Cortes (parliament) along with other officers loyal to Franco's memory. The coup fails.

1982–96 In 1982, Felipe González's Socialist Workers' Party – the PSOE – are elected to office with the votes of nearly ten million Spaniards. It's an electoral landslide and the PSOE, buoyed up by the optimism of the times, promises change and progress. But González finds it hard to deliver and loses the enthusiasm of the left, his electoral power base. The left feels that González has followed a semi-monetarist policy, putting economic efficiency above social policies and rating the control of inflation as more urgent than the reduction of unemployment. Nevertheless, Spain's economy grows dramatically, the country becomes a respected member of the EU, and the PSOE attempt to deal with Spain's deep-seated separatist tendencies by permitting a large degree of regional autonomy. No effort is made to hunt down Franco's thugs – part of an accommodation between left and right designed to stop Spain from degenerating into a cycle of political revenge.

1996 At the general election, the Conservative Popular Party become the largest party in the Cortes, but do not get an overall majority. They enlist the support of Catalan and Basque nationalist deputies to form an administration. More regional autonomy is promised as part of the deal.

Flora and fauna

Despite their reputation as package-holiday destinations, Menorca and more especially Mallorca have much to offer birders and botanists alike. Separated from the Iberian Peninsula some fifty million years ago, the Balearic archipelago has evolved (at least in part) its own distinctive flora and fauna, with further variations between each of the islands. Among the wildlife, it's the raptors inhabiting the mountains of northwest Mallorca – particularly the black vulture – which attract much of the attention, but there are other pleasures too, especially the migratory birds which gather on the islands' saltpans and marshes in April and May and from mid-September to early October. The islands are also justifiably famous for their fabulous range of wild flowers and flowering shrubs.

Some of the islands' most important habitats have, however, been threatened by the developers. This has spawned an influential conservation group, **GOB** (Grup Balear d'Ornitologia i Defensa de la Naturalesa), which has recently launched several successful campaigns. It helped save the S'Albufera wetlands in Mallorca from further development, played a leading role in the black vulture re-establishment programme, and successfully lobbied to increase the penalties for shooting protected birds. GOB provide the latest environmental news in its quarterly periodical

Socarrell, which is available from larger book-shops. The group has offices in Palma (c/Veri 1-3), Maó (c/Cami d'es Castell 59) and Ciutadella (c/Mallorca s/n). Another useful contact is Graham Hearle, Aptdo 83, Sa Pobla (☎971 862418; e-mail, *grahamhearle@mx3.redestb.es*), the GOB/RSPB (Royal Society for the Protection of Birds) representative in Mallorca; he sometimes organizes birders' meetings in Port de Pollença.

The account of the islands' flora and fauna given below serves as a general introduction and includes mention of several important birding sites, cross-referenced to the descriptions given in the *Guide*. For more specialist information, some recommended **field guides** are listed on p.261.

Habitats

The Balearic Islands are a continuation of the Andalucian mountains of the Iberian Peninsula, from which they are separated by a submarine trench never less than 80km wide and up to 1500m deep. Mallorca, the largest of the islands, comprises three distinct geographical areas with two ranges of predominantly limestone hills falling either side of a central plain, **Es Pla**. Mallorca's northwest coast is dominated by the **Serra de Tramuntana** (in Castilian, Sierra del Norte), a slim, ninety-kilometre-long range of wooded hills and rocky peaks, fringed by tiny coves and precipitous seacliffs, that reaches its highest point at Puig Major (1447m). Also edged by steep seacliffs is the **Serres de Llevante**, a range of more modest hills that runs parallel to the island's east shore and rises to 509m at the Santuari de Sant Salvador.

Menorca has less topographical diversity, dividing into two distinct but not dramatically different zones. The rolling sandstone uplands of the northern half of the island are punctuated by wide, shallow valleys and occasional peaks, the highest of which is Monte Toro at 357m. To the south lie undulating limestone lowlands and deeper valleys. Both parts of the island are trimmed by dramatic seacliffs and scores of rocky coves.

Mallorca and Menorca have a temperate Mediterranean climate, with winter frosts a rarity, but there are significant differences between the two. The Serra de Tramuntana both protects the rest of Mallorca from the winds that blow from the north and catches most of the rain. Menorca, on the other hand, has no mountain barrier to protect it from the cold dry wind (the tramóntana) which buffets the island, giving much of its vegetation a wind-blown look and prompting the island's farmers to protect their crops with stone walls.

Mallorcan flora

The characteristic terrain of Mallorca up to around 700m is garigue, partly forested open scrubland where the island's native trees – Aleppo pines, wild olives, holm oaks, carobs and dwarf palms – intermingle with imported species like ash, elm and poplar. Between 700m and 950m, garigue is gradually replaced by maquis, a scrubland of rosemary, laurel, myrtle and broom interspersed with swaths of bracken. Higher still is a rocky terrain that can only support the sparsest of vegetation, such as an assortment of hardy grasses and low-growing rosemary.

Across much of the island, this indigenous vegetation has been destroyed by cultivation. However, the Aleppo pine and the evergreen holm oak – which traditionally supplied acorns for pigs, wood for charcoal and bark for tanning – are still common, as is the carob tree, which prefers the hottest and driest parts of the island. Arguably the archipelago's most handsome tree, the carob boasts leaves of varying greenness and conspicuous fruits – large pods which start green, but ripen to black-brown. The dwarf palm, with its sharp lance-like foliage, is concentrated around Pollença, Alcúdia and Andratx. The wild olive is comparatively rare (and may not be indigenous), but the cultivated variety – which boasts silver-grey foliage and can grow up to 10m in height – is endemic and has long been a mainstay of the local economy. There are also orange and lemon orchards around Sóller and literally millions of almond trees, whose pink and white blossom adorns much of Mallorca in late January and early February.

Mallorca has a wonderful variety of flowering shrubs. There are too many to list in any detail, but look out for the deep blue flowers of the rosemary, the reddish bloom of the lentisk (or mastic tree), the bright yellow broom which begins blossoming in March, the many types of tree heather and, especially around C'an Picafort, the autumn-flowering strawberry tree. Rockroses are also widely distributed, the most

common members of the group being the spring-flowering grey-leafed cistus, with its velvety leaves and pink flowers, and the narrow-leafed cistus whose bloom is white.

In spring and autumn the fields, verges, woods and cliffs of Mallorca brim with wild flowers. There are several hundred species and only in the depths of winter – from November to January – are all of them dormant. Amongst well-known species there are marigolds, daisies, violets, yellow primroses, gladioli, poppies, hyacinths, several kinds of cyclamen, the resinous St John's wort with its crinkled deep green leaves and, abundant in the pine woods near the sea and in the mountains, many types of orchid. Two common mountain plants are the pampas-like grass ampelodesmus mauritanica, giant clumps of which cover the hillsides, and a local variety of the sarsaparilla, smilax balearica, which flourishes in limestone crevices where its sharp thorns are something of a hazard for walkers. Other common and prominent plants are the giant-sized agave (century plant), an imported amaryllid with huge spear-shaped, leathery leaves of blue-grey coloration, which produces a massive flower spike every ten years (just before it dies). There's also the distinctive asphodel, whose tall spikes sport clusters of pink or white flowers from April to June. The asphodel grows on overgrazed or infertile land and its starch-rich tubers were once used by shoemakers to make glue. Another common sight is the prickly pear, traditionally grown behind peasants' houses as a windbreak and toilet wall. A versatile plant, the smell of the prickly pear deflects insects (hence its use round toilets) and its fruit is easy to make into pig food or jam.

Finally, many islanders maintain splendid gardens and here you'll see species that flourish throughout the Mediterranean, most famously bougainvilleas, oleanders, geraniums and hibiscus.

Mallorcan birds

The diverse birdlife of Mallorca has attracted ornithologists for decades. The island boasts a whole batch of resident species and these are supplemented by migrating flocks of North European birds that descend on the island in spring and autumn. The Serra de Tramuntana is a haven for predatory birds, such as ospreys, red kites, Eleanora's falcons, kestrels, peregrines, several sorts of eagle and, rarest of all, black vultures. The last-mentioned, with their two-metre wingspan, breed on the seacliffs in November and, although there are only about fifty of them remaining, there's a reasonable chance of a sighting in the vicinity of Puig Massanella (see p.138) or the Boquer valley (see p.149). The sea-cliffs of the Cap de Formentor (see p.151) are a good area to spot nesting colonies of **seabirds**, including shearwaters and shags.

Characteristic birds of the lower wooded slopes include wood pigeons, crossbills, firecrests and blue tits, whilst the island's scrubland provides excellent cover for a variety of **warblers** and **small songbirds**, such as nightingales and larks. These two types of terrain – and their associated birdlife – are seen to their best advantage again in the **Boquer valley**, near Port de Pollença (see p.149).

Two areas of special note are the S'Albufera wetlands, part of which has recently been designated a nature reserve, and the saltpans – Salines de Llevant – near Colònia de Sant Jordi. The marsh of **S'Albufera** and its surrounds (see p.157) is the most important birdwatching spot in the whole of the Balearics, its resident species augmented by hundreds of migrating birds, which find fresh water here after their long journey north or south. Amongst scores of species, the shorter grasses shelter moorhens, coots and crakes, while the reeds hide herons, egrets, flamingoes, green sandpipers, the occasional kingfishers, and the distinctive hoopoe (though this relatively common bird prefers cultivated fields), with its long beak and punkish orange and black head-feathers. On the opposite side of Mallorca are the Salines de Llevant (see p.191), where the saltpans are especially attractive to waders and terns, including the black-tailed godwit, little egret, black and whiskered tern, sandpiper, redshank, heron and avocet. In both areas, the abundance of prey attracts raptors, most frequently marsh harriers, kestrels and ospreys.

Other Mallorcan fauna

Mallorca's surviving **mammals** are an uninspiring bunch. The wild boar and red fox were eliminated early in the twentieth century, leaving a motley crew of mountain goats, wild sheep, pine martens, genets, weasels and feral cats, as well as such commonplace smaller mammals as hedgehogs, rabbits, hares and shrews. As far as **reptiles** go, there are four types of snake – all hard to come by – and two species of gecko (or broad-toed lizard), the lowland-living wall gecko and the mountain-dwelling disc-fingered version. With any luck, you'll spot them as they heat up in the sun, but they move fast since warm gecko is a tasty morsel for many a bird. Off the south coast of Mallorca, the desolate island of Cabrera has a large concentration of the rare, blue-under-sided **Lilfords wall lizard**.

Among **amphibians**, Mallorca has a healthy frog population, concentrated in its marshlands but also surviving in its mountain pools (up to around 800m). There are also three types of toad, of which the **Mallorcan midwife toad**, hanging on in the northern corner of the island, is the rarest. With no natural predators, its evolution involved a reduction in fecundity (it produces only a quarter of the number of eggs laid by its mainland relative) and the loss of its poison glands. However, with the introduction of the viperine snake, the resident midwife toads were all but wiped out – only about 500 pairs remain.

Common **insects** include grasshoppers and cicadas, whose summertime chirping is so evocative of warm Mediterranean nights, as well as over 200 species of moth and around 30 types of **butterfly**. Some of the more striking butterflies are red admirals, which are seen in winter, and the clouded yellow and painted ladies of spring. One of the more unusual species is the two-tailed pasha, a splendidly marked gold-and-bronze butterfly that flits around the coast in spring and late summer, especially in the vicinity of strawberry trees.

Menorcan flora and fauna

Far flatter than its neighbour, Menorca's indigenous vegetation is almost all **garigue**, though intensive cultivation has reduced the original forest cover to a fraction of its former size – nowadays only about fifteen percent of the island is wooded. Native trees are the holm oak, the dwarf palm, the carob and, commonest of all, the **Aleppo pine**, which has bright green spines, silvery twigs and ruddy-brown cones. Olive trees are endemic and dramatically illustrate the effects of the *tramóntana*, with grove upon grove bent almost double under the weight of the wind.

Menorca's soils nourish a superb range of **flowering shrubs** and **wild flowers**. There is less variety than on Mallorca, but the islands have many species in common. Menorca also boasts a handful of species entirely to itself, the most distinguished of them being the dwarf shrub **daphne rodriquezii**, a purple-flowering evergreen present on the cliffs of the northeast coast. In addition, the cliffs of much of the coast have a flora uniquely adapted to the combination of limestone yet saline soils. Here, **aromatic inula**, a shrubby perennial with clusters of yellow flowers, grows beside the **common caper**, with its red pods and purple seeds, and the **sea aster**.

The mammal, amphibian and insect populations of Mallorca and Menorca are very similar, but Menorca does excel in its **reptiles**. Of the four species of lizard which inhabit the Balearics, Menorca has populations of three. There are two types of wall lizard – Lilfords, a green, black and blue version, and the olive green and black-striped Italian lizard – as well as the Moroccan rock lizard, with olive skin or reticulated blue-green coloration. The **birds** of Menorca are less inspiring than those of Mallorca and, in particular, there are very few species of raptor – the marsh harrier is the most common. The island's best birdwatching spot is the marshland round the lake of S'Albufera, near the village of Es Grau (see p.212).

Books

Most of the following books should be readily available in the UK or North America, although a few are obtainable only in Mallorca and Menorca. We have given UK and US publishers for each title, unless the book is published in one country only; o/p means out of print.

In the UK, Books on Spain (PO Box 207, Twickenham, London TW2 5BQ ☎ & fax 0181/898 7789) can supply all manner of rare and in- and out-of-print books about Spain. Their comprehensive catalogue, available free from the above address, includes sections on topics such as travel, Spain since 1900, plus other regions including the Pyrenees, Portugal and Latin America.

Impressions and travel accounts

Tom Crichton, *Our Man in Majorca* (Robert Hale, UK, o/p). The American sailor, adventurer and journalist Tom Crichton was briefly a package-tour representative on Mallorca in the early 1960s. With the encouragement of Robert Graves, he published this account of a comical, disaster-filled fortnight. A book for the sunbed.

Paul Richardson, *Not Part of the Package* (Picador, UK). Richardson spent a year observing and enjoying the razzle-dazzle of Ibiza. His idiosyncratic tales are diverting and revealing in equal measure – and, by implication, throw light on the way mass tourism works in the Balearics as a whole.

George Sand, *A Winter in Majorca* (M&N Publishing, Mallorca). Accompanied by her lover, Frédéric Chopin, Sand spent the winter of 1838–39 resident in the monastery of Valldemossa, on Mallorca. These are her recollections, ponderous in style and very critical of the islanders. Readily available in Valldemossa and Mallorca's better bookshops.

Gordon West, *Jogging Round Majorca* (Black Swan, UK). This gentle, humorous account of an extended journey round Mallorca by Gordon and Mary West in the 1920s vividly portrays the island's pre-tourist life and times. The trip had nothing to do with running, but rather "jogging" as in a leisurely progress. West's book lay forgotten for decades until a BBC Radio 4 presenter, Leonard Pearcey, stumbled across it in a secondhand bookshop and subsequently read extracts on air. The programmes were very well received, and the book was first reprinted in 1994.

History

David Abulafia, *A Mediterranean Emporium: the Catalan Kingdom of Majorca* (Cambridge University Press, UK & US). Serious-minded, detailed study of medieval Mallorca.

Raymond Carr, *Spain 1808–1975* and *Modern Spain 1875–1980* (Oxford University Press, UK & US). Two of the best books available on modern Spanish history – concise and well-considered narratives.

J. H. Elliott, *Imperial Spain 1469–1716* (Penguin, UK & US). The best introduction to Spain's "golden age" – academically respected as well as being a gripping yarn.

Desmond Gregory, *Minorca, the Illusory Prize: History of the British Occupation of Minorca between 1708 and 1802* (Fairleigh Dickinson University Press, UK & US). Exhaustive, scholarly and well-composed narrative detailing the British colonial involvement with Menorca.

Bruce Laurie, *Life of Richard Kane: Britain's First Lieutenant Governor of Minorca* (Fairleigh Dickinson University Press, UK & US). Detailed historical biography providing an intriguing insight into eighteenth-century Menorca.

Geoffrey Parker, *The Army of Flanders and the Spanish Road (1567–1659)* (Cambridge University Press, UK & US). Sounds dry and academic, but this fascinating book gives a marvellous insight into the workings of the Spanish army, then the most feared in Europe.

Hugh Thomas, *The Spanish Civil War* (Penguin, UK; Touchstone, US). Exhaustively researched, brilliantly detailed account of the war and the complex political manoeuvrings surrounding it, with sections on Mallorca and Menorca. First published in 1961 and now in its third edition, it remains easily the best book on the subject.

Fiction and general background

Barbara Catoir, *Miró on Mallorca* (Prestel, UK & US). Lavishly illustrated book covering Miró's lengthy residence in Cala Major, just outside Palma. There's discussion of the work Miró produced in this period and of his thoughts on the island. Too hagiographical for some tastes.

Juan Goytisolo, *The Virtues of the Solitary Bird* and *Makbara* (Serpent's Tail, UK & US). Born in Barcelona in 1931, Goytisolo is widely acclaimed as being one of Spain's leading novelists. The first of these two titles (from 1988) is a deep and powerful study of pain and repression, the second (from 1980) explores the Arab culture of North Africa in sharp and perceptive style.

William Graves, *Wild Olives* (Pimlico, UK). The son of Robert Graves, William was born in 1940 and spent much of his childhood in Palma and Deià, sufficient inspiration for mildly diverting accounts of his Mallorcan contemporaries. The book's real focus, however, is his troubled family life and his difficult relationship with his father. Published in 1995, the centenary of Robert's birth.

John Hooper, *The New Spaniards: A Portrait of the New Spain* (Penguin, UK & US). Well-constructed and extremely perceptive portrait of post-Franco Spain; an excellent general introduction. Highly recommended.

Ramon Llull, *Selected Works of Ramon Llull*, ed. Anthony Bonner (Princeton, UK & US); *Doctor Illuminatus: A Ramon Llull Reader*, ed. Anthony Bonner (Mythos, UK; Princeton/Bollingen, US). Not for the faint-hearted, the Mallorcan scholar and philosopher Ramon Llull wrote lengthy and heavy-going treatises on mysticism and Christian zeal in the thirteenth century. His works were some of the first to be written in Catalan.

Juan Masoliver (ed), *The Origins of Desire: Modern Spanish Short Stories* (Serpent's Tail, UK & US). Enjoyable selection of short stories from some of Spain's leading contemporary writers, including Mallorca's own Valentí Puig and Carme Riera.

Ana María Matute, *School of the Sun* (Quartet, UK; Columbia University Press, US). The loss of childhood innocence on the Balearics, where old enmities are redefined during the Civil War.

Manuel Vazquez Montalban, *Murder in the Central Committee*, *The Angst-ridden Executive*, *Off Side* and others (Serpent's Tail, UK & US). Riveting tales by Spain's most popular crime thriller writer, a long-time member of the Communist Party and now a well-known journalist resident in Barcelona. Original and wonderfully entertaining.

Miranda Seymour, *Robert Graves: Life on the Edge* (Doubleday, UK). Lengthy account of Robert Graves's personal life with lacklustre commentary on his poetry and novels. Much detail on Graves's residence in Deià, Mallorca. Published in 1995, to mark the centenary of Graves's birth.

Llorenç Villalonga, *The Doll's Room* (o/p). Subtle portrait of nobility in decline in nineteenth-century Mallorca by an island writer. An interesting read, but rather stodgy in style. First published in 1956.

Specialist guidebooks

Herbert Heinrich, *Twelve Classic Hikes through Mallorca* (Editorial Moll, Mallorca). Heinrich has published a number of Mallorcan hiking guides in German. This was his first (and best) English volume, a compilation of some of the most enjoyable and less demanding one-day hikes in the mountains of northwest Mallorca. The descriptions are a bit patchy, but the topographical sketches are extremely helpful. Widely available in Mallorca. Also, *Walking in Southwest Mallorca* (Editorial Moll, Mallorca). Several good one-day hikes and useful topographical sketches.

Gaspar Martí, *Walking Tours around the Historical Centre of Palma* (Ajuntament de Palma, Mallorca). Detailed and enjoyable exploration of Palma's historical nooks and crannies. Beautiful sketches illuminate the text. Published by Palma Town Hall and available in all leading Palma bookshops.

June Parker, *Walking in Mallorca* (Cicerone, UK). Highly recommended: detailed and accurate accounts of over seventy Mallorcan hikes, to suit almost all levels of fitness.

Flora and fauna

John Busby, *Birds in Majorca* (Christopher Helm, UK). Well-illustrated catalogue of Mallorcan birdlife.

John and Margaret Goulding, *Menorca* (Windrush, UK; Interlink, US). A general travel guide with detailed and informative lists describing Menorca's flora and fauna.

Oleg Polunin and Anthony Huxley, *Flowers of the Mediterranean* (Hogarth, UK). Useful if by no means exhaustive field guide.

Ken Stoba, *Birdwatching in Mallorca* (Cicerone, UK). An excellent introduction to Mallorca's birdlife and major birdwatching sites.

Language

Most of the inhabitants of Mallorca and Menorca are bilingual, speaking Castilian (ie Spanish) and their local dialect of the Catalan language (either *Mallorquín* or *Menorquín*) with equal facility. *Català* (Catalan) has been the islanders' everyday language since the Reconquest and absorption into the Kingdom of Aragón and Catalunya in the thirteenth century, whereas Castilian was imposed much later from the mainland as the language of government – and with special rigour by Franco. As a result, Spain's recent move towards regional autonomy has been accompanied by the islanders' assertion of Catalan as their official language. The most obvious sign of this has been the change of all the old Castilian town and street names into Catalan versions. On paper, Catalan looks like a cross between French and Spanish and is generally easy to understand if you know those two, although when spoken it has a very harsh sound and is far harder to come to grips with.

Some background

When Franco came to power in 1939, publishing houses, bookshops and libraries were raided and *Català* books destroyed. While there was some relaxation in the mid-1940s, the language was still banned from the radio, TV, daily press and, most importantly, schools, which is why many older people today cannot read or write *Català* (even if they speak it all the time); in the Balearics, the best-selling Catalan-language

newspapers still have modest sales figures compared with the most popular Castilian-language daily papers. The linguistic picture has been further muddied by the emigration of thousands of mainland Spaniards to the islands, and nowadays it's estimated that Castilian is the dominant language in around forty percent of island households.

Català is spoken by over six million people in total in the Balearics, Catalunya, part of Aragón, most of Valencia, Andorra and parts of the French Pyrenees; it is thus much more widely spoken than several better-known languages such as Danish, Finnish and Norwegian. It is a Romance language, stemming from Latin and more directly from medieval Provençal. Spaniards in the rest of the country belittle it by saying that to get a *Català* word you just cut a Castilian one in half (which is often true!), but in fact the grammar is much more complicated than Castilian and there are eight vowel sounds, three more than in Castilian.

Getting by in Mallorca and Menorca

Although Catalan is the preferred language of most islanders, you'll almost always get by perfectly well if you speak Castilian (Spanish) as long as you're aware of the use of Catalan in timetables and so forth. Once you get into it, Castilian is one of the easiest languages there is, the rules of pronunciation pretty straightforward and strictly observed. You'll find some basic pronunciation rules below for both *Català* and Castilian, and a selection of words and phrases in both languages. Castilian is certainly easier to pronounce, but don't be afraid to try *Català*, especially in the more out-of-the-way places – you'll generally get a good reception if you at least try communicating in the local language.

Castilian/Spanish: a few rules

Unless there's an accent, words ending in d, l, r, and z are **stressed** on the last syllable, all others on the second last. All **vowels** are pure and short; combinations have predictable results.

A somewhere between the A sound of back and that of father.

E as in get.

I as in police.

O as in hot.

U as in rule.

C is lisped before E and I, hard otherwise: *cerca* is pronounced "thairka".

CH is pronounced as in English.

G works the same way, a guttural H sound (like the *ch* in loch) before E or I, a hard G elsewhere – *gigante* becomes "higante".

H is always silent.

J the same sound as a guttural G: *jamón* is pronounced "hamon".

LL sounds like an English Y: *tortilla* is pronounced "torteeya".

N as in English unless it has a tilde (accent) over it, when it becomes NY: *mañana* sounds like "man-yarna".

QU is pronounced like an English K.

R is rolled, RR doubly so.

V sounds more like B, *vino* becoming "beano".

X has an S sound before consonants, normal X before vowels.

Z is the same as a soft C, so *cerveza* becomes "thairvaitha".

Català: a few rules

With *Català*, don't be tempted to use the few rules of Spanish pronunciation you may know – in particular the soft Spanish Z and C don't apply, so unlike in the rest of Spain it's not "Barthelona" but "Barcelona", as in English.

A as in hat if stressed, as in alone when unstressed.

E varies, but usually as in get.

I as in police.

IG sounds like the "tch" in the English scratch; *lleig* (ugly) is pronounced "yeah-tch".

O varies, but usually as in hot.

U somewhere between the U sound of put and rule.

Ç sounds like an English S; *plaça* is pronounced "plassa".

C followed by an E or I is soft; otherwise hard.

G followed by E or I is like the "zh" in Zhivago; otherwise hard.

H is always silent.

J as in the French "Jean".

LL sounds like an English Y or LY, like the "yuh" sound in million.

N as in English, though before F or V it sometimes sounds like an M.

NY replaces the Castilian Ñ.

QU before E or I sounds like K; before A or O as in "quit".

R is rolled, but only at the start of a word; at the end it's often silent.

T is pronounced as in English, though sometimes it sounds like a D, as in *viatge* or *dotze*.

TX is pronounced like English CH.

V at the start of a word sounds like B; in all other positions it's a soft "F" sound.

W is pronounced like a B/V.

X is like SH in most words, though in some, like *exit*, it sounds like an X.

Z is like the English Z in zoo.

Phrasebooks, dictionaries and teaching yourself

Spanish

Numerous Spanish phrasebooks are available in Britain, the most user-friendly being the *Rough Guide Spanish Phrasebook*. Harrap's small dictionaries are reliable. For teaching yourself the language, the BBC tape series *España Viva* is excellent.

Many of the books available in North America are geared to New World, Latin American usage; more old-fashioned publications may be better for Spain itself. Cassells, Collins and Langenscheidt all produce useful dictionaries; Berlitz publishes separate Spanish and Latin American Spanish phrasebooks.

Català

It's much harder to track down books that can help you with *Català*. In Britain, there's only one English–Catalan phrasebook in print, *Parla Català* (Pia), and for a dictionary you're limited to the version published by Routledge. For teaching yourself the language, there's the excellent *Catalan in Three Months* (Stuart Poole, UK), a combined paperback and tape package. Spanish speakers can also use a total immersion course called *Digui Digui*, a series of books and tapes published by L'Abadia de Montserrat.

Words and phrases

Basics

	Spanish	Catalan
Yes, No, OK	*Sí, No, Vale*	*Sí, No, Val*
Please, Thank you	*Por favor, Gracias*	*Per favor, Gràcies*
Where, When	*Dónde, Cuando*	*On, Quan*
What, How much	*Qué, Cuánto*	*Què, Quant*
Here, There	*Aquí, Allí, Allá*	*Aquí, Allí, Allà*
This, That	*Esto, Eso*	*Això, Allò*
Now, Later	*Ahora, Más tarde*	*Ara, Més tard*
Open, Closed	*Abierto/a, Cerrado/a*	*Obert, Tancat*
With, Without	*Con, Sin*	*Amb, Sense*
Good, Bad	*Buen(o)/a, Mal(o)/a*	*Bo(na), Dolent(a)*
Big, Small	*Gran(de), Pequeño/a*	*Gran, Petit(a)*
Cheap, Expensive	*Barato/a, Caro/a*	*Barat(a), Car(a)*
Hot, Cold	*Caliente, Frío/a*	*Calent(a), Fred(a)*
More, Less	*Más, Menos*	*Més, Menys*
Today, Tomorrow	*Hoy, Mañana*	*Avui, Demà*
Yesterday	*Ayer*	*Ahir*
Day before yesterday	*Anteayer*	*Abans-d'ahir*
Next week	*La semana que viene*	*La setmana que ve*
Next month	*El mes que viene*	*El mes que ve*

Greetings and responses

	Spanish	Catalan
Hello, Goodbye	*Hola, Adiós*	*Hola, Adéu*
Good morning	*Buenos días*	*Bon dia*
Good afternoon/night	*Buenas tardes/noches*	*Bona tarda/nit*
See you later	*Hasta luego*	*Fins després*
Sorry	*Lo siento/disculpéme*	*Ho sento*
Excuse me	*Con permiso/perdón*	*Perdoni*
How are you?	*¿Cómo está (usted)?*	*Com va?*
I (don't) understand	*(No) Entiendo*	*(No) Ho entenc*
Not at all/You're welcome	*De nada*	*De res*
Do you speak English?	*¿Habla (usted) inglés?*	*Parla anglès?*
I (don't) speak Spanish/Catalan	*(No) Hablo Español*	*(No) Parlo Català*
My name is ...	*Me llamo ...*	*Em dic ...*
What's your name?	*¿Como se llama usted?*	*Com es diu?*
I am English	*Soy inglés(a)*	*Sóc anglès(a)*
Scottish	*escocés(a)*	*escocès(a)*
Australian	*australiano/a*	*australià/ana*
Canadian	*canadiense/a*	*canadenc(a)*
American	*americano/a*	*americà/ana*
Irish	*irlandés(a)*	*irlandès(a)*
Welsh	*galés(a)*	*gallès(a)*

Hotels and transport

	Spanish	Catalan
I want	*Quiero*	*Vull (pronounced "fwee")*
I'd like	*Quisiera*	*Voldria*
Do you know ... ?	*¿Sabe ... ?*	*Vostès saben ... ?*
I don't know	*No sé*	*No sé*
There is (is there?)	*(¿)Hay(?)*	*Hi ha(?)*

Hotels and transport (continued)

	Spanish	Catalan
Give me . . .	Deme . . .	Doneu-me . . .
Do you have . . . ?	¿Tiene . . . ?	Té . . . ?
. . . the time	. . . la hora	. . . l'hora
. . . a room	. . . una habitación	. . . alguna habitació
. . . with two beds/ double bed	. . . con dos camas/ cama matrimonial	. . . amb dos llits/ llit per dues persones
. . . with shower/bath	. . . con ducha/baño	. . . amb dutxa/bany
for one person (two people)	para una persona (dos personas)	per a una persona (dues persones)
for one night (one week)	para una noche (una semana)	per una nit (una setmana)
It's fine, how much is it?	Está bien, ¿cuánto es?	Esta bé, quant és?
It's too expensive	Es demasiado caro	És massa car
Don't you have anything cheaper?	¿No tiene algo más barato?	En té de més bon preu?
Can one . . . ?	¿Se puede . . . ?	Es pot . . . ?
. . . camp (near) here?	¿ . . . acampar aqui (cerca)?	. . . acampar a la vora?
Is there a hostel nearby?	¿Hay un hostal aquí cerca?	Hi ha un hostal a la vora?
It's not very far	No es muy lejos	No és gaire lluny
How do I get to . . . ?	¿Por donde se va a . . . ?	Per anar a . . . ?
Left, right, straight on	Izquierda, derecha, todo recto	A l'esquerra, a la dreta, tot recte
Where is . . . ?	¿Dónde está . . . ?	On és . . . ?
. . . the bus station	. . . la estación de autobuses	. . . l'estació de autobuses
. . . the bus stop	. . . la parada	. . . la parada
. . . the railway station	. . . la estación de ferrocarril	. . . l'estació
. . . the nearest bank	. . . el banco más cercano	. . . el banc més a prop
. . . the post office	. . . el correo/la oficina de correos	. . . l'oficina de correus
. . . the toilet	. . . el baño/aseo/servicio	. . . la toaleta
Where does the bus to . . . leave from?	¿De dónde sale el autobús para . . . ?	De on surt el auto bús a . . . ?
Is this the train for Barcelona?	¿Es este el tren para Barcelona?	Aquest tren va a Barcelona?
I'd like a (return) ticket to . . .	Quisiera un billete (de ida y vuelta) para . . .	Voldria un billlet (d'anar i tornar) a . . .
What time does it leave (arrive in . . .)?	¿A qué hora sale (llega a . . .)?	A quina hora surt (arriba a . . .)?
What is there to eat?	¿Qué hay para comer?	Què hi ha per menjar?
What's that?	¿Qué es eso?	Què és això?

Days of the week	Spanish	Catalan
Monday	lunes	dilluns
Tuesday	martes	dimarts
Wednesday	miércoles	dimecres
Thursday	jueves	dijous
Friday	viernes	divendres
Saturday	sábado	dissabte
Sunday	domingo	diumenge

Numbers	Spanish	Catalan		Spanish	Catalan
1	un/uno/una	un(a)	19	diecinueve	dinou
2	dos	dos (dues)	20	veinte	vint
3	tres	tres	21	veintiuno	vint-i-un
4	cuatro	quatre	30	treinta	trenta
5	cinco	cinc	40	cuarenta	quaranta
6	seis	sis	50	cincuenta	cinquanta
7	siete	set	60	sesenta	seixanta
8	ocho	vuit	70	setenta	setanta
9	nueve	nou	80	ochenta	vuitanta
10	diez	deu	90	noventa	novanta
11	once	onze	100	cien(to)	cent
12	doce	dotze	101	ciento uno	cent un
13	trece	tretze	102	ciento dos	cent dos (dues)
14	catorce	catorze	200	doscientos	dos-cents
15	quince	quinze			(dues-centes)
16	dieciseis	setze	500	quinientos	cinc-cents
17	diecisiete	disset	1000	mil	mil
18	dieciocho	divuit	2000	dos mil	dos mil

Glossary

Albufera Lagoon (and surrounding wetlands).

Altar major High altar.

Ajuntament Town Hall.

Aparcament Parking.

Avinguda (Avgda) Avenue.

Badia Bay.

Barranc Ravine.

Barroc Baroque, the art and architecture of the Counter-Reformation, dating from around 1600 onwards, elements of which – particularly its ornate gaudiness – remained popular in the Balearics well into the twentieth century.

Basílica Catholic church with honorific privileges.

Cala Small bay, cove.

Camí Way or road.

Ca'n At the house of (contraction of *casa + en*).

Capella Chapel.

Carrer (c/) Street.

Carretera Road, highway.

Castell Castle.

Celler Cellar or a bar in a cellar.

Churrigueresque Fancifully ornate form of Baroque art named after the Spaniard José Churriguera (1650–1723) and his extended family, its leading exponents.

Claustre Cloister.

Coll Col, mountain pass.

Convent Convent, nunnery or monastery.

Correu Post office.

Coves Caves.

Cyclopean Prehistoric style of dry-stone masonry comprising boulders of irregular form.

Església Church.

Estany Small lake.

Festa Festival.

Finca Estate or farmhouse.

Font Water fountain or spring.

Gòtic Gothic.

Illa Island.

Jardí Garden.

Llac Lake.

Majolica Fine pottery coated with an opaque enamel and decorated with metallic colours. The term originally referred to Mallorcan-made pottery only, but was adopted by the Italians in the 15th century to describe their own products.

Mercat Market.

Mirador Watchtower or viewpoint.

Modernisme (Modernista) Literally "modernism" ("modernist"), the Catalan form of Art Nouveau, whose most famous exponent was Antoni Gaudí.

Monestir Monastery.

Mozarabe Christian subject of medieval Moorish ruler; hence **Mozarabic**, a colourful building style that reveals both Christian and Moorish influences.

Mudéjar Moor subject to medieval Christian ruler. Also a style of architecture developed by Moorish craftsmen working for Christians, characterized by painted woodwork with strong colours and complex geometrical patterns; revived between the 1890s and 1930s and blended with Art Nouveau forms.

Museu Museum.

Nostra Senyora The Virgin Mary (lit. "Our Lady").

Oficina d'Informació Turística Tourist office.

Palau Palace, mansion or manor house.

Parc Park.

Passeig Boulevard; the evening stroll along it.

Pic Summit.

Plaça Square.

Plateresque Elaborately decorative Renaissance architectural style, named for its resemblance to silversmiths' work (*platería*).

Platja Beach.

Pont Bridge.

Port Harbour, port.

Porta Door, gate.

Puig Hill.

Rambla Avenue or boulevard.

Rei King.

Reial Royal.

Reina Queen.

Reixa Iron screen or grille, usually in front of a window.

Renaixença Rebirth, often used to describe the Catalan cultural revival at the end of the nine-teenth and beginning of the twentieth centuries. Architecturally, this was expressed as *Modernisme*.

Retaule Retable or reredos, a wooden, ornamental panel behind an altar.

Riu River.

Romeria Pilgrimage or gathering at a shrine.

Salinas Saltpans.

Salt d'aigua Waterfall.

Santuari Sanctuary.

Sant/a Saint.

Serra Mountain range.

Talayot Cone-shaped prehistoric watchtower.

Taula T-shaped prehistoric monolith.

Torrent Stream or river (usually dry in summer).

Urbanització Modern urbanization or estate development.

Vall Valley.

Index

A

accommodation 34
airlines
  in Australia 14
  in Britain 4
  in Ireland 9
  in North America 11
Alaior 218
Alaró 114
Alcúdia 153–154
Alfabia, Jardins d' 112
Algaida 165
Andratx 131
Arenal d'En Castell 213
Artà 170

B

Badia de Palma 91
bail bonds 31
banks 29
Banyalbufar 130
bars 45
Bendinat 96
Biniaraix 109
Binibeca Vell 211
Binidali 211
Binissalem 43, 152
Binisues 223
books 259–261
Bóquer Valley 149
bullfighting 49
Bunyola 113
buses
  from Britain 7
  in Mallorca and Menorca 30

C

Cabrera island 190
Cala Blanca 236
Cala Bona 178
Cala Bóquer 149
Cala d'Alcaufar 210
Cala de Algaiarens 236
Cala de Deià 117, 119
Cala d'Or 183
Cala En Porter 212

Cala En Turqueta 235
Cala Esmeralda 184
Cala Figuera 185
Cala Fornells 99
Cala Gamba 93
Cala Gran 183
Cala Llombards 186
Cala Llonga 184
Cala Macarella 225
Cala Major 95
Cala Millor 178
Cala Mitjana 224
Cala Mondragó 185
Cala Morell 236
Cala Pi 192
Cala Pregonda 216
Cala Rajada 174–176
Cala Sant Vicenç 145
Cala Santa Galdana 224
Cala Santandría 236
Cala Santanyí 186
Cala Tirant 215
Cala Trebalúger 225
Cala Tuent 135
Cales Coves 211
Cales de Mallorca 181
Calvià 97
Camp de Mar 100
camping 36
Campos 192
Ca'n Pastilla 93
Ca'n Picafort 157
Cap de Cavalleria 215
Cap de Favaritx 213
Cap de Formentor 151
Cap de Ses Salines 187
Capdellà 129
Capdepera 173
Capocorp Vell 192, 242
car rental 32
casas de huéspedes 34
Castell d'Alaró 113
Castell de Bellver 84
Castell de Santueri 183
Castell del Rei 144
Castell Santa Agueda 223

Castilian 262–266
Castilian food glossaries 38–42
Catalan 262–266
Catalan food glossaries 38–42
children, travelling with 55
Chopin, Frédéric 122, 123
CIUTADELLA 225–234
  accommodation 227
  Ajuntament 229
  arrival 227
  bars 233
  cafés 233
  Castell de Sant Nicolau 232
  Cathedral 229
  ferry terminal 227
  listings 233
  Museu Diocesà 230
  Museu Municipal 231
  orientation 227
  Palau Salord 229
  parking 227
  Plaça d'es Born 228
  restaurants 233
  Sant Crist 231
  Ses Voltes 232
  tourist information 227
climate table xiii
Colònia de Sant Jordi
  189–190
Colònia de Sant Pere 172
consulates in Mallorca 90
contraceptives 27
Cornadors Circuit 109
Costa de Los Pinos 178
Coves d'Artà 176
Coves del Drac 180
Coves d'es Hams 181
credit cards 29
crime 52
currency exchange 29
cycling 33

D

Deià 115–121, 125
dentists 27
dictionaries 263
disabled travellers 22

doctors 27
drinking, eating and 37
driving
  licences 31
  rules 31
  to the Balearics 7

E

eating and drinking 37
electricity 55
Els Calderers 168
emergencies 27, 52
Ermita de Betlem 171
Ermita de Nostra Senyora del
  Puig 142
Es Castell 209
Es Grau 212
Es Mercadal 221
Es Migjorn Gran 222
Es Trenc 191
Escorca 136
Esporles 129
Estellencs 130
euro, The 28
exchange, currency 29
exchange rate 28

F

fauna, flora and 255–258, 261
Felanitx 182
Ferreries 222
ferries
  between Mallorca and Menorca
    33
  from Britain 8
  from Ibiza and Formentera 18
  from mainland Spain 16
festivals 50–51
fincas 36
flights
  between Mallorca and Menorca
    33
  from Australia 13
  from Britain 3
  from Ibiza and Formentera 18
  from Ireland 9
  from mainland Spain 16
  from North America 10
flora and fauna 255–258, 261
fly–drive 32
fondas 34
food
  glossaries 38–42
  vegan 42
  vegetarian 42

football 49
Formentor peninsula 151
Fornalutx 109
Fornells 214–215
Fundació Pilar i Joan Miró 95

G

Galilea 129
Gaudí, Antoni 71
glossary 267–268
Golden Farm 208
Gordiola Glassworks 164
Gorg Blau 135
Graves, Robert 115–117
Grup Balear d'Ornitologia i
  Defensa de la Naturalesa
  (GOB) 255

H

health 27
hikes 119, 125, 138, 149
history
  of Mallorca and Menorca
    241–250
  of Spain (principal dates)
    251–254
hostals 35
hostels, youth 35
hotels 35

I

Illa Dragonera 132
Illetes 96
Inca 152
information offices 24
insurance 20
Internet sites 26
IVA 28, 41

J

Jardins d'Alfabia 112

K

Kane, Camí d'En 217
Kane, Richard 216, 248

L

La Granja 128
La Mola 208
language 262–266
Las Maravillas 94
laundries 55
Le Shuttle 7

Lilfords wall lizard 191, 257
Lluc monastery 136–138
Llucalcari 118
Llucmajor 192
Llull, Ramon 79, 165

M

Magaluf 98
Mallorcan Primitives (painters)
  72, 76
Manacor 169
MAÓ 197–206
  accommodation 199
  airport 197
  Ajuntament 201
  arrival 197
  bars 205
  bus stands 199
  cafés 204
  Carrer Isabel II 201
  Claustre del Carme 201
  ferry terminal 199
  gin distillery, Xoriguer 203
  hotels 200
  listings 205
  Museu de Menorca 202
  nightclubs 205
  orientation 199
  parking 199
  Plaça Constitució 201
  Plaça Espanya 201
  Plaça S'Esplanada 203
  quayside 203
  restaurants 204
  Sant Francesc 202
  Santa Maria 201
  tapas bars 204
  tourist information 197, 199
  Xoriguer gin distillery 203
maps 24
March, Banca 82
March, Joan 80
March, Palau (Palma) 80
March, Palau Joan
  (Cala Rajada) 174
Massanella, Puig de 135, 138
Maura, Antoni 80
Miró, Joan 95, 123
Mola, General 81
monastery accommodation
  35, 138, 144, 165, 168, 182
Monestir de Lluc 136–138
Monte Toro 221
Montuiri 166
mopeds 32
Muro 158

N

Na Macaret 213
Naveta d'es Tudons 235, 242
navetas 196, 242
newspapers 46

O

opening hours 47
Orient 113

P

packages
  from Britain 5
  from Ireland 10
PALMA 59–91
  accommodation 65
  airport 61
  Ajuntament 79
  arrival 61
  Banys Àrabs 75
  bars, late-night 88
  bars, tapas 85
  Basílica de Sant Francesc 78
  buses 64, 90
  cafés 85
  Can Rei 83
  Can Solleric 80
  Castell de Bellver 84
  Cathedral 68
  City walls 74
  El Puig de Sant Pere 80
  ferry terminal 63
  Gran Hotel 82
  harbourfront 81
  hotels 65
  L'Àguila 83
  La Llotja 81
  listings 89
  Mallorcan Primitives (painters)
    72, 76
  mansions 76
  Museu d'Art Espanyol
    Contemporani 82
  Museu de la Catedral 72
  Museu de Mallorca 75
  Museu Diocesà 73
  nightclubs 89
  nightlife 87
  old town 75
  orientation 64
  Palau de l'Almudaina 73
  Palau March 80
  Parc Cuarentena 81
  Parc de la Mar 74
  parking 65
  Passeig d'es Born 79
  performing arts 88

Plaça Cort 79
Plaça Major 82
Plaça Weyler 82
Poble Espanyol 83
restaurants 86
Sant Miquel 83
Santa Eulalia 77
tapas bars 85
theatres 82, 88
tourist offices 61, 64
train stations 64
Palma Nova 97
Parc Natural de S'Albufera
  (Mallorca) 157, 257
pearls, artificial 166, 169
Peguera 99
pensions 34
Petra 167
petrol 31
pharmacies 27
phrasebooks 263
Platges Son Saura 235
Platja de Binimel·Là 216
Platja de Canyamel 177
Platja de Formentor 151
Platja de Palma 94
Poble Espanyol (Palma) 83
police 52
Pollença 141–144
Port d'Addaia 213
Port d'Alcúdia 154–157
Port d'Andratx 132–134
Port d'es Canonge 130
Port de Maó 207–209
Port de Pollença 146–148, 149
Port de Sóller 110–112, 119
Port de Valldemossa 128
Portals Nous 96
Portals Vells 98
Porto Colom 181
Porto Cristo 178–180
Porto Petro 184
post 45
public holidays 48
Puig de Massanella 135, 138
Puig d'es Teix 125
Puig Major 135
Puig Randa 165
Puigpunyent 129
Punta Prima 211

R

racions 38
radio 47

Randa 165
restaurants 39
robberies 52

S

S'Albufera (Mallorca) 157, 257
S'Albufera (Menorca) 213
S'Algar 210
S'Arenal 94
S'Illot 178
Sa Calobra 135
Sa Mesquida 208
Salines de Llevant 191, 257
Salvator, Ludwig 121
Sant Elm 131
Sant Esteve 209
Sant Jaume Mediterrani 220
Sant Lluís 210
Sant Tomás 222
Santa Ponça 99
Santanyí 185
Santuari de la Victòria 154
Santuari de Nostra Senyora de
  Cura 165
Santuari de Sant Salvador 182
Serra, Junipero 78, 167
Ses Paisses 171, 242
Ses Voltes 232
sexual harassment 53
Shuttle, The 7
Sineu 167
SNTO offices 23
Sóller 105–108
Sóller train 105
Sometimes 94
Son Bou 220, 243
Son Catlar 235
Son Marroig 121
Son Parc 214
Son Vitamina 211
Spanish embassies and
  consulates 19
Spanish language 262–266
Spanish National Tourist
  Offices 23
speed limits 31

T

Talatí de Dalt 207, 242
Talayotic
  culture 196, 241
  sites (Menorca) 206, 242

talayots 196, 241
tapas 38
taulas 196, 242
taxis 31
teaching 54
Teix, Puig d'es 125
telephones 46
television 47
time zone 55
tipping 41
toilets, public 55
Torralba d'En Salort 219, 242
Torre d'En Gaumes 220
Torrellafuda 236
Torrent de Pareis 135, 136
tour operators
  in Britain 6
  in North America 13
Tourist Offices, Spanish
  National 23
trains
  from Britain 6
  in Mallorca 30
  to Sóller 105
travel agents
  in Australia 15
  in Britain 4
  in Ireland 9
  in North America 12
travel insurance 20
travellers' cheques 29
Trepucó 206

V

Vall de Bóquer 149

Valldemossa 122–124, 125
vegan food 42
vegetarian food 42
visas 19

W

wine 42
wiring money 29
work 54

X

Xoriguer gin distillery 203

Y

youth hostels 35

Stay in touch with us!

ROUGH*NEWS* is Rough Guides' free newsletter.
In three issues a year we give you news, travel
issues, music reviews, readers' letters and the
latest dispatches from authors on the road.

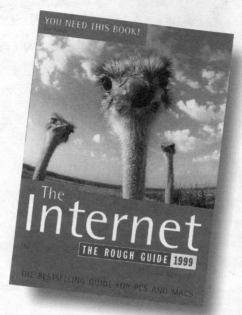

¿Qué pasa?

WHAT'S HAPPENING?
A ROUGH GUIDES SERIES –
ROUGH GUIDES PHRASEBOOKS

Rough Guide Phrasebooks
represent a complete shakeup
of the phrasebook format.
Handy and pocket sized, they
work like a dictionary to get you
straight to the point. With clear
guidelines on pronunciation,
dialogues for typical situations,
and tips on cultural issues, they'll
have you speaking the language
quicker than any other
phrasebook.

Czech, French, German, Greek,
Hindi & Urdu, Hungarian, Indonesian,
Italian, Japanese, Mandarin Chinese,
Mexican Spanish, Polish, Portuguese,
Russian, Spanish, Thai, Turkish,
Vietnamese

Further titles coming soon...

Thurs: Palma

Fri: Port d'Andrátx
Camp de Mar

Sat: Soller
Port de Soller
Fundacio Miro
Palma Nova

Sun: Valldemosa
Deia
Port de Soller
Soller (Fiesta)

Mon: Port de Soller

Tues: Lluc
Port de Pollensa.

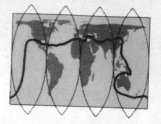